09192462

GW00707248

To, A02

From,

Gu/LIS

GU ⟶ TA

18 NOV 2011

GU TO WE

SURREY
COUNTY COUNCIL

Overdue items may incur charges
as published in the current
Schedule of Charges.

L21

Handbook of Library Training Practice and Development

For Ann

Handbook of Library Training Practice and Development

Volume Three

Edited by

ALAN BRINE
De Montfort University, UK

ASHGATE

Published by
Ashgate Publishing Limited
Wey Court East
Union Road
Farnham
Surrey, GU9 7PT
England

Ashgate Publishing Company
Suite 420
101 Cherry Street
Burlington
VT 05401-4405
USA

www.ashgate.com

British Library Cataloguing in Publication Data
Handbook of library training practice and development
    Vol. 3
    1. Library employees - In-service training 2. Library
    employees - Training of
    I. Brine, Alan, 1967-
    020.7'155

ISBN 978-0-7546-7044-5
e-ISBN 978-0-7546-9487-8

Mixed Sources
Product group from well-managed
forests and other controlled sources
www.fsc.org Cert no. SGS-COC-2482
© 1996 Forest Stewardship Council
FSC

Printed and bound in Great Britain by
TJ International Ltd, Padstow, Cornwall

CONTENTS

LIST OF FIGURES

LIST OF BOXES

LIST OF TABLES

NOTES ON CONTRIBUTORS

Barbara Allan is Director of Learning and Teaching at the University of Hull Business School where she is also Director of the Centre for Innovations in Learning and Teaching. Her current focus is on enhancing the student experience through projects such as the virtual graduate school, the alumni e-mentoring project, and the 'world of work' project. Her previous experience includes managing academic and workplace libraries, and freelance work in the design and delivery of training programmes including events for CILIP and ASLIB/IMI. She has extensive experience of teaching in the UK and also Singapore, Egypt, Iceland, Ireland and Portugal. In the past ten years, she has been involved in a wide range of national and regional e-learning and e-mentoring initiatives. Barbara has written numerous articles and also books on e-learning, project management and work-based learning. Working with Dina Lewis, she co-authored *Virtual Learning Communities* (published by the Open University Press in 2005). Her latest book, *Blended Learning*, was published by Facet Publishing in 2007. Barbara is a Fellow of the Higher Education Academy and a Member of the Chartered Institute of Library and Information Professionals (CILIP). In her spare time she is completing a Doctorate in Education on the theme of 'temporal experiences of e-learners'.

Susie Andretta has worked in the field of Information Management for 20 years, and in the last ten has focused on information literacy, integrating this practice in a range of disciplines and at all levels of provision. Her publication profile includes a book, *Information Literacy: A Practitioner's Guide* (Chandos Publishing, 2005), which promotes information literacy education as the foundation of independent and lifelong learning, and explores its empowering effect on the facilitator and the learner. In January 2006 she edited a special issue of *Italics*, the online journal of the Higher Education Academy – Information and Computer Sciences, entitled 'Information Literacy: Challenges of Implementation'. The issue looked at the problems of integrating information literacy within the Higher Education sector. At this time, Susie also developed Facilitating Information Literacy Education (FILE), a continuing professional development course commissioned by the London Health Libraries as part of their Learner Support Programme and currently co-sponsored by the National Library for Health. FILE was created in response to the preliminary findings from her research on information literacy as a new way of learning. In 2007 she edited a book, *Change and Challenge:*

Information Literacy for the 21st Century (Auslib Press), which examines the implementation of information literacy education from a range of UK-based and Australian perspectives. Her latest work, 'Information Literacy from the Learner's Perspective. A UK Study', is published in *Information Literacy as the Crossroad of Education and Information Policies in Europe* (Basilli, C. (ed.), CNR, 2008). This publication presents her use of the relational model of information literacy to enhance the learning experience of information professionals as researchers and as information literacy facilitators.

Andrew Booth is a lecturer/researcher with experience of a wide range of aspects of evidence based practice. His 15 years' experience as a health information professional include managing national information services at the King's Fund Centre and, since November 1994, the School of Health and Related Research, University of Sheffield where he is Director of Information Resources. His current brief is to develop an information resource to support evidence based healthcare both within the University of Sheffield and Trent Region. He also co-ordinates a module on Systematic Reviews and Critical Appraisal for a Masters in Health Services Research and Technology Assessment, and he is currently developing a Masters in Health Informatics. He has researched and published extensively on literature searching and critically appraising the evidence, and his recent research outputs include three published systematic reviews for the NHS Health Technology Assessment Programme, with a further two in progress. He is the compiler of the ScHARR Guide to Evidence Based Practice and the World Wide Web resource, Netting the Evidence. He is the Chair of the LINC Health Panel Research Working Party and is on the Steering Groups of EPI-Centre: the Centre for Evidence Based Health Promotion, University of London, and ARIF: the Aggressive Research Intelligence Facility at the University of Birmingham.

Helen Booth is a researcher in Information Management and has previously worked on projects on electronic resources for the Department of Information and Communications and the Centre for Research in Library and Information Management (CERLIM) at Manchester Metropolitan University. She has also been involved with the LearnHigher project and in the creation of online tutorials for Intute.

Frances Boyle is currently the Executive Director of the Digital Preservation Coalition. Her previous incarnations have included IT Development & Strategy Manager for Oxford University Library Services and time in the information units of Cancer Research UK and the Royal Society of Chemistry. She has been a member of the UKSG Committee and was a past Chair of the JIBS User Group Committee. She has presented and written widely on the subject of electronic resources management, IT library based initiatives and now digital preservation over a number of years.

Alan Brine is the Head of Technical Services at De Montfort University library. Previous to this he was the Manager for Information Science at the Learning and Teaching Support Network Centre for Information and Computer Sciences at Loughborough University. This supported departments across the UK delivering teaching and research in library and information science in the UK, achieved through a mixture of collaborative activities and publications. He has presented a number of papers on his research at international conferences including IFLA, many of which have been published in the professional press, and has also written 'Continuing Professional Development: A Guide for Information Professionals'. He is a Chartered Member of CILIP and is professionally active in its groups, especially PTEG, providing training for members. He acts as a mentor to candidates for both certification and chartership with CILIP. In his spare time he has completed a Doctorate in information science at Loughborough University on the theme of 'Information Needs at Historic Houses'.

Carol Brooks has a wide range of experience in training and development, having worked in the public sector and the Territorial Army for over 30 years. She undertook a Level 4 NVQ in Human Resources and Training Development in 2004 and has been an NVQ Assessor and Internal Verifier since 1995. Her current post is as Operations Manager (South) for Derbyshire County Council. Currently Carol heads up the Mentor Support Network for the Personnel, Education and Training Group of CILIP and led the team in devising the Mentor Training, which is accredited with the CILIP Seal of Recognition. In addition she runs a coaching and development company, providing life coaching and training services. A Fellow of CILIP since 2005, Carol was also awarded an Honorary Fellowship in 2007 for services to continuing professional development.

Sheila Corrall is Professor of Librarianship and Information Management and Head of the Department of Information Studies at the University of Sheffield. She has previously worked as a senior manager and strategic director in public, special, national and academic library and information services. Her interests include strategic planning, organizational structures, staff development and managing change. Sheila has published three books and more than 50 articles on professional and management topics and has served on many committees of national bodies. In 2002 she became the first President of the Chartered Institute of Library and Information Professionals (CILIP), and in 2003 received the International Information Industry Lifetime Achievement Award for her contribution to the information profession.

Ross Harvey is Visiting Professor at the Graduate School of Library and Information Science, Simmons College, Boston. Previous positions include Professor of Library and Information Management at Charles Sturt University, New South Wales, Australia, and academic positions in Australia, Singapore and New Zealand. He is an Associate Fellow of the Australian Library and Information

Association. Ross has published widely in the fields of preservation of library and archival material, bibliographic organization, and library education. His current research interests include the preservation of library and archival material, especially in digital form.

Margaret Kendall is Principal Lecturer (Continuing Professional Development) in the Centre for Learning and Teaching at Manchester Metropolitan University (MMU). Prior to taking up this position, she spent 15 years in the Department of Information and Communications at MMU, during which time she taught on the undergraduate and postgraduate Library and Information Management programmes, undertook research and latterly, as Senior Learning and Teaching Fellow, took a leading role in the Faculty in the uses of learning technology. Her previous experience as a practitioner included employment as Team Leader in Manchester public libraries and as Head of Libraries and Learning Resources at Manchester College of Arts and Technology.

Graham Matthews is Professor of Information Management in the Department of Information Science, Loughborough University. He has also held professorial posts at Liverpool John Moore's University (LJMU) and the University of Central England (UCE). Teaching interests include management in information and library services and collection management. His major research interest is preservation management and he has led or been involved in many projects in that area, including an overview of preservation management training. He has been a member of National Preservation Office committees on education and training. He is Chair of the Chartered Institute of Library and Information Professionals Preservation and Conservation Panel.

Beryl Morris is the Director of Hudson Rivers. Beryl established Hudson Rivers in 1992 and leads the company's work in training and development. Previously she was a Chief Officer with the London Borough of Newham, responsible for Cultural Services. She has also worked as a Senior Lecturer at Manchester Metropolitan University, as Assistant Polytechnic Librarian at the Polytechnic of East London and as a Management Adviser with the Industrial Society. She works with a diverse range of clients in the public and private sectors, including universities, local authorities, commercial and government organizations, and specializes in training in leadership, management, customer service and communication skills.

Kath Owen has worked in Nottinghamshire public libraries throughout her career, starting as a Saturday Assistant when her children were small. This proved an ideal grounding for her future development. Already a qualified teacher, she studied for a postgraduate library qualification part-time. Since then she has progressed through a number of posts, taking opportunities to gain experience through secondments whenever they looked interesting. This path led her to work as a front line librarian, a member of headquarters staff with responsibility for prison and hospital services, a training and development officer and a Principal Librarian with geographic and strategic responsibilities. She is currently Service Manager, Customers, Staff and Development. She became a member of CILIP's Chartership Board in 2003 and is now Vice-Chair. She achieved her Fellowship in 2007. She has been involved for many years in the East Midlands branch of CILIP and in other regional networks.

Chris Powis is Deputy Director (Academic Services) in the Department of Information Services at the University of Northampton. He previously worked in Oxford and Bristol before arriving at Northampton's previous incarnation as Nene College. Although a historian by background, most of his earlier professional life was as a business subject librarian. His involvement in the EduLib Project in the 1990s as one of the national Development Officers led to an interest in how librarians can develop as teachers. He was active in what was the Institute of Learning and Teaching in Higher Education (now the Higher Education Academy), speaking as an advocate for the professionalization of teaching in Higher Education. He has subsequently spoken, written and led training in this area in the UK and internationally, and was co-author, with Jo Webb, of *Teaching Information Skills: Theory and Practice* (Facet, 2004). He was awarded a National Teaching Fellowship in 2004 and a CILIP Fellowship in 2007. Chris is active in CILIP, as a UC&R (University, College and Research Group) committee member, as a mentor and previously as a member of a regional assessment panel.

Richard Sayers is Director, Capability Development for CAVAL, an Australian not-for-profit company owned by 12 universities. Richard is a qualified librarian, trainer and group facilitator; working with high profile clients such as UNESCO in Australia and overseas. Prior to joining CAVAL, Richard worked as a senior library and information manager in government agencies and universities in Australia. His responsibilities now include CAVAL's international training and consulting programs and Horizon – Australasia's first Executive Leadership Program for Senior Library Managers. Richard is the author of two books, the first published by UNESCO, and is currently ALIA's representative on IFLA's Continuing Professional and Workplace Learning Section. He is a Fellow of the Australian Institute of Professional Facilitators, Associate Fellow of the Australian Library and Information Association and Member of the Australian Institute of Training and Development and Australian Institute of Management.

John Vincent is the Networker for 'The Network – tackling social exclusion in libraries, museums, archives and galleries' (see: <www.seapn.org.uk>). Having worked in Hertfordshire and Lambeth, and now via The Network, John has always been involved in training – for library and other local authority staff, parents and carers, and other agencies. He specializes in training around community engagement and equalities, especially tackling social exclusion; working with looked-after children and young people; and developing services for LGBTs (lesbians, gay men, bisexuals and transgendered people). John still works directly with young people, most recently researching study/revision techniques with a group of Year 9 students in a secondary school in Enfield.

Jane Walton is a chartered librarian who has worked in further education, local authority and specialist libraries. She was until recently the Head of Development at MLA Yorkshire where she advised the sector on issues related to education, inclusion and professional development. Jane worked with the Museums Association and CILIP to develop their mentoring schemes and related continuing professional development programmes, and has also developed a mentoring network for CIPD West Yorkshire. Jane's current role is leading the Make Your Mark campaign in Wakefield which aims to promote enterprise amongst young people. Jane continues to develop her mentoring skills and is an active advocate of mentoring as part of personal and professional development.

Jo Webb is Academic Services Manager at De Montfort University where she is responsible for library services in support of learning, teaching and research, including academic learning development. She read Modern History at Oxford before taking an MLib at Aberystwyth and subsequently studying for a part-time MBA. Before moving to De Montfort, initially as a subject team leader, Jo worked at Cranfield University and the History Faculty Library in Oxford. Jo has written and spoken on a wide range of topics in library and information services, including staff development for library support staff, collection management and business information. Together with Chris Powis, she wrote *Teaching Information Skills: Theory and Practice* (Facet, 2004), and with Pat Gannon-Leary and Moira Bent, *Providing Effective Library Services for Research* (Facet, 2007). She was awarded a National Teaching Fellowship in 2005 for her impact on the student learning experience, both within her own institution and through influencing the community of practice through her active involvement with UC&R, of which she is currently Vice Chair, and from 2007 a Fellow of CILIP. She is also an NVQ Internal Verifier and Assessor, and a CILIP mentor.

Terry L. Weech is an Associate Professor at the Graduate School of Library and Information Science, University of Illinois. His professional positions have included Head of Government Documents, Illinois State Library; Research Associate, University of Illinois Library Research Center; and teaching positions at the University of Iowa, University of North Carolina, Chapel Hill, Emporia State University, and the University of Illinois. At the Graduate School of Library and Information Science, University of Illinois he has been Coordinator of Advanced Studies and Director of Development and the International Liaison for the School. His research interests include collection development, library systems and networks, library administration, economics of information, and international library education. He has been active professionally at the national and international level in areas of intellectual freedom, quality assessment, education and training of librarians, and library co-operation. Internationally he has served as Chair of the Education and Training Section of IFLA (International Federation of Library Associations and Institutions) and he has lectured in more than 20 countries. A list of his international activities can be found at: <http://people.lis.uiuc.edu/~weech/TLWHOME1.htm>.

FOREWORD

The two *Training Handbooks* that I compiled some 20 years ago, and the various surveys and reports on training at that period, showed how provision in the UK varied in coverage and effect. The challenges identified at that time are still relevant, but have been augmented by new concerns. This new volume will support us in addressing our current developmental needs.

The librarianship and information management environment still needs its traditional skills, but its professionals are surrounded by competitors – some serious, others lightweight – who expect to perform the same functions from new perspectives. The opportunities offered by convergence with new technologies and interdisciplinary roles need to be grasped to achieve professional expansion and influence. A common information territory is not a threat, and isolationism not an answer.

Some unease has surfaced in the face of competition. Fundamentally this is a crisis of professional identity: so many organizations in a range of information contexts; the erosion of the institutional basis of libraries; access to information is common property; users of our services have high expectations based on their searching skills. From our side of the equation, poor presentation of our own value, the potential collapse of the concept of professionalism, the fragmentation of professional education, lack of clarity of purpose in professional organizations, and the myriad providers of training with conflicting agendas challenge coherence.

But these are exciting times; our core skills remain in demand and we have the potential to do so much more in academic, public and commercial environments. The improvement of our key skills is our guarantee of our own future relevance. We can add to that core base various generic organizational skills, transferable skills, pedagogic skills, and networking and advocacy skills. There is everything to gain.

A perpetual confusion of new challenges, emerging solutions, competing partners, relentless technological progress and the threat to all employees of the impending economic downturn are just the current set of problems confronting us. Previous challenges have been overcome by the absolutely crucial strategy of implementing and monitoring effective training and development. This generation of professionals can win out by the same means.

Ray Prytherch
June 2008

INTRODUCTION

ALAN BRINE

Staff development in the library and information sector has changed dramatically over the last 20 years. When the first volume of the *Handbook of Library Training Practice* was published, the importance of training in libraries could not be underestimated. Prytherch noted in his preface at the time that training was developing and was distinctly patchy, resulting in an overall picture of some adequately developed areas, with others actively trying to improve provision in their areas (Prytherch 1986). This picture of poor provision in some areas and acceptable practice in others led to the publication of the previous two volumes of the handbook.

During the period since those two volumes were published, staff development has grown within libraries and across the profession. Personal and professional development is now central to individuals, organizations and the profession. Consequently the title of the book has been altered to reflect these changes. Oldroyd describes how the profession has changed in the academic sector by reviewing SCONUL (Standing Conference on University Libraries) members, showing that 88 per cent of members have staff development as an explicit part of the senior management portfolio (Oldroyd 2004). She goes on to state that most of the posts with this responsibility have arisen since the start of the new millennium. This is encouraging and it indicates that training and development is a core part of professional development in the library and information sector.

There are now opportunities for staff development both internally within organizations and externally. One only has to take a look at the courses offered by CILIP (Chartered Institute of Library and Information Professionals) and the long list of groups that CILIP acts as an umbrella for to give a glimpse of the possibilities (CILIP 2008a and 2008c). CILIP is the body that represents library and information professionals in the UK and offers a professional qualification in the form of chartership. The routes to this accreditation are defined, administered and monitored by CILIP for the profession as a whole. According to Griffin, CILIP and Aslib are the major providers of training for information professionals in the United Kingdom (Griffin 2008). He goes on to describe other training opportunities provided by the UK eInformation Group (UKEIG), City Information Group (CIG) and the Special Libraries Association. These are specialist training providers who have particular expertise in certain areas. UKEIG targets aspects of training related to electronic information provision while CIG represents business and commercial information practitioners. As already noted, there are many specialist groups that are a part of the CILIP community. The Personnel, Training and Education Group is one of these and they offer courses on mentoring and fellowship as well as others to support professional development (PTEG 2008). Other groups, like the Career Development Group, support chartership candidates (CDG 2008), or provide training in specific areas of practice, such as the University, College and Research Group (UC&R 2008).

Other bodies also exist in areas of practice and provide training and networks that ensure that good practice is shared throughout the community. SCONUL is one such example in the Higher Education sector (SCONUL 2008), while BIALL operates in the law sector (BIALL 2008) and the School Library Association in the schools sector (SLA 2008). The support they offer varies but the fact that they exist shows that training and development is paramount to both individuals and organizations throughout the library and information community.

Not only is the profession providing a lead in staff development, but most employers now see the importance of developing their staff and provide their own training programmes. De Montfort University, for example, runs its own programmes for health and safety, personnel, information technology and library-related specialities. From this we can see that not only do employers take training seriously but they also provide a broad training programme for all staff. In addition to this, De Montfort also has a senior manager who is responsible for staff development. This is not untypical of the Higher Education sector, but this pattern is not replicated across all sectors; for example, school libraries are not blessed with the resources in either financial or staffing terms that would enable staff development to take place in a similar manner, and other sectors are equally hard pressed.

The importance of staff and their development is now paramount to organizations. They are now seen not just as employees but as the organization's greatest asset which, when given development opportunities, will deliver a service to meet the changing needs of the users. In a fast-changing and dynamic world, this is of the utmost importance.

Although training in libraries is developed in most parts of the country, access to that training is patchy. Some employers place great emphasis on ensuring that their staff are well placed to deliver the services that are required. In addition, the level at which librarians are operating is significantly higher than previously. Individuals will have some access to training, much of it provided internally by their employer, and this will be appropriate in a library context in some cases, and sometimes not. This volume will address aspects of service provision that are emerging or significant areas in which the library profession is now involved. Additionally it will review areas becoming more prominent and of increasing importance to practitioners. Additionally the concept of professional librarianship both here and abroad is considered, as the role of the librarian has changed and promises to continue to do so in the electronic age. The text will also help the reader to focus on possible career paths and think about the acquisition of skills.

The key features of this handbook are a focus on training currently taking place in the library and information sector, both in the United Kingdom and also in the United States and Australia. It also focuses on good practice within the sector in the hope that others can adapt their own training programmes to take advantage of what are simply 'good ideas'. Through the practices exhibited within this volume, organizations and individuals will be given the tools to create or find programmes for development that will enhance the skills sets of those involved. This can help to deliver a programme that is both innovative and, hopefully, more engaging. One of the key aspects of, and reasons for producing, this volume is to aid the development of skills for the future for the individual, teams, departments and, by default, organizations. As a result of the information contained within this volume, individuals can, with or without their employer, develop their skills, and consequently enhance their career development. Expanding existing skills and introducing new ones through training opportunities will enable practitioners to improve their career prospects and look for different or more advanced roles within the sector.

STRUCTURE OF CHAPTERS

The contributors have all been asked to conform to a standard layout and structure for their chapter, while still giving flexibility where needed for the topic under consideration. Not all chapters stick rigidly to this pattern as the topic does not lend itself to this structure, either because they are an overview of provision or because they are trying to convey a different view of training, as in the international sections.

At the outset each topic will provide:

- Definitions
- The importance and need for this training
- Suggested training programmes
- Methods of training and means of implementation, with examples
- Monitoring and evaluation of training
- Bibliographies and resource guides

Authors have based their content on the above requirements but have been allowed to let the substance of the chapter speak for itself, so that the training provision being described and the exemplars give clear routes for staff development. All of the contributors have used their own style of presentation and the book does not seek to change that, ensuring that the message regarding the training and development is delivered as originally intended by the author and is not lost due to overprescribed standardization of presentation. To this end, all of the material provided by each author is included with their chapter, including appendices, for easier access and referral for the reader.

As in the previous volumes of the handbook, contributors have been asked to include the best current practice and real examples of training so that: 'Readers can fully understand the intention and format of various activities' (Prytherch 1986). This volume is an extension of the *Handbook of Library Training Practice* that was published previously (Prytherch 1986). As in previous volumes the intention is to: 'Suggest ways forward, to alleviate that lack of information and advice that impedes progress in training' (Prytherch 1986). As in the previous handbooks, this one is intended to provide a blueprint of good training practice and help both individuals and organizations to spot opportunities and methods for development for both libraries and library and information professionals.

This handbook has a distinctly different structure to previous volumes and focuses on aspects of practice within libraries that are currently delivering new and enhanced services. Services that, in an ever-changing technological world, are central to the development of staff, ensuring that users receive the provision that is required. To this end this handbook is divided into sections that cover areas that are key to the delivery of services at the present.

The first section presented in the volume is that of teaching and training users. In this section we have three chapters that review evolutionary good practice that makes use of e-learning trends that are now impacting on education in the United Kingdom. E-learning has become more established in education in the United Kingdom and is now developing as a delivery mechanism. Programmes are actively taking methods of e-learning forward. Examples of developments in this area include the Pathfinder project established by the Higher Education Academy (Higher Education Academy 2008) and the JISC e-learning programme (JISC 2008). Consequently the first chapter, from Margaret Kendall and Helen Booth, is dedicated to virtual learning, to give some examples of good practice using learning technologies. This provides not only the background to the area under discussion but exemplars of training methods and delivery that any practitioner can use to their advantage.

Following this Jo Webb and Chris Powis discuss pedagogical development in Chapter 2. This provides a template for the development of programmes for delivery of training for users. Library and information professionals will be able to use this chapter as a way to develop their own training programmes to deliver enhanced skills development for users. The subsequent chapter provided by Susie Andretta reviews information literacy and then, in the context of an existing programme, reviews the continuing professional development requirements of library and information professionals who are delivering information literacy training and programmes for users. These three chapters provide the reader with a grasp of one of the central tenets of the modern library and information professional's skills set, the ability to enhance the user's ability to understand and access information, rather than just doing it for them. The need for users of library and information services to be able to use increasingly complex information resources in all formats, including electronic, is of the utmost importance due to factors such as changes in primary and tertiary education and technological developments in the home and at work. Changes have led to an increasing dependence on technology and less analytical application of that technology by users in their search for information. One of the challenges for the profession is to ensure that the need for appropriate training is not overrun by further technological developments.

The second section of the book is on the management of resources, of which two aspects of resource management are covered here that have developed since the previous volumes of the handbook were published. Graham Matthews writes on preservation management in Chapter 4 and gives an overview of its development and of its importance. All organizations have assets that need preserving, whether they are more traditional materials or of a digital nature. They have value to the organization and are important assets. It had been hoped to include developments in the sector on training in the area of digital preservation, but it was not possible to get a chapter included in the time required for publication. Chapter 5 includes a treatise on the management of electronic resources by Frances Boyle. A key development in the library and information sector is the changing nature and increasing use of electronic resources which have become an omnipresent part of service provision. Although this is a discrete chapter in this book, it is argued that they are just part of an overall picture of information provision, and should be treated as part of training provision rather than as a separate identity. In addition to this, electronic resources provision is constantly changing, whether through the increasing number of resources or sources and methods of access. Some guidance is therefore provided here for training and development in this complex area of information provision.

The third section of the book looks at services to users and how library and information professionals can develop in the area of customer service and inclusion, which are increasingly important in the changing climate in the sector. Inclusion is particularly relevant in the public library sector, but as with any training programmes provided in this book, they are applicable to any sector and can be applied to different circumstances and adapted. John Vincent delivers training in this area and in Chapter 6 he provides an overview of what it means and how to make best use of training to deliver targeted services to all sections of the community, especially the disadvantaged. This is particularly valuable as readers will notice that other authors also refer to the importance of social inclusion in this volume, both in the United Kingdom and overseas. Chapter 7 sees Beryl Morris discourse on customer service and gives readers an update on training in this area of service delivery. This topic has been covered in a previous volume of the handbook, but practices have developed during this period and an update is necessary to promote good practice for library and information professionals. Different modes of service delivery have provided new challenges for library and information services that have required careful planning and innovative solutions to ensure that the user is central to the services ethos.

The next section of the book is made up of four chapters which have a common theme: that of management. One of the challenges to the library and information sector is management of staff and service. Management is difficult to deliver in a formal educational setting and does to some extent require practical experience to be able to get maximum benefit from training. To this end we have three chapters that review different aspects of this topic. Initially first line management is discussed, looking at aspects of practice including budgets, project management, performance measurement and quality assurance that will be new to recently appointed and aspiring managers. Barbara Allan provides an overview of these areas and combines that with the addition of blended learning as a method of delivery for training. In this section other crucial aspects of management are provided. To complement this, Carol Brooks gives the reader an overview of recruitment, selection and interviewing, and induction, enabling practitioners to plan both their own training, and the training of others, in a key area of development for library staff.

The sector is looking for the next generation of leaders and programmes are being developed to enhance this process. Sheila Corrall's chapter on aspects of strategic development for librarians as managers is intended to provide guidance in an area that is both difficult to deliver training in and to access. Managers in libraries that are operating at this level are often time-limited and consequently need training that is appropriate. Aspects of management that include change, service development, structure and organizational culture are covered and provide readers with the tools for their own development.

Subsequently Jane Walton reviews mentoring in Chapter 11 to give a picture of current practice in the sector. Mentoring is now a key aspect of training and development for library and information professionals and is fully endorsed by CILIP as best practice in the development of chartered librarians, a defined standard of practice for professional library and information professionals. Mentoring is of great importance to the development of staff and enables experience to be shared amongst staff to the benefit of the organization or institution that they work in.

Professional development is the overarching heading for the fifth section and looks at aspects of training and development that individuals can utilize to improve their professional development and enhance their skills. Kath Owen reviews the national and vocational qualifications currently available in the library and information sector in Chapter 12. The sector has reviewed its qualification structure in recent years and those offered by the professional body and additional training providers have changed to reflect the current landscape; this is conveyed for the reader's benefit.

In the following chapter in this section of the book, Barbara Allan provides an overview of communities of practice, which is a different approach to a traditional activity within the library community that is normally described as collaborative working and networking. Groups facilitate informal mentoring and professional development, and these are often a way to develop a wide range of skills including management and leadership, even if those opportunities are not forthcoming in their place of work. The final chapter in this section is a review of evidence based practice. Andrew Booth reviews a topic that has risen to prominence since the latter half of the 1990s alongside the need to justify services and keep up to date with a rapidly changing body of knowledge. Professionals need to employ the skills required for evidence based practice to deliver services and continually develop professionally.

The final section of the book is given over to international developments to give the reader a comparison with practice in other parts of the world. Chapters 15 and 16 do not follow the same format as the previous chapters in this volume as they are providing an overview of the country concerned. The first of these is written by Ross Harvey and Richard Sayers who have described current trends and practices in Australia. In combination with the subsequent chapter, written by Terry L. Weech on professional developments in the United States, the reader gets a clear picture of practice in other parts of the globe that enables them to make conclusions regarding directions and methods that could be taken by individuals responsible for their own training and for that of others in different organizational cultures.

SKILLS FOR THE FUTURE

As a profession it is important that those working in the library and information sector are appropriately skilled to carry out their roles, and are able to develop their careers and use their skills to bring good practice to other organizations and areas of service provision which they choose to undertake. Underlying this is the requirement to ensure that individuals have the appropriate competences, and to believe that they have them, so that they can move forward with their careers. In 2003 the Information Services National Training Organisation (ISNTO) reported on the fact that the sector felt that 44 per cent of the skills required for the future are already held by existing staff, and in addition that they could provide 41 per cent of its future needs by training existing staff or recruiting to new posts (ISNTO 2003). This is a heavy emphasis on training for those staff in post and it is borne out in practice as the rapidly changing environment that libraries are working in requires a changing workforce to meet users' future needs. Klagge identified that statistical measurement, customer service techniques, process improvement methods, coaching and facilitating were necessary for middle managers (Klagge 1998). This is certainly the case now for middle managers and is actually more widespread than this, with many staff at all levels of the organization being involved with customer delivery and with the increasing use of electronic resources. Geleijnse (1997) wrote that new skills were necessary for the digital library. Many organizations rely now on a hybrid model that uses both electronic resources and more traditional resources, and this means that they require both new skills and existing ones. A planned and continuing programme of training and development is required to keep staff skills current.

There are frameworks that the individual and organization can use to measure their skills against and address those areas that they feel need to be developed. There are the ILS NVQs currently available in the UK that can be undertaken for staff who wish to gain a qualification and also ensure that their skills set is current. In addition to this is the European Computer Driving Licence which gives a grounding in IT competences (ECDL 2008). These enable individuals to not only give themselves an opportunity to develop but also the confidence to carry out their work. The Learning and Skills Council has been created and has taken on the work of the aforementioned ISNTO. This may deliver an enhanced and more fully integrated framework of competences for the sector, but the outcomes are not fully known yet and as such cannot be included in this publication (Learning and Skills Council 2008).

However, during this period the Body of Professional Knowledge has been produced by CILIP which provides an overview of the areas of competence that are required to practise in the sector (CILIP 2008b). This was developed by reviewing existing competences toolkits, including those of the Learning and Teaching Support Network (LTSN 2002) and TFPL (TFPL 2008), and by gaining feedback from the profession. Coupled with a mentoring programme, members of the profession can update their skills with support and a focus on development that were not available before.

REFLECTION AND RECORDING

Training and development opportunities are abundant; however, it cannot happen unless the individual is committed to their own development. All organizations have those who are keen to develop and who relish a challenge, but also have those staff who are not keen to change and who are reluctant to develop, sometimes due to their own lack of confidence. Organizations and professional bodies can provide support, but the individual is the only one who can undertake the training and develop their skills.

As part of their development, the individual must be aware of their own learning style. Learning styles are more prevalent in the sector's literature and some staff are more aware of them, so that development can be maximized. The individual must endeavour to learn in the way that they get the most benefit to ensure that any training undertaken is appropriate and achieves the required end result. Beryl Morris covers this in her chapter on customer service.

Reflective practice is inherently bound with the individual's learning style. Part of development is the ability to review and reflect on the training that has been undertaken. Only then can the individual gain the maximum benefit and make decisions about their needs and future developmental path. It is reflection that is key to the profession's practice; it forms part of the chartership and certification process at CILIP, as the individual is required to show that the training they have undertaken has been fully evaluated by them and used to re-engineer their developmental plans as required for their needs.

As a part of this process, it is essential to undertake the recording of skills development as both a record of the individual's progress and proof of that development; it also enforces the practice of reflection. Brine says that building a portfolio gathers evidence that provides an indication of the individual's level of skills. This must follow a process of identification of skills achieved and required through a SWOT analysis and a training needs analysis (Brine 2005). Using the frameworks noted above will give the individual something against which to register their own personal skills set. The creation and building of a portfolio is an onerous and extensive task, but once created, it is easy to keep up to date. Good practice guidelines in creating portfolios can be found through attending workshops by professional bodies or using texts such as Brine and Watson (Brine 2005, Watson 2008).

At the time that the two previous volumes of the handbook were published, training was underdeveloped and underprovided for in the sector. The picture is quite different now and the opportunities for individuals to grow their professional abilities and increase their potential are quite literally staggering. However, everyone's potential is limited by their desire to improve or develop in conjunction with changes in working practices and by budgetary and time constraints. Some individuals are more driven than others and part of the challenge of management is encouraging and enabling all staff to develop. This safeguards both the organization and the profession for the future.

FUTURE DEVELOPMENTS

Developments in technology are changing the way that services are delivered and also the working practices of staff working in the library and information sector. Corrall tells us that: 'There is no room for complacency as the changes currently in train are arguably more profound and more extensive than those experienced in previous eras' (Corrall 2004). This was in the context of academic libraries, but it is fair to say that changes in the electronic environment are more pervasive than this. The emergence of web 2.0 technologies, as it is sometimes termed, has led to a change in the way that individuals can and do communicate. The sector is now entering a new phase of development where individuals are looking at their own development and analysing how to incorporate these technologies, or trying to determine how to harness them to best effect to provide an enhanced service to the user. The ability to access news feeds more easily using RSS allows users to be quickly updated; different methods of social networking take place via tools such as Facebook and MySpace. White says that: 'Rather than go to conferences to find people with the same academic interests, you can join or organise a community on the web' (White, quoted in Chillingworth 2007).

This tells us that people can more easily build a community of practice without travelling great distances to share common interests and goals. Other tools include photo-sharing libraries such as Flickr, but the one thing that they all have in common is that the content is user generated. This is not always good news, as sites which are shared are open to abuse, like any system, unless appropriate safeguards are put in place. For example, Wikipedia is an attempt to use the knowledge of the herd to provide information to everyone, but entries could be amended by anyone and this makes it possible to represent things inaccurately either by mistake or on purpose. This changes the way that we should be thinking about our services and the needs of our users.

The working environment is changing and we have to address changes in the way that people may wish to learn and communicate and even how they will want new services delivered. This presents huge challenges as the sector investigates and helps to define the use of these technologies. As is always the case, the profession is already trying to promote itself and provide services through these methods, including, for example, using Facebook, as the University of Kentucky did, until it found its profile disabled when Facebook discovered it was not an individual (SLA-IT 2008). The sector will learn through its experiences and adapt to new methods of working, as it has always done. Anderson tells us that a balanced approach ensures that the benefits of using the technology are equally as important as real world concerns (Anderson 2007). What should be added to this is a note of caution. As with any major developmental changes, there is always a concern that library and information workers will be sidelined because of technological changes. Holmes tells us: 'In the end users will decide. And the changes which do happen will happen much more slowly' (Holmes 2008).

Learning using electronic methods, such as virtual learning environments, is becoming more embedded and is slowly becoming more commonplace across education, but this process has already taken years to become an established method of delivery and practice is still developing and evolving. The sector has always coped with changes and it is important to keep that in the forefront of one's mind. Changes to professional development, and the recording of that development, provide a more rigorous approach to training and development that individuals can use to effectively manage their careers. This volume will help individuals to guide their training and development, and provide organizations with ideas on how to encourage and support their staff. It is important to note that ideas are transferable between sectors and some of the examples within these pages can be adapted, adjusted and adopted to fit the local context and enhance existing programmes for development.

REFERENCES

Anderson, P. (2007), *What is Web 2.0? Ideas, Technologies and Implications for Education* (London: JISC). <http://www.jisc.ac.uk/publications/publications/twweb2.aspx>.

BIALL (2008), The British and Irish Association of Law Librarians: home page. <http://www.biall.org.uk/home.asp>.

Brine, A. (2005), *Continuing Professional Development: A Guide for Information Professionals* (Oxford: Chandos).

CDG (2008), Career Development Group: home page. <http://www.careerdevelopmentgroup.org.uk/>.

Chillingworth, M. (2007), 'Breaking New Ground', *JISC Inform*, 18 (Summer), 11–13.

CILIP (2008a), Training, events and conferences. <www.cilip.org.uk/training>.

CILIP (2008b), 'Body of Professional Knowledge' (London: CILIP). <http://www.cilip.org.uk/qualificationschartership/bpk>.

CILIP (2008c), Chartered Institute of Library and Information Professionals: home page. <http://www.cilip.org.uk>.

Corrall, S. (2004), 'Rethinking Networked Competence for the Networked Environment' in Oldroyd, M. (ed.).

ECDL (2008), ECDL (European Computer Driving Licence). <www.bcs.org/ecdl/>.

Geleijnse, H. (1997), 'Human Resource Management and the Digital Library', *International Journal of Electronic Library Research*, 7:1, 25–42.

Griffin, D. (2008), 'Grow your Professional Abilities', *Information World Review*, 242 (January), 17–18.

Higher Education Academy (2008), Pathfinder. <http://www.heacademy.ac.uk/ourwork/learning/elearning/pathfinder>.

Holmes, D. (2008), 'Web 2.0 is No Revolution – Wait for Users to Decide', *Library and Information Gazette*, 7–20 March, 5.

Information Services National Training Organisation (ISNTO) (2003), *Skills Foresight in the Information Services Sector 2003–2009* (Bradford: ISNTO).

JISC (2008), E-learning Programme. <http://www.jisc.ac.uk/whatwedo/themes/elearning/programme_elearning.aspx>.

Learning and Skills Council (2008), Learning and Skills Council: home page. <http://www.lsc.gov.uk/>.

Klagge, J. (1998), 'Self Perceived Needs of Today's Middle Managers', *Journal of Management Development*, 17:7, 481–91.

LTSN-ICS (2002), *Recording Skills Development for Information and Library Science* (Loughborough: LTSN-ICS (Information Science)). <http://www.ics.heacademy.ac.uk/resources/links/is_skills.php>.

Oldroyd, M. (ed.) (2004), *Developing Academic Library Staff for Future Success* (London: Facet).

Prytherch, R. (ed.) (1986), *Handbook of Library Training Practice* (Aldershot: Gower).

PTEG (2008), Personnel, Training and Education Group: home page. <http://www.cilip.org.uk/specialinterestgroups/bysubject/pteg/>.

SCONUL (2008), Standing Conference on University Libraries. <http://www.sconul.ac.uk>.

SLA (2008), School Library Association. <http://www.sla.org.uk/>.

SLA-IT (2008), Blogging Section of SLA-IT: Weblog of the Blogging Section of SLA's Information Technology Division. <http://sla-divisions.typepad.com/itbloggingsection/2006/09/librarys_facebo.html>.

TFPL (2008), *TFPL Skills Toolkit* (London: TFPL). <http://skillstoolkit.tfpl.com>.

UC&R (2008), University, College and Research Group: home page. <http://www.cilip.org.uk/specialinterestgroups/bysubject/ucr/>.

Watson, M. (2008), *Building your Portfolio: A CILIP Guide* (London: Facet).

TEACHING AND TRAINING USERS

CHAPTER 1

TEACHING AND TRAINING USERS OF UNIVERSITY LIBRARIES VIA LEARNING TECHNOLOGIES

HELEN BOOTH AND MARGARET KENDALL[1]

INTRODUCTION

The first part of this chapter provides a review of the literature on the uses of learning technologies in Higher Education in the UK, with particular reference to their use by librarians. Whilst the authors recognize that there have been significant developments in the use of learning technologies in other library sectors (for example, the Knowledge Web initiative, MLA 2004), they consider it would not be possible to do justice to all within the scope of one chapter.

The second part provides examples from Manchester Metropolitan University (MMU), which serves approximately 33,000 students mainly taught on campus rather than by distance learning.

DEFINITIONS

As a starting point, librarians need to be aware of the terminology for learning technologies within Higher Education and identify how they are being used within their own institutions. Users of university libraries include undergraduate and postgraduate students, researchers and academic staff.

The general term 'e-learning' is often used to refer to any use of information and communication technology to support and facilitate learning. In its *Strategy for E-learning* (HEFCE 2005) the Higher Education Funding Council puts the emphasis on embedding the use of technologies for appropriate pedagogic purposes, and explains that: 'For HE this will encompass flexible learning as well as distance learning, and the use of ICT as a communications and delivery tool between individuals and groups, to support students and improve the management of learning.' A recent definition by JISC explains that e-learning 'can cover a spectrum of activities from the use of technology to support learning as part of a "blended" approach (a combination of traditional and e-learning approaches), to learning that

---

1   With thanks to Mary Harrison, Rosemary Jones and Emily Shields.

is delivered entirely online. Whatever the technology, however, learning is the vital element' (JISC 2006).

In a review of over 300 studies of blended learning since 2000, Sharpe et al. identified three different ways in which the term blended learning was being used. The most common use was to refer to 'supplementary resources for courses that are conducted along predominantly traditional lines through an institutionally supported virtual learning environment' (Sharpe et al. 2006). They also found some examples of 'transformative course level practices underpinned by radical course designs' and occasionally 'students taking a holistic view of the interaction of the technology and their learning, including the use of their own technologies'.

Commercial Virtual Learning Environment (VLE) systems such as Blackboard, which provide integrated communication tools and facilities for delivering content online are common in many universities. Although the predominant use of VLEs is to enhance the student experience through support for traditional forms of teaching (Britain and Liber 2004), it is possible to incorporate additional tools to support group work with which students may be familiar and consider their 'own'. For example, Campus Pack (2006) provides software for blogs, wikis and podcasts designed to work with Blackboard (Campus Pack 2006).

TRAINING NEEDS

Changing Approaches to Learning and Teaching

Levy explains how research into student approaches to learning over the last few decades has led to changes in the way students are being taught (Levy 2005). Increasing emphasis is placed on constructivist approaches which encourage learning building on prior experience through activity either individually or in groups (for example, case studies, projects, debates and role play). Physical study spaces in libraries are being redesigned in order to accommodate these changing needs, for example, flexible seating areas with wireless access for group work (Weaver 2006).

As well as face to face activities, much collaborative and enquiry-based activity can also take place online through virtual learning environments. However, as discovered by Markland, the quality of online resources provided by academic staff may be variable, as may the extent to which they seek the support of librarians for the identification of relevant resources (Markland 2003). Markland also found that the abilities of students in seeking and evaluating information gave considerable cause for concern. Both staff and students need opportunities to develop skills in information literacy, defined by CILIP as 'knowing when and why you need information, where to find it and how to evaluate, use and communicate it in an ethical manner' (CILIP 2004).

Learner Profiles

As Allan explains, it is important to think about learning first and technology second when planning training (Allan 2002). This includes identifying who the learners are, what they will gain from the training and how their needs will be met. Rowntree has created a useful checklist covering demographic factors, motivation, learning styles, subject background and resources (Rowntree 2000). The level of study should also be considered and Bloom's taxonomy may be helpful here (available through Krumme 2002) as it identifies five levels of learning, from Level 1 – knowledge reproduction to Level 5 – synthesis and evaluation. The higher levels will be more appropriate for third year undergraduates, postgraduates and academic staff.

Collaboration in Course Design

There are many recommendations in the literature for librarians to work in partnership with academic staff and learning technologists. Secker believes that there is a need to move to a more integrated approach; for librarians to 'work alongside teaching staff to build programmes that are integrated into the curriculum' (Secker 2004).

At the University of Birmingham it was found that librarians are supporting, not creating, content and the conclusion was made that librarians need greater input at the creation stage. (Kent 2003). This was also the case at the University of Sheffield where, according to Stubley, it was found that it was essential for librarians to know not just the content of resource lists but also how the courses are to be taught in order to support and encourage learning (Stubley 2002). It was again recommended that librarians have more input in identifying and recommending relevant information resources for the list.

According to Harris: 'One of the biggest problems faced by institutions within the Information Environment has little to do with understanding new technologies, implementing standards or financing research but finding ways in which traditionally isolated groups of people within an institution can work together' (Harris 2005).

Several projects have been funded by JISC to investigate the linking of digital library resources with Virtual Learning Environments. The DELIVER (Digital Electronic Library Integration within Virtual EnviRonments) project had 'a clear focus on finding a common ground in which learning technologists, librarians and academic staff could present the best experience or environment to students. As such the project was as much focused on changing processes and cultural attitudes as developing new tools' (Secker 2005).

The DiVLE (Linking Digital Libraries with VLEs) programme funded ten projects to further investigate the issues of linking digital libraries and VLEs in order to 'reduce barriers to learning technologists and library staff working together' (Harris 2005).

Formative evaluation of the DiVLE project was carried out by the Centre for Research in Library and Information Management (CERLIM) based at Manchester Metropolitan University, under the name Link[ER]. The final report from Link[ER] draws the conclusions that:

> There is evidence that library staff need the same standard of VLE training as academics, and that this is not always provided. There are warnings of the impact that the move to an integrated digital library and VLE teaching environment may well have upon the job roles and practices of the teaching community. These outcomes of the DiVLE programme are valuable lessons for institutional e-learning policies which must be taken on board if the VLE with integrated digital library facilities is to become a key teaching and learning environment (Brophy, Markland and Jones 2003).

Roberts, Schofield and Wilson explain how new academic teams have evolved at Edge Hill College, highlighting the importance of shared understanding of pedagogic principles in developing the curriculum and embedding information literacy skills (Roberts, Schofield and Wilson 2005). Working in collaborative teams can be challenging and may involve a willingness to reach a consensus about the use of language, as Scales, Matthews and Johnson explain in their analysis of the process undertaken in the revision of an online information literacy course with partners from the Distance Degree Program: '... we recognised that our assumptions about learning objectives derived from our training – how they are expressed and assessed, even what they are – were different from the assumptions about the concept of "objectives" possessed by the DDP staff, who were experts in distance course design and implementation' (Scales, Matthews and Johnson 2005). It is likely that the DDP staff used the term objective to mean a specific learning outcome assessed through completion of an associated assignment.

Supporting Use of VLEs

Specific training on how to use the VLE may be provided as part of a student's taught programme or through central provision. Library staff may be involved to a greater or lesser extent, for example, at Birmingham University (Kent 2003) subject librarians include an introduction to WebCT in their library induction sessions for students. Individual students will inevitably seek help, for example, when studying in the library in the evenings or at weekends. Some students with special educational needs, such as assistive technologies, will need additional support. At the University of Central Lancashire, the library service has a specialised learning resources unit for users with disabilities.

Forsyth explains that whilst students' needs in the use of VLEs are mainly technical, staff needs are more complex, ranging from technical training in the use of the software to staff development in curriculum design for online learning (Forsyth 2003). At Birmingham University it was found that user needs differed widely. Some staff needed training on how to use the new software, while others needed help with the creation of materials. A module on E-learning in Higher Education was designed, which incorporated various 'e-tivities', including reflective learning journals, which became part of portfolios of e-learning practice (Kent 2003).

Librarians at the University of Sheffield created a user needs survey of academic staff, incorporating questions about the individual's use of the VLE, the reactions of their students to the technology, the requirements of the member of staff and their use of resources, either library-based or Internet-based (Stubley 2002).

At the University of Waterford, the library service took the lead in introducing the use of the virtual learning environment, including user training and support for e-learning (Quinlan and Hegarty 2006). Care was taken to 'position' VLE training as a mainstream academic staff development activity, rather than a specific 'library' or 'computer' event and training was not carried out in the library but in a new staff training area. According to Quinlan and Hegarty, library policy is to encourage the use of new technologies for the delivery of effective teaching and learning. The librarian's experience in traditional library roles such as conducting reference interviews and delivering training on electronic resources meant that they were 'well-equipped to establish individual lecturer needs and to work towards empowering staff to efficiently and effectively exploit the VLE' (Quinlan and Hegarty 2006).

EXAMPLES FROM MANCHESTER METROPOLITAN UNIVERSITY

Learning technology is used in a variety of ways at Manchester Metropolitan University (MMU) to help its 33,000 students develop the skills necessary to find resources, evaluate their quality and use them effectively in their academic work. The university is located on seven different campuses throughout the city and in Cheshire, so there are local variations in practice, according to the subjects taught and the willingness of academic staff to make time available. In some cases, assessment of the extent to which specific learning objectives have been achieved is formative rather than summative, for example through quizzes undertaken in class using an electronic voting system. In other cases, for example at the Business School, information literacy teaching through an online tutorial in the VLE is embedded into the first year curriculum with marks associated for its completion (Donnelly et al. 2006).

Whichever approach is used, a common look and feel to the training is given through the InfoSkills toolkit, developed as an outcome of the JISC-funded Big Blue project, managed jointly by MMU library and Leeds University library in 2002. The kit includes PowerPoint slides and handouts for the Foundation year, each year of undergraduate study and for postgraduates, which can be adapted by trainers to include examples relevant to specific subject areas and a customizable online tutorial, structured around 'Five steps to success': five key stages in planning searches, using a range of resources, evaluating information, using information effectively and reviewing the process (Donnelly et al. 2006).

Training the Trainers

Given the size of the university and its location on seven campuses, training the trainers sessions are particularly useful, with key staff being designated as 'InfoSkills Champions' on each campus who come together for specific training sessions and then cascade the information gleaned to others, customizing as appropriate. One example is training in the use of interactive whiteboards (Jones, Peters and Shields 2006). In a similar fashion, 'EndNote Champions' have also been selected (see below) and these are directly responsible for training in the use of EndNote software (Harrison, Summerton and Peters 2005).

Interactive Whiteboard Training

The seven library sites have adopted interactive whiteboards (IWBs) in order to enhance learning experiences for students taking part in library training sessions. The IWBs are used in conjunction with ACTIVstudio2 software,[2] which allows trainers to increase the interactivity of their training sessions, for example, through the use of electronic flipcharts.

A one-day training session for an InfoSkills trainer from each campus gave an introduction to the IWBs, demonstrated the various functions and showed how the technology could be used in delivering InfoSkills sessions to students. The aim was that participants would then disseminate this knowledge to other staff at their various library sites. Small group hands-on workshops involved the participants in games and activities to show how the various features could be used in delivering InfoSkills training. These activities were designed to be fun, as well as practical.

---

2   ACTIVStudio 2. <http://rols.ramesys.com/product1.aspx?Product_ID=782&Category_ ID=122&>.

It was essential that staff enjoyed using the IWBs and built their confidence in the workshop environment before integrating the technology into their own training sessions.

At the end of the day, most staff were confident about using the IWBs in their own teaching. Those who did not feel confident were encouraged to introduce the boards into their teaching gradually, at their own pace. Checklists were given out with four levels of proficiency comprising basic functions, PowerPoint tools, Flipcharts and advanced functions, with specific goals for each in order for staff to incorporate the use of the boards into their teaching. The goals have clear tasks, which increase in difficulty, and confidence is built as the tasks are completed and the next level is reached. The trainers were able to monitor the progress of staff through the checklists and therefore were able to assess the level of uptake of the technology and the different ways it has been used in delivering training sessions. Each participant was also given training materials to enable them to run similar workshops at their own library. The central InfoSkills team members were available to assist with training at the various sites but it was felt that encouraging staff to lead their own sessions would mean greater ownership of the technology at site level.

The central InfoSkills team also created 'A Guide to ACTIVstudio2 and the Interactive Whiteboards' which was posted on the library's Intranet and available to all library staff. This was designed to help the training day participants reinforce their own learning and to support them in delivering their own training sessions to other library staff. This guide was written to be more accessible to library staff and more relevant to their needs than the guides provided by the technology supplier.

An online guide with step-by-step instructions for using the ACTIVstudio software was also created and a WIKI was set up on the Intranet as a forum for staff from all library sites to share ideas and experiences and to discuss problems. The WIKI was also used to let staff know about times of sessions using IWBs that are being held by their colleagues which they may attend to observe practical use of the technology.

The incorporation of IWBs into teaching has been much faster than anticipated and some staff are now reluctant to teach without them. The technology seems to have encouraged staff to develop more interactive training and to become more involved with their learners; feedback from staff and students has been positive. Future goals are to ensure that the positive experiences of staff using IWBs continue and that new staff are properly trained and encouraged to incorporate the technology into their teaching.

EndNote Software[3]

As demand for training in the use of the bibliographic software was high, library services managers at each of the library sites nominated one member of their team to become an 'EndNote Champion' and a training the trainers session was devised. This took the form of a presentation on the advantages of the library delivering EndNote training followed by the three-hour training workshop which had been developed for academic staff and postgraduate students. This comprised PowerPoint presentations and live demonstrations of the key software functions, and hands-on exercises after each function had been explained. Finally there was an informal discussion on what was expected from the new trainers. The Champions were asked to use the workshop template to ensure that EndNote training was standardized throughout the University. They were given PowerPoint slides and a complete training script that they could use as it was or adapt to their needs. Trainers also needed to make their workshops more relevant to the needs of their learners by including databases from their subject area in their sessions. They were provided with promotional literature, booking forms, feedback forms and workshop checklists. Training documentation was made available on the library's Intranet and an e-mail discussion list was created to enable trainers to share their experiences and communicate news.

Cascading training in this way has been successful in meeting the needs of academic staff and postgraduate students; for example, 39 workshops were held in a one-year period. As well as benefiting the academic staff and students, the initiative has had many benefits for the library service. Library staff members have been able to meet the needs of their key users and have better communication with academic staff. The programme has also allowed promotion of library resources, with the result that users have an increased awareness of what is available from the library in their own subject areas.

On an annual basis since 2004, MMU's Research Support Librarian has organized a small conference for the EndNote Champions. Usually lasting 2½ hours, this meeting provides the opportunity for new trainers to meet the rest of the team and for informal group discussion about the successes and failures of the previous year. A short programme of presentations by individual Champions is organized as a way of keeping the Champions up-to-date with new developments. For example, in 2007 the programme included a presentation on the recently launched web-based version of EndNote, My EndNoteWeb; a presentation on a simple method for explaining field codes to workshop participants; an introduction to the new INFORMS tutorial on working with images; and a look at the new version of EndNote – EndNote X – which MMU will be adopting in the summer of 2007.

---

3   EndNote. <http://www.endnote.com/>.

Workshops conclude with a discussion aimed at identifying issues to be addressed in the coming year. The workshops are very useful for keeping EndNote training on the agenda and in persuading less active members of the team to schedule more EndNote training sessions.

Activote

The Activote audience response system[4] has been used since September 2005 in InfoSkills sessions for undergraduate and postgraduate students of Education and Social Care. The age, background and experience of the learners is very varied, particularly on the vocational postgraduate courses. Many of the courses involve large periods off campus on placement, meaning that knowledge of electronic sources is vital to complete studies without having to come onto campus regularly.

Throughout an InfoSkills session students are asked a number of pre-prepared questions that relate to the presentation. The students vote (up to six multiple choice answers) and the results are displayed on the screen for discussion. The aim is to be as participative as possible with varied activities to engage with all learners. An activity of some kind takes place every ten minutes (either voting or another activity) to keep the learners' interest. For most of the quizzes, students work individually, but peer instruction has also been found helpful. For example, the group is asked a difficult question (usually about Boolean logic or plagiarism). If the majority get it wrong, rather than give them the correct answer, they are asked to spend a few minutes talking to a neighbour about what they answered and why. The vote is retaken after a few minutes and – hopefully! – more students have come to the right answer. This creates a useful opportunity to give the group a chance to discuss amongst themselves.

In this example, the voting system is not used for assessment purposes, only for instant feedback to the students. It is possible to use the software over a long period in 'named' mode so that the tutor (but no one else) can know who answered what. This could give valuable information about an individual student's understanding over time.

INFORMS Tutorials

The INFORMS software enables the creation of short, interactive tutorials to guide students and staff in using electronic resources. The software was originally developed at the University of Huddersfield, and a service to share the tutorials created by staff at different institutions was hosted by them. At the time of writing,

---

4   Activote. <http://www.prometheanworld.com/uk/server/show/nav.1689>.

the service was being moved to a new home at Intute.[5] INFORMS uses split screens that have access to the live web-based resource on the right with the guide to the resource appearing on the left. The library service has created many guides to electronic resources which are made available from the library website.[6]

Feedback from staff about the EndNote training asked for it to be extended to undergraduates (Harrison, Summerton and Peters 2005). As it would not be feasible to run hands-on workshops given the numbers of students at MMU, an INFORMS tutorial was seen as a solution. EndNote is not a web-based resource, however, but is held on the hard drive of the user's computer. Library staff therefore needed to provide additional instructions in order for the user to be able to load up EndNote to appear on the right of the screen. The tutorial was designed to incorporate images, which had not been previously included in INFORMS tutorials.

The first version of the tutorial was developed by three EndNote Champions over six weeks, then user tested in April 2005 by members of staff who had not used it before and students of the Department of Information and Communications. The tutorial consists of an introduction to the software, instructions on use of the features and practical exercises, and should take about 45 minutes. There are 15 steps for users to work through at their own speed, either linearly or by jumping to the sections that are most relevant to their needs. The tutorial can be used as a stand-alone resource for users to complete on their own, or it can be incorporated into workshop sessions by library or academic staff.

Feedback from the user testing was highly positive, with users particularly commenting on the ease of navigation, the clarity of the instructions, the convenience of having the table of contents constantly present and the fact that the instructions are available on the same page as the EndNote resource. Negative points related to the re-sizing of the EndNote window to gain the split-screen, which some users found confusing.

Improvements based on the user testing feedback were incorporated into the final version, which was launched in June 2005. Since then, in addition to the original tutorial on the basics of using EndNote, members of the EndNote training team developed an additional three tutorials: an advanced tutorial on working with import filters; an advanced tutorial on editing output styles (something virtually impossible to teach in a drop-in facility owing to the need for administrative rights to the PC); and the aforementioned tutorial on working with images. The tutorials are available to other UK HE and FE libraries to be copied and adapted to their own needs.

---

5   Intute. <http://www.intute.ac.uk>.
6   MMU Library. <http://www.mmu.ac.uk/library>.

LearnHigher

LearnHigher is 'Britain's biggest collaborative HEFCE funded Centre for Excellence in Teaching and Learning'.[7] Based at Liverpool Hope University, LearnHigher is a partnership between 16 universities and the Higher Education Academy. The aim of the five-year programme is to 'build and disseminate a sound evidence base in learning development'. Each of the partners will contribute resources in 20 learning areas, which are 'research-driven, peer-reviewed and evaluated'. LearnHigher will also create a portal, through which resources and materials will be available to 'staff in both support roles and/or teaching roles' to use in course delivery. In the future resources will also be available for students to support their learning development. The focus of LearnHigher is 'not to endlessly create new resources but to understand what the role of resources is within formal and informal learning, what works in what context and why'. This focus drives the creation of reusable learning objects, which can be shared by many HE institutions and by many disciplines within institutions.

The learning area for which MMU is responsible is information literacy and the steering group includes staff from the Department of Information and Communications (which offers undergraduate and postgraduate courses in librarianship), library staff, staff from the central Learning Support and Learning and Teaching unit. An example of a reusable learning object created as part of the LearnHigher project, involving staff at MMU in partnership with the Intute Virtual Training Suite, is the Internet Detective resource,[8] now in its third edition, published in March 2006. The third edition is a complete rewrite of the second edition which was published in 1999 and produced by the DESIRE Project. The tutorial is designed to help HE and FE students develop the practical skills needed to think critically in order to evaluate the quality of Internet resources when carrying out research for their academic work. It is freely available online to students, can be worked through at their own pace and includes interactive elements, such as quizzes. At MMU it is widely used by many departments and has been incorporated into a WebCT version (available for download from the Internet Detective website). The use of a WebCT version gives staff more flexibility in the delivery of the tutorial; for example, staff have the option of making the tutorial part of blended learning courses and of releasing it to students in sections over time, rather than all at once. It also enables staff to track student progress and to include further graded quizzes, as well as self tests.

During the 2006–07 academic year, a customized and revised version of the university library's InfoSkills tutorial for physiotherapy students included the

---

7 LearnHigher. <http://www.learnhigher.ac.uk>.
8 Internet Detective. <http://www.vts.intute.ac.uk/detective>.

Internet Detective in the 'evaluating information' section. Further customized versions for other subjects are planned for the 2007–08 academic year.

SUMMARY

Changes in the way in which students are being taught, particularly through blended learning approaches, require changes in teaching and training of users of academic libraries in information literacy. The literature gives examples of partnerships between librarians and academic staff and identifies a need for improvements in the training of librarians in the use of learning technologies, particularly virtual learning environments. Examples discussed from Manchester Metropolitan University under the umbrella term of InfoSkills include training the trainers sessions in the use of interactive whiteboards and the use of EndNote software, incorporating an electronic voting system into lecture sessions, creating online tutorials using INFORMS software and the development of reusable learning objects.

REFERENCES

Allan, B. (2002), *E-learning and Teaching in Library and Information Services* (London: Facet).

Britain, S. and Liber, O. (2004), *A Framework for Pedagogical Evaluation of Virtual Learning Environments* (JISC). <http://www.jisc.ac.uk/uploaded_documents/VLE%20Full%20Report%2006.doc>.

Brophy, P., Markland, M. and Jones, C. (2003), *Link^{ER}: Linking Digital Libraries and Virtual Learning Environments: Evaluation and Review. Final Report: Formative Evaluation of the DiVLE Programme, CERLIM, Manchester.* <http://www.cerlim.ac.uk/projects/linker/>.

Campus Pack (2006), <http://www.learningobjects.com/products/campus-pack.html>.

CILIP (2004), *A Short Introduction to Information Literacy.* <http://www.cilip.org.uk/professionalguidance/informationliteracy/definition/introduction.htm>.

Donnelly, K., Jones, R., Matthews D. and Peters, K. (2006), 'Blended Learning in Action: The InfoSkills Programme at Manchester Metropolitan University's Library Service', *The New Review of Academic Librarianship*, 12:1, 47–57.

Forsyth, R. (2003), 'Supporting E-learning: An Overview of the Needs of Users', *The New Review of Academic Librarianship*, 9:1, 131–40.

Harris, N. (2005), 'The DiVLE Programme: Outputs and Outcomes', *VINE: The Journal of Information and Knowledge Management Systems*, 35:1/2, 64–9.

Harrison, M., Summerton, S. and Peters K. (2005), 'EndNote Training for Academic Staff and Students: The Experience of the Manchester Metropolitan University Library', *The New Review of Academic Librarianship*, 11:1, 31–40.

HEFCE (Higher Education Funding Council for England) (2005), *Strategy for E-learning*. <http://www.hefce.ac.uk/pubs/hefce/2005/05_12/>.

JISC (2005), *Pedagogy and Virtual Learning Environment (VLE) Evaluation and Selection*. <http://www.jisc.ac.uk/uploaded_documents/bp5.pdf>.

JISC (2005b), *Planning and Evaluating Effective Practice for E-learning Workshop Materials*. <http://www.jisc.ac.uk/elp_workshop content.html>.

JISC (2006), *eLearning strategic theme*. <http://www.jisc.ac.uk/whatwedo/themes/elearning.aspx>.

Jones, R., Peters, K. and Shields, E. (2006), 'Providing for the Next Generation: Adopting Interactive Whiteboards' in G. Walton and A. Pope.

Kent, T. (2003), 'Supporting Staff Using WebCT at the University of Birmingham in the UK', *Electronic Journal of E-Learning*, 1:1, 1–10. <http://www.ejel.org>.

Krumme, G. (2002), *Major Categories in the Taxonomy of Educational Objectives* (University of Washington). <http://faculty.washington.edu/krumme/guides/bloom1.html>.

Levy, P. (2005), 'Pedagogy in a Changing Environment' in P. Levy and S. Roberts.

Levy, P. and Roberts, S. (2005), *Developing the New Learning Environment: The Changing Role of the Academic Librarian* (London: Facet).

Markland, M. (2003), 'Embedding Online Information Resources in Virtual Learning Environments: Some of the Implications for Lecturers and Librarians of the Move towards Delivering Teaching in the Online Environment', *Information Research*, 8:4, July. <http://informationr.net/ir/8-4/paper158.html>.

MLA (Museums, Libraries and Archives) (2004), *The Knowledge Web*. <http://www.mla.gov.uk/resources/assets//I/iik_kw_pdf_5038.pdf>.

Quinlan, N. and Hegarty, N. (2006), 'Librarians Outside the Box: Waterford Institute of Technology's Library-based Virtual Learning Environment (VLE) Training and Development Programme', *New Library World*, 107:1/2, 37–47.

Roberts, S., Schofield, M. and Wilson, R. (2005), 'New Academic Teams' in P. Levy and S. Roberts.

Rowntree, D. (2000), *Who Are Your Distance Learners?* <http://www-iet.open.ac.uk/pp/D.G.F.Rowntree/distance_learners.htm>.

Saumure, K. and Shiri, A. (2006), 'Integrating Digital Libraries and Virtual Learning Environments', *Library Review*, 55:8, 474–88.

Scales, J., Matthews, G. and Johnson, C. (2005), 'Compliance, Cooperation, Collaboration and Information Literacy', *The Journal of Academic Librarianship*, 31:3, 229–35.

Secker, J. (2004), *Electronic Resources in the Virtual Learning Environment* (Oxford: Chandos).

Secker, J. (2005), 'DELIVERing Library Resources to the Virtual Learning Environment', *Program: Electronic Library and Information Systems*, 39:1, 39–49.

Sharpe, R., Benfield, G., Roberts, G. and Francis, R. (2006), *The Undergraduate Experience of Blended Learning: A Review of UK Literature and Practice* (The

Higher Education Academy). <http://www.heacademy.ac.uk/research/Sharpe_Benfield_Roberts_Francis.pdf>.

Stubley, P. (2002), 'Information Needs and WebCT', *Information Management Report*, October, 16–19.

Walton, G. and Pope, A. (2006), *Information Literacy: Recognising the Need*, Staffordshire University, 17 May 2006 (Stoke on Trent: Chandos).

Weaver, M. (2006), 'Flexible Design for New Ways of Learning', *Library and Information Update*, 5, 54–5.

CHAPTER 2

TRAINING FOR PEDAGOGICAL DEVELOPMENT

JO WEBB AND CHRIS POWIS

DEFINITIONS

Library and information staff are increasingly involved in facilitating learning through teaching, training, learning development and enhancement activities. Once perceived principally as an activity for those working within Higher Education institutions, teaching and supporting learning are now core activities for many library and information services staff, irrespective of the sector in which they work. In fact, these skills in enhancing learning are a vital part of our professional role as we must ensure that all our users are able to maximize the added value of libraries and information services.

This chapter will start with our definitions of learning and teaching, most of which are drawn from a previous work (Webb and Powis 2004).

The *learner* is the person who is the object of our learning and teaching activities. This may be an adult or a child, someone within or outside formal education. The learner may be employed or seeking work, retired or returning to education after an absence.

Learning is the process of active engagement with experience. It is what people do when they want to make sense of the world. It may involve the development or deepening of skills, knowledge, understanding, awareness, values, ideas and feelings, or an increase in the capacity to reflect. Effective learning leads to change, development and the desire to learn more (Museums, Libraries and Archives Council 2004).

Pedagogy is the art and science of teaching. Its Greek word root applies principally to teaching children, but it is most often applied in a general sense to any form of teaching. The practice of pedagogy is a focus for debate, with divergent theories and ideologies of learning and teaching feeding intense debates. Common areas of conflict include its emphasis on teaching children (whereas it is claimed adults require a completely different approach, called andragogy) or that it is teacher- rather than learner-centred. For further discussion of andragogy, consult Knowles

(1990). It is helpful to be aware of some of the key theories and principles. The websites run by James Atherton (2005) are an excellent introduction to this area.

A *teacher* is someone who organizes learning and helps the learner to construct meaning. Often the role of the teacher is to shape the learning environment and guide the learner to reach specific goals. Learning can take place without a teacher being present, but even in these cases a teacher will have at least prepared the environment or materials required for learning to take place.

Teaching is the process when a teacher shapes the learning experience for an individual or group. Teaching may be face-to-face or via ICT; it may be formal, in a classroom, or in a wide variety of informal settings.

A *learning and teaching event* is a discrete experience built around specific aims, objectives and learning outcomes. There is usually an identifiable learner or group of learners and someone leading the activity in the role of a teacher. Those activities may be part of formal or informal learning programmes, in physical and virtual environments, linked to education, work or leisure. The number and ages of the learners may also vary, ranging from informal work one-to-one with adult learners to leadership of modules within the university curriculum.

So a consideration of training for pedagogical development must include not only development for traditional information skills teaching in formal education but also informal interaction through, for example, roving support in a library. Changes in learning design, culture and expectations also require a greater understanding of learning and pedagogy as staff working in libraries have an increased responsibility for creating, developing and maintaining effective learning environments, both physical and virtual. We are also required to be more inclusive in our practice, supporting the widest community of users, including disabled and neurodiverse learners. It should therefore also be clear that in order to work effectively in a dynamic learning-centred library, staff need an understanding of pedagogy both to enhance their own practice and to ensure that the service meets its goals.

An understanding of the theory of teaching and of learning enables teachers, trainers and learning facilitators to be more effective in their work. As a starting point, if we understand how children and adults learn, the barriers to learning that may be encountered and the influence of individual differences and diversity, we will develop empathy for the individual learner and his or her learning needs. Building on this understanding of the nature of learning, we can start to understand how teachers and teaching shape the learning experience and then design and develop effective learning and teaching opportunities, whether in the form of structured teaching and training sessions, designing web or Intranet pages and online learning activities, or just in enhancing the way that we work face-to-face. This will shape not only an individual encounter with a learner, but should also influence how we create learner-centred environments.

ANALYSIS OF TRAINING NEEDS

The Higher Education Academy[1] produces a Professional Standards Framework for the self-assessment of teaching and supporting learning (Higher Education Academy 2006). Although designed to be used within Higher Education as either a personal self-assessment or course accreditation tool, its flexible and inclusive approach means it can be valuable in identifying needs in pedagogic development in both formal and informal learning environments. One of the benefits of the framework is the way it can be applied to staff with differing levels of experience and training.

The Professional Standards Framework is divided into three parts: core activities, core knowledge and professional values. The six areas of core activity in teaching and supporting learning are:

- The design and planning of learning activities and/or programmes of study
- Teaching and/or supporting learning
- Assessment and giving feedback to learners
- Developing effective environments and student support and guidance systems
- Integration of scholarship, research and professional activities with teaching and supporting learning
- Evaluation of practice and continuing professional development

The core activities are then linked with core knowledge:

- The subject material
- Appropriate methods for teaching and learning in the subject area and at the level of the academic programme
- How students learn, both generally and in the subject
- The use of appropriate learning technologies
- Methods for evaluating the effectiveness of teaching
- The implications of quality assurance and enhancement for professional practice

The third strand is the development of professional values, which are:

- Respect for individual learners

---

1   Higher Education Academy. <http://www.heacademy.ac.uk>.

- Commitment to incorporating the process and outcomes of relevant research scholarship and/or professional practice
- Commitment to development of learning communities
- Commitment to encouraging participation in higher education, acknowledging diversity and promoting equality of opportunity
- Commitment to continuing professional development and evaluation of practice

With a couple of adjustments to remove some of the HE-specific context – 'academic programmes', 'participation in *Higher* Education', this is a simple but comprehensive tool.

Following this framework, the first consideration in determining training needs should be to identify how a knowledge of pedagogy will be applied and if necessary what areas of knowledge, practice and values should be given priority. Different groups of staff will necessarily have a range of, and very possibly quite different, training needs. It may be helpful to consider what level of knowledge of pedagogy is essential for all members of staff, including library support staff involved in actively supporting users, and also for any staff who have some responsibility for training colleagues, including supervisors.

The areas for potential training fall into the following areas:

- Communication and presentation skills
- Knowledge of learners, motivation, learning styles and theories
- Delivery methods
- Planning
- Course structure and pedagogic design
- Auditing (or pre-assessment)
- Assessment (formative, summative)
- Evaluation including learner feedback
- Strategy and policy development to enhance learning and teaching

These are discussed in more detail in the following section.

OBJECTIVES OF SUGGESTED TRAINING PROGRAMMES

The nature of training and development for pedagogy clearly depends on the experience and needs of the learner. The new librarian faced with his or her first classes will usually be delivering another's materials, and will want to concentrate on presentation skills and delivery methods above anything else. A basic understanding of how learning takes place, different delivery methods and principles of feedback will probably suffice until the teacher is more experienced and therefore able to place pedagogy within his or her practical experience. As teachers take more control over their teaching, they will need to add a greater depth to their knowledge and add planning and assessing learners to simple survival skills. How to motivate, how to develop and encourage learners to learn outside of the classroom or formal teaching setting, generally only come with experience.

An understanding of pedagogy, learners and context is also important for less formal learning and teaching experiences. For many newer professionals, the process of the reference interview may not have been as central to their training as those in mid-career, but it offers some helpful models for understanding how to support learners in informal learning situations. For example, those principles of the reference interview – separating out expressed needs from actual wants, enabling the learner to become independent and embodying reflective and ethical professional practice – are also valid in tutorial situations.

The following can be found in most training and development programmes in teaching and learning and can provide a basic framework for developing pedagogic practice.

Communication and Presentation Skills

One starting point for the development of sound pedagogic practice is the development of effective presentation skills. If a teaching or learning event is to be successful, it needs to be well presented and understandable to the learners. This means rather more than designing attractive PowerPoint slides. Instead, presentation skills encompass the following:

- Ability to speak in front of other people. This includes speaking clearly without excessive use of notes, not speaking to a screen and a sense of presence as a teacher
- Ability to structure a presentation or talk. A well-structured, well-paced and well-timed presentation is easy to follow and facilitates understanding
- Sound skills in designing PowerPoint, or other, presentations
- Awareness of other presentation technologies and understanding of when to use visual aids – and when not to

These are not strictly pedagogic in nature but they are crucial in delivering effective teaching. Communication and presentation skills are often forgotten in practice with the assumption that they will be picked up on the job or come naturally. Many of us will start our careers without any experience of delivering to an audience beyond the occasional presentation at university or college. Yet being able to make others understand sometimes complex information is at the very heart of professional practice.

Effective communication skills may be simply about effective spoken skills, but increasingly the skills set will also include use of technologies ranging from PowerPoint or other presentation software, including interactive whiteboards, to recording spoken word or other presentations to embed within online learning environments.

Any teaching is a performance and should be approached as such. This does not mean that we need to train library staff to be actors, but it does mean that an understanding of voice control, movement and how the learners perceive the teacher should be included in training.

E-learning offers different challenges. The absence of the person in e-learning does not lessen the need to understand how good presentation works – in fact it makes it more important. Holding the learners' attention is vital but the high drop-out rates from e-learning show how much more difficult this is to do online (Packham et al. 2004).

In face-to-face teaching the delivery and timing of the teacher's inputs are important. Simple things like how and when to give out handouts will sometimes make or damage the effectiveness of a learning and teaching event.

Knowledge of Learners and Learning

To be effective, teaching should have the learner at its heart. This requires an understanding of how learning takes place and those variables that affect the learning experience. There are many different theories of learning, none of which are entirely satisfactory, often based on conflicting assumptions about human nature and society. In summary, however, effective learning tends to occur because of a combination of behaviour modification, personal development, appropriate social context, personal experience and good design. For staff involved in designing and developing learning programmes, an awareness of some of the key learning theories, especially cognitivist and constructivist approaches, and key theorists like Piaget (1950), Vygotsky (1978) and Bloom (1956), are essential.

Linked to theories of learning is the interaction between personality and learning, in the form of theories of learning styles and preferences. This is another substantial area for research and debate, often simplified into an awareness of either Kolb's experiential learning cycle (1984) or the VARK learning styles preferences (n.d.), to the extent that 'If you are a visual learner, you will use mindmaps ...' Although such simplifications are dangerous, a session on learning styles and diversity can be a valuable trigger in encouraging all library staff to understand individual differences and hence sensitivity in supporting the learning needs of library users.

The session below is an outline course on learning styles for library and information staff at De Montfort University. It is in two parts: the first session covers learning styles and an opportunity to find out your own styles. The second session explores how to apply your understanding of learning styles to working with others.

The motivation of our learners in approaching our teaching is often problematic. In educational settings we are often service teaching, sometimes as part of a subject but often as an add-on. Students have an interest in their subject and rarely in information skills per se. Understanding this motivation, or lack of it, and having techniques to overcome an initial lack of enthusiasm is critical to engaging the learner. Without such engagement it is unlikely that learning will take place in any meaningful sense. In public libraries there can be different issues: the challenges of dealing with groups often excluded from society or with people there on a voluntary basis who may not share a common understanding of the purpose of the course.

Table 2.1 Session plan – learning styles 2

Topic	Activity	Resources	Time
Aims of session and recap session 1			
Recap	Learning differences Taking responsibility for own learning Being sensitive to others' needs Using learning preferences to enhance learning identity and learning confidence	Slides and examples of VARK, Gardner, Kolb etc. for Sarah	
Presentation 'Learning Styles – what's the point?'	Learning styles? Learning strategies? Disposition or choice? Using language of preference and strength rather than deficit and weakness	New slide	

Topic	Activity	Resources	Time
What might be the impact on your professional role? • Within teams and groups within the workplace • As supervisors and managers of other people • As people involved in supporting learning	Think about situations – giving information, teaching concepts, processes Using VARK and Kolb or Serialist and Holists, think about how you could enhance the experience for a colleague or student or group. Use your own learning preferences to maximize your engagement with this task – then translate your ideas into something that would have generic application (could work in learning preference groups if enough attendees) Use flip-chart or post-its, coloured pens or whatever else you need to create and present your ideas	Flip-charts Pens Post-its Planning chart	
Feedback/presentations			
Evaluate and close			

Note: With thanks to Mary Pillai, Academic Team Manager, Centre for Learning and Study Support, Department of Library Services, De Montfort University.

Delivery Methods

The interaction between librarian (as teacher) and learner lies at the heart of the learning experience. As previously discussed, this interaction can be within a classroom, across an enquiry desk, online or as the author of learning materials. To make it effective in achieving the desired learning outcomes needs a knowledge and understanding of delivery methods. Choosing the appropriate method(s) for groups, individuals and material requires not just a portfolio of methods but an ability to tailor and amend them as needed. This requires experience allied to understanding, so training courses should provide an opportunity to find out about different delivery methods, see them demonstrated and have opportunities for participants to try out different methods for themselves.

Planning

Planning teaching should be grounded in an understanding of learning outcomes, not as a straitjacket but as an essential outline of the final product – what is it that you want to achieve from the interaction with your learners. Delivery, assessment and evaluation will all stem from this fundamental iteration but an understanding of the pedagogy underpinning the design of learning outcomes will enable the teacher to respond flexibly to the learners as the teaching develops.

The aims of the teaching should encompass the overall intention of the teaching – what is it intended to achieve. Learning outcomes should relate to those aims and offer steps towards achieving them. At a minimum level, anyone involved in designing learning and teaching opportunities should be able to devise aims and intended learning outcomes and recognize the importance of communicating those aims and learning outcomes/objectives to learners.

Course Structure and Pedagogic Design

Teaching, in our context, is often as a part of another course or learning programme. The typical one-hour, 'one shot', workshop where information skills has been shoehorned into a student's timetable is still common across all forms of formal education. This means that we need to be aware of how our teaching fits into the wider learner experience. Understanding how teaching works across contexts and subjects other than information skills is critical to providing an effective, holistic learning experience. Librarians can be somewhat arrogant in thinking that only they fully understand information skills and are uniquely placed to deliver its teaching. This is simply not the case. Academics, for example, will embody successful information-seeking behaviours for their students. To be successful in our teaching we need to be fully embedded in the wider subject and/or context to be successful.

It is important to have a grasp of the underlying principles behind course design so that our workshops or online learning objects can integrate into an existing programme rather than being seen as no more than an add-on. It may be helpful to conceptualize this as a curriculum or a learning journey for students. This approach refocuses attention on the needs of the learners rather than the performative elements of teaching inputs. After all, learning does not only take place during teacher input but also while learners are engaging actively with each other or with resources, and when they reflect on the learning and teaching event.

This means that a wider understanding of notions of syllabus and curriculum should also be included in training for pedagogical development. Key issues for consideration here include:

- Overall selection of topics and themes should be appropriate for the nature and level of the learning programme (so, for example, community learning initiatives are set at the right level for the target groups)
- Currency of content
- How the curriculum is designed, especially if this is more than a single workshop, and in particular how themes and ideas are introduced, developed and reinforced

Auditing

Learners will bring a range of experience, knowledge and needs to any teaching session and teachers need to audit their learners to match their teaching to them. Teaching without knowing your learners can result in bored, patronized and disengaged learners. The teacher should know techniques to discover learner needs and how to incorporate them into planning before and during a teaching session.

Assessment

Librarians are often unable to offer summative assessment (that is, offering a formal mark or grade) as part of their teaching. This does not mean that they do not take any part in assessment. For teaching to be effective it needs to include some check on whether learning outcomes have been met and a way of offering feedback to the learners in order to reinforce or amend their understanding. This formative element needs an understanding of the assessment process but it is often ignored or misunderstood by librarians. We are generally supportive and developmental in our teaching but rarely map this onto any formal ideas of assessment. However, these traits lie at the heart of good assessment practice.

Teachers should understand the difference between summative and formative assessment and know how to plan and deliver assessment using a range of methods.

They should understand the importance of feedback on learner performance and be able to provide constructive and developmental written and verbal feedback.

Evaluation Including Learner Feedback

The effectiveness of teaching can be measured through assessment but it should also include personal reflection informed by feedback from learners and other parties. This can include the design of feedback methods (including but not exclusively questionnaire-based) and techniques like peer observation, reflective logs/diaries and mentoring relationships.

Teachers should be able to use a variety of methods to gain feedback during and after formal teaching. They should understand the basic principles underpinning good feedback and be able to place it within an overall process of reflection on their teaching. This may typically include questionnaire and other written feedback methods but should also cover peer observation and an understanding of the body language of learners for instant feedback.

Equality and Diversity, and Inclusive Practice

The diverse nature of our learners will not be confined to their learning styles or motivation. Gender, ethnicity, educational experience and disability will all influence the learning experience and need to be understood and placed in a learning context. Many organizations offer some training in diversity awareness, and anyone involved in teaching and supporting learning should be encouraged to reflect on how these principles could be applied in a learning context. For more staff with some practical experience of working with diverse groups of learners, a facilitated session on inclusive practice in learning and teaching can be helpful.

METHODS OF TRAINING AND MEANS OF IMPLEMENTATION WITH EXAMPLES

There are many different ways of developing practice and expertise in pedagogy. These may be formal programmes leading to a range of academic qualifications or they may be delivered informally within the workplace. Choosing an appropriate method will depend on the experience, need and level of the teacher/librarian. It is probably of little use for a newly qualified librarian to undertake a Masters qualification in teaching and learning immediately on starting his or her teaching career. Needs would probably be better met through the support of a good mentor in conjunction with attendance on short courses and professional meetings. Someone with more experience will be able to apply personal experience to a greater depth of academic input and be better able to benefit from a more academic approach.

Learning on the Job

In reality many people learn how to teach and support learning through practice and reflection. Typically, a newly qualified librarian will first observe one or more experienced colleagues and then take on teaching using materials developed by another colleague. There are advantages and dangers in this approach but it is often simply the most practical way to begin teaching. Some people will thrive in this 'sink or swim' environment, and if the teaching mentor is sensitive to the worries and fears of their mentee it can be an effective introduction. The dangers lie not only in the obvious worry that the mentor might impart bad practice but also that the new teacher tries to copy the style and methods of their mentor without understanding the pedagogy underpinning them. It is important for new teachers to discover their own style of delivery and not to mimic others.

Even at this informal level of learning in pedagogic practice, it is helpful to identify key staff development outcomes.

Discrete Short Course or Workshop

Initial development in pedagogy is often best achieved through short courses or events organized by CILIP Training and Development (or equivalent) or by CILIP special interest groups (including University, College and Research Group libraries (UC&R), Education Libraries Group (ELG) or Colleges of Further and Higher Education (CoFHE)) where experienced and novice teachers can discuss teaching rooted in their context. This mirrors the experience of many teachers who update their knowledge and skills through contact, and discussion of teaching, with other subject specialists. Placing teaching in a wider context is laudable but ignoring the specialist needs of librarians would leave out an element of any pedagogical education.

Typically such short courses last no longer than a day and concentrate on particular issues like motivating students or sharing practice, or attempt to cover basic pedagogical principles. They are invariably popular, something that reinforces the notion that there is a need for such development. The example below is the programme for a one-day introductory course on teaching skills for librarians condensed from the EduLib programme.

Courses leading to a qualification will almost always be general in nature, allowing the learner to put a theoretical framework onto his or her experience. Often they will also expose librarians to learning alongside colleagues from other disciplines. This is often cited as a major strength of this approach and it does have much to recommend it; an understanding of the wider context in which we teach, exposure to the experience of other teachers, reinforcement that we do actually teach. For academic or specialist librarians it can give real insights into the pedagogy of the disciplines that they support. We would recommend that librarians with a fair proportion of teaching responsibility follow this route.

Courses are available through both colleges and universities. The most widely recognized college route, open to anyone interested and in a role where suitable experience can be acquired, is the suite of awards offered by City and Guilds. Accredited by City and Guilds, these courses are available wherever there is access to a Further Education college and often also via distance learning route. Of particular relevance are the Diploma in Delivering Learning (C&G 7302), Teaching Adult Learners (C&G 7307) and Tutoring Online (C&G 7516).

Table 2.2 Teaching skills for librarians

Aim

To enable participants to understand theories of teaching and learning and to map these on to their experience of teaching. To provide them with strategies to plan, deliver, assess and evaluate their teaching activities.

Objectives

At the end of the workshop participants will:

- Be able to relate theories of teaching and learning to their experiences of teaching
- Be able to plan a teaching and learning event
- Be able to match appropriate teaching methods to learning needs
- Have strategies to assess the effectiveness of their teaching
- Have strategies to evaluate their teaching

The Workshop

Please note that times, apart from start, finish and lunch, are approximate.

9.45–10.00	Registration
10.00–10.05	Welcome and introduction
10.05–11.30	The nature of teaching and learning
11.30–11.45	Break
11.45–12.00	Planning your teaching
12.00–1.00	Once you've got them – delivering teaching
1.00–1.45	Lunch
1.45–2.30	Delivering teaching cont.
2.30–3.00	Assessment and feedback
3.00–3.15	Tea
3.30–4.00	Critical incidents

Note: Much of the material was developed for Edulib, a JISC-funded project under the eLib project. Sample programme outline for a course delivered by Chris Powis, July 2008.

Formal Courses with Certification

Most UK universities now run a Teaching in Higher Education course at postgraduate certificate or diploma level. Although some institutions limit the courses to academic staff, many welcome librarians as long as they fulfil the admission requirements (usually a set number of hours teaching per year). Others, for example, the University of Northampton, have librarians on the course development and delivery teams.

However, it is also important to recognize that there are significant differences in our teaching context – particularly in the amount of time we have with students, the nature of assessment and the motivation of learners towards information skills. This difference is also found between, say, historians and physicists and reflected in the staff development organized through subject-specific routes like the HEA Subject Centres. We should not be afraid of recognizing these differences and following pedagogical development alongside other librarians as a companion to seeking more generic teaching development. For those new to the profession, and to teaching, it can seem very exposing to be alongside academic or teaching colleagues.

The online FOLIO course is a good example of a subject-based approach where the target audience is health librarians (Booth et al. 2005). Although the subject matter is generic in its coverage of the issues, the context is based around the participant's experience.

Reading/Self-development

The literature on teaching and learning is immense and anyone wishing to keep up to date faces a formidable task. As teaching is usually only one of the librarian's responsibilities, it can seem too daunting. However, there is a growing literature on teaching for librarians and we would recommend that accessing this should be a basic requirement for self-development (for example, see Secker, Boden and Price 2007; or Webb and Powis 2004).

Key issues are covered in the press, particularly the weekly *Times Higher Education Supplement* (THES) and the *Times Education Supplement* (TES), and the features in these papers provide a good starting point to investigate pedagogy as well as linking the librarian into the wider debates on teaching and learning.

Peer observation, both as observer and observee, is an easily arranged but immensely powerful tool to aid self-analysis and reflection on teaching and learning. Although simply observing another teacher can be informative in itself, it is more developmental if done using a more formal structure. Key issues for comment should be identified before the session and analysis made under agreed headings.

Recommendations and actions should also be included in the final reporting process. This can appear daunting, especially for the new teacher, appearing as it does to be about identifying weaknesses. This aspect is there but so too is the identification of personal strengths and good practice. Linking these (ideally confidential) reports to further reading and discussion can form an excellent developmental tool. For further information, look at Brown et al. (1993).

Action Learning Sets, or similar discussion forums, can add an extra dimension to reflection on teaching. Such sets have been run for librarians who teach in the East Midlands, and although the commitment required is significant, they can form a mutually supportive, confidential and innovative developmental tool.

One-off Events on Aspects of L&T

We have already noted above the short courses run by CILIP Training and Development, UC&R, CoFHE and other groups. Such events are certainly also common across the education sector and we would recommend that librarians who can access them do so. These range from internal seminars, often run by Schools or Faculties as well as by staff development or learning and teaching departments, to conferences or regional staff development consortia days (for example, the M25 group of universities in London or the M69 group in the East Midlands). They will usually concentrate on a particular aspect of pedagogy, for example, assessment or research-informed teaching, and are valuable networking as well as developmental events.

Research and Evaluation Activities

The importance of practitioner-based research into teaching and learning is often overlooked by librarians. The emphasis of our research is still more likely to be in traditional areas of concern for the profession such as user behaviour, information literacy or use of resources, but we should look to engage in or with pedagogical research projects. Work done in Centres of Excellence in Teaching and Learning (CETLs), through JISC-sponsored projects in Further and Higher Education and in small-scale work, will be relevant, and librarians should be actively engaged in seeking funding from these bodies or working as partners with others to make bids. Involvement in such research informs the researcher's own practice and encourages the reflective process which is so important in teaching.

EduLib

EduLib was a JISC-funded project running from 1996 to 1999, aimed at developing the teaching skills of librarians. An initial pool of 12 development officers was trained not only in pedagogy but also in how to cascade such knowledge to the rest of the Higher Education library sector. Two national iterations of the final EduLib project were run at venues across the UK, some local variants were also held and at least one international course based on EduLib was delivered (in Finland in 1999). A set of EduLib materials to aid staff development in teaching and learning was also sent to each UK university (McNamara and Core 1998). Although the original cascade idea did not work consistently across the UK, EduLib did raise the profile of pedagogical development for academic librarians and was adapted for use in Australia (Peacock 2001). Many of the short courses or professional workshops being held over ten years later owe a considerable debt to the original EduLib materials and ethos.

MONITORING AND EVALUATION OF TRAINING

Any consideration of the monitoring and evaluation of training and development activity should first consider the purpose of such evaluation. Embarking on what could be a time-consuming exercise without knowing what you are looking for or what ends you are hoping to achieve will lead to wasted effort and what may be a lessening of motivation to continue with such activity in the future.

It is perhaps too obvious to claim that any training and development in pedagogy will enhance the quality of teaching. A greater understanding of the nature of teaching and learning, a better grasp of teaching techniques and a wider knowledge of assessment should only help enhance teaching. Monitoring the effectiveness of development in this is, however, very difficult. Librarians are often not part of formal assessment where an increase in grades or pass rates can be seen as evidence of better teaching (although other factors can and do have a bearing on increased achievement of students). Long-term monitoring of teaching is also difficult when librarians are commonly restricted to single or limited exposure as a small element on a course, however integrated they may be, or when working with adult learners in the community.

Where these conditions apply, it is best to track enhanced teaching through triangulating feedback across the full range of your teaching, taking peer observation, session feedback and any improvement in student performance together. Where a training event has concentrated on a single issue, learner engagement perhaps, this feedback can be mined for specific improvements based on the learning that took place during the training event.

Initial training and development may be geared around an improvement in the librarian's confidence as a teacher. Increases in confidence can be monitored through peer observation and especially through reflection. The latter can be structured, with a mentor perhaps, or self-led.

Monitoring the development of new skills and/or innovative practice is also best done through self- or group reflection, although students can be asked specific questions about the effectiveness of new techniques. The use of feedback forms, usually immediately after a teaching event, is probably the most common form of monitoring and evaluation. This applies to the development event itself and to subsequent teaching. However, these are of limited value unless they are targeted at specific issues. There is little to be gained by asking if training and development has been effective before the teacher has had a chance to integrate any learning that has taken place into their practice. Likewise, asking students whether they have gained anything from a teaching session is likely to elicit unconsidered and limited feedback if done immediately after the session. If possible such feedback should be sought once the students or trainees have had a chance to process and reflect on their learning and to put it into practice.

Formal feedback on training should not formulaically reproduce feedback forms from previous events. Asking questions on the catering, environment and performance of the trainer are worthwhile if they can be changed, but this is often not the case. It is far better to target issues about the application, relevance and applicability of the training. It should be questioned whether a paper form is the best way to achieve this. E-mail and other online applications can make the timely collection of feedback much easier and strong consideration should be given to their use.

The agencies that validate formal courses in teaching and learning monitor the quality of those courses. Individual universities, the Higher Education Academy, City and Guilds and others will demand that courses undergo vigorous validation and review procedures. Librarians may have input to these quality procedures and those taking them will usually have routes to contribute to the quality process (through course representatives or other feedback mechanisms).

Action learning and peer observation have been mentioned as powerful developmental tools above, but they can also serve as a forum for the gathering of feedback on the effectiveness of development activities. If questions are asked specifically related to any development that has taken place before the teaching being monitored or discussed, they can serve as a useful monitoring tool on the development as well as the teaching. It is important to retain confidentiality with this methodology, though, and the collation of such feedback by training co-ordinators or managers should be handled sensitively.

The overall focus of any training for pedagogical development should be to develop effective and innovative teachers applying pedagogical theory within a framework of values. The monitoring and evaluation of this cannot be achieved through one simple methodology, and a more sophisticated framework involving reflection, peer observation and more formal mechanisms should be applied to recognize that more holistic goal.

REFERENCES

Atherton, J.S. (2005), 'Learning and Teaching'. <http://www.learningandteaching. info>.

Bloom, B. (ed.) (1956), *Taxonomy of Educational Objectives: The Classification of Educational Goals* (New York: Longmans).

Booth, A., Ayiku, L., Sutton, A. and O'Rourke, A. (2005), 'Fulfilling a Yearning for E-learning', *Library and Information Update*, October 2005. <http://www.cilip.org.uk/publications/updatemagazine/archive/archive2005/october/boothoct05.htm>.

Brown, S. et al. (eds) (1993), *Observing Teaching*, SCED Paper 79 (Birmingham: SEDA Publications).

Higher Education Academy: home page. <http://www.heacademy.ac.uk>.

Higher Education Academy (2006), *The UK Professional Standards Framework for Teaching and Supporting Learning in Higher Education*. <http://www.heacademy.ac.uk/ourwork/policy/framework>.

Knowles, M.S. (1990), *The Adult Learner: A Neglected Species*, 4th edn (Houston: Gulf Publishing).

Kolb, D. (1984), *Experiential Learning* (Englewood Cliffs: Prentice Hall).

McNamara, D. and Core, J. (1998), *Teaching for Learning in Libraries and Information Services: A Series of Educational Workshops*, The EduLib Project and its Teaching Materials (Hull: EduLib Project).

Museums, Libraries and Archives Council (2004), *Inspiring Learning for All*. <http://www.inspiringlearningforall.gov.uk/introduction/what_do_we_mean/what_do_we_mean/default.aspx>.

Packham, G., Jones, P., Miller, C. and Thomas, B. (2004), 'E-learning and Retention: Key Factors Influencing Student Withdrawal', *Education and Training*, 46, 6/7, 335–42.

Peacock, J. (2001), 'Teaching Skills for Teaching Librarians: Postcards from the Edge of the Educational Paradigm', *Australian Academic and Research Libraries*, 32, 1. <http://alia.org.au/publishing/aarl/32.1/full.text/jpeacock.html>.

Piaget, J. (1950), *The Psychology of Intelligence* (London: Routledge & Kegan Paul).

Secker, J., Boden, D. and Price, G. (2007), *The Information Literacy Cookbook: Ingredients, Tasters and Recipes for Success* (Oxford: Chandos).

VARK: A Guide to Learning Styles: home page. <http://www.vark-learn.com/english/index.asp>.

Vygotsky, L. (1978), *Mind in Society: The Development of Higher Psychological Processes* (Cambridge, MA: Harvard University Press).

Webb, J. and Powis, C. (2004), *Teaching Information Skills: Theory and Practice* (London: Facet).

CHAPTER 3

FACILITATING INFORMATION LITERACY EDUCATION (FILE)

SUSIE ANDRETTA

INTRODUCTION

This chapter outlines the FILE course commissioned by London Health Libraries[1] as part of its Learner Support Programme (LSP), and developed by the School of Information Management at London Metropolitan University as a continuing professional development (CPD) programme which is also accredited as a postgraduate module. Whilst the first delivery of this course is targeting a specific section of the information community operating within the health sector, the purpose and structure of FILE enable the customization of its provision to address the CPD needs of any information community of practice that deals with information literacy education. FILE, therefore, is relevant to a wide range of information professionals who are interested in becoming reflective practitioners (Schön 1991), and developing the competence and the confidence required to facilitate information literacy practices associated with diverse populations of users. The chapter consists of two main parts. The first introduces the context in which the phenomenon of information literacy (IL) has emerged, presents some of the definitions of information literacy, outlines the continuing professional development (CPD) requirements of information practitioners who are involved in its provision, and explains the relational approach of information literacy underpinning the FILE course. The second part offers an outline of FILE, gives a profile of its first cohort, presents examples of formative and summative assessment strategies implemented to record the participants' progress as information literacy facilitators, and reports on the preliminary feedback generated by this cohort.[2] Concrete examples of the participants' work are given for the first four components of the assessed portfolio, as the writing of this chapter runs concurrent with the submission of these components. The impact of component 5, together with a long-term evaluation of the course, will be covered by a later publication.

---

1   London Health Libraries. <http://www.londonlinks.ac.uk/>.
2   The online evaluation the participants completed at the end of the taught part of FILE is available at: <http://freeonlinesurveys.com/rendersurvey.asp?sid=m2buodhd6v2ogjo27444 7>. Throughout the rest of this chapter we shall refer to this as the FILE evaluation survey.

SETTING THE SCENE FOR INFORMATION LITERACY:
A CONSTANTLY CHANGING INFORMATION ENVIRONMENT

Increased access to digital information necessarily requires an ability to evaluate it in terms of quality and relevance (Whitworth 2007). However, in practice there is a gap of evaluative competences and attitudes at both employee and student levels. For example, O'Sullivan found in a survey of 6,000 corporate workers in the US that 80 per cent went for free information on the Internet rather than using the resources provided by the company or by libraries (O'Sullivan 2002). The majority also had difficulties in determining the quality (credibility and accuracy) of the information retrieved. More recent research by the Economist Intelligence Unit (EIU 2006) eliciting the view of 386 senior executives worldwide discovered that only 4 per cent of this sample was very satisfied with data integration and analysis, while 40 per cent admitted that their workers often make poor decisions because of inadequate data. A similar scenario is found in Higher Education (HE), where a study by Lorenzo and Bziuban on information literacy practices in three English-speaking countries (US, Australia and UK) observed that even the students who are 'digital natives' (Lorenzo and Bziuban 2006), and therefore familiar with the technology and the web environment, are not equipped with the ability to assess the quality of the information at their disposal.

One of the factors associated with this problem is the employers' overemphasis on ICT literacy at the expense of information literacy, or the ability to fully capitalize on the information that is available through digital technology:

> *A great deal of attention has been paid to the development of 'computer literacy', and computer literacy is now a core skill for many posts. The focus is on the ability to use computers and standard software applications, but stop short of being able to structure, find, evaluate and use the information to which a computer provides access* (Abell and Oxbrow 2001).

In the UK the potential for interactive technologies and communication systems to create a professional workforce has long been associated with e-learning practices which identify information literacy as a necessary e-oriented skill. However, the criticism made by Abell and Oxbrow remains valid as it is the area of ICT that is specifically singled out as 'a priority for the new Skills Strategy' (DfES 2003).[3] The main concern here is that the mastery of self-directed learning practices envisaged by the UK e-learning initiative is not embedded in an appropriate information literacy framework, but relies on a computer literacy approach which falls short of covering the complex, critical and ethical interaction with information (Whitworth 2007).

---

3   Cited in Andretta 2005b.

A REVIEW OF INFORMATION LITERACY'S DESCRIPTIONS

There is a vast body of literature on what the phenomenon of information literacy entails; however, a full account of this debate goes beyond the scope of this chapter and has been given elsewhere (Snavely and Cooper 1997; Plotnick 1999; Bruce 1999; 2002; Bruce and Candy 2000; Virkus 2003; Andretta 2005a; Koufogiannakis and Wiebe 2006). Here we briefly explore the publications that are deemed relevant for those who wish to become more familiar with the evolving roles of information literacy as a catalyst for educational change through its promotion of independent learning, and as a social developer through its promotion of lifelong learning.

By associating information literacy with the learning how to learn approach the American Library Association (ALA) defined its role as a necessary framework for the support of learning and knowledge dissemination.

> *To be information literate, a person must be able to recognize when information is needed and have the ability to locate, evaluate, and use effectively the needed information. [...] Ultimately, information literate people are those who have learned how to learn. They know how to learn because they know how knowledge is organized, how to find information, and how to use information in such a way that others can learn from them* (ALA 1998).

Clearly, the learn how to learn approach addresses the requirements for continuous learning practices associated with a knowledge-based economy: 'In recognition of the requirements for a lifelong learning strategy generated by the Knowledge-based economy which is characterised by the need for continuous learning of both codified information and the competencies to use this information' (OECD 1996).

Information literacy as the foundation of lifelong learning is also promoted at international level, emphasizing the importance of this phenomenon as a social developer (Abid 2004). Its emancipatory role is confirmed by both the Prague Declaration (Thompson 2003) and the Alexandria Proclamation (Alexandria Proclamation 2005) which promote information literacy as a basic human right because of its association with lifelong learning initiatives. Therefore, as an enabler of social inclusion through personal and social empowerment, information literacy assumes the role of the functional literacy for the twenty-first century (Andretta 2007b).

The need for the learn how to learn approach in education was recognized as far back as the late 1960s in response to the constantly changing nature of knowledge, and the need to focus on the process of knowledge construction rather than on the accumulation of static knowledge.

We are faced with an entirely new situation in education, where the goal, if we are to survive, is the facilitation of change and learning. The only person who is educated is the person who has learned how to learn; the person who has learned how to learn, adapt and change; the person who has realised that no knowledge is secure; that only the process of seeking knowledge gives a basis for security. Changingness, a reliance on process rather than upon static knowledge, is the only thing that makes any sense as a goal for education in the modern world (Rogers 1969).

A few decades on and the realization that education cannot rely on the acquisition of static knowledge is found in the work of Bruce (Bruce 2002) and Bundy (Bundy 2003) who promote information literacy as a catalyst for educational change. In a subsequent paper, Bundy argues for an education that focuses on the questions used to investigate knowledge as these rarely change, rather than concentrate on the answers that always change (Bundy 2005). This view is further elaborated by a recent study on *Ensuring the Net Generation is Net Savvy* which sees information literacy as the connector of the fragmented knowledge that characterizes the current HE environment (Lorenzo and Bziuban 2006).

This review would be incomplete without mentioning the information literacy frameworks produced by the Association of College and Research Libraries (ACRL 2000) and the Australian and New Zealand Institute for Information Literacy (Bundy 2004) as these offer clear guidelines on the effective integration of information literacy in education and learning through the promotion of critical thinking and an iterative knowledge-construction process. A more detailed account of these frameworks is given elsewhere (Andretta 2005a); the main point to be stressed in this chapter is that both frameworks provide detailed and comprehensive information literacy standards that cover the iterative stages involved in the accomplishment of an information goal. These include the clear formulation of an information need, the retrieval and critical evaluation of the sources which are scrutinized in terms of relevance and credibility, the application of information which acknowledges the related social and ethical concerns, and the final integration of the information into the learner's knowledge base (which leads to effective dissemination practice).

CPD REQUIREMENTS OF INFORMATION LITERACY EDUCATORS

According to Lichtenstein, information professionals need to assume the role of 'professional information navigators [...] who can train people to be information literate and operate effectively in our contemporary, complex and largely unregulated information environment' (Lichtenstein 2000). Bruce goes further by arguing that information literacy educators must themselves be information literate: 'The whole point of IL is that you are helping people learn how to learn and how to engage in that process. There is no point in teaching IL if you are not experiencing it in your own learning' (cited in Newton and Boden 2006).

A similar point is made by this author (Andretta 2005a) who argues that the principle of independent learning underpinning the process of information literacy must also be viewed by information professionals as an opportunity to further their own lifelong learning practice:

> *Provision of information literacy, which is based on the process of recursive learning, therefore requires an equivalent process of reflection on practice to be undertaken by the information literacy educator. If information literacy is about learning how to learn, for the reflective information literacy practitioner this necessarily becomes a question of learning how to learn how to learn* (Andretta 2005a).

Such a perspective leads to a redefinition of the information professional's role as one of teacher (Lantz and Brage 2006), or facilitator (Andretta 2005b) of information literacy education associated with a learner-centred approach and reflective practices (Andretta 2005a). Stubbings and Franklin also claim that the role of the academic librarian must include that of educator (Stubbings and Franklin 2006). Information literacy, therefore, becomes intrinsically linked with learning, although this view brings particular challenges in HE when attempting to establish collaboration between library and faculty staff: 'One cannot help but think that as librarians become pro-active advocates of information literacy, and reclaim the role of educator, faculty staff must perceive this development as an encroachment on their professional territory, and therefore resist such a change' (Andretta 2006a).

According to Stubbings and Franklin there is a need to advocate for information literacy within the context of the academic library (Stubbings and Franklin 2006). Here information literacy educators face the additional challenge of dispelling the misconceptions about information literacy held by faculty staff and students alike. In particular, library staff are constantly battling against the problem of moving beyond the stand-alone induction approach in an attempt to demonstrate that information literacy is not an issue to be tackled somewhere outside the curriculum, nor it is solely about ICT skills or searching the Internet. Advocacy, in this case, involves using a number of marketing strategies that present information literacy as a way of combating plagiarism, or as a method for implementing personal development planning (PDP). The problem of adequate access to the users is also experienced by the FILE participants who, while exploring the challenges of delivering information literacy education during the second session of the course,[4] stressed the need to move from a just-in-case approach, characterized by the stand-alone one-hour induction, to a just-in-time type of provision characterized by flexible delivery that is fully customized to address the diverse users' needs and competences, taking into account the environmental factors that may hinder the training.

Booth[5] argues that the strategy of advocacy is particularly crucial within the context of the health information sector where information literacy educators need to substantiate the impact of their practice on evidence-based medicine and patient care (Booth 2006). This necessarily stresses the importance of evaluation in promoting evidence-based advocacy. According to Booth this requires a shift in the way the impact of information literacy training is measured so that educators do not stress what they do, but focus on what they can achieve, and in particular on what contribution they are making to the objectives of the organization. Instead of presenting data on the number of people who received training in a year, information literacy educators should emphasize the effect of the training on patient care. He illustrates this with the following examples: '15 people out of 350 changed their clinical positions as a result of the training',[6] rather than limiting the evaluation to the number of people who received training within a given period of time, such as '350 people were trained last year'.[7]

In terms of CPD, therefore, information literacy educators must employ advocacy to stress the impact of their practice not only on the users, but also on the organization as a whole. The following quote illustrates how FILE encouraged this participant to advocate her information literacy practice in a much more focused (and by implication more effective) manner. She confirms her ability to target the advocacy of information literacy at specific users thanks to FILE: 'The opportunity to "sell" the course (i.e. the information literacy activities and strategies developed for the portfolio) really helped as I have trouble with getting people to attend my courses. It made me focus on a particular group rather than trying to promote everything to everybody.'[8]

---

4   The file illustrating this point can be found at: <http://www.ilit.org/file/files/wk2am discussionssession.doc>.

5   Extract from Andrew Booth's talk on 'Information literacy training: How can we know we are not wasting our time?' presented during the third session of FILE, 14 February 2007. The PowerPoint presentation and pod-cast of the talk are available at: <http://www.ilit.org/file/file3.htm>.

6   Ibid.

7   Ibid.

8   Extract from the FILE evaluation survey.

Furthermore, as the role of information literacy becomes associated with strategies of independent and lifelong learning, it follows that the educators responsible for its provision must be fully conversant with pedagogical practices that address the diversity of their users' learning needs and attitudes (Markless and Streatfield 2007). The feedback from another participant points to the usefulness of one of FILE's assessed components in increasing her awareness of the users' requirements, and in acknowledging their learning needs:

> *Bringing all the 'pieces' of the course together in this activity [Component 4] has demanded considerable thought and planning and highlighted the need to approach my training sessions from many different angles: the learning level of the cohort, the context of the training, setting achievable learning outcomes and much more. I go away with a much firmer grip on how to style IL training sessions.*[9]

FILE AND THE RELATIONAL MODEL

The relational model of information literacy promoted by Bruce, Edwards and Lupton is taken as the starting point of FILE, based on the premise that our conception of this phenomenon is influenced by the way we perceive learning and teaching (Bruce, Edwards and Lupton 2007). Bruce, Edwards and Lupton identify six conceptual frames of information literacy including:

- The Content frame
- The Competency frame
- The Learning to Learn frame
- The Personal Relevance frame
- The Social Impact frame
- The Relational frame

A full account of the six frames approach is given elsewhere (Andretta 2006a); here it suffices to say that each frame reflects a unique view of information literacy, characterized by its own interpretation of information, curriculum focus, learning, teaching, content, and assessment or impact. The frames are self-explanatory, so that the Content frame focuses on the accumulation of knowledge associated with the world of information, the Competency frame measures the level of information skills developed, the Learning to Learn frame stresses the independent and lifelong learning approaches we wish to associate with continuing professional development (CPD) programmes, while frames four and five aim to promote information use that leads to emancipation at personal or social levels respectively,

---

9   Ibid.

and finally the Relational frame focuses on the awareness of the complex learning and information relationship.

The Relational frame has major implications for information literacy facilitators as it stresses the link between learning and information use, promoting a change in the learner's awareness, rather than measuring learning in terms of the knowledge that one accumulates: '[...] a qualitative change in a person's way of seeing, experiencing, understanding, conceptualising something in the real world – rather than a change in the amount of knowledge which someone possesses' (Bruce 1997).

Such a shift in awareness is what makes the Relational approach the catalyst for educational change advocated by Bruce in her 2002 paper. In practice Competency and Content are the two most popular frames adopted to implement information literacy education (particularly in HE), and this is demonstrated by the findings of a workshop run at the Information Literacy conference organized by Staffordshire University in May 2006.[10] Statements presented by Bruce, Edwards and Lupton to describe the six frames of information literacy were used to elicit the view of the conference's participants about their institution's approach towards the implementation of information literacy education (Bruce, Edwards and Lupton 2007). The results[11] demonstrate a dominant preference for information literacy as a set of competencies or skills. For example, 73 participants (out of 150) selected the Competency frame as their first choice, while 49 participants chose information literacy that is associated with the knowledge about the world of information (the Content frame) as their second choice. Even more revealing though is the fact that out of the 150 conference delegates, no one selected the Social Impact frame, raising serious concern over the lack of awareness of information literacy within the HE sector as a social enabler (Andretta 2007a).

The same activity was completed by the FILE participants at the start of the course in session one (17 January) and at the end in session five (14 March). Here the lack of selection of the Social Impact frame in session one, shown in Table 3.1, echoes the findings generated by the Information Literacy conference workshop. Such an omission suggests that, in the UK at least, these two perspectives have not permeated the professional consciousness of information literacy educators. This is particularly curious in respect to the health sector where one would expect a strong association between the Social Impact frame and the aim of promoting information literacy to underpin evidence-based medicine and optimize patient care (two very clearly defined social contexts). It should be noted that in session five

---

10   'Information Literacy: Recognising the Need', Staffordshire University, 17 May 2006. <http://www.staffs.ac.uk/infolitconf/>.
11   For full details of the findings, see Poster 1: 'Institutional perspectives of information literacy', available at: <http://www.staffs.ac.uk/infolitconf/susie_andretta/index.php>.

only one participant of FILE chose this frame as a second option, thus illustrating that greater emphasis needs to be placed on the relationship between information literacy and the Social Impact frame in a future delivery of the course.

**Table 3.1 Selections of the six frames of information literacy
by FILE participants**

Statements illustrating the six frames of information literacy	Session one: 17 January 2007		Session five: 14 March 2007	
	First choice	Second choice	First choice	Second choice
Information literacy is knowledge about the world of information	0	5	0	0
Information literacy is a set of competencies or skills	7	4	2	3
Information literacy is a way of learning				1
Information literacy is a personalised investigation of a subject and is different for different people/groups	4	2	2	6
Information literacy is viewed within a social context	0	0	0	1
Information literacy is a complex of different ways of interacting with information	2	2	9	2

As Table 3.1 illustrates, preference for the Competency frame is found in the selections made by the FILE participants in session one, with seven out of 13 opting for the information skills approach as their first choice and nine going for the Knowledge or Competency frames as their second choice. This indicates a similarity between the views of the FILE cohort at the beginning of the course and the views of the conference's participants. By contrast, the Relational frame attracts only four selections, pointing to the need of increasing the FILE participants' awareness of the appropriateness of this approach in acknowledging the diverse perceptions of information literacy by learners and facilitators. To counteract the traditional provision of information literacy where this is defined solely as a set of distinct skills, or a self-contained discipline, the relational approach proposes the strategy of mediating information skills and content by focusing on the interaction between learner and information and facilitating the variation in learning styles and information use. This is also the ultimate aim of FILE which encourages the participants to go beyond the conception of evaluating information literacy in terms of content and/or skills and adopt a more reflective Relational approach. The impact of this strategy is confirmed by the selection of the Relational frame in columns four and five of Table 3.1 which clearly shows a shift away from information skills (11 out of 13 chose this frame during the first session) towards a Relational perspective (11 out of 13 selected this frame in session five).

Increased awareness of the six frames of information literacy promoted by Bruce, Edwards and Lupton was fostered by Component 2 of the FILE portfolio, where the participants, working in teams, were asked to correlate the information literacy strategy proposed to support a specific group of users with the appropriate information literacy frame(s) (Bruce, Edwards and Lupton 2007). The results[12] illustrate the teams' effective use of a combination of information literacy approaches. For example, group two adopted the Relational frame to foster information literacy practices of clinical research physicians by emphasizing the users' relationship with information through active reflection, aiming to strengthen their existing information practice. Group four, on the other hand, promoted a combination of Competency and Learning to Learn approaches for staff nurses to further this group's professional development by enhancing their ICT competences and problem-solving skills. Group three adopted a similar combination of Competency and Learning to Learn frames to address the ICT requirements of clinical staff, ranging from surgeons to managers, and improve patient care. Meanwhile group one combined ICT skills with reflective and iterative assessment strategies included in a BTEC Certificate in Food and Beverage Service programme for hospital catering staff. The rationale here was that improved access and dissemination of online information would lead to a successful completion of the course. Finally group five emphasized the importance of developing information literacy and ICT competences of junior doctors in combination with independent learning strategies, although these were not openly associated with the Learning to Learn frame.

INTERNAL AND EXTERNAL INFORMATION HORIZONS OF INFORMATION LITERACY

FILE adopts the Relational approach in its provision by starting with the basic pedagogical premise that information literacy is characterized by the relationship between learner and information. This concept is based on the phenomenographic perspective of learning which focuses on the relationship between subject and phenomenon (Marton and Booth 1997). An account of how the phenomenographic approach has influenced the Relational frame is found in other works (Bruce 1997;

---

12   The PowerPoint presentations produced by the five teams as part of Component 2 are available at: <http://www.ilit.org/file/eportfolios07.htm>.

2002; Lupton 2004; Edwards 2006; Bruce, Edwards and Lupton 2007; Hughes, Bruce and Edwards 2007; Andretta 2007c). For the purpose of this chapter we will explore the basic tenets of the Relational approach to illustrate that the dynamics of the learner–information relationship have an impact on the overall learning experience. This relationship is shown by Figure 3.1[13] as either an external horizon or an internal one, while the circle at the centre represents the focal awareness of the learner, also described as the engagement with the phenomenon or process (Bruce 1997; Edwards 2006).

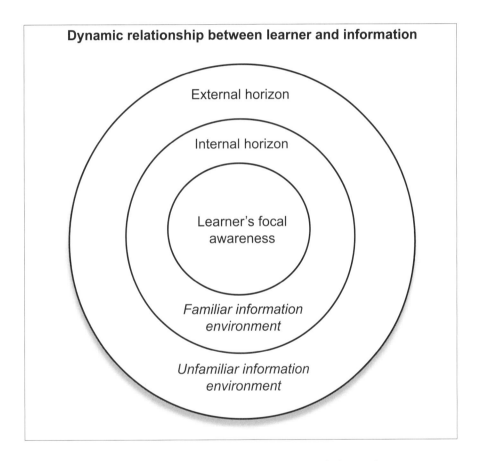

Figure 3.1 Dynamic relationship between learner and information

---

13   This is part of the Doctoral research currently undertaken by the author and exploring the information literacy conceptions of information professionals who are currently attending the Masters in Information Services Management at London Metropolitan University.

THE EXTERNAL HORIZON AND BEYOND

The external horizon is characterized by fuzzy awareness, where the existence of information may be acknowledged, but remains outside the subject's focus, demonstrating poor retention (or ownership) and poor transfer of the information (and of the learning) process. An example of poor retention and transfer is given by a Masters student describing her attempt to learn how to use concept maps:

> [Concept mapping] was recommended to me before but I didn't understand what it was about. (The student was introduced to concept maps during her PhD which she started a few years ago but never completed). Many times my supervisor said OK you are going to write a chapter about this, let's sit on the floor with a huge sheet of paper, put this here and I put this here, what's the relationship between [those], is there something in the middle, put it here, draw a line, and I would do it with her, and take that home and by the time I got home I had completely lost it.[14]

Despite her attempts to internalize concept mapping, this process remained unfamiliar. When prompted to explain what went wrong during the PhD she attributed this failure to a lack of understanding concept mapping as a method for structuring knowledge. In other words she was going through the activity without conceptualizing the purpose driving it: 'I didn't see that it was about establishing relationships between concepts. To me it was just putting down a map of ideas, but I wasn't seeing how it was that the connecting [would enable me] to write a structured essay or a structured chapter or something like that [...] it's about organising knowledge.'

It is clear that information literacy education needs to foster the ability to conceptualize/organize knowledge by introducing the learner to the principles underpinning these processes. This is in line with the perspective proposed by Laurillard who argues that educators: '[...] have to appeal to the conceptual apparatus that supports [learning]' (Laurillard 1993). In FILE this is achieved by introducing the participants to user profiling, formulation of learning outcomes and reflective practice.

Beyond the external horizon information is unknown, demonstrating a total lack of awareness from the part of the learner. Evidence of such an extreme level of unfamiliarity was first encountered by this author (Andretta 2005a; 2006b) during a study of first-year students attending an information literacy module as part of their undergraduate degree. To put it simply, when faced with information systems that were unfamiliar, the students felt intimidated and were unable to interact with

---

14   Extract from an interview undertaken as part of the author's Doctoral research. All the subsequent quotes in this paragraph are taken from the same interview.

these resources. The strategy used to address this type of unfamiliarity consisted of an iterative learning process involving the students' engagement with interactive learning resources to foster familiarity and confidence. These offered guidelines on a number of information systems through step-by-step examples and exercises facilitated through face-to-face support as well as online tutorials on-demand. The introduction to the newspaper database gives a good example of how students moved from an unfamiliar to a familiar information environment: 'At the beginning this [the newspaper database] was very unfamiliar. It soon became one of my favourite databases and was especially useful for my research into the history of the press' (Andretta 2005). In this case, increased confidence generated by variation in practice that leads to a familiarization with the database is complemented by the usefulness of this resource in accomplishing an academic task, for example, an essay on the history of the press. This further strengthens the learner's motivation to engage with the newspaper database because he/she perceives it as a relevant source of information. As a result, a successful change of the student's attitude ensues and the learner moves from intimidated to confident and enthusiastic use of the resource. The implication here is that information literacy educators need to advocate the importance of information literacy by stressing its usefulness to their users/learners and enhance their motivation to engage with it. The feedback from a FILE participant shows that the usefulness of the training is promoted through the adoption of shared information literacy resources developed as part of the portfolio:

> *[...] I've just run a training session for library assistants on searching the databases such as Medline. Used my Boolean presentation as part of it [Component 4 of FILE] and bits of both Jane's and Louise's presentations around selecting search terms and introduced the citation matcher into my session for the very first time. All down to FILE and my wonderful colleagues! One lady said she learnt more this afternoon than in the last 3 years together and has been 'inspired'.*[15]

Unfamiliarity breeds anxiety at all levels of provision, and this is manifested by the difficulties the learner expects to encounter when engaging with the information process, or task for the first time. This point is confirmed by the findings from a survey[16] of postgraduate students attending the Applied Information Research (AIR) module on the Masters in Information Services Management at London Metropolitan University. At the beginning of the module the students were asked to identify what they perceived as the challenging aspects of research and were required to rank these in terms of difficulties (1 being low and 10 being high). Overwhelmingly the literature review was seen as one of the most challenging research tasks, and the difficulties associated with this pointed to a total lack of

---

15   Extract from e-mail correspondence from a FILE participant, received 15 March 2007.
16   The AIR online survey is available at: <http://www.ilit.org/air/indexair.htm>.

experience as the most likely cause of the expected challenges: 'Not experienced so 9.' Other comments justified the perception of the literature review as challenging (rated as 9 or 10 by the students) with similar concerns of unfamiliarity:

- Never done this in the past
- I am not sure what this is!
- Never had to do one thus far
- Never written one
- Have no prior knowledge

In order to ensure a successful outcome of the learning experience, information literacy educators need to be aware of the learners' level of anxiety and devise strategies that ideally eliminate this obstacle altogether. In FILE the problem of anxiety was addressed by promoting a safe and supporting learning environment '[…] where one feels able to participate fully without fear of failure'.[17] This approach also aimed to boost the participants' professional confidence which in some cases is undermined by the lack of a supportive work environment: '[…] I feel more confident about the work I do and encouraged to aim higher as I do not necessarily receive this encouragement in my workplace. The tutor and my colleagues have both been incredibly supportive.'[18]

THE INTERNAL HORIZON

By contrast, the internal horizon reflects the spontaneous centre of attention in the experience examined. In other words, this shows what information the learner is aware of, has internalized and can apply to similar or new contexts. As alluded to earlier, the employment of a conceptual framework is necessary to facilitate the process of internalization and transfer. A Masters student defines this as:

> the guiding principle or what underlies this case, to see how I can apply it in what I am going to study or write about or I am being asked to understand (i.e. the focal awareness shown as the circle in the centre of the diagramme). For example, if I were just now in the Indexing module and the lecturer tells us something, gives us an example of how to build a notation or something, well I can assume that that can be applied to other cases of the same.[19]

Effective facilitation of information literacy, therefore, means encouraging the learner to shift their awareness from an unfamiliar to a familiar information environment where the process is internalized by discerning the guiding principle(s)

---

17   Extract from the FILE evaluation survey.
18   Ibid.
19   Extract from an interview undertaken as part of the author's Doctoral research.

that determine the task, rather than focusing on the task per se. In order to achieve this FILE adopts the following strategies:

- *Start with the learner to establish the internal and external horizons of information literacy.* Learners' needs are identified through an initial diagnostic activity to enhance their motivation by learning about the things they do not know, and increase their confidence by identifying the things they do know (Andretta 2005a). In FILE this is achieved through the analysis of the personal statements that the participants have produced as part of the initial application to the course, and the examination of their input to the pre-course survey. The statements illustrate a high degree of motivation, an acute awareness of the users' information needs profiles (what they know, or internal horizon) and the desire to explore information literacy and pedagogical strategies in depth (what they do not know, or external horizon), although in most cases the participants had a much greater understanding of information literacy than they were aware of and FILE simply facilitated the process of acknowledging their current professional value as information literacy facilitators. This point was confirmed by a clear preference, expressed in the pre-course survey, for a participatory and active style of learning (involving demonstration followed by practice and reflection) which all the participants employ or plan to adopt in their information literacy training practice. This approach implies a shift from the perspective of training the 'average user' to a process of facilitation of learning (promoted by the Relational frame) that focuses on individual, and therefore diverse needs. Comments from the FILE evaluation survey confirm that the participants have taken on board the importance of profiling their users to enhance their training practices:

  'I started profiling my trainees with the use of questionnaires which directly helps me target the needs of the user group. With clearer targets I am able to set more appropriate activities for the session that aims to match the learning needs of my users with the outcomes they often request via the profiling questionnaires.'[20]

- *Formulate learning outcomes that require the learners to create, not just find, information* (Whitworth 2006; 2007; Williams 2006; Williams and Minnion 2007). This is achieved through an assessment strategy based on real world and problem-solving conditions that are relevant to the participants' practice (Lantz and Brage 2006), and are therefore transferable to the workplace. The portfolio is devised specifically to ensure that the participants develop innovative information literacy education strategies that are fully integrated in their CPD agenda, and produce learning resources that can be shared by

---

20   Extract from the FILE evaluation survey.

a larger community of practice. Again comments from the evaluation seem to illustrate that this aim was successfully achieved:

'[Component 4] was useful because it gave plenty of ideas for use in further training, and because I was using material I could develop back at work it increased my confidence.'[21]

• *Employ an iterative learning approach that encourages reflection* 'both "in action" whilst actively engaging with information and "on action" at completion' (Hughes, Bruce and Edwards 2007). As we will see in a later section, the portfolio promotes reflective formative and summative assessment strategies.

THE DEVELOPMENT OF THE LEARNER SUPPORT PROGRAMME'S PILOT

The precursor of FILE was developed as a pilot 'training the trainers' course commissioned by London Health Libraries (LHL) as part of its LSP agenda. The pilot was implemented by the Information Management School at London Metropolitan University between January and March 2006, and its impact was evaluated in September of the same year. The evaluation of the pilot was based on the following objectives:

• Identify the impact of the pilot on the participants' current professional practice by gathering individual examples of activities learned during the pilot and implemented within a specific period of time (at the end of the pilot 11 out of 12 were planning immediate use of what they learned, therefore the timescale of the impact was also evaluated)
• Prioritize the topics that participants identified at the end of the pilot and ensure that these would be addressed by FILE
• Identify other areas of CPD needs to inform future LHL training programmes

Two data-gathering methods were devised to implement these objectives. First an online survey[22] was used to gather information on the impact of the pilot, the

---

21   Ibid.
22   The survey evaluating the Learner support programme is available at: <http://freeonlinesurveys.com/rendersurvey.asp?sid=g721lwsqcgyyorh211278>. Although a 50 per cent response rate for this survey provided a valid set of data on which to develop the subsequent course, it was decided that in order to ensure a 100 per cent response rate any future survey would need to be integrated in the assessment strategy. This strategy provided a 100 per cent response rate in both the pre-test survey which was used to write Component 1 of the portfolio and the FILE evaluation survey completed after the end of the taught part of the course in preparation for Component 5.

participants' suggestions for improvements and their expected future training needs. The survey's findings were used to inform the discussion of the focus group held in September, six months after the course had ended. Here the responses project a positive impact of the pilot as participants gave a number of examples where the training had a beneficial effect on their practice, including giving greater consideration to learning outcomes and differing learning styles, and assuming more teaching or training responsibilities within the organization. The section in the survey that explored suggestions to improve the course prioritized the formulation of lesson plans and learning outcomes, emphasized the exploration of information literacy from a learner-centred perspective, and placed a greater focus on reflective practice as an information literacy facilitator. All of these aspects were fully integrated in the learning outcomes and the syllabus of FILE.

THE OUTLINE OF FILE

Following the pilot London Health Libraries commissioned the Information Management School to develop FILE. The course was validated by London Metropolitan University in October 2006 as a 20-credit postgraduate module and scheduled to run between January and May 2007. FILE promotes a new model of provision combining the flexible approach to CPD training (not confined to the traditional schedule of three hours each week for the duration of a semester) with the academic status of an accredited module. As a stand-alone CPD course, FILE addresses the demand for information literacy training needs of information professionals. At the same time the accredited status ensures that the quality of the information literacy training programme is established through 'a never-ending cycle of practice and reflection' (Andretta 2005a), and monitored through rigorous academic quality assurance procedures. This approach is in line with the recommendations by a study commissioned by the National Library for Health (Urquhart, Spink and Thomas 2005) on 'Assessing Training and Professional Development Needs of Library Staff', which supports the combination of accreditation and reflective training. An additional long-term benefit needs to be considered here: as an accredited postgraduate module FILE can also be used for the completion of a postgraduate degree following the Accreditation to Prior Learning (APL) route.

The delivery of FILE is based on blended provision involving five separate sessions of six hours each (30 hours in total). In addition to the face-to-face delivery, 170 hours are allocated to independent study where the participants are asked to complete a portfolio of assignments and contribute to peer-based evaluation of individual and group practice via a blog.[23] As alluded to earlier, the learning resources produced

---

23   <http://facilitatingileducation.blogspot.com/>.

by the FILE participants are available online through a dedicated webpage[24] to encourage practice-sharing amongst the authors, and enable further dissemination of these resources to a wider health information community of practice. Informal feedback illustrates that FILE was successful in establishing the initial community of practice amongst its participants:

> *It's been a real thought-provoking and exciting course for me and I have appreciated the opportunity not only to work with you [the FILE tutor] but with all my colleagues [the other participants of FILE]. They all have inspired me to believe in the work I do and to aim higher and higher in getting the IL message across the [organization].*[25]

Another instance of the information literacy community emerging from FILE is illustrated by the fruitful collaboration between the Learner Support Programme (LSP) Steering Group, representing London Health Libraries, and the FILE co-ordinator (also author of this chapter). Such a positive relationship has enabled the sharing of good practice between information professionals in HE and the healthcare sectors which has resulted in useful feedback from the LSP group on the evaluation strategies employed to assess the medium-term impact of the pilot. In addition, the development of FILE was based on a two-way exchange between the FILE facilitator who provided the expertise on information literacy education and the LSP working group who contributed a practical view of the challenges faced by information literacy educators in the NHS. This collaborative approach '[…] was the making of the course and really helped to cement the link between theory and practice'.[26] The remaining part of this chapter demonstrates how FILE has successfully promoted a full integration of the information literacy theoretical framework into reflective practice.

LEARNING OUTCOMES

FILE aims to develop or enhance the participants' professional practice as information literacy facilitators. The course is based on the following learning outcomes:

1. Identify diverse information literacy requirements of the users they support
2. Develop a learning strategy that appropriately addresses the needs of a targeted group of users
3. Facilitate a range of information literacy activities

---

24   <http://www.ilit.org/file/indexfile.htm>.

25   Extract from e-mail correspondence from a FILE participant, received 28 February 2007.

26   Extract from e-mail correspondence from a member of the LSP steering group, received 23 March 2007.

4. Reflect on the process and the impact of information literacy practice on their professional development

THE FILE PORTFOLIO: FORMATIVE AND SUMMATIVE ASSESSMENT STRATEGIES

The portfolio aims to enhance information literacy facilitation by fostering reflective practice on users' profiling, learning diversity and information literacy strategies to address these, as well as promoting a reflective attitude towards the participants' CPD. The portfolio consists of five components which offer evidence of reflective practice as well as concrete examples of information literacy facilitation that the participants implement during the course. A full outline of the components and the schedule underpinning the delivery of FILE is available in a document found on the FILE home page.[27] This section gives a summarized version of the components to demonstrate how these map onto the learning outcomes of the course, and to give an overview of the underpinning professional and pedagogical rationale. It should be noted that each component was devised to build competences and confidence required to tackle the next assignment, and the following feedback illustrates how Component 4 in particular capitalized on the experience of the previous assignments, making the portfolio a foundation for future practice:

> *This was the most useful component because it brought together all the skills we had developed by completing the previous components. It felt as though the successful completion of this component was what the whole course was aimed at. The process I went thorough to complete this component (which is also linked to the previous 'C3' component) is what I will attempt to replicate and build upon in my own practice.[28]*

Component 1: Professional development targets. Here the participants produce a written CPD profile on entry reflecting on their initial expectation of FILE and on what they consider effective training within the context of the information (and learning) needs of their users. As mentioned earlier, data gathered from a pre-course online survey[29] and the personal statements from the application forms[30] are used as the basis for this reflection (Learning Outcome 4).

Component 2: Group-based presentation using PowerPoint. The group-based presentation focuses on the profiling of targeted users selected from one of the

---

27 <http://www.ilit.org/file/indexfile.htm>.
28 Extract from the FILE evaluation survey.
29 For a copy of the online survey please contact the author.
30 This refers to the application form produced by London Health Libraries to select the participants for FILE.

following groups: home care workers, NHS support staff, clinical researchers, or a subgroup of perioperative staff, such as surgeons, clinical staff, theatre nurses, OPDs, modern matrons and staff nurses.[31] In addition the teams devise appropriate information literacy strategies to address the needs of the targeted users and these are contextualized within the six frames approach promoted by Bruce, Edwards and Lupton (2007). The quality of delivery and the content of the presentation are reflected upon by the individual members of the team and provide a rationale for the team-assessed mark calculated on a scale of 1 to 10 (Learning Outcome 1).

Component 3: Individual presentation of the information literacy activity using PowerPoint. The individual presentation articulates the learning objectives for a specific information literacy activity which are mapped onto appropriate assessment strategies developed in response to the profile of the audience targeted (this group of users is different from the one covered in the team presentation). Playback of the video-recorded presentations is used as the main source of reflection on the overall performance of the participants accompanied by peer/tutor-based feedback (Learning Outcome 2).

Component 4: Implementation of a training session covering the information literacy activity presented in the previous component. The session is delivered by each participant to the rest of the FILE cohort and complements the individual presentation by offering the opportunity to experience hands-on information literacy facilitation. Most importantly the impact of the session is reflected on through the analysis of the participants' feedback elicited through the evaluation activity completed by the cohort at the end of each session (Learning Outcome 3).

Component 5: Overall evaluation of FILE and professional targets completed approximately two months after the end of the taught part of the course. Here the participants produce an overall evaluation of FILE in meeting the original expectations (outlined in Component 1), as well as setting and achieving future professional targets to demonstrate competent facilitation of information literacy practice in their place of work (Learning Outcome 4).

FILE AND THE CHALLENGES OF A HYBRID STATUS

Because FILE sits outside of the traditional delivery of academic and CPD courses, this poses specific challenges for its facilitator and participants. A major challenge faced by the facilitator is the need to keep to a tight schedule. Time management in the delivery of the course is crucial and involves a careful balance between pace

---

31   The types of users vary according to the sector the cohort operates in, as indicated at the beginning of this chapter; the first cohort of FILE is drawn from the health information sector and therefore the list of users explored in the assignments reflects this.

of delivery, coverage of content, practice of curricular activities and the formative assessment work. This must be complemented by proactive support of the participants through provision of immediate feedback on their performance. With the exception of Component 5, all the other assignments are completed within the taught part of FILE and detailed feedback is provided for each component within a 24-hour turnaround. Whilst all participants commended the quality and timing of the feedback produced by the tutor, some complained that five sessions were insufficient to cover the syllabus:

> [...] sometimes there was a lot to pack into the day and by the end we felt tired so couldn't take it all in properly. It would have been useful to maybe have another week to finish all the other activities off which had to be rushed due to lack of time.[32]

This is a fair comment which refers to the over-running of a number of assessment activities at the expense of the coverage of the programme. In future a reduced size of cohort and an extended schedule will be employed to address this problem.

Time management is also an important factor for the participants as they need to meet assessment deadlines which occur within a relatively short period of time (the first four components are completed in approximately eight weeks),[33] while working full-time as information professionals. This was one aspect participants were asked to comment on during the evaluation survey and their responses illustrate that the majority found the time intervals between the taught sessions sufficient to complete the assignments, claiming that the timing was just right: 'Any longer would have made each component drag out too much, any shorter would make it difficult to fit this in with working full time.'[34]

The majority also welcomed the extra week allocated to complete Component 2 (the group-based assignment) which gave the teams three weeks as opposed to the normal two weeks allocated to Components 1, 3 and 4, although one argued that the extended time should apply to these components as well. The feedback seems to confirm that the assessment timetable worked, although such a consistent adherence to the deadlines is mainly due to the high degree of motivation and dedication exhibited by the FILE participants who, despite work and family commitments, submitted the first four components on time.

---

32   Extract from the FILE evaluation survey.
33   For the schedule of the sessions and the components: < http://www.ilit.org/file/indexfile. htm>.
34   Extract from the FILE evaluation survey.

A BLENDED LEARNING ENVIRONMENT

A course like FILE necessarily requires a combination of face-to-face and virtual learning environments. Such a flexible delivery involves the use of accommodation equipped with fully networked computers to ensure that participants interact with the online resources complementing the face-to-face activities. For instance, in session two the participants were asked to evaluate examples of PowerPoint presentations available on the FILE website, and feed their findings into the evaluation criteria used to assess the presentations in Components 2 and 3. The quality of the peer-based feedback and of the reflection expressed in the individual evaluations produced for the second component illustrate the active engagement by all participants with the evaluation process assessing the teams' performance, the quality of the users' profiling and the appropriateness of the information literacy strategy devised. A similar outcome was achieved in Component 3 where the participants demonstrated evidence of clear design and effective layout in the presentations, illustrating that they all achieved a good balance between readability and content coverage. In all cases this enhanced the clarity of the presentation and in particular of the IL activity proposed.[35] Effective design and clear coverage are important communication strategies that information literacy facilitators need to employ to ensure that their dissemination practices enhance rather than hinder the training. This is in line with the ALA's view that information literacy also involves the ability to foster learning in others through effective communication (ALA 1989).

The availability of ICT and online facilities during the taught part of the course also ensures that the participants are not limited in their choice of information literacy activities required to complete Components 3 and 4, thus enabling them to explore the e-learning culture and information practices associated with users within the health information sector. Some of the information literacy strategies they produced include the detailed exploration of health-related resources which are embedded within the needs of specific professional groups, such as: an exploration of Intute as a portal of reliable sources of information for nursing and midwife professional groups; the introduction to the CAM Specialist Library for Health Visitors; the demonstration of the standard search facility of the Maternity and Infant Care Database for Midwives; or an introduction to the Citation Matcher for first-year medical students. The remaining strategies facilitate competences that operate within the online environment, but that are transferable across a range of systems and groups of health professionals (although in some cases these resources target the needs of specific groups). Examples here include: the use of MeSH to support advanced searches in PubMed; referencing electronic resources with the Harvard system to support scholarly activities; the evaluation of websites in terms

---

35   PowerPoint presentations available at: <http://www.ilit.org/file/eportfolios07.htm>.

of quality and bias; the use of the PICO model[36] to formulate a search question, or underpin evidence-based medicine (EBM); effective use of Boolean logic underpinning transferable searching competences, or the application of Boolean operators in a search engine such as Google; and the distinction between popular versus scholarly as well as primary versus secondary sources of information within the context of academic work.

WHAT THE FILE PARTICIPANTS SAY ABOUT THE COURSE

To gather an overall evaluation of the course, the concluding question of the survey asked the participants the following question: '*If a colleague asked you "Would you recommend FILE?" what would you answer?*' The responses are examined here under some of the main themes generated by the feedback. First of all the participants find the course suitable for both novice and experienced trainers, thus confirming the accomplishment of the original aim of FILE with its dual purpose of developing or enhancing professional practice in information literacy education

> *I would recommend it, especially if the person was new to training and wanted to develop the ability to analyse IL needs and formulating learning outcomes. I think that the course was also excellent in the way that it developed the confidence of the participants. However, I would also recommend FILE to the more experienced trainers, as it did make one more aware of issues surrounding IL and to reflect on one's own practice.*[37]

Confidence boosting is another benefit that the participants associate with this course, supporting the view that FILE promotes information literacy as the foundation of an emancipating lifelong learning attitude:

> *[...] the course has given me confidence in training, I have learnt so much from the tutor and colleagues. It has inspired me to look afresh at the training I do, but to also look beyond that and learn more about IL in general and to keep updating my ideas.*[38]

This in turn strengthens the participants' sense of professional status: 'I have really enjoyed the course and it has been valuable to share resources and ideas with colleagues and the course tutor. I also now feel much more aware of the value of the work we do.'[39] And it enhances their confidence as information literacy educators: 'The support and encouragement from the tutor and colleagues has also

---

36   PICO stands for: Patient, Population, Problem; Intervention; Comparison; Outcome.
37   Extract from the FILE evaluation survey.
38   Ibid.
39   Ibid.

made a real difference to the way that I think about my work, I have gained in confidence and now believe that I DO know what I am talking about!'[40]

CONCLUSION

FILE offers an example of effective integration of CPD training within an academic environment (ensuring quality of provision). This leads to a qualification that can be used towards the completion of a postgraduate degree, thus making this kind of course more appealing in the long term. Most importantly, this course emphasizes the adoption of a range of information literacy frames to address the diversity of the users' professional needs and attitudes. In particular, the Relational frame orientation of FILE enables the creation of a reflective space for its participants, where they can examine the role and impact of their information literacy practice on the users they support. Ultimately the aim of FILE is to promote the professional development of confident information literacy educators that feeds into evidence-based advocacy of information literacy. This is particularly important for information professionals operating in the health sector which is characterized by a culture of EBM (Sackett et al. 1996). Increasingly, however, the issue of evidence-based advocacy for information literacy education is becoming crucial in all sectors, given the need to illustrate concrete evidence of its valid contribution in the face of rapidly diminishing user education budgets.

ACKNOWLEDGEMENTS

My thanks go to the FILE participants whose feedback is presented in this chapter as invaluable evidence of the successful impact of the course on their information literacy practice. I am also grateful to Liz Osborne (Chair of the LSP working group at the time this chapter was written) for her comments, and to Christine Bruce for her insightful feedback on an earlier draft of this work. I am particularly indebted to Christine for the inspiring effect her work on the Relational approach of information literacy has had on my research, my reflective experience as an information literacy educator and the development of FILE.

REFERENCES

Abell, A. and Oxbrow, N. (2001), *Competing with Knowledge: The Information Professional in the Knowledge Management Age* (London: Library Association Publishing).

---

40   Ibid.

Abid, A. (2004), 'Information Literacy for Lifelong Learning', Paper presented at the *World Library and Information Congress: 70th IFLA General Conference and Council*, 22–27 August 2004, 1–38.

Alexandria Proclamation on Information Literacy and Lifelong Learning, IFLA, National Forum on IL and UNESCO, November 2005. <http://www.bibalex. org/infolit2005/AlexProclamation.htm>.

American Library Association (ALA) (1989), *Presidential Committee on Information Literacy: Final Report*. <http://www.ala.org/ala/mgrps/divs/acrl/ publications/whitepapers/presidential.cfm>.

Andretta, S. (2005a), *Information Literacy: A Practitioner's Guide* (Oxford: Chandos Publishing).

Andretta, S. (2005b), 'From Prescribed Reading to the Excitement or the Burden of Choice. Information Literacy: The Foundation of E-learning', *Aslib Proceedings* 57:2, 181–9.

Andretta, S. (ed.) (2006a), 'Information Literacy: Challenges of Implementation', *ITALICS* 5:1. <http://www.ics.heacademy.ac.uk/italics/vol5iss1.htm>.

Andretta, S. (2006b), 'Information Literacy: The New Pedagogy of the Question?', in G. Walton and A. Pope (eds).

Andretta, S. (ed.) (2007a), *Change and Challenge: Information Literacy for the 21st Century* (Adelaide: Auslib Press).

Andretta, S. (2007b), 'Information Literacy: The Functional Literacy for the 21st Century', in S. Andretta (ed.), 1–13.

Andretta, S. (2007c), 'Phenomenography: A Conceptual Framework for Information Literacy Education' in *Aslib Proceedings* 59:2, 152–68.

Association of College and Research Libraries (ACRL) (2000), *Information Literacy Competency Standards for Higher Education*. <http://www.ala.org/ acrl/ilcomstan.html>.

Booth, A. (2006), 'Where is the Harm in EBLIP? Current Perspectives, Future Developments', *Journal of the European Association for Health Information Libraries* 2:3, August 2006, 34–41.

Bruce, C. (1997), *The Seven Faces of Information Literacy* (Adelaide: Auslib Press).

Bruce, C. (1999), 'Information Literacy. An International Review of Programs and Research', *Auckland '99 Lianza Conference*, 9–12 November 1999. <http:// www2.auckland.ac.nz/lbr/conf99/bruce.htm>, no longer available.

Bruce C.S. (2002), 'Information Literacy as a Catalyst for Educational Change: A Background Paper', White Paper prepared for UNESCO, the US National Commission on Libraries and Information Science, and the National Forum on Information Literacy, for use at the *Information Literacy, Meetings of Experts*, Prague, Czech Republic, 1–17. <http://www.nclis.gov/libinter/ infolitconf&meet/papers/bruce-fullpaper.pdf>.

Bruce, C. and Candy, P. (eds) (2000), *Information Literacy Around the World, Advances in Programs and Research* (Wagga Wagga: Centre for Information Studies).

Bruce, C., Edwards, S. and Lupton, M. (2007), 'Six Frames of Information Literacy Education: A Conceptual Framework for Interpreting the Relationship between Theory and Practice' in S. Andretta (ed.) 37–58.

Bundy, A. (2003), 'One Essential Direction: Information Literacy, Information Technology Fluency', Paper presented at *eLit 2003 Second International Conference on Information and IT Literacy*, Glasgow Caledonian University, 11–13 June 2003.

Bundy, A. (ed.) (2004), *Australian and New Zealand Information Literacy Framework Principles, Standards and Practice*, 2nd edn (Adelaide: Australian and New Zealand Institute for Information Literacy).

Bundy, A. (2005), 'Changing and Connecting the Educational Silos: The Potential of the Information Literacy Framework', Paper presented at the *Lilac 2005 Conference*, Imperial College, UK, 5 April 2005.

Department for Employment and Skills (DfES) (2003), *Towards a Unified E-learning Strategy.* <http://www.dfes.gov.uk/consultations2/16/>.

Economist Intelligence Unit (2006), *Business Intelligence: Putting Information to Work* (London: Economist Intelligence Unit).

Edwards, S. (2006), *Panning for Gold. Information Literacy and the Net Lenses Model* (Adelaide: Auslib Press).

Hughes, H., Bruce, C. and Edwards, S. (2007), 'Models for Reflection and Learning: A Culturally Inclusive Response to the Information Literacy Imbalance' in S. Andretta (ed.), 59–84.

Koufogiannakis, D. and Wiebe, N. (2006), 'Effective Methods for Teaching Information Literacy Skills to Undergraduate Students: A Systematic Review and Meta-Analysis', *Evidence Based Library and Information Practice*, 1:3, 3–43. <http://eprints.rclis.org/archive/00007655/01/koufogiannakis_eblip.pdf>.

Lantz, A. and Brage, C. (2006), 'Exploring the Challenge of Applied Information Literacy through Reality-Based Scenarios', *ITALICS* 5:1. <http://www.ics.heacademy.ac.uk/italics/vol5iss1.htm>.

Laurillard, D. (1993), *Rethinking University Teaching. A Framework for the Effective Use of Educational Technology* (London: Routledge).

Lorenzo, G. and Bziuban, C. (2006), 'Ensuring the Net Generation is Net Savvy', *Educause Learning Initiative*, September 2006.

Lupton, M. (2004), *The Learning Connection. Information Literacy and the Student Experience* (Adelaide: Auslib Press).

Markless, S. and Streatfield, D. (2007), 'Three Decades of Information Literacy: Redefining the Parameters' in S. Andretta (ed.), 15–36.

Marton, F. and Booth, S. (1997), *Learning and Awareness* (Mahwah, New Jersey: LEA).

Newton, A. and Boden, D. (2006), 'Information Literacy Development in Australia', *Library and Information Update*, January/February, 5:1–2, 42–3.

Office of Economic Co-operation and Development (OECD) (1996), *The Knowledge-Based Economy* (Paris: OECD).

O'Sullivan, C. (2002), 'Is Information Literacy Relevant in the Real World?' *New Library World* 30:1, 7–14.

Plotnick, E. (1999), 'Information Literacy', *ERIC Digest*.

Rogers, C. (1969), *Freedom to Learn* (Columbus, Ohio: Merrill).

Sackett, D.L., Rosenberg, W.M.C., Muir Gray, J.A., Haynes, R.B. and Scott Richardson, W. (1996), 'Evidence Based Medicine: What It Is and What It Isn't', *British Medical Journal* 312, 71–2.

Schön, D. (1991), *The Reflective Practitioner: How Professionals Think in Action* (Aldershot: Ashgate).

Snavely, L. and Cooper, N. (1997), 'The Information Literacy Debate', *Journal of Academic Librarianship* 23:1, 9–14.

Stubbings, R. and Franklin, G. (2006), 'Does Advocacy Help to Embed Information Literacy into the Curriculum?' *ITALICS* 5:1. <http://www.ics.heacademy.ac.uk/italics/vol5iss1.htm>.

Thompson, S. (2003), *The Prague Declaration* (US Commission on Libraries and Information Science). <http://www.nclis.gov/libinter/infolitconf&meet/post-infolitconf&meet/FinalReportPrague.pdf>.

Urquhart, C., Spink, S. and Thomas, R. (2005), 'Assessing Training and Professional Development Needs of Library Staff', *National Library for Health*, May 2005. <http://www.library.nhs.uk/nlhdocs/nlh_cpd_report100505.doc>.

Virkus, S. (2003), 'Information Literacy in Europe: A Literature Review', *Information Research* 8:4. <http://informationr.net/ir/8-4/paper159.html>.

Walton, G. and Pope, A. (eds) (2006), *Information Literacy: Recognising the Need* (Oxford: Chandos Publishing).

Whitworth, A. (2006), 'Communicative Competence in the Information Age: Towards a Critical Theory of Information Literacy Education', *ITALICS* 5:1. <http://www.ics.heacademy.ac.uk/italics/vol5iss1.htm>.

Whitworth, A. (2007), 'Communicative Competence in the Information Age: Towards a Critical Pedagogy' in S. Andretta (ed.), 85–113.

Williams, P. (2006), 'Exploring the Challenges of Developing Digital Literacy in the Context of Special Educational Needs Communities', *ITALICS* 5:1. <http://www.ics.heacademy.ac.uk/italics/vol5iss1.htm>.

Williams, P. and Minnion, A. (2007), 'Exploring the Challenges of Developing Digital Literacy in the Context of Special Educational Needs' in S. Andretta (ed.), 115–44.

RESOURCE MANAGEMENT

CHAPTER 4

PRESERVATION TRAINING

GRAHAM MATTHEWS

INTRODUCTION

Preservation

In the United Kingdom (UK) in the 1980s, a new approach to preservation in libraries began to be developed. White, at the beginning of his chapter, 'Conservation', in the *Handbook of Library Training Practice*, published in 1986, attests to this: 'The vagaries of fashion are such that, had this book been compiled two or three years ago, I doubt very much that anyone would have been called upon to contribute a chapter on conservation. Today, conservation is very much the 'in' thing' (White 1986). He then dismissed that this was merely fashionable by outlining actual factors that had contributed to this renewed approach, such as the impact on libraries of the Florence floods of 1966, research in the United States (US) which revealed the extent of the brittle book problem (acidic, decaying paper) brought about by changes in paper production, and inadequate environments for and storage of books as libraries became more user-centred (White 1986).

Following the publication of the Ratcliffe report in 1984 (Ratcliffe with Patterson 1984), which criticized many aspects of preservation and conservation in the UK, the National Preservation Office (NPO) was established. Since then preservation in the UK has developed in many ways. At this time, 'No longer the preserve of the rare book librarian or the archivist, preservation was seen as one of the tools of collection management to ensure access to books and information by library users' (Feather 1996). That training was central to this is underlined by the fact that following its establishment, the Education and Training Panel was one of two panels set up by the NPO.

Whilst there have indeed been new developments in the last 25 years or so, older, traditional skills and practices, including 'good housekeeping', are still at the heart of effective preservation, as noted by Feather: 'Preservation, in its broadest sense as an aspect of collection management, and oriented towards the provision of access to users, is a comparatively new element in librarianship, although it derives from many much older areas of activity and draws on long-established expertise' (Feather 1996, 137). It is in this broad context of preservation and its management in libraries that training must be considered.

Developments in Preservation Training in the UK

Furthermore, a brief overview of developments in training for preservation management in the UK also provides a contextual background for those responsible for its delivery today. In his research in the early 1980s, Dr Ratcliffe found little evidence of preservation training in libraries (Ratcliffe with Patterson 1984). A dozen or so years later, following their survey of preservation in British libraries Feather, Matthews and Eden found that:

> *Training is still neglected in many libraries, and in others is necessarily constrained by small numbers and other calls on staff time ... One in five of our respondents provide some in-house training schemes for existing staff which are intended, wholly or partly, to increase their awareness of preservation issues, or to give them some appropriate basic training in prevention and repair of damage. Rather more, just over 25% include some mention of preservation in their induction programmes for newly appointed staff* (Feather, Matthews and Eden 1996).

In some large research libraries, however, training was not just at this basic level. Here:

> *... there are training courses organised by consortia of libraries for their mutual benefit, which can, of course, draw on a far wider range of expertise than any one small library could offer. There is widespread evidence of the use of videos and other training material, not least that prepared by the National Preservation Office, among those libraries who do offer some staff training ... Where there is a preservation manager in post, or an identifiable person with responsibility for preservation policy, that postholder is often used as a trainer* (Feather, Matthews and Eden 1996).

Preservation training was thus undertaken in a limited number of libraries and what there was, was mixed, ranging from the basic to the more sophisticated. The level and depth varied greatly, partly because of the commitment of staff time and the varying expertise of trainers and the availability of material resources. A key driver at this time was the NPO, with its annual seminar, its production of videos, leaflets, posters, Survival Kit, provision of speakers and advice, and so on. Professional associations also played their part as different aspects of preservation were addressed. The main function of training at this point was to raise awareness of preservation (Feather, Matthews and Eden 1996).

Five years or so later, the author and colleague Thebridge undertook a review of preservation management training (Thebridge and Matthews 2000). Reflecting developments in practice, the review did not just consider training for preservation but preservation management. Among its findings were that training in preservation management of relevance to libraries was available but was not co-ordinated. There was some in-house training. Publicly available training resources were limited but a small number were well used. Many wrote their own or tailored publicly available materials to their institutional requirements. The research underlined the importance of training being available to all levels of staff. It also found that many relevant topics crossed domains – archives, libraries, museums – and whilst there are domain-specific requirements, there were common issues where training resources might be shared. With regard to subject coverage, provision was good with regard to disaster management, but the main 'gap' was a lack of management training for middle and senior managers. The research also highlighted that those responsible for preservation in the library must have both professional and managerial competencies – as emphasized in an earlier review of management training and development in museums (Holland 1998) – and that preservation must interlink with other aspects of their roles and training. 'The research also emphasised the relationship between education and training: The basic education of information workers needs to have at its heart a preservation ethos, if the principles of preservation management are to filter through to general library management training' (Thebridge and Matthews 2000). Developments in education and preservation have been considered elsewhere (see, for instance, Cloonan 1994; Feather 2000; Feather and Lusher 1988; Matthews and Walker 2004). Education was a key theme within the NPO's 2000 annual conference, *Training for Preservation Management: The Next Step* (Thebridge 2000).

Since 2000, one of the major developments relating to preservation training has been the growing use of the Internet by individual institutions, professional associations, companies, collaborative networks and others involved in preservation (or specific aspects of it) and conservation to disseminate advice and information, some of it relevant to training, and to advertise events such as conferences, seminars and training. The NPO, professional bodies and others have tried to keep preservation on the wider library agenda with varying degrees of success. The establishment in England of regional Museum, Library and Archive Councils (MLAs) and their national equivalents during this period has also resulted in a variety of activity relating to preservation, and there has been some closer cross-domain working. More recently the establishment of Collections Link (2007) has attempted to bring together resources relating to preservation from across the sector.

But the biggest impact has been the growth in digitization activities which have moved forward rapidly since 2000. Digitization brings with it its own preservation issues, relating to the preservation of digitally born objects and digitization as preservation (see, for example, Bremer-Laamanen and Stenvall 2004; de Lusenet

2006; Deegan and Tanner 2006; Muir 2004; Reed 2006; Webb 2004). With both there is a need for appropriate training (see the JISC Digital Preservation Training Programme 2007).

At an international level, the major organizations active in preservation for libraries are: the International Federation of Library Associations (IFLA) through its Preservation and Conservation Core Activity (2007), the European Commission on Preservation and Access (2007), and UNESCO, in particular its Memory of the World (2007) project. Their websites are useful for keeping up to date with initiatives, training and conferences, finding expertise and guidance. National or other major libraries often take on a key leadership role within their countries, and their websites offer information and advice. In the UK and Ireland, the NPO, funded by national and research libraries, has done this since the mid 1980s.

WHAT IS PRESERVATION? DEFINITIONS AND TERMINOLOGY

Preservation in libraries can be defined as: '… all managerial, technical and financial considerations applied to retard deterioration and extend the useful life of materials to ensure their continued availability' (Eden et al. 1998). Preservation is an umbrella term encompassing a range of activities, including conservation, which need to be planned and managed. It is a key aspect of collection management. In recent years it has increasingly become associated with the term collection(s) care, particularly in museums. Many of the activities it incorporates are preventative. Up to the early 1990s preservation and conservation were often incorrectly used interchangeably (for example, much of what White refers to would today be regarded as preservation). Conservation, a major element of preservation management, involves the maintenance and/or repair of individual items and requires considerable specialist education, training and expertise.

WHY IS PRESERVATION NECESSARY?

The principal causes of deterioration in libraries that preservation must address are:

- Poor handling
- Inadequate storage
- Incorrect temperature and Relative Humidity (RH) levels
- Inappropriate lighting
- Pollution
- Pests (such as rodents, insects)
- Fire

- Flood
- Theft
- Vandalism

Inattention to dealing with these can result in loss of, or disruption to, access to library materials for users. Rare items, or those that are unique, may be lost forever. Librarians have a duty to ensure access not just for the present but for future generations. Replacing stock or carrying out binding or conservation work also adds to expenditure which may be avoided by good practice.

PRESERVATION MANAGEMENT

To counter these causes of deterioration, good preservation management seeks prevention rather than intervention and should be based on a preservation needs assessment which identifies preservation requirements and facilitates prioritization of planned preservation activities and their funding.

Preservation policy and strategy should be based on such assessments and must address the dual responsibilities of custodial care and providing access to collections now and in the future. The different requirements of various formats (for example, microfilm, photographs, digital objects) held in collections in libraries must also be taken into account. Since the mid 1990s, as mentioned above, considerable attention has been paid to developing techniques for the preservation of digital materials, including those born digitally and those digitized from some other format. In the UK, the Digital Preservation Coalition, established in 2001, aims 'to secure the preservation of digital resources in the UK and to work with others internationally to secure our global digital memory and knowledge base' (Digital Preservation Coalition 2007).

Since 2000, there has been considerable debate about digitization taking over from microfilm, the most common preservation surrogate used in the twentieth century, but it has yet to demonstrate proven long-term archival qualities. The technology of digitization is, however, developing rapidly. (For up to date information about preservation and digitization, see PADI, a subject gateway to international preservation resources, managed by the National Library of Australia.)

Disaster management is perhaps the aspect of preservation management that has seen most activity in the last 30 years or so as librarians have faced a range of natural and man-made incidents. Effective disaster management should be based on institution-specific risk assessment which feeds into the drawing up of a disaster plan, addressing the four key stages: prevention, preparedness, reaction and recovery. Other related aspects of preservation include: sound security, effective monitoring and regular inspection and maintenance of environments and buildings in which collections are housed and when building work or refurbishment is taking place. Care must also be taken when items are moved for exhibitions or loans.

Before you Begin – Getting an Overview of the Subject

For those new to preservation, who wish to gain a general understanding of the subject, or for those wishing to refresh their knowledge, further information on the above subjects is available in textbooks and manuals, such as: Feather 1996; Feather 2004; Gorman and Shep 2006; Harvey 1993; Ogden 1999; Swartzburg 1995. The chapters on preservation which review activity in *British Librarianship and Information Work* (Walker 2006; 2007) provide an overview of recent and current areas of activity, and further references to useful sources of information.

Leaflets produced by authoritative bodies can also provide advice and insight into specific aspects and offer further sources. Many of these are now available to download from websites (in the US, the Northeast Document Conservation Centre (NEDCC) has nearly 60 on topics such as: Planning and Prioritizing, the Environment, Emergency Management, Storage and Handling, Photographs, Reformatting, Conservation Procedures; the NPO provides leaflets, too – see below for examples).

The CoOL (Conservation OnLine 2007) website provides a wide range of information and links to various aspects of preservation and conservation on an international scale. It is also worth signing up to Conservation DistList where announcements can be found about training events and queries can be posted (Conservation DistList 2007).

WHY? THE PURPOSE OF PRESERVATION TRAINING

Training plays a vital part in the success of preservation management. It can raise awareness of issues and practical factors in all levels of staff; and it has significance for managers in terms of overall library planning and strategy: 'Training can contribute more to the success of preservation than anything else, by getting people to understand what is at stake and what they can do about it' (de Lusenet 1998).

WHO?

Staff with responsibility for special collections will have need of specialist training but all staff in a library can contribute to preservation management, from caretakers and cleaners who may notice something amiss with, say the environment, a rise in temperature or a potential source of water ingress that could cause damage to collections, to front line counter staff who may observe inappropriate handling of individual items at the photocopier or spot initial damage to a returned book and put it aside for minor repair. Those with responsibility for building maintenance and security also have a key role, as do senior managers who can underline their commitment by taking part in exercises and simulations, for instance. It is important that good practice is sustained and management can set a good example and encourage motivation in others.

It is also important that users are aware of basic good practice and understand its significance. Information on websites, posters and leaflets can help promote this. Personal intervention, advice and instruction may occasionally be necessary if misuse of materials is observed.

WHAT? THE CONTENT OF PRESERVATION TRAINING

In the mid 1980s, Meadows (1987, 22) provided a simple list of requirements for conservation (preservation) training which still apply today:

1. Basic knowledge for junior staff
2. Policy-related knowledge for senior staff
3. Detailed knowledge for specialist staff

Basic Knowledge for All Staff

With regard to the first category, it is important that all staff, not just junior staff, should have a knowledge of and appropriate basic skills in those fundamental aspects of preservation which contribute to 'good housekeeping' and 'collection care'.

The following core aspects should be included in the library's induction programme:

*   Handling of different kinds of library materials
*   Cleaning and repair
*   Environmental conditions
*   Security
*   Disaster management

An outline of some of the topics to be covered in each of these is provided below, together with a reference to a source of further concise information about it. (Reference should also be made to items under 'Additional Resources' below.)

Handling of different kinds of library materials
Books, newspapers, photographs, DVDs, for example, are different in their composition and size and have different requirements regarding handling and

storage. Instruction should include, for example, how to take a book off a shelf and put it back, how to open it; what to do and not to do when photocopying materials; carrying library materials, using a trolley; placing material in different kinds of storage (for example, cabinets, cases, boxes); using equipment properly (for example, CD players, microfilm reader/printers). An understanding of book structure can help, as can an introduction to protective measures such as boxing. For further information, see the NPO leaflet, Good Handling Principles and Practice for Library and Archive Materials (National Preservation Office and British Library Collection Care and Handling Team 2000).

Cleaning and repair
Cleaning and repair should be carried out carefully on items of general stock using methods and materials that will not cause further damage. Only very minor tasks such as repairing small tears on a page or pasting part of a spine which has come slightly apart should be undertaken. Refer other cases to experts.

All staff should be able to identify signs of damage (such as loose binding, cracks in protective cases) and need to be aware of procedures for dealing in-house with such items; for example, put aside for minor repair, or for dispatch to binders, or to conservators. Staff on issue desks should be alert to such damage on returned items.

They should be aware of procedures for dusting books and shelves and should also seek to protect stock from dirt (for example, from users' food and drink; dust during building work). For more information, see the NPO leaflet, *Cleaning Books and Documents* (Bendix and Walker 2006).

Environmental conditions
Staff should be aware of environmental conditions and the impact that inappropriate levels of heat, humidity and light, for example, can have on items within collections. They should know how to read and interpret simple equipment (such as thermometers) used to record and/or monitor environmental conditions, and when, how and to whom they should report any inconsistencies or system failures. They should realize the impact that damp and mould can have on collections and report any instances promptly and in line with institutional procedures. They should also look out for signs of insect activity. For more details, including relevant standards and use of equipment, consult the NPO leaflet, Managing the Library and Archive Environment (Henderson 2007).

Security
If adequate security measures are not in place, this can lead to theft and loss of material. All staff must be aware of standard security procedures (and systems for special collections/areas as appropriate), ranging from locking of doors and windows to more sophisticated detection and alarm systems, and what to do if they

'go off'. A comprehensive manual on security, Security in Museums, Libraries and Archives: A Practical Guide, is available (Resource: the Museums, Libraries and Archive Council 2003).

Disaster management All staff should be trained to be vigilant and look out for threats to the library, its staff, users, collections and facilities; they should also know what action to take in such situations, including raising the alarm, knowing to whom to report and how. Staff, for instance, may spot a leaking pipe or smouldering electrical equipment. All staff should receive practical training in, for example, their roles in evacuating the building, using fire extinguishers, and handling damaged materials. They should also be aware of health and safety issues relevant to them and users. For an overview of disaster management, a disaster control plan template and further sources of information, see the M25 Consortium of Academic Libraries Disaster Management Group website.

Knowledge for Senior and Specialist Staff

With regard to Meadows' second and third categories – that is, senior and specialist staff, for example, those managers with responsibility for preservation, or aspects of it (for example, security, special collections) – as part of the preservation management training review undertaken by Thebridge and Matthews, a list of skills for preservation management was devised (Thebridge and Matthews 2000). (Table 4.1 is adapted and updated from this.) Its primary concern was the needs of middle and senior managers, and it thus has a focus on preservation management, but the list represents the topics that need to be considered for inclusion in training programmes aimed at all levels of staff, including those with non-managerial roles.

This preservation-related list is, of course, in addition to generic management skills that underpin them, including communication (verbal and written), presentation, ICT (word-processing, spreadsheets, e-mail, web design), project management, time management, an ability to work independently and with others (networking, consultation). Certain activities will also require specialist expertise or consultancy (for instance, with regard to specific conservation options/treatments, risk assessment of building, facilities and services).

Anyone with responsibility for preservation management in libraries, if not a conservator, will need an awareness of conservation techniques and procedures so that they may understand and consider options available and their financial and strategic implications. They should of course be prepared to take specialist advice on such issues and, if this is not available in-house, should find out where it might be available elsewhere, commercially or otherwise. (ICON's Conservation Register can be used to find conservators with particular skills and/or in a geographical location.)

Likewise, those managing digital preservation will require specific expertise relating to that. A Digital Preservation Training Programme was recently developed in a JISC-funded project led by the University of London Computer Centre in partnership with the Digital Preservation Coalition and Cornell University (University of London Computer Centre 2007).

Table 4.1 Skills required for preservation management
(as required by middle/senior library manager
with responsibility for preservation)

Preservation management

Awareness of preservation issues and techniques

Current awareness (personal and for others) (e.g., digitization and preservation, impact of climate change)
Knowledge of printed and electronic sources, organizations and individuals (local, regional, national and international) relating to preservation

Building(s) management

Environmental control
Storage and shelving
Disaster management/emergency planning
Service/business continuity
Security
Inspection and maintenance
Risk assessment and management
Planning and supervising minor building work
Building conservation, e.g., listed building procedures

Collections management/collection care

Knowing your collections and their use
Cleaning and repair programmes
Handling of library materials (different formats/media)
Understanding structure of the book and other library materials and causes of deterioration
Knowledge of protective/preventive measures (e.g., boxing, packaging)
Valuing items and collections
Minor repair work
    – also understanding limitations of stock and of staff skills
Awareness of conservation procedures and techniques – options available

Preservation needs assessment/surveys and their use
Selection for preservation
Awareness of cataloguing and record-keeping requirements
Cataloguing and record-keeping
Surrogacy (and options)
  – reprographics
Knowledge of preservation requirements of different library materials (e.g., books, photographs, microfilm, digital objects)
Valuing items/collections
Stock control and stock moves
Awareness and understanding of appropriate standards and benchmarks
Condition assessment (and treatment options)
Exhibitions and loans

Financial planning and monitoring

Budget control
Funding applications (and awareness of sources/schemes/initiatives)
Fund-raising
Costing routine work and special projects (e.g., binding, conservation, microfilming, digitization)
Building insurance
Collection insurance

Human resource management

Management of staff (different grades and responsibilities)
Liaison with archivists and conservators – knowledge of their activities and capabilities
Liaison with contractors/external services/suppliers – ability to select as appropriate
Meetings and minute-taking
Drawing up job specifications and advertisements
Health and safety

Policy and strategy

Undertaking in-house surveys and pilot schemes
Drafting and writing policy and strategy documents
Drafting and writing working documents (e.g., disaster control plans)
Awareness of regional and national policies and strategies; networking
Methods of integrating preservation policy with other library policies
Methods of effectively implementing policy
Performance management – justifying the value of preservation management through performance indicators (evidence-based practice)
Advocacy and negotiation

Promotion and marketing

    Communication – verbal and written
    Presentation
    Organizing events for users and 'friends' of the library
    Liaison with graphic designers and printers
    Targeting an audience
    Convincing senior management, library committee members, local politicians
    Writing annual reports and newsletters
    Creating/updating websites/pages

Training

    User awareness/education
    Staff training (all levels) – induction and CPD
    Identifying and liaising with external trainers
    Identifying and adapting training materials
    Identifying and negotiating with external suppliers
    Devising training programme(s) and materials
    Integrating preservation training into general staff training

---

Note: Adapted and updated from Thebridge and Matthews 2000.

HOW?

Preservation needs to be integrated into overall library management and training in libraries.

> *Instruction in preservation demands an active political effort from the management of the library, and active work on attitudes from the staff. Not through a once-off course, but through a continuous process that never stops ... it has to be part of the active everyday activity of the institution ... Instruction must be based on a holistic policy where preservation is balanced in relation to the use of the collections* (Larsen 1997).

Analysis of Training Needs

A programme of training needs to be developed that meets individual library requirements and those of particular library staff roles, for example, caretakers and cleaners, library assistants, professionals with responsibility for special collections and different media or formats, and those tasked with determining preservation policy and strategy. It should begin with induction and also needs to build in 'repeat' or 'refresher' sessions to meet the needs of staff joining the institution or taking on new roles. Existing levels of expertise (basic, intermediate, advanced) should be taken into account. Training methods and activities will vary; externally available resources may be used or adapted for use. In-house staff and or trainers may lead training or external trainers may be brought in. Local networks may facilitate such events and enable sharing of resources. External training events should also be part of the programme. Professional bodies, regional MLAs, conservators and specialist companies all offer training and diaries of events (see below) that should be consulted regularly to keep abreast of what is on offer, what it covers, who is offering it and what it costs.

To determine the content and scope of such a training programme, those planning it should undertake an analysis of preservation training needs in the library. This may be done in the context of how overall training needs are analysed. Table 4.1 can be taken as a checklist against which current training activity can be compared, and where there are gaps these may be considered for inclusion, or exclusion confirmed if not appropriate to local circumstances. But, for a more specific approach, carrying out a preservation needs assessment will indicate preservation priorities and areas where training is required. The preservation training programme can thus be devised in line with the library's preservation policy and have clear objectives, both from the point of view of the library and those to be trained. Resources required need to be identified and costs budgeted.

Methods

As many aspects of the subject are of a practical nature, demonstrations and practical, activity-based, 'hands-on' workshops and exercises are essential. Diagrams and photographs in books and on websites can be useful aids but there is nothing like first-hand experience under expert guidance. Exhibitions, of different kinds of conservation treatments, for example, can be useful. If these are not possible within the institution, consider contacting local institutions or commercial binders to see if a visit might be arranged. There are few up to date videos/DVDs available and they are expensive to produce but those undertaking, say, disaster management exercises or simulations may wish to consider recording these and then viewing the results and reflecting on them. Seminars can introduce topics and offer a means of sharing experience, discussing specific issues or questions and determining actions. Surveys (for example, of environmental conditions around the library) or risk assessments (of parts of the building) can be carried out as exercises with groups of staff with different expertise, followed by debriefing sessions where issues can be discussed and fed back into procedures.

Monitoring and Evaluation of Training

The literature offers little on the monitoring and evaluation of preservation training. Quizzes have been used informally. General procedures should be followed both from the individual's point of view and that of the institution. Lessons from feedback, observation and review should be considered and implemented as appropriate. One example which those considering this aspect of training might find useful is the logbook provided for use with preservation microfilming training at the National Library of Australia (Brown 2003). The logbook includes tables and tick boxes to record performance against learning outcomes (elements of competency) and learning activity criteria.

EXAMPLES OF TRAINING AND TRAINING RESOURCES

The following examples from the UK and elsewhere should provide guidance, inspiration and encouragement to those looking to develop training programmes and training resources for preservation in their institutions.

In-house – General

Oxford University Library Services. Conservation and Collection Care. <http://www.bodley.ox.ac.uk/dept/preservation/workofdept/pagethree.htm>.

The webpages offer an introduction to the library and its collections, followed by introductions to key aspects of preservation and conservation. There is also a series of links to further information on a range of topics, including: security, emergency control planning, environmental control, library material, photographic media, audio-visual media and reformatting. A glossary is also provided.

Oxford University Library Services. Conservation and Collection Care. Training Notes. <http://www.bodley.ox.ac.uk/dept/preservation/training/training.htm>.

The training notes are attractive with colourful illustrations, photographs and diagrams which add to the words. Advice is given on how long it will take to read through them. Topics addressed include: handling library material, increasing preservation awareness, housekeeping, book moves, environmental monitoring and control, dealing with mould, dealing with pests, and service continuity. Each of the broad topics, where appropriate, are further subdivided. Handling library material, for example, covers: clean hands, food and drink, removing books from shelves, carrying, handling, book structures, supporting books in use, note taking, stationery, books not in use, bookmarks, photocopying, and shelving books. This guidance is aimed at users as well as staff.

Regional initiatives in preservation training are developing, too. The MLA North East and Durham University Collections Care Framework recently received the Award for Care of Collections 2007, Conservation Awards 2007.

The scheme which started in July 2002 provided advice and training in collection care to libraries, archives and museums with paper based collections throughout the north east. In April 2006 it expanded to provide preservation advice on museum objects as well, in partnership with the NE Museums Hub. The North East Collections Care Framework responds to requests for advice on storage conditions, disaster planning, benchmarks and other preservation issues, and can organise training days on practical topics such as the care, handling and cleaning of collections (Durham University 2007).

For further information, see MLA North East Collections Care Stewardship (2007) and Hingley (2006).

The MLA South West has developed a series of fact sheets, *Signposts to Collection Care*, on topics such as: handling and packing, preventive conservation, emergency planning (MLA South West 2007). Whilst the focus is on museums, they also contain information of relevance to libraries and archives.

As indicated above, at basic knowledge, the NPO offers leaflets on a range of preservation topics addressing basic and managerial aspects. As well as hard copy, these are available on the NPO website (National Preservation Office 2007).

The California Preservation Program offers useful information on its website including a section on Preservation Education for Staff and Users that provides information on responsibilities for staff, addresses preservation in public and school libraries and gives links to training tools (California Preservation Program 2007). Additionally, there is an e-discussion facility.

Whilst such services and sources are available externally, they serve as examples or may be adapted for use internally.

External

A couple of examples of online courses on preservation exist:

Dean J.F. (2007), Cornell University Library. Library Preservation and Conservation Tutorial Southeast Asia. <http://www.library.cornell.edu/preservation/librarypres ervation/meolda/index.html>.

The tutorial, supported by the National Endowment for the Humanities, focuses on libraries and archives in developing countries and includes an introduction to methods of education and training, a self-assessment of preservation activity, case studies and resources.

Northeast Document Conservation Center (2007). Education. Online Courses. <http://www.nedcc.org/education/online.php>.

The Northeast Document Conservation Center's Preservation 101 online course is in the process of being completely revamped with new content, new resources, and a new design. This self-paced course will cover the preservation of paper collections and related formats. Participants will learn how to identify deteriorated materials, how to properly care for collections, and how to set priorities for preservation. Whether one seeks to learn about preservation basics or explore a specific topic in depth, this course provides essential information for both professionals caring for library and archival materials and individuals eager to preserve family collections.

Subject-focused

The following are illustrative of the kind of training and resources available for an aspect of preservation – disaster management (or emergency planning as it is also known).

In the UK, as part of the Renaissance South East Sharing Skills programme, specialists from Harwell Document Restoration Services have been contracted to provide tailored training, advice and support to help museums, libraries and archives in the south east get to grips with emergency planning throughout 2007. The training comprises three parts: Writing an emergency plan, practical training on salvaging your collection and individual support for writing an emergency plan:

Having done the training you will be fully equipped to write your own Emergency Plan using the templates provided here, and materials provided at the training courses. The Emergency Planning Advisor will provide 121 advice and individual feedback to help museums, libraries & archives complete their plans, including visiting sites if needed (MLA South East. Emergency Planning 2007).

The website also provides a list of emergency suppliers and the trainer's PowerPoint presentations introducing emergency planning and covering reaction and recovery.

Sources from outside the UK may also be of use. For example, the California Preservation Program Disaster Plan Exercise includes instructor guidelines, a role-playing exercise with scenario, and questions for group discussion. Also on the website is a generic disaster plan workbook, a disaster plan template and a guide to resources (including case histories) (California Preservation Program Disaster Plan Exercise 2007). The Library of Congress provides a rationale for training for emergency planning and suggestions on how to do it (Library of Congress 2007). Also in the United States, as part of its response to the aftermath of Hurricane Katrina, Heritage Preservation produced a DVD, *Field Guide to Emergency*

Response, accompanied by a DVD that shows procedures and practices (Heritage Preservation 2006).

It is also worth considering an international initiative of the International Council of Museums, Module 4, Museums Emergency Programme Education Initiative Teamwork for Integrated Emergency Management Course.

> *The course reflects a capacity building approach to emergency management by combining training workshops with practical experience gained over an extended period of time. The course guides participating institutions through the processes of undertaking risk assessment and implementing emergency plans and strategies that are suitable for their own institutions, taking into account local contexts, traditions, and methods* (International Council of Museums 2007).

WHERE TO FIND TRAINING EVENTS

Regular scanning of the following websites should ensure relevant training events in the UK are identified:

National Preservation Office[1]

Look at 'What's new' on the home page. For example,
What's new October 16th 2007
NPO conference. Second life for collections [collection surrogacy]
Three training days, on:

> Managing the library and archive environment
> How clean are your books?
> Understanding and caring for bookbindings

Two leaflets:

> Specifying library and archive storage
> Knowing the need: meeting the need (report on the state of preservation of the UK library and archive collections

The NPO offers a preservation management consultancy, and for its preservation assessment survey offers documentation, database, workshops and introductory on-site training – prices available on the website. In addition to the *NPO e-Journal*, the NPO offers a range of publications of interest to trainers, including reports

---

1   National Preservation Office. <http://www.bl.uk/npo>.

and guides, some of its conference proceedings, and free leaflets on a range of topics such as *Building Blocks for a Preservation Policy*; *Guidance for Exhibiting Library and Archival Materials*; *Managing the Digitisation of Library, Archive and Museum Materials*; *Photocopying of Library and Archive Materials*; *Preservation of Photographic Material*; and *Prevention and Treatment of Mould Outbreaks in Collections*. It also provides a comprehensive and up to date Training and Events Calendar, covering mainly the UK, but with select international events.

Collections Link[2]

> *[T]he new national advisory service for collections management managed by MDA in partnership with the Institute of Conservation (ICON) and the National Preservation Office (NPO). Collections Link provides fast, easy access to current best practice in 16 areas of professional collections management. All of the content of the site has been provided by authoritative national bodies and experts with years of experience in their field* ('Welcome to Collections Link', Collections Link 2007).

It provides details of courses and conferences, highlighting new ones and offers a database of training search facility.

Websites of regional MLAs and their national equivalents should also be consulted.

Professional Bodies

The journals, newsletters and websites of professional bodies should be scanned. They may have an annual training programme, but specialist subject or regional groups' activities should also be consulted.

Chartered Institute of Library and Information Professionals (CILIP). Training, events and conferences: <http://www.cilip.org.uk/training/>.

Society of Archivists. Events: <http://www.archives.org.uk/events.asp>.

Museums Association. MA Events: <http://www.museumsassociation.org/maevents&_IXMENU_=events>.

ICON (The Institute of Conservation). Education and Training: <http://www.icon.org.uk/index.php?option=com_content&task=view&id=6&Itemid=7>.

---

2   Collections Link. <http://www.collectionslink.org.uk/>.

Educational Institutions

It is worth identifying universities and colleges active in preservation-related matters and checking their websites. See, for example:

UCL Centre for Sustainable Heritage. CSH Short courses: <http://www.ucl.ac.uk/sustainableheritage/short_courses.htm>. This offers a three-day course, 'Surviving a Disaster', in collaboration with English Heritage.

Commercial companies and conservators may also offer training. As mentioned above, ICON's Conservation Register can be used to find conservators (ICON 2007).

Moving beyond the UK, the following are useful:

European Commission on Preservation and Access (ECPA)[3] provides a calendar of events (conferences, workshops, seminars).

International Preservation News, published three times per year by the International Federation of Library Associations' Preservation and Conservation Core Activity (IFLA PAC), contains an Events and Training section.

FUTURE

Preservation training has to compete for resources with other aspects of library management. In recent years, 'traditional' preservation has also had to vie with the demands of digital preservation. There are few positions in libraries solely devoted to preservation; it is still an activity carried out in the main in national, research and special libraries. It is, however, from its basic aspects upwards, to varying degrees, a component of the role of all members of staff and has a vital part to play in ensuring accessibility to, and provision of, training resources for general use The momentum built up in the UK in the 1990s by the NPO has been lost, but it and other bodies are still active in offering training courses and expertise, and the Internet offers access to a range of sources offering advice and examples for those looking to develop in-house materials. Those libraries with in-house staff with relevant expertise, such as conservators and archivists, and librarians experienced in aspects of preservation, may be better placed to plan and undertake institutional training themselves and/or with institutional trainers. For those without this, for example, in smaller organizations, sending staff to external courses, bringing in trainers or commercial companies, or developing training themselves remain the main options. These have financial and time implications – it seems likely that to

---

3   ECPA. <http://www.knaw.nl/ecpa/>.

maximize effective use of limited resources in this kind of organization, it may be necessary to continue to develop preservation training collaboratively at local or regional level. Thus whilst the Internet brings helpful resources from around the world much closer, seeking out potential local collaborators and partners nearer to home should not be overlooked, and it may be more suited to local circumstances.

REFERENCES

Bendix, C. and Walker, A. (2006), *Cleaning Books and Documents*, rev. edn (London: National Preservation Office).

Bowman, J.H. (ed.) (2006), *British Librarianship and Information Work 1991– 2000* (Aldershot: Ashgate).

Bowman, J.H. (ed.) (2007), *British Librarianship and Information Work 2001– 2005* (Aldershot: Ashgate).

Bremer-Laamanen, M. and Stenvall, J. (2004), 'Selection for Digital Preservation: Dilemmas and Issues' in J. Feather (ed.).

Brown, H. (2003), *Training in Preservation Microfilming – Log Book* (Canberra: National Library of Australia). <http://www.nla.gov.au/preserve/micro/screen/logbooksc.pdf>.

California Preservation Program (2007). <http://calpreservation.org/index.html>.

California Preservation Program. Disaster Plan Exercise (2007). <http://calpreservation.org/disasters/exercise.html>.

California Preservation Program. Preservation Education for Staff and Users (2007). <http://calpreservation.org/education/index.html>.

Centre for Sustainable Heritage, UCL. Short Courses from CSH. <http://www.ucl.ac.uk/sustainableheritage/short_courses.htm>.

Chartered Institute of Library and Information Professionals (CILIP). Training, Events and Conferences (2007). <http://www.cilip.org.uk/training>.

Cloonan, M.V. (1994), *Global Perspectives on Preservation Education* (Munich: Saur).

Collections Link (2007). <http://www.collectionslink.org.uk/>.

Conservation DistList (2007). <http://palimpsest.stanford.edu/byform/mailing-lists/cdl/aboutcdl.shtml>.

Conservation in Crisis: Proceedings of a Seminar at Loughborough University, 16–17 July 1986 (1987) (London: The National Preservation Office, The British Library).

Conservation OnLine (2007), Educational Opportunities in Museum, Library and Archives Conservation/Preservation. <http://palimpsest.stanford.edu/bytopic/education/>.

de Lusenet, Y. (1998), 'The Case of the Dutch Hamster: Promoting Awareness and Preservation Management Training in Europe', *Liber Quarterly* 8:4, 458–71.

de Lusenet, Y. (2006), 'Moving with the Times in Search of Permanence' in G.E. Gorman and S.J. Shep (eds).

Dean J.F. (2007), Cornell University Library. Library Preservation and Conservation Tutorial Southeast Asia. <http://www.library.cornell.edu/preservation/library preservation/meolda/index.html>.

Deegan, M. and Tanner, S. (eds) (2006), *Digital Preservation* (London: Facet Publishing).

Digital Preservation Coalition (2007). <http://www.dpconline.org/graphics/index. html>.

Digital Preservation Coalition (2007). Mission and Goals. <http://www.dpconline. org/graphics/about/mission.html>.

Durham University. University Library. Conservation (2007). <http://www.dur. ac.uk/library/asc/conservation/>.

Eden, P., Dungworth, N., Bell, N. and Matthews, G. (1998), *A Model for Assessing Preservation Needs in Libraries* (London: British Library Research and Innovation Centre).

European Commission on Preservation and Access (ECPA) (2007). <http://www. knaw.nl/ecpa/>.

Feather, J. (1990), 'Staff Training for Preservation', *Library Management* 11:4, 10–14.

Feather, J. (1996), *Preservation and the Management of Library Collections*, 2nd edn (London: Library Association Publishing).

Feather, J. (2000), 'The Role of Library and Archive Schools' in S. Thebridge (ed.).

Feather, J. (ed.) (2004), *Managing Preservation for Libraries and Archives: Current Practice and Future Developments* (Aldershot: Ashgate).

Feather, J. and Lusher, A. (1988), 'The Teaching of Conservation in LIS Schools in Great Britain' (British Library Research Paper 49) (London: British Library).

Feather, J., Matthews, G. and Eden, P. (1996), *Preservation Management. Policies and Practices in British Libraries* (Aldershot: Gower).

Forde, H. (2007), *Preserving Archives* (London: Facet Publishing).

Gorman, G.E. and Shep, S.J. (eds) (2006), *Preservation Management for Libraries, Archives and Museums* (London: Facet Publishing).

Harvey, R. (1993), *Preservation in Libraries: Principles, Strategies and Practices for Librarians* (London and Melbourne: Bowker Saur).

Henderson, J. (2007), *Managing the Library and Archive Environment* (London: National Preservation Office). <http://www.bl.uk/services/npo/pdf/environment. pdf>.

Heritage Preservation (n.d.), *Emergency Response and Salvage Wheel*, rev. edn (Washington, DC: Heritage Preservation).

Heritage Preservation in support of the Heritage Emergency National Task Force (2006), *Field Guide to Emergency Response* [with instructional DVD] (Washington, DC: Heritage Preservation).

Hingley, S. (2006), 'The North East Collections Care Scheme', *NPO e-Journal*, 4 (May). <http://www.bl.uk/services/npo/journal/4/hingley.html>.

Holland, G. (1998), *Review of Management Training and Development in the Museums, Galleries and Heritage Sector: The Final Report, December 1997* (Bradford: Museum Training Institute).

ICON. Conservation Register (2007). <http://www.conservationregister.com/find-a-conservator.asp?id=2>.

ICON. Education and Training (2007). <http://www.icon.org.uk/index.php?option=com_content&task=view&id=6&Itemid=7>.

International Council of Museums (2007), 'Museum Emergency Programme. Preparedness and Response in Emergency Situations. Module 4. Museums Emergency Programme Education Initiative Teamwork for Integrated Emergency Management Course. <http://icom.museum/mep_module4.html>.

International Federation of Library Associations Preservation and Conservation Core Activity (PAC). <http://www.ifla.org/VI/4/pac.htm>.

International Federation of Library Associations Preservation and Conservation Core Activity, *International Preservation News*. <http://www.ifla.org/VI/4/ipn.html>.

JISC Digital Preservation Training Programme (2007). <http://www.jisc.ac.uk/whatwedo/programmes/programme_preservation/programme_404/project_dptp.aspx>.

Larsen, S.B. (1997), 'Teaching Preservation in Large Research Libraries', *Liber Quarterly*, 7, 518–28.

Library of Congress (2007), Preservation. <http://www.loc.gov/preserv/>.

M25 Consortium of Academic Libraries Disaster Management Group Website. <http://www.m25lib.ac.uk/m25dcp/>.

Matthews, G. and Thebridge, S. (2001), 'Preservation Management Training and Education: Developing a Sector-wide Approach', *New Library World* 102:1170–1171, 443–51.

Matthews, G. and Walker, A. (2004), 'A Snapshot Survey of Preservation Education in Library Schools', *NPO e-journal*, 2. <http://www.bl.uk/services/npo/journal/2/training.html>.

Meadows, A.J. (1987), 'Conservation and Preservation: Some Questions Answered' in *Conservation in Crisis*, 19–22.

MLA North East Collections Care Stewardship (2007). <http://www.mlanortheast.org.uk/stewardship.htm>.

MLA South East. Emergency Planning (2007). <http://www.mlasoutheast.org.uk/whatwedo/standards/emergencyplanning/>.

MLA South West. Document Library. Collections. *Signposts to Collection Care* (2007). <http://www.mlasouthwest.org.uk/index.php?ID=739>.

Muir, A. (2004), 'Issues in the Long-term Management of Digital Material' in J. Feather (ed.).

Museums Association. MA Events (2007). <http://www.museumsassociation.org/maevents&_IXMENU_=events>.

National Preservation Office (1994), *Preservation: A Training Pack for Library Staff* (London: National Preservation Office).

National Preservation Office (2007). <http://www.bl.uk/services/npo/npo.html>.

National Preservation Office. Leaflets (2007). <http://www.bl.uk/services/npo/publicationsleaf.html>.

National Preservation Office and British Library Collection Care and Handling Team (2000), *Good Handling Principles and Practice for Library and Archive Materials* (London: National Preservation Office). <http://www.bl.uk/services/npo/pdf/handling.pdf>.

Northeast Document Conservation Center (2007). <http://www.nedcc.org/home.php>.

Northeast Document Conservation Center. Education. Online Courses (2007). <http://www.nedcc.org/education/online.php>.

Northeast Document Conservation Center. Resources. Preservation Leaflets (2007). <http://www.nedcc.org/resources/leaflets.list.php>.

Ogden, S. (ed.) (1999), *Preservation of Library and Archival Materials: A Manual*, 3rd edn (Massachusetts: Northeast Document Conservation Center). Available as leaflets by topic at: <http://www.nedcc.org/resources/print.php>.

Oxford University Library Services. Conservation and Collection Care (2007). <http://www.bodley.ox.ac.uk/dept/preservation/workofdept/pagethree.htm>.

Oxford University Library Services. Conservation and Collection Care. Training Notes (2007). <http://www.bodley.ox.ac.uk/dept/preservation/training/training.htm>.

PADI. Preserving Access to Digital Information (2007). <http://www.nla.gov.au/padi/>.

Prytherch, R. (ed.) (1986), *Handbook of Library Training Practice* (Aldershot: Gower).

Ratcliffe, F.W. with Patterson, D. (1984), Preservation Policies and Conservation in British Libraries: Report of the Cambridge University Library Conservation Project (London: British Library).

Reed, B. (2006), 'Challenges of Managing the Digitally Born Object', in G.E. Gorman and S.J. Shep (eds).

Resource: The Museums, Libraries and Archive Council (2003), *Security in Museums, Libraries and Archives: A Practical Guide* (London: Resource). <http://www.mla.gov.uk/resources/assets//S/security_manual_pdf_5900.pdf>.

Society of Archivists. Events (2007). <http://www.archives.org.uk/events.asp>.

Swartzburg, S.G. (1995), *Preserving Library Materials: A Library Manual*, 2nd edn (Metuchen, NJ: Scarecrow Press).

Thebridge, S. (ed.) (2000), *Training for Preservation Management: The Next Step. Proceedings of the National Preservation Office Annual Seminar held on 26th October 1999 at the British Library and Thebridge, S. and Matthews, G. Review of Preservation Training in the UK and Abroad. The Main Findings from the Library and Information Commission Research Report 48* (London: National Preservation Office).

Thebridge, S. and Matthews, G. (2000), *Review of Current Preservation Management Training in the UK and Abroad* (London: Library and Information Commission).

UCL Centre for Sustainable Heritage. Short Courses from CSH (2007). <http://www.ucl.ac.uk/sustainableheritage/short_courses.htm>.

UNESCO Memory of the World Programme (2007). <http://portal.unesco.org/ci/en/ev.php-URL_ID=1538&URL_DO=DO_TOPIC&URL_SECTION=201.html>.

University of London Computer Centre (2007), Digital Preservation Training Programme. <http://www.ulcc.ac.uk/dptp/>.

Walker, A. (2003), *Basic Preservation Guidelines for Library and Archive Collections*, rev. edn, 2006 (London: National Preservation Office). <http://www.bl.uk/services/npo/pdf/basic.pdf>.

Walker, A. (2006), 'Preservation' in J.H. Bowman (ed.).

Walker, A. (2007), 'Preservation' in J.H. Bowman (ed.).

Webb, C. (2004), 'The Malleability of Fire: Preserving Digital Preservation' in J. Feather (ed.).

White, D. (1986), 'Conservation' in R. Prytherch (ed.).

ADDITIONAL RESOURCES

Books

Adcock, E.P. (comp. and ed.) with the assistance of M.-T. Varlamoff and V. Kremp (1998), *IFLA Principles for the Care and Handling of Library Materials* (Paris: IFLA). Available at: <http://www.ifla.org/VI/4/news/pchlm.pdf>.

Boomgarden, W.L. (1993), *Staff Training and User Awareness in Preservation Management* (Washington, DC: Association of Research Libraries).

Boylan, P. and Woollard, V. (2006), *Running a Museum. The Trainer's Manual: for Use with Running a Museum: A Practical Handbook* (Paris: UNESCO). Available at: <http://unesdoc.unesco.org/images/0014/001478/147869E.pdf>.

Clements, D.W.G., McIlwaine, J.H.,Thurston, A.C. and Rudd, S.A. (1989), *Review of Training Needs in Preservation and Conservation* (Paris: UNESCO RAMP Study PGI-89/WS/15).

Deegan, M. and Tanner, S. (2006), *Digital Preservation and the Future of Culture* (London: Facet).

Ford (sic), H. (1991), *The Education of Staff and Users for the Proper Handling of Archival Materials: A RAMP Study with Guidelines* (Paris: UNESCO RAMP Study PGI-91/WS/17).

Heritage Preservation (2005), *A Public Trust at Risk: The Heritage Health Index [Summary] Report on the State of America's Collections. A Project of Heritage Preservation and the Institute of Museum and Library Services* (Washington, DC: Heritage Preservation). Summary report <http://www.heritagepreservation.org/

HHI/summary.html>; Full report <http://www.heritagepreservation.org/HHI/full.html>.

McIlwaine, J. (comp.) (2005), *First, Do No Harm. A Register of Standards, Codes of Practices, Guidelines, Recommendations and Similar Works Relating to Preservation and Conservation in Libraries and Archives* (Paris: IFLA Preservation and Conservation). Available at: <http://www.ifla.org/VII/s19/pubs/first-do-no-harm.pdf>.

Walker, A. and Foster, J. (2006), *Knowing the Need: A Report on the Emerging Picture of Preservation Need in Libraries and Archives in the UK* (London: National Preservation Office). Available at: <http://www.bl.uk/services/npo/pdf/knowing.pdf>.

Websites

Canadian Conservation Institute (2007). <http://www.cci-icc.gc.ca/main_e.aspx>.

Heritage Preservation. The National Institute for Conservation (2007). <http://www.heritagepreservation.org/>.

International Federation of Library Associations. Safeguarding our Documentary Heritage (2000). <http://www.ifla.org/VI/6/dswmedia/en/index.html>.

National Library of Australia. Preservation (2007). <http://www.nla.gov.au/preserve/>.

reCollections. Caring for Collections across Australia (2007). <http://archive.amol.org.au/recollections/foreword.htm>.

soliNET. Preservation and Access (2007). <http://www.solinet.net/preservation/>.

United Kingdom and Ireland Blue Shield Organisation (2007). <http://www.bl.uk/blueshield/>.

CHAPTER 5

MANAGEMENT OF ELECTRONIC RESOURCES

FRANCES BOYLE

DEFINITIONS

What are we talking about? This beguiling question will doubtless be familiar to all library practitioners (at whatever level) who operate within the electronic resources landscape. However, not only are we dealing with a dynamic area but also one which has multifarious meanings to many players across all sectors of the information world. The overarching ethos that must be understood before staff venture towards electronic resources is that this is not the ordered proven print world. This is a much more chaotic world in which, for the foreseeable future anyway, there are no absolute solutions or system that can be implemented in a prescriptive foolproof fashion.

An even more fundamental question to pose is whether electronic resources should remain a discrete area in library management? If one considers libraries and information units from all sectors then one could argue that electronic resources are pervasive across all areas, procedures and processes of library operations. From backroom activities such as acquisitions and cataloguing to front line service delivery and outreach activities, the 'electronic resource' is omnipresent. It is perhaps interesting to reflect whether it is strategically prudent to consider electronic resources not as isolated entities but rather as 'atoms' of information that only reach their full potential and value when 'lubricated' into the complex information cycle by a range of information practitioners that make them 'fit for purpose'. I would suggest that in the twenty-first century training needs for all information professionals are focused on networks of one type or another. So managing connections is just as important as managing the collections, be they print or virtual. As such the major challenges and stress points for training and staff development in this area stem from the realization that it is the deployment, support and embedding of these resources within the teaching, learning and research environments which pose the greatest challenges for staff at all levels. Indeed one also needs to consider to what extent electronic resources management training is embedded into training programmes for all library staff.

Electronic resources are themselves constantly changing, mutating, coalescing and linking. Thus their management and aligned processes also operate in a fluid environment. This calls for a keen sense of direction and a flexible and agile mind set, not for the faint of heart.

Though technical and business level skills are critical, the softer interpersonal skills are equally as valuable and as such time and resources need to be invested to develop the desired skills set. These softer skills may include communication and presentation skills, negotiating, project management, creative decision making, multitasking and problem solving – though of course the range and depth of these will be dependent on the precise role that the individual fulfils.

To first principles then and to define the scope of the electronic resources remit that we are dealing with. For the purposes of this chapter I have used those that have been defined in recent UKSG and Facet publications (UKSG 2007a; Lee and Boyle 2004). This is a pragmatic decision as much time could be spent debating a taxonomy that could be adopted. This elasticity of definition is indicative of the breadth of the area and the diversity of skills, duties and responsibilities that institutions expect from their electronic resources practitioner(s). However, there are generic themes traversing the management of the electronic resource portfolio which will create a suite of transferable skills. There will be peculiar issues and challenges, and thus training needs, for each of the core specific types; for example, datasets, full text databases, e-journal, e-books, and so on, and the attendant technologies that surround them.

ANALYSIS OF TRAINING NEEDS

The parameters of the electronic resource landscape are fluid and may vary from institution to institution. We only have to look at the plethora of job titles that abound in this area, and the variety of 'homes' within institutions' organizational structures that electronic resources staff find themselves, to appreciate the developing nature of this area.

As with any training programme, one needs to define what the core competencies are for that area. One must also consider whether the organization/department has a commitment to promote career progression and staff development, indeed what are the institution's values? I feel that in any emerging area (and there may be much debate whether electronic resources have 'emerged' – but we should best leave that to other fora) the proactive support and opportunities for career progression and development are even more critical to the enrichment and progress of the library in the wider context. How the organization deals with these issues will impact on the 'buy in' from the staff. For instance, if new specialist staff are recruited on short-term fixed contracts, then this 'bought in' expertise and skills base will need to be shared and cascaded to the established staff posts. In this scenario the key issue in effective staff training practice is the management of the relationships between the two groups of staff and how this information sharing environment can be fostered.

For existing library staff, their move to the electronic resources area may be an organic, gradual transition during which time they have developed confidence and skills resulting in a positive and rewarding experience. However, there will be instances when the move to dealing with, or managing, some aspect of electronic resources may have been thrust upon them, which may affect their motivation and confidence. So the team members tasked with managing electronic resources may be from diverse professional and operational backgrounds, for example, reader services, systems, technical services, but they may also have different aspirations, expectations and experiences. These variations may lead to tensions and misunderstandings once they find themselves working together closely in a new team or unit. Alternatively they may meld into a balanced innovative team with a positive approach to the exciting world of electronic resources. This wide baseline of existing skills and experiences will inevitably impact on the training requirements. Another scenario to consider is that there may not always be a centralized dedicated electronic resources team, but rather a range of staff distributed across various established teams which deal with overlapping components of the jigsaw. This second scenario will inevitably mean that the softer skills set of communication and negotiating will be more important to ensure that there is cross-team co-operation and collaboration. I would suggest that the two scenarios throw up different priorities for the training needs, particularly in the softer side of the skills set.

The following is a general list of some of the skills, experience and competencies that library and information services staff would need for working in the electronic resources area within the emerging digital campus. I have not attempted to earmark them into different types of library staff, for example, professional, para professional, administrative, and so on, as there is often disparity between levels of responsibility and duties that institutions/organizations expect from similar grades of staff. I would hope that most of these would be required across all sectors of the information world.

SKILLS, COMPETENCIES, KNOWLEDGE (IN NO PARTICULAR ORDER)

Managing relationships:

* Liaison – with vendors, publishers, users (staff, student, external visitor) library and institutional colleagues

- Negotiating – with vendors, users, library colleagues, organizational colleagues, for example, computing, learning technologists, funders, and so on
- Influencing skills – with vendors, users and colleagues

Information and Communications Technology:

- Management of content – e-books, e-journals, datasets
- Access authentication – remote access issues, VPN, Shibboleth
- Delivery/presentation of the platform on which the electronic resources are presented and managed, for example, user interface – web, portal, ERM systems
- E-learning – virtual learning environments, virtual research environments. How can we embed the electronic resource into the teaching/learning and research environments
- Institutional repositories – how these are becoming part of the electronic resource landscape
- Digital assets – management, preservation
- Linking technologies, for example, resolvers, federated searching
- Reference handling software, for example, RefWorks, EndNote, and so on

Content management:

- An appreciation of the attendant IPR/licensing issues for electronic resources
- An awareness of the scholarly communication issues, for example, open access
- An understanding of the supply chain, for example, aggregators, vendors, publishers
- An understanding of new business systems for acquisitions, for example, may not be able to transfer acquisition models from the print to the electronic world
- Collection management – an understanding of the overall collection policies that the library may have

Outreach:

- PR/marketing – to colleagues, to end users, and so on
- User education – to colleagues, to end users, and so on

Management:

- Budget management – pricing models – the black art of demystifying the 'bundle spreadsheet'

- Bigger picture – understanding/appreciating the potential 'glue' to other digital campus developments, for example, e-learning, personnel student portfolios
- Management of change – may be part of new team, part of strategic move from print to electronic-only collections, and so on
- Project management – may be setting up new team, creating and implementing new service with cross-team matrix management role
- Analytical and evaluation skills – which deal, which bundle? What ERM?
- Workflow creations and implementation for new processes and procedures

Any needs analysis must be contextualized by the role and background the individual plays and the remit of the department/section that the post resides in. If we scan just one sector, for the sake of argument the UK Higher Education sector, the plethora of job titles, remits and organizational structures is striking. We have e-services posts, electronic resources librarians/managers/co-ordinators, e-strategy co-ordinators and e-services developers, to list just a few.

The scope and level of training will depend on circumstances, some of which have been explored earlier. As with all training there is a recurrent aspect to it which should not be overlooked. Indeed sometimes it is the already skilled experienced staff member that presents most of the training and development challenges to a manager. They may be more difficult to persuade that they should ensure that their awareness and skills are kept up to date, following the old adage 'You can't teach an old dog new tricks'. In these cases the training development opportunity must be presented in a sensitive way to ensure that it is not perceived as a criticism of their current skills or performance – if this is not the case. The feeling of wasting years of professional experience on refining the existing systems and procedures, for them only to be changed, may well prompt a sense of genuine loss which cannot be underestimated.

OBJECTIVES OF TRAINING

There are broadly two aspects to training. Firstly, the continued professional development and growth of the individual, and secondly, to ensure that person is equipped and confident so that they have the skills and knowledge to enable them to carry out their duties efficiently and effectively – in effect that they are fit for purpose. Senior managers of these posts, though, must realize that however willing their team member is, in this rapidly growing arena, there will always be new situations and systems to encounter.

To that end I would suggest that there is no such thing as the consummate electronic resources librarian/manager. As we are dealing with a dynamic area, then development and opportunities for professional growth and training need to be ongoing throughout a career. Useful experience may be gained from the staff member becoming the trainer rather than the trainee, particularly when sharing experience or best practice with fellow practitioners from other institutions.

I would also suggest that effective training programmes cannot be devised in isolation from either the external or institutional environment. This is because the 'purpose' referred to earlier may well change when the department or the home organization's strategic direction or imperatives change. In the UK there has been, and continues to be, ongoing changes affecting the HE sector which will inevitably have a knock-on effect on the expectations of all stakeholders within learning organizations.

It is essential that even if the content of any training event or course is on target, the level must also be appropriate for the potential trainee as well. If it is not, then you may hinder the person's development rather than contribute to it. As we progress through our careers, individuals will discover the type and format of learning experience that best suits them, be that formal presentation, shared experience fora, self-guided computer-assisted learning (CAL) and so on. Whilst it is always beneficial to stretch a learner, and even to encourage one 'to think out of the box', as it were, adults learn in different ways and indeed certain modes of delivery complement certain types of information exchange. So a mixed bag of training events and styles is perhaps the most balanced approach to take.

METHODS OF TRAINING

As in all areas of library and information work, there are a gamut of training organizations and events that are offered within the electronic resources arena; though it is only in the recent past that there have been dedicated events for training in this area. They range from in-house, to external, to vendor-led, and from the specific topic session, for example, vendor-run product sessions, to the broader crystal ball gazing sessions and all shades in between.

External Events

There are a host of external events run by a variety of organizations. In the field of electronic resources, the current major players in the UK are a mix of professional bodies, commercial providers that are often vendors, practitioner-led bodies and events sponsored by the LIS community. The style and format they adopt varies but often it is a mix of formal presentations and some more participative exercise, for example, workshops, panel sessions or focus groups.

There is often a significant cost associated with attending these external events, though this can often be mitigated if the library or individual is a member of the organizing body. Of course if the event is being run by an external supplier specifically for library staff as a result of a recently purchased product or system, then these costs should be negotiated at the time of product purchase. Indeed they may well not come out of the library budget at all or indeed be offered at no extra cost as part of the vendor's implementation package which will include support and documentation. Whilst this type of training is invaluable when there are specific detailed issues and procedures to be explored around a new dataset or rollout of a new system – for example, a new ERM – it must always be remembered that this is a vendor-centric approach to training. However, this type of training can also be viewed as a team-building exercise. There is often a positive vibe and a palpable team spirit when an entire team is trained collectively. It can often be a positive and rewarding event with much informal transfer of skills and experience.

Most external events clearly state the objectives of the event in the supplementary information; this should in theory make it easier to gauge whether an event is what an individual or manager is looking for. It is always useful to read this before making the decision to attend. One should look at the subject matter that is being focused on, the speakers, the mode of training, for example, workshop, formal lectures, and so on. Other considerations to make might include networking opportunities, what audience the event is geared for, the organizing body – have they a good reputation? – the location and facilities, and so on.

An example of an informative and concise outline about an event is the following, which was organized by the UKSG: 'E-Journal Technical Update Edinburgh. Thursday 15 February 2007, Edinburgh University Library. Everything you always wanted to know about e-journals but were afraid to ask ...' (UKSG 2007b). For this particular event there was also a full outline of the topics that were going to be covered and, more importantly, what was not going to be covered. This would prove invaluable in making an informed decision on the relevance of the event.

Another very helpful resource that may be tapped is that many of the presentations given at external events are published on the organizing bodies' websites post-event. The full details of the above quoted event can be found on the UKSG's website. The UKSG is an organization that offers a wealth of training opportunities in the area of electronic resources management. They run an annual conference, and both the formal lecture programme as well as the workshops offer a broad approach to the electronic resources landscape. The strength of the UKSG is that it encapsulates all players in the supply chain, for example, librarians, publishers, subscription agents, technology vendors, and so on.

If one looks at their 2007 programme (UKSG 2007c) the topics covered range from e-textbooks, COUNTER and open-access/institutional repositories to cataloguing e-books, Google Scholar and federated access management, all of which are within the consciousness of many an electronic resources practitioner.

As well as the formal sessions there is also an accompanying exhibition (a feature of many conferences) where many vendors are present. This affords an excellent opportunity to meet suppliers, view new features and products and to discuss any specific issues that may be outstanding with the supplier.

The UKSG conference is usually spread over three days and whilst this is an appreciable time for a staff member to be out of the library, the positive gains from attending should not be underestimated. An important tool in any working life is the informal professional network that is built up over the years with fellow practitioners. These contacts can often act as a sounding base for new ventures and also provide a much needed realistic perspective of a new service or product. Thus the networking opportunities that a large busy conference affords are another tangible benefit for both the participant and hopefully the home organization. The UKSG conference, though, remains a manageable size and is not an overpowering anonymous event. It does, however, have an international, albeit European, slant, which is reflected in both the speakers and the delegates.

So, reviewing the events that UKSG offers, there is a mix of short subject-specific seminars, usually over a single day and the broader approach to industry-wide themes and issues at the annual conference. Another format that the UKSG offers is brainstorming 'In Forum' events that are aimed primarily at special librarians to facilitate ideas exchange and discussion.

The following are different types of organization that provide training and development events – this is not an exhaustive list by any means:

- CILIP[1] – professional body
- JISC[2] – a funding body and government agency

CILIP, or to give it its full name, the Chartered Institute of Library and Information Professionals, runs a host of training events, including workshops and conferences.

The 2007 workshop programme includes some events that would be of interest to the electronic resources practitioner. It is noted also that the events are hosted across the country. The cost and time involved in travelling to events is an important factor and a consideration that may dictate what events are attended. They also offer the opportunity to hold the event in the home organization if there were to be a minimum number of attendees. Some courses that would be of interest include:

- E-Content and e-services showcase

---

1   CILIP. <http://www.cilip.org.uk/training/>.

2   JISC. <http://www.jisc.ac.uk/>.

- Electronic copyright
- Elementary statistics
- Blogs and wikis
- Getting the most out of Google

If training end users is a major part of the electronic resources practitioner's remit, then CILIP offer numerous courses on presentation and training techniques. The annual conference organized by CILIP is 'Umbrella' and its 2007 programme has streams on 'E-content' and 'information Literacy'.

The CILIP special interest group that deals with issues broadly in the electronic resources area is the UK eInformation Group (UKeiG). Their remit states that 'UKeiG is a respected and well-established forum for all information professionals, users and developers of electronic information resources in all formats' (UKEIG 2007) – in effect the core business of electronic resources in the broadest sense, for example, not just subscription-based information products but the more challenging aspects of interlinking and embedding the resources and technologies to underpin user-focused services. UKeiG is a personal subscription-based group, though one does not have to be a CILIP member to be eligible. Indeed if you are a CILIP member, one could select membership of UKeiG as one of the two special interest groups one is entitled to join.

Their 2007 programme offers a mixture of workshops and seminars that are open to everyone at a cost, though members of the group attract discounts. Also a popular series of fact sheets are published on a range of subjects – these are available to members on the group's website. Subjects covered include 'OpenURLs', 'TopTips on Reference Managing' and 'e-Books', to list just a few. This at your desk, self-paced learning approach is very useful and is particularly valuable for a quick update for background research on a new topic. The themes of the seminars are just as varied and range from developing digital collection policies to the challenges of e-science.

The strength of this organization, as well as others such as JIBS,[3] is that it is practitioner-led and run and as such is more likely to reflect the actual issues that are of interest to the community at that time. It again acts as a forum for information exchange and support. Like many of the above, the group has a suite of alerting tools, for example, monthly journal, alerting service, blogs and mailing lists to facilitate discussion, problem solving and information sharing amongst practitioners.

In general a very rewarding way to keep up to date professionally and '*carpe diem*' in respect to training and professional development is to become involved with

---

3   JIBS. <http://www.jibs.ac.uk>.

one of the organizing committees of these bodies. Not only will this afford one the opportunity to influence the topics that will be presented, but again it is a great opportunity to mix with fellow professionals from other organizations and indeed sectors. Obviously any commitment to an external body will be an additional work load so this must be considered carefully by both the manager and the individual. The influencing power of these groups on the industry must not be forgotten. Most service providers and vendors are only too keen to share the platform at practitioner-organized events. From their perspective these offer a direct route to many of their existing and potential customers at one event. The JIBS User Group, in its own words, is: 'One of the major means of feedback for end-users of the UK's networked resources' (JIBS 2007). It is another practitioner-led group that offers training events to the community. Recent topics covered include federated searching and a comparison of some of the major A&I datasets, for example, Web of Knowledge, Scopus and Google Scholar. This is again a subscription-based group, but here it is an institutional not a personal subscription, the major benefit of which is that all of the institutions' staff are deemed members and as such would benefit from the event discount that is available.

JISC, the Joint Information Systems Committee, has as its mission: '... to provide world-class leadership in the innovative use of Information and Communications Technology to support education and research' (JISC 2009), and as such is one of the main grant funders for research in the LIS world. JISC offers a number of events with an annual conference. The sessions on offer in the 2007 programme included:

- Is e-content out of control
- UK Access management federation
- Repository ecology: EThOS, the new UK e-theses service, national and institutional repository interaction

Another useful resource provided by JISC is the JISC Fact Files (JISC 2005). Though these are a little out of date, they do still provide some useful background to the wider electronic resources area. Titles include 'Providing Links to Your Content from Other Services' and 'Adding Value with RSS'.

Another very useful body is the JISC infoNet which '... aims to be the UK's leading advisory service for managers in the post-compulsory education sector promoting the effective strategic planning, implementation and management of information and learning technology to support the core activities of learning, teaching, research and business processes' (JISC 2008). The resources found here would be very useful for practitioners who are operating at a middle management level and involved in project management. The toolkits that are available provide a rich resource and range from 'Project Management' and 'Risk Management' to 'Systems Selection' and 'Effective Use of Virtual Learning Environments' (JISC 2008).

Vendor-led Training

As mentioned previously, the vendors, be they publishers, aggregators or service providers, all offer some sort of training and support resources. The quality and effectiveness of this varies depending on both the provider and the circumstances of the library. This type of training is particularly efficient and cost effective if there are large groups of staff that need to be trained on a new system or product. Additionally the vendor may be geared up to provide training for large groups of end users. This may be a useful component in any outreach activity which the library is planning to support a new service. Test account and 'sandpits' are often provided by the vendors as user support tools and could be rolled out by the library to end users. These are very useful in circumstances when the staff cannot be released for an off-site event, or as post-formal training aides to try out some of the skills that have been learnt at a previously attended event. They have the added advantage of staff being able to test drive new products in private so that they do not have to feel self-conscious or nervous in front of colleagues.

IN-HOUSE TRAINING OPPORTUNITIES

In most organizations there is a raft of training opportunities available, though perhaps not always run or sponsored by the library. For the practitioners working in larger organizations, particularly the education sector, there will often be a structured training and development department available to all organization staff. The range of courses available from the host organization may not cover the occupation-specific skills of the electronic resources practitioner but may offer the support and soft skills that are requisites within the professional environment. For example, these may be general management skills such as time management, personnel training or negotiation skills, and so on. There will be a double whammy effect from attending these courses. Firstly, library and information staff are mixing and learning in the same environment as their library customers. This is a great opportunity to hear their perceptions and priorities from the library. Secondly, the style and the content of the course delivery will reveal something about the organization's culture, which in turn may facilitate the library's future dialogue with the corporate and academic stakeholders within the institution.

An example of a tool that is available from a central institution is 'The Learning Needs Analysis Toolkit' (University of Oxford 2007). The site offers tools to assess your own organization and whether it is a 'learning organization'. This could be implemented within the library to some advantage to assess if the existing training and staff development programmes that are in place are effective.

Many people prefer to learn informally from colleagues in a shared best practice environment, often in a 'train the trainer' scenario. Useful sessions may be shared if colleagues from neighbouring institutions visit each other's libraries and perhaps discuss common issues and challenges. There are often collaborative organizations based on a local or regional area. One of the most active of these is Nowal Consortium[4] based in the north west of England. Nowal offers training opportunities from its Staff Development and Training stream. They not only offer training courses and support for core competencies but there is also a programme of staff eExchange of experience' events, and a scheme for job shadowing which would work well within the area of electronic resources.

There are also related training needs for staff who are not directly involved in the management of electronic resources but have either an outreach or a liaison role. These staff need to be kept abreast of resources in their areas of responsibility but also may need an understanding of some of the wider issues relating to electronic resources. This is when the library 'expert(s)' must ensure that colleagues are kept abreast of developments, if only the headlines. A pragmatic and enjoyable training pathway to follow is when libraries run a series of training events for colleagues. This should not become too burdensome but it should facilitate open discussion and debate. Many institutions adopt this strategy – whether they are regular 'training hours' or a shared repository of training modules, presentations and documentation available through the staff Intranet. There are many online tools that can be utilized from VLEs, Wikis, websites and social networking software.

Another very active regional consortium that offers an extensive staff development programme is cpd25 (M25 Consortium of Academic Libraries 2008), the staff development organization allied to the M25 Consortium of Academic Libraries Their current events programme includes sessions on e-books, Web 2.0 technologies and access to electronic resources issues.

Another common route to a quick download of expertise to share amongst colleagues is to invite a leading practitioner in that area from another institution to talk to staff. This might work particularly well for the wider strategic themes surrounding electronic resources management. For instance, the move to e-only – this has not only technical but also many cultural and policy issues surrounding it. A respected professional recounting how their institution successfully dealt with and managed these issues would hopefully inspire staff. It would also lead to an appreciation of the broader issues and hopefully trigger staff to begin to explore their own views and possible solutions if the same policy were adopted in their library.

As with all information areas, there is a wealth of professional literature that is available. In this particular area, publications that are of interest include *Ariadne* (UKOLN 2008) and *Serials* (UKSG 2008).

---

4   NOWAL. <http://www.nowal.ac.uk/training/clip/about_clip.htm>.

MONITORING AND EVALUATION OF TRAINING

To ensure an effective use of training opportunities, one would hope that any subject-specific training was set against a background of a supportive organization where staff development is firmly on the agenda.

In some organizations there are formal staff development reviews and appraisal procedures which are held regularly. These will give staff the opportunity to voice any training or development issues that they have. Ideally there will be a record kept of the training pathways and this perhaps could be taken to any future employers as well. Many libraries ask that staff report back to colleagues if they have attended an external training event. This may take many forms: a cascade of training to other colleagues in the team, a report in the staff newsletter, a verbal report at a staff meeting. This feedback is invaluable both to colleagues but also the sponsoring body. If the event did not match expectations, then the manger may think twice before sending other staff to similar events. Likewise an 'approved' training event or conference would encourage colleagues to attend future meetings.

A more tangible and encouraging result from successful training would be to see staff actively engaging both within and outside the organization in debate on matters virtual. Their active participation in the many JISCmail[5] lists and discussion groups would contribute to an active involvement in their areas of responsibility. There are over a hundred lists on JISCmail under the electronic resources heading, including LIS-E-Books, LIS-E-Journals, JISC-E-Collections, and JISC-Shibboleth, to name but a few. There are regular alerts available in this area which offer timely news about many aspects of electronic resource management from the community's, the funders' and the vendors' perspectives.

For those more experienced practitioners, another route to developing and expanding skills and experience is to become involved in an externally funded project in emerging areas. JISC regularly holds calls for projects in many areas. Of the current streams on repositories, e-learning, e-infrastructure and e-resources overlap in the wider electronic landscape. Participation in collaborative externally funded projects not only extends professional competencies but also builds up the profile of the library and the individual.

Another useful by-product of the project culture is that there are often toolkits produced as project deliverables which are interesting and allow the practitioner

---

5   JISCmail. <http://www.jiscmail.ac.uk/>.

to review and be informed of development in their areas. Over recent years these include Intute,[6] COUNTER[7] and JORUM.[8]

CONCLUSION

The challenges and issues faced in training of library staff in the area of electronic resources are not that different from other library specialist areas. The major difference is the speed at which the area is developing, with the attendant impact on all other aspects of information work. On the positive front, it is pleasing how open the debates from all sectors of the information world have become. At many fora the same questions are being asked by all stakeholders, which can only contribute to the richness of the debate and development taking place.

This area will continue to grow and as such the LIS community must ensure that its members of staff are confident, motivated and skilled in all aspects of their area of responsibility. Otherwise the opportunities that are available for libraries to become partners in delivering the strategic objectives of the organization in the emerging era of the digital campus will be lost as other stakeholders take up the challenge.

REFERENCES

JIBS (2007). <http://www.jibs.ac.uk>.
JISC (2005), e-Resources Fact Files. <http://www.jisc.ac.uk/publications/publications/pub_factfiles>.
JISC (2008), JISCinfoNet. <http://www.jiscinfonet.ac.uk>.
JISC (2009), JISC. <http://www.jisc.ac.uk>.
Lee, S.D. and Boyle F. (2004), *Building Electronic Resources Collections* (London: Facet).
M25 Consortium of Academic Libraries (2008), cpd25. <http://www.cpd25.ac.uk/>.
UKEIG (2007), UK eInformation Group: home page. <http://www.ukeig.org.uk/>.
UKOLN (2008), *Ariadne*. <http://www.ariadne.ac.uk/>.
UKSG (2007a), *E-Resources Management Handbook* (UKSG). <http://serials.uksg.org/link.asp?id=6tuu9n7wfl18>.
UKSG (2007b), E-Journal Technical Update. <http://www.uksg.org/events/150207prog.pdf>, no longer available.
UKSG (2007c), *30th Annual UKSG Conference and Exhibition*. <http://www.uksg.org/events/conference07>.

---

6   Intute. <http://www.intute.ac.uk/>.
7   COUNTER. <http://www.projectcounter.org/>.
8   JORUM. <http://www.jorum.ac.uk/>.

UKSG (2008), *Serials.* <http://uksg.metapress.com/link.asp?id=107730>.
University of Oxford (2007), 'The Learning Needs Analysis Toolkit'. <http://tall.
conted.ox.ac.uk/lnat/>.

SERVICES TO USERS

CHAPTER 6

INCLUSION: TRAINING TO TACKLE SOCIAL EXCLUSION

JOHN VINCENT

INTRODUCTION

This chapter looks at social exclusion (and other current social policy) and how it applies to libraries. It then outlines good practice for delivering training courses and makes some suggestions for developing our personal awareness of this area.

WHAT IS SOCIAL EXCLUSION, AND WHY IS IT RELEVANT TO LIBRARIES?

There has been a long history in the UK of public libraries developing services to meet the needs of 'disadvantaged' people (see, for example, Muddiman 2000; Coleman 1981; Clough and Quarmby 1978) – including the only partially successful 'community librarianship' model of the 1970s and 1980s (see Black and Muddiman 1997; Vincent 1986) – but this has had a renewed focus (and a new name) since 1997.

The earliest use of the term 'social exclusion' seems to have been by René Lenoir, the former French Secretary of State for Social Action, who used it in 1974 to refer to '… individuals and groups of people who were administratively excluded from state social protection systems (e.g. the physically disabled, single parents, and the uninsured unemployed)' (Todman 2004). More recently, social exclusion has become a central part of the European Commission's social policy agenda (see Room et al. 1992), and was introduced as a concept to the UK in the 1990s (see, for example, Walker and Walker 1997), with the Labour Government's establishing of a Social Exclusion Unit in the Cabinet Office in 1997.

The Government's earliest definitions of social exclusion were quite broad and limited: '… a shorthand term for what can happen when people or areas suffer from a combination of linked problems such as unemployment, poor skills, low incomes, poor housing, high crime, bad health and family breakdown' (see, for example, Social Exclusion Unit 2001). By 2001, the Government's definition had developed further:

Social exclusion is something that can happen to anyone. But some people are significantly more at risk than others. Research has found that people with certain backgrounds and experiences are disproportionately likely to suffer social exclusion. The key risk factors include: low income; family conflict; being in care; school problems; being an ex-prisoner; being from an ethnic minority; living in a deprived neighbourhood in urban and rural areas; mental health problems, age and disability [emphasis in original] (Social Exclusion Unit 2001).

Whilst there are still clearly some socially excluded groups missing from this list (for example, homeless people, LGBTs[1]), it gives a clearer picture of who may be excluded and some of the reasons for this.

At the same time, however, some organizations continue to narrow the definition, with some defining social exclusion almost entirely in terms of anti-poverty work;[2] and, much more recently, the Government itself has refocused its definition to refer to a 'small minority' – in *Reaching Out* (Cabinet Office 2006), they identify that '… against this background of success, the persistent and deep-seated exclusion of a small minority has come to stand out ever more dramatically'. This Action Plan therefore focuses specifically on early years, children and teenagers, and adults 'living chaotic lives' (Cabinet Office 2006, p. 11).

It is important not to allow these narrower definitions themselves to exclude people. Janie Percy-Smith at the Policy Research Institute, Leeds Metropolitan University, took a different approach (Percy-Smith 2000). Concerned about the narrowing of definitions to poverty and spatial issues, she defined seven 'dimensions' of social exclusion:

- Economic (for example, long-term unemployment; workless households; income poverty)
- Social (for example, homelessness; crime; disaffected youth)
- Political (for example, disempowerment; lack of political rights; alienation from/lack of confidence in political processes)
- Neighbourhood (for example, decaying housing stock; environmental degradation)
- Individual (for example, mental and physical ill health; educational underachievement)
- Spatial (for example, concentration/marginalization of vulnerable groups)

---

1   LGBTs is the accepted term for lesbians, gay men, bisexuals and transgendered people.
2   Whilst they do define 'social justice' fairly broadly, nevertheless the Institute for Public Policy Research, for example, sees a large part of the issue as being related to economics and poverty (Pearce and Paxton 2005).

- Group (concentration of above characteristics in particular groups, for example, disabled, elderly, ethnic minorities)

Tackling Social Exclusion at Government Level

Since April 2006, responsibility for social exclusion at Government level has rested with the Social Exclusion Task Force within the Cabinet Office.[3] Also since April 2006, the Department for Communities and Local Government has been established, with part of its remit being for community cohesion, equalities and community capacity-building.[4]

Prior to 2006, social exclusion was the responsibility of the Social Exclusion Unit (SEU), and material from their website has been archived.[5] The SEU tackled a number of important areas, such as rough-sleeping, truancy, the education of looked-after children, and mental health, and their reports can be found on the archived website.

How, Then, Does Social Exclusion Affect Libraries? Aren't We 'Open to All'?

Research into the work of public libraries has found clear evidence of the barriers to take-up of service, including institutional (issues around the way that libraries are organized and present themselves), personal and social, perceptions and awareness, and environmental (for example, location, appearance) – and it was very clear that libraries were by no means 'open to all' (Department for Culture, Media and Sport 1999; Muddiman et al. 2000a; 2000b; 2000c). Until these barriers are removed, libraries are clearly still tackling social exclusion – on their journey towards social inclusion.

Social inclusion occurs at a later stage, once socially excluded groups and individuals gain access to the mainstream. However, it is vital that work on inclusion also involves diversity[6] – we are not looking for a society which is 'all the same'.

---

3   Social Exclusion Task Force. <http://www.cabinetoffice.gov.uk/social_exclusion_task_force/>.

4   Department for Communities and Local Government. <http://www.communities.gov.uk/index.asp?id=1165628>.

5   Social Exclusion Unit. <http://www.socialexclusion.gov.uk/>.

6   Diversity has been defined as: '... adding another dimension to "equal opportunities". It encompasses all types of difference beyond those covered by the legislation and focuses in particular on the needs of the individual. It is also concerned with the culture of the organisation, and adds value through a sort of enlightened self-interest, usually in association with a well-developed business case' (Sanglin-Grant 2003).

There is also now a number of 'toolkits' that can be used to assess progress in tackling social exclusion. These include, for example:

- The earliest toolkit was the six-point plan drawn up by the Department for Culture, Media and Sport (DCMS) (1999) which gives a very useful starting point in terms of assessing where a service has reached
- An 'Access for All' toolkit that has been developed nationally by the Museums, Libraries and Archives Council (MLA) (2004a) and which can be used as part of an assessment against *Inspiring Learning for All* (MLA 2004b)[7]
- A toolkit that has been developed by Suffolk County Council for use in any council service (Suffolk County Council 2002)
- A toolkit that has been developed by an Exeter-based community group to assess progress primarily in the voluntary and community sector (Magne and McTiernan 2004)

The historical background to libraries' progress from equal opportunities to tackling social exclusion, and from social exclusion to community cohesion, has been outlined in two recent chapters (Vincent and Pateman 2006; Pateman and Vincent 2007).

As well as understanding social exclusion issues, library staff need a broad awareness of other social policy developments. At the time of writing (Spring 2007), major issues include community/social cohesion[8] and community engagement.

Community Cohesion

The community cohesion agenda has been developed as a response to the disturbances in towns and cities in England (including Bradford, Burnley, Oldham and Stoke-on-Trent) in 2001 (see, for example, Home Office 2001a; Home Office 2001b), and, more recently, to the London bombings of 2005. In June 2006, the Department for Communities and Local Government established a Commission on Integration and Cohesion:

> *The Commission, a fixed term advisory body, is considering how local areas can make the most of the benefits delivered by increasing diversity – but will*

---

7   *Inspiring Learning for All* 'describes what an accessible and inclusive museum, archive or library which stimulates and supports learning looks like. It invites you to: find out what the people that use your services learn; assess how well you are achieving best practice in supporting learning; improve what you do' (MLA 2004b).

8   Whilst definitions differ, community cohesion has been seen as the bringing together of divided communities, whilst social cohesion is about people's own interpersonal relationships.

also consider how they can respond to the tensions it can sometimes cause. It will develop practical approaches that build communities' own capacity to prevent problems, including those caused by segregation and the dissemination of extremist ideologies (Department for Communities and Local Government 2008).

A cohesive community is defined as one where:

- There is a common vision and a sense of belonging for all communities
- The diversity of people's different backgrounds and circumstances is appreciated and positively valued
- Those from different backgrounds have similar life opportunities
- Strong and positive relationships are being developed between people from different backgrounds and circumstances in the workplace, in schools and within neighbourhoods (Local Government Association 2004, 7)

The role (or potential role) of libraries in creating cohesive communities is, so far, under-recognized. Certainly the setting in many libraries is right; the recent study, published by MLA (Harris and Dudley 2005), suggests that there are four 'essential attributes' of the public library, which have a bearing on its place 'in the public realm' and therefore on community cohesion. These are:

- Library as resource
- Library as expertise
- Library as place
- Library as symbol (of a public resource providing for the public good) (Harris and Dudley 2005)

More about the role of libraries in community cohesion and social inclusion can be found in a briefing paper written for the then South East Museums, Libraries and Archives Council (Vincent 2005).

Community Engagement

Community engagement is currently seen as the key to involving local people in service provision:

> *Community engagement is the process of involving communities in the planning, development and management of services. It may also involve other issues which concern us all, or it may be about tackling the problems of a neighbourhood, such as crime, drug misuse or lack of play facilities for children* (Scottish Centre for Regeneration 2006).

For local authorities, there has been an even greater emphasis on this way of working with the publication of the local government white paper, *Strong and Prosperous Communities* (Department for Communities and Local Government 2006a), which emphasizes the need for consultation and engagement.

For libraries, it is also a way of ensuring that staff really do get involved with their local communities (rather as the 'community librarianship' approach had intended back in the 1970s) (see, for example, CSV Consulting 2006a; 2006b).

THE LINK BETWEEN THE GOVERNMENT/WIDER AGENDA AND THE LOCAL LIBRARY

Whilst all these strategies and directions may be 'out there', they also need to be focused locally. Most public library services have written a social inclusion strategy or policy (and many are going on to develop similar strategies to cover topics such as community cohesion and community engagement) which will fall within the overall local authority strategy.

This local libraries strategy (see, for example, Tameside Metropolitan Borough Council 2003) will set out the aims and objectives of the service, with, for example, details of communities that are under-served and need to be targeted; plans for a specific period; and staff development and training targets.

TRAINING NEEDS OF LIBRARY STAFF

At a national level, over the last five years or so, there has been considerable work to identify training needs of library (and museum and archive) staff in terms of tackling social exclusion and the wider social issues mentioned above.

For example, at Government level, the report *Libraries, Museums, Galleries and Archives for All* identified that 'resources were needed for staff training in social inclusion issues, as well as for actual work in this area' (Department for Culture Media and Sport 2001).

The national research project funded by the then Library and Information Commission,[9] 'Public Library Policy and Social Exclusion', the results of which were published as *Open to All?* (Muddiman et al. 2000a; 2000b; 2000c), stressed the need for training: '... public libraries also need to ensure that they have high quality training in place for all their staff. This should include thorough induction

9   The Library and Information Commission became part of Resource which, in turn, has become the Museums, Libraries and Archives Council.

training, as well as in-depth training in all aspects of service provision, particularly focusing on tackling social exclusion ...' (Muddiman et al. 2000a). Incidentally, similar concerns were raised within the archives domain: 'The archive profession is seeking not only additional resources ... but also clear guidance, networks, training and support ... to promote social inclusion more successfully and establish sustainable partnerships ...' (National Council on Archives 2001).

In the research paper on workforce development produced for the then Resource by Demos (Demos 2003), it was made clear that there were very real skills gaps – and that different kinds of people were needed to work in libraries (and museums and archives):

> *Skills needs for the 'new agenda' involve both changing roles and increasing awareness. First, the 'learning agenda' changes the role of people working in the sector in [a] way that can be summarised as a shift from simply providing or presenting information towards teaching, instruction and guidance. Engagement and empathy with users in all respects will be needed. The importance of developing sector specific learning skills has been highlighted; as one stakeholder said, 'museums and libraries aren't schools.' Second, the 'access and inclusion agenda' necessitates a new set of skills to be developed, including outreach, collections reinterpretation, marketing and market research ... Third, there is a need to increase awareness of these agendas and buy-in from workers across whole organisations* (Demos 2003).

The Chartered Institute of Library and Information Professionals (CILIP) also considered training to be essential to the required transformation of libraries if they were to deal properly with social inclusion. The report of the CILIP Executive Advisory Group stressed the importance of training and the need for 'Leadership of a workforce committed to social inclusion' (CILIP 2004).

In terms of public libraries, training to implement the People's Network[10] was carried out across the UK to an agreed standard. In addition,

> *A number of progressive authorities used the programme as a catalyst to address some of the cultural barriers to learning and development. The programme was linked to achieving service objectives and staff and line managers encouraged to take active responsibility and 'own' their development through*

---

10   'The People's Network, completed in 2002, was a major lottery funded government-led initiative to bring equality of internet access to the whole UK population, by installing PCs, broadband connection and software in all public libraries; training library staff to support users and creating a wealth of quality digital materials relevant to local needs.' Museums, Libraries and Archives Council website. <http://www.mla.gov.uk/webdav/harmonise?Page/@ id=73&Document/@id=18376&Section[@stateId_eq_left_hand_root]/@id=4332>.

personal development plans, action learning and planned opportunities to apply learning at work (MLA 2004c).

This process highlighted some key training issues around:

- Building capacity to deliver and own organizational change
- Changing staff roles from providing information to advice, coaching, mentoring, instruction and guidance in accessing, using and interpreting that information
- Conceptual and practical understanding of digitization and its impact on new users, for example, the need for training and a qualification in content creation
- Management and staff ownership of the new skills needed
- Extending the basic ICT training provided for library staff to the museum and archive workforce
- Upgrading and sustaining ICT skills in the future across museums, libraries and archives
- Leadership skills (MLA 2004c)

The MLA workforce development strategy then goes on to outline skills gaps which libraries (and museums and archives) had identified as needing to be filled – these include:

- Learning and access, for example, facilitating learning, coaching, mentoring, marketing and new audience development skills
- Service delivery, for example, customer care, communication, presentation, interpersonal, multidisciplinary team working, cross-domain team working and project management skills
- User and non-user consultation and understanding (MLA 2004c)

Interestingly, whilst these areas clearly relate to the training required for tackling social exclusion, nothing specific about training in diversity, inclusion (or wider political awareness) appears to have been identified at this stage. Indeed, whilst there has been considerable investment in training to meet two strands of *Framework for the Future* (Department for Culture, Media and Sport 2003) – the People's Network and reader development – there has been less focus generally on the third strand which includes tackling social exclusion.

'The Network – tackling social exclusion' runs courses for all levels of library staff (and others), and, from these, there is clear, first-hand evidence of training needs. The areas most frequently asked for include:

- What is social inclusion/exclusion? Definitions

- Practical ideas and solutions – things we could use tomorrow, that would not be just tokenistic
- How to reach the hard-to-reach, and how to find out what socially excluded people want, rather than just making assumptions
- Staff issues, including attitudes and our image
- How to overcome language barriers

OBJECTIVES OF THE TRAINING

The objectives of courses on tackling social exclusion can, obviously, be quite wide, including, for example:

- Creating a greater awareness and understanding of social exclusion
- Giving more understanding of how it impacts on children and young people
- Identifying socially excluded groups of children and young people
- Examining the strengths and weaknesses of current provision
- Exploring strategies for developing social inclusion policies and practices
- Developing a shared vision of service priorities
- Instigating an action plan

These objectives have been taken from a course created by Anne Harding and the author.[11]

As noted below, depending on who is to deliver the training, the objectives may be broader or narrower; most training aims to give staff the tools to be able to deliver more effective services for socially excluded people.

The pilot phase of the project, 'Welcome to Your Library' (WTYL), found that 'Training is best undertaken as part of a wider commitment to serving the under-served' (Carpenter 2004), and:

> *In the course of the WTYL project work has begun to raise awareness and influence staff thinking through training courses. In LB Enfield, the WTYL Project Officer worked in conjunction with library managers and The Network to organise and deliver a series of six day-long training modules to all permanent staff, entitled Welcome To Your Library.*

---

11   <http://www.seapn.org.uk/documents/Children.pdf>.

The aim of the training was:

- To define social exclusion and place the work of the library service in this area within the Government and council's agenda
- To provide information and dispel myths about asylum-seekers and refugees nationally and locally
- To consult with staff about WTYL's recommendations on simplifying joining procedures (Carpenter 2004)

WHO SHOULD DELIVER THIS TRAINING?

Background

In 2001–2002, the then Resource (now the Museums, Libraries and Archives Council) commissioned work to develop a cross-domain[12] training package to raise awareness of social inclusion issues, particularly among managers. After trials of different training methods and materials, the working group produced a report (Resource 2003) which identified the following issues:

- Social exclusion/inclusion work is complex, fast-changing and relies on a combination of an emotional and a cognitive response. People's experiences are so different, and their reactions to the issue so varied, that training has to be tailored to 'where they are'
- Therefore, having a one-size-fits-all programme is unlikely to be effective, except at the most general level – or with a group that has already worked at some of this and has a level of shared experience and understanding
- Any training needs the scope to be able to 'go with the flow', to take up issues as they arise, to pursue specific points (some examples from the pilots were sources of funding; why Travellers are considered to be socially excluded; the role of volunteers). Having a course that is fairly prescriptive is not the best approach – the materials, the PowerPoint presentations are needed , but we also need the scope to move outside this
- Feedback from (a few) experienced trainers on both the pilots suggests that they would feel very uneasy about taking on this kind of training (Resource 2003)

Therefore, there seems to be a dilemma about who should/could provide this training.

---

12   Libraries, archives and museums are each a domain.

Cascading Training

There can be benefits in cascading[13] training – for example, this has been effective in equipping library staff to use the People's Network, as this quote shows:

> *Staff generally feel confident in using computers, finding information themselves, and using the packages. But the support role is still rather daunting. They are not as confident in this. We are trying to address this through cascade training, and the emphasis we've placed on the Educator role* (Tavistock Institute 2004).

However, whilst many people have the knowledge, skills and ability to train, they may not have the experience and skills to enable them to deal with emotional reactions such as those noted in the Resource report above, and therefore the training session may not work successfully; moreover, if this is the training group's first experience of social exclusion issues, they may actually be put off this work forever!

Training Led by Your Manager

With some areas of training (for example, passing on work-based skills), it can be effective if it is led by your own manager, especially as they will be able to deal with practical and work-based issues as they arise.

Training in tackling social exclusion often creates emotional responses in groups (for example, someone may feel that their partner did not get a new job because a refugee had been appointed instead; someone may have had a past experience of mental health issues themselves or in their family; or someone is adamant that Travellers exclude themselves and refuse to discuss this group in the context of social inclusion), and having the training course led by a manager with whom the person has got to work on a day-to-day basis may make for awkward work relationships in the future.

In addition, the manager's presence as course-leader may well deter staff from saying what is really on their minds. For example, if someone is struggling with the media images of asylum-seekers or LGBTs, and wants to clarify this via an exploration of what their own feelings towards these groups are, this is likely to involve the discussion of quite negative views which the person may be inhibited from expressing by their manager's presence.

---

13   Whereby a person attends a course and then goes back to their organization and delivers the training themselves. This has been shown to work successfully with some topics (such as training in aspects of the use of the People's Network), but not with areas where participants need to engage emotionally.

One example: on a recent course, a participant was concerned that ex-prisoners were being seen as socially excluded, when, in his view, having left prison, they could, presumably, get a job just like anyone else. This needed a sympathetic discussion about the realities of ex-prisoners' lives – and chances in the job market – for the participant to understand why there were barriers to their getting jobs.

One county library service and a unitary authority within its borders have developed an introductory course together, involving the county's social inclusion manager and an experienced manager from the unitary authority: this has meant that staff gain from both the managers' first-hand experience, but are also not being trained just by their direct line manager.

TRAINING METHODS

Successful Training Approaches

Those library services that are providing successful training are using a mixed approach which includes:

- In-house training, drawing on local policies and strategies (for example, Enfield Council's own Social Inclusion Strategy) and using local staff's expertise and local case studies
- Training involving local community organizations
- Training by external trainers who bring expertise in a specific area (for example, tackling social exclusion generally; working with particular communities)

In addition, staff are encouraged to undertake their own self-development and research, using the wide range of materials available (especially via the Internet) – see below.

Role Play and Case Studies

Whilst some trainers regularly use role play, The Network does not. This is for two main reasons:

- One of the key aims of a social inclusion course is to enable participants to explore areas which they may not understand/have experience of in a setting which provides them with a level of safety – this sense of safety can be undermined by the use of role plays and putting people on the spot
- Participants do not all have the same levels of 'acting' skills, and, for example in a scenario where someone plays the librarian and someone plays

a difficult user, if the 'difficult user' is too convincing, it has been known to reduce the 'librarian' to tears – again, not a good way to build confidence!

Case studies are, however, a very successful way of involving a group in drawing from and developing information and skills they have learned from the course. For example, on our LGBT awareness course, participants can work on a number of case studies to grapple with the sorts of complaints they may receive. For example: a member of the public complains to you about having *Gay Times* on display in the magazines section next to the photocopier, as she was concerned that her son might see it and, as she puts it, she does not want him 'perverted'. She then goes on to complain about the money she thinks the council is wasting on buying 'this sort of filth'. How would you deal with this?

Training Methods Used by The Network

Every trainer needs to develop a working method and style with which they are comfortable. The author delivers on average one or two courses a week, mostly on his own, but, on occasions, with a co-trainer, and uses the following methods:

- A mix of whole-group and small group sessions
- Input from the trainer and discussion
- Flipchart and handouts (with occasional back-up from PowerPoint), and with notes from the flipchart being written up later and sent back to participants
- Case studies
- Working groups to tackle specific issues

The content of an introductory course on tackling social exclusion might typically contain the following:

- What would we like from today's course?
- What is social exclusion, and where has the idea come from? Is there a difference between 'social inclusion' and 'social exclusion'? What are the key principles for ensuring that we are working to tackle social exclusion?
- Where do we fit into the Government agenda and the national picture?
- What are the major barriers to the take-up of library services for socially excluded people? And how are we successfully dealing with some of these barriers? Reports-back on tackling barriers
- Which barriers can we identify that we are not successfully tackling, and what can we do about them? What can we do in our workplace? Reports-back on how to tackle these barriers

The first session, 'What would we like from today's course?', gets participants talking to each other (and is therefore a good, natural ice-breaker, without any gimmicks[14]), and is a useful check on participants' expectations, as well as giving the trainer and the group a way of self-assessing what has been covered.

The second session is probably the one that is most in demand, and covers the different terms (social exclusion, social inclusion, social/community cohesion, social justice), as well as placing social inclusion within its Government context. This session also includes looking at who might be socially excluded (emphasizing the real dangers of making assumptions and stereotyping – not all frail elderly people, for example, would either be or consider themselves to be excluded). Starting with the list[15] in 'Preventing Social Exclusion' (Social Exclusion Unit 2001), the group then goes on to consider who else might be excluded, and why; those on a recent course identified:

- People who are just unaware of what we provide
- People of different faiths/religions
- People of different nationalities and with English as a Second Language (ESOL) needs
- Travellers
- People with basic skills needs
- People who cannot access our services
- Homeless people
- Gender – for example some women, some men are excluded
- Poor people
- Older people
- Drug abusers
- People with facial disfigurements
- Young people who are not in employment, education or training (NEET)

The third session looks at where libraries fit into the bigger picture (see below).

The fourth session begins with a whole-group discussion of the barriers to take-up of library services, especially by socially excluded people. These are written up on the flipchart, divided into barriers which might be institutional (charges, joining procedures, staff attitudes, and so on), perception (the library image, young people's view of libraries as not being cool), social (people with basic skills needs, competing leisure facilities) and environmental (location, access, parking).

---

14   Such as interviewing your neighbour and then telling the group key things about them, or having the trainer throw a ball at group members, with the person who catches it having to say something about themselves!
15   Low income; family conflict; being in care; school problems; being an ex-prisoner; being from an ethnic minority; living in a deprived neighbourhood in urban and rural areas; mental health problems; age; disability.

Immediately following that is an opportunity for participants to celebrate some of the work that their library authority has developed, which is successfully challenging some of these barriers. Experience has shown that most library staff spend very little time discussing positive developments – much of their work in meetings is problem-solving – and, given that there are already enough people criticizing libraries,[16] this is a good moment to think about what we are doing well. Perhaps not surprisingly, people find this quite hard to do!

The last session involves a re-look at the barriers, with the group's choosing which they think are most critical, and then working in small groups to investigate this barrier and to come up with some recommendations for ways to start challenging it – and these recommendations can be at the national and local level, with the intention being that everyone can then go away with some action that they can take.

Finally, after the course, the notes of the sessions are written up and sent back to the training co-ordinator in the library service, partly so that they can circulate them to all participants, but also partly so that recommendations from the course members can be fed into service improvement plans (in one authority, the senior manager responsible for training, and/or one of her colleagues, sits in on every course to learn first-hand what staff are concerned about and to hear what recommendations they make).

'Understanding the Bigger Picture'

It is essential that all library staff have an understanding of both where the library fits into a 'bigger picture' and where their own job then fits into this structure. It is clear that this is often a weak area for library staff.

In terms of tackling social exclusion, one way of doing this (which has proved effective in practice) is to trace briefly the development of social inclusion in the UK from its introduction in 1997, including the establishment (and disbanding in 2006) of the Social Exclusion Unit, and the roles of DCMS, MLA and the local authority, in order to show the impact that all of these have on staff's everyday work. It also gives an opportunity to introduce the key documents and reports, for example, *Libraries for All* (DCMS 1999) and *Framework for the Future* (DCMS 2003) in their context.

In addition, it connects library staff to broader issues: for example, all library staff will know about the People's Network and the library's role in lifelong learning, but do they know that MLA has been instrumental in rolling out the former (and

---

16   For example, the Libri Trust (Coates 2004).

channelling the funding for the training in its use), and has devised *Inspiring Learning for All* (MLA 2004b) as a means of evaluating the latter?

In some recent courses, staff have particularly highlighted this session as important learning that they were taking away with them. It is also a good way of empowering front line staff who may say 'I'm only a Library Assistant – what can I do?' but then see that their day-to-day work does actually fit into a much bigger picture. Library staff are faced with continuous change, and it can only help them understand it if they also see what is driving the changes.

Change is critical to this work. As the final report of the 'Welcome to Your Library' project noted:

> *There needs to be a clear commitment from senior management to fundamental change backed up with human and financial resources to deliver this across the entire service. This change is not a short-term project but a long-term process. It is part of a much wider cultural shift required so that public libraries play a much more proactive role in identifying and meeting community needs* (Carpenter 2004).

The Next Stages of Training

After the introductory training, staff will need to undertake more specific training to meet the needs of specific groups identified within the service's social inclusion strategy (and also those that staff themselves identify as needing more support in serving, noted during a training needs analysis or from feedback during the introductory sessions). These further modules could include sessions on socially excluded groups identified during the second session of the introductory course (see above).

WHAT SORTS OF ISSUES MAY THERE BE?

Library Staff's Reluctance to Engage with Social Inclusion

The majority of library staff are welcoming and work hard to understand what tackling social exclusion really involves. However, a small minority do not behave like this. As was noted in *Open to All?*:

> *However, there may also be a core of staff who do not want to change, do not want the public library to change in an inclusive direction, and who will do their utmost to frustrate attempts to do so. In these cases, public libraries need*

> *to have very clear aims, policies and mechanisms in place, and management*
> *has to accept a real responsibility for dealing with this core* (Muddiman et
> al. 2000a).

On a training course, staff may not take part fully, or may take every opportunity
to disagree or challenge statements made – they may also use the 'we tried this ten
years ago and it didn't work then' technique!

Some of this is clearly as a result of fear of change – is it going to threaten their
jobs, or their comfortable routine? Some of it may be from staff who have worked
in libraries for a while and believe that libraries perform certain functions only
(the 'I'm not a social worker' syndrome). Some may be from staff who have an
antipathy to certain minority groups. And some of this opposition may be from
staff who want their library to remain theirs – a club for members only! All of these
fears and assertions need to be challenged – and it is this that makes some of the
training complex to deliver.

Prejudice

Opposition to tackling social exclusion is going to come from any staff who are
prejudiced (bearing in mind that we all 'shorthand' or stereotype and are therefore
potentially prejudiced):

> *Prejudice is the process of 'pre-judging' something. In general, it implies*
> *coming to a premature judgement about something without having any direct*
> *experience or evidence. It can mean a positive or negative attitude, but we*
> *usually use the word in a negative sense. These premature judgements are*
> *generally based on stereotypes* (Woodcraft Folk 2006).

Some of this prejudice will come from a lack of awareness of the issues facing a
particular group; for example, media coverage of refugees, asylum-seekers and
migrant (or guest) workers frequently misleads by confusing the three groups (see,
for example, ICAR 2005), and a training course (with space for people to discuss
and examine issues in some depth) can begin to help participants understand the
differences.

At the same time, some staff may be hostile.[17] Training may go some way to
assisting changes in attitudes, but this is going to be more difficult to achieve, and
trainers need to take this on board. A couple of examples:

---

17   Whilst it is going to be very rare that a training course includes someone who expresses
outright hatred of a socially excluded group, nevertheless trainers should be aware of the
Government's definitions of discrimination (Home Office 2008) and hate crime: 'Hate crime
can take many forms including: physical attacks – such as physical assault, damage to property,

- On one LGBT awareness course, a participant declared that it was 'all [the trainer's] fault' for raising the topic – if nothing was said, then prejudice and discrimination would never occur! However, during the course of the half-day training course, she clearly recognized that she had been wrong and, at the end, said so
- On another course, one participant said that she was being socially excluded for being made to touch magazines and books with LGBT content (which, she said, were 'polluting' her). Despite considerable discussion, she did not shift her position

With cases such as these, trainers and managers need to consider what else the library service might wish or need to do; using their equal opportunity policy, for example.

MONITORING AND EVALUATION

As noted elsewhere, evaluation of training courses can be something of a hit-and-miss affair, with some respondents appearing to spend more time commenting on the refreshments and lunch (and on the trainer's appearance!) than on the course itself.

We therefore use three broad methods of evaluating courses, depending on the needs of the participants and their managers. These include:

- Using the checklist of issues that the group has raised in the 'What would we like from today's course?' session as a means of the group identifying their own learning – and what remains either not covered or needs to be followed up by further training and/or individual work (this would be run as a whole-group discussion)
- Using a 'broad-brush' approach, with, for example, an invitation to participants to comment on the course, perhaps identifying something they particularly liked, something they thought could be improved, and something that they will take away and follow up (this would be undertaken using feedback forms)
- Using the organization's own feedback forms

---

offensive graffiti, neighbour disputes and arson; threat of attack – including offensive letters, abusive or obscene telephone calls, groups hanging around to intimidate and unfounded, malicious complaints; and verbal abuse or insults – offensive leaflets and posters, abusive gestures, dumping of rubbish outside homes or through letterboxes, and bullying at school or in the workplace' (Home Office 2008).

We also invite participants to keep in touch and let us know what they have done as a result of the training, and this can give valuable feedback, with the added bonus that the participant is using knowledge gained from the course at a later date. For example, a participant in a recent course about developing services for looked-after children has e-mailed to let us know how she has taken forward the work from the day (and to ask some follow-up questions). Ideally, managers too would be following up with the participants after a period of time, to see what they have retained from the course, and how it has affected their day-to-day practice.

In addition, evaluation of the impact of the training needs to be carried out. Ideally, this would involve people from socially excluded groups, who could identify the difference that the training has made to service provision to them, as well as using the Generic Learning Outcomes in *Inspiring Learning for All* (MLA 2004b) (and the Generic Social Outcomes).

INDIVIDUAL LEARNING – WHAT CAN I DO AND WHERE CAN I START?

So far, this chapter has concentrated on courses and more formal training approaches. However, we all need to develop awareness of and keep up to date with social exclusion issues. Where to start?

Background

Check if your organization has a social inclusion strategy/policy (in a public library setting, there may be an overall authority policy as well as one specifically for the library service). Is there a regional policy too? For instance, your MLA region may have developed a strategy (for example, MLA North East, n.d.); and the regional Government Office may also have a strategy.[18]

Find Out About Your Area

If you work for a public library service, they will be producing a community profile (if they have not done so already) – this will give you a range of information beyond the bare numbers available from the census.

Again, there will be a range of information available for your authority, area, region (a worked-up example for the East Midlands is available on the 'Welcome to Your Library' website[19]).

---

18   Government Office South West's statement. <http://www.gosw.gov.uk/gosw/peoplesc/socialinc/?a=42496>.
19   Welcome to Your Library. <http://www.welcometoyourlibrary.org.uk/editorial.asp?page_id=78>.

Essential Background Reading

Open to All? (Muddiman et al. 2000a, 2000b, 2000c).
Framework for the Future (DCMS 2003).
The two chapters in J. Bowman (ed.), *British Librarianship and Information Work 1991–2000* (Vincent and Pateman 2006) and J. Bowman (ed.), *British Librarianship and Information Work 2001–2005* (Pateman and Vincent 2007).

Absolutely Essential Websites

Department for Communities and Local Government <http://www.communities.gov.uk/>.
The Network – tackling social exclusion <http://www.seapn.org.uk>.
Welcome to Your Library <http://www.welcometoyourlibrary.org.uk>.
CILIP's Community Services Group <http://www.cilip.org.uk/specialinterestgroups/bysubject/communityservices/about/Aims.htm>.

Keeping Up to Date

If your organization belongs to The Network, then you can receive the monthly newsletter (which is also published on The Network website).

Welcome to Your Library produces a regular e-digest which you can request via the WTYL website.

Many of the relevant Government websites offer RSS feeds which will enable you to keep up to date with new postings on their websites.

CONCLUSIONS

More than ever before, libraries have got to engage with their different communities, and, to do this successfully, library staff need to be fully trained and involved. This chapter has looked at some of the issues likely to be faced when training to tackle social exclusion, and also gives pointers to running successful developmental programmes for staff and to sources of information for our own self-learning and development.

Tackling social exclusion is still high on the Government's priority list, and, given the many issues that we face in the UK today, needs to remain high on everyone's priorities, linked to developing issues such as community engagement, integration, cohesion, personalization of services, and so on.

It is vital that libraries of all kinds recognize the importance and value of this work, give it the priority it needs, and ensure that resources for training and staff development are made available. As DCMS states: 'It is essential that public library staff and their leaders are equipped with the skills to deliver a public library service for the 21st Century.'[20]

Libraries *do* have a key role to play in tackling social exclusion – let us work together to ensure that all library staff are trained and equipped to do so.

REFERENCES

Black, A. and Muddiman, D. (1997), *Understanding Community Librarianship: The Public Library in Post-modern Britain* (Aldershot: Avebury).

Bowman, J. (ed.) (2006), *British Librarianship and Information Work 1991–2000* (Aldershot: Ashgate).

Bowman, J. (ed.) (2007), *British Librarianship and Information Work 2001–2005* (Aldershot: Ashgate).

Cabinet Office (2006), *Reaching Out: An Action Plan on Social Exclusion* (London: Cabinet Office). <http://www.cabinetoffice.gov.uk/media/cabinetoffice/social_exclusion_task_force/assets/reaching_out/reaching_out_full.pdf>.

Carpenter, H. (2004), *Welcome To Your Library Project: Developing Public Library Services for Asylum Seekers and Refugees in the London Boroughs of Brent, Camden, Enfield, Merton, Newham – Final Report* (London: London Library Development Agency). <http://www.welcometoyourlibrary.org.uk/content_files/files/WTYL_PC_FINAL_REPORT.pdf>.

Chartered Institute of Library and Information Professionals (CILIP) (2004), *Making a Difference – Innovation and Diversity. The Report of the Social Inclusion Executive Advisory Group to CILIP* (London: CILIP). <http://www.cilip.org.uk/NR/rdonlyres/6315E6DA-785D-4A08-9FCD-33C07A57CAA1/0/sereport2.pdf>.

Clough, E. and Quarmby, J. (1978), *A Public Library Service for Ethnic Minorities in Great Britain* (London: Library Association).

Coates, T. (2004), *Who's in Charge? Responsibility for the Public Library Service: A Report by Tim Coates* (London: Libri).

Coleman, P. (1981), *Whose Problem: The Public Library and the Disadvantaged* (London: Association of Assistant Librarians).

CSV Consulting (2006a), *Community Engagement in Public Libraries: A Report on Current Practice and Future Developments* (London: Museums, Libraries and Archives Council).

CSV Consulting (2006b), *Community Engagement in Public Libraries: A Toolkit for Public Library Staff* (London: Museums, Libraries and Archives Council).

---

20   DCMS. <http://www.culture.gov.uk/what_we_do/Libraries/improving_libraries.htm>.

Demos (2003), *Towards a Strategy for Workforce Development: A Research and Discussion Report Prepared for Resource* (London: Demos).

Department for Communities and Local Government (2006a), *Strong and Prosperous Communities: The Local Government White Paper*, Vol. 1: Cm 6939-I; Vol. 2: Cm 6939-II (London: The Stationery Office). Volume 1: <http://www.communities.gov.uk/documents/localgovernment/pdf/152456.pdf>. Volume 2: <http://www.communities.gov.uk/documents/localgovernment/pdf/154067.pdf>.

Department for Communities and Local Government (2006b) 'Commission on Integration and Cohesion'. <http://www.communities.gov.uk/communities/commissionintegration/>.

Department for Communities and Local Government (2008), Department for Communities and Local Government: home page. <http://www.communities.gov.uk/corporate/>.

Department for Culture, Media and Sport (1999), *Libraries for All: Social Inclusion in Public Libraries – Policy Guidance for Local Authorities in England* (London: DCMS). <http://www.culture.gov.uk/images/publications/Social_Inclusion_PLibraries.pdf>.

Department for Culture, Media and Sport (2001), *Libraries, Museums, Galleries and Archives for All: Co-operating across the Sectors to Tackle Social Exclusion* (London: DCMS). <http://www.culture.gov.uk/PDF/libraries_archives_for_all.pdf>.

Department for Culture, Media and Sport (2003), *Framework for the Future: Libraries, Learning and Information in the Next Decade* (London: DCMS). <http://www.culture.gov.uk/reference_library/publications/4505.aspx>.

Harris, K. and Dudley, M. (2005), *Public Libraries and Community Cohesion: Developing Indicators* (London: MLA).

Home Office (2001a), *Building Cohesive Communities: A Report of the Ministerial Group on Public Order and Community Cohesion* (London: Home Office).

Home Office (2001b), *Community Cohesion: A Report of the Independent Review Team Chaired by Ted Cantle* (London: Home Office).

Home Office (2008) 'Hate Crime'. <http://www.homeoffice.gov.uk/crime-victims/reducing-crime/hate-crime/?version=2>.

ICAR (2005), 'What Role Do the Media Play?' <http://www.icar.org.uk/?lid=5026>.

Local Government Association (2004), *Community Cohesion – An Action Guide: Guidance for Local Authorities* (London: Local Government Association).

Magne, S. and McTiernan, A. (2004), *Open Hearts, Open Minds: A Social Inclusion Self-assessment Handbook for Staff Working with the Public and Those who Support Them* (Exeter: Exeter Community Initiatives).

Muddiman, D. (2000), 'Public Libraries and Social Exclusion: The Historical Legacy' in D. Muddiman et al., Vol. 3.

Muddiman, D., Durrani, S., Dutch, M., Linley, R., Pateman, J. and Vincent, J. (2000a), *Open to All? The Public Library and Social Exclusion – Volume 1:*

Overview and Conclusion, Library and Information Commission Research Report 86 (London: Resource).

Muddiman, D., Durrani, S., Dutch, M., Linley, R., Pateman, J. and Vincent, J. (2000b), *Open to All? The Public Library and Social Exclusion – Volume 2: Survey, Case Studies and Methods*, Library and Information Commission Research Report 86 (London: Resource).

Muddiman, D., Durrani, S., Dutch, M., Linley, R., Pateman, J. and Vincent, J. (2000c), *Open to All? The Public Library and Social Exclusion – Volume 3: Working Papers*, Library and Information Commission Research Report 86 (London: Resource).

Museums, Libraries and Archives Council (MLA) (2004a), *'Access for All' Toolkit: Enabling Inclusion for Museums, Libraries and Archives* (London: MLA).

Museums, Libraries and Archives Council (MLA) (2004b), *Inspiring Learning for All* (London: MLA). <http://inspiringlearningforall.gov.uk>.

Museums, Libraries and Archives Council (MLA) (2004c), *Learning for Change: Workforce Development Strategy* (London: MLA).

MLA North East (n.d.), *Decoding Diversity* (Newcastle upon Tyne: MLA North East).

National Council on Archives (2001), *Taking Part: An Audit of Social Inclusion Work in Archives* (Sheffield: NCA). <http://www.ncaonline.org.uk/materials/takingpart.pdf>.

Pateman, J. and Vincent, J. (2007), 'From Social Inclusion to Community Cohesion' in J. Bowman (ed.).

Pearce, N. and Paxton, W. (eds) (2005), *Social Justice: Building a Fairer Britain* (London: Politico's Publishing).

Percy-Smith, J. (ed.) (2000), *Policy Responses to Social Exclusion: Towards Inclusion?* (Buckingham: Open University Press).

Plous, S. (2008), 'Understanding Prejudice'. <http://www.understandingprejudice.org/>.

Resource (2003), *Cross-domain Training for Social Inclusion: Report on Lessons from Phase One* (London: Resource).

Room, G. et al. (1992), *National Policies to Combat Social Exclusion*, Second Annual Report of the EC Observatory on Policies to Combat Social Exclusion (Brussels: European Commission).

Sanglin-Grant, S. (2003), *Divided by the Same Language? Equal Opportunities and Diversity Translated*, A Runnymede Trust Briefing Paper (London: Runnymede Trust). <http://www.runnymedetrust.org/uploads/publications/pdfs/DividedByLanguage.pdf>.

Scottish Centre for Regeneration (2006), 'What is Community Engagement?' <http://www.communitiesscotland.gov.uk/stellent/groups/public/documents/webpages/scrcs_006876.hcsp#TopOfPage>.

Social Exclusion Unit (2001), 'Preventing Social Exclusion: A Report by the Social Exclusion Unit'. <http://www.cabinetoffice.gov.uk/media/cabinetoffice/social_exclusion_task_force/assets/publications_1997_to_2006/preventing.pdf>.

Suffolk County Council (2002), *Aspiring to Inclusion: A Handbook for Councils and Other Organisations* (Ipswich: Suffolk County Council).

Tameside Metropolitan Borough Council, Libraries Service Unit (c2003), *Social Inclusion Strategy: Summary 2004/5–2006/7* (Tameside: Tameside Metropolitan Borough Council) <www.tameside.gov.uk/libraries/inclusion/strategy.pdf>.

Tavistock Institute (2004), *Books and Bytes: New Paradigms for the 21st Century Library – An Evaluation of the People's Network and ICT Training for Public Library Staff Programme* (London: Big Lottery Fund).

Todman, L. (2004), *Reflections on Social Exclusion: What s it? How is it Different from U.S. Conceptualizations of Disadvantage? And, Why Americans Might Consider Integrating it into U.S. Social Policy Discourse*, Paper given at the 'City Futures' Conference, Chicago, 8–10 July 2004. <http://www.uic.edu/cuppa/cityfutures/papers/webpapers/cityfuturespapers/session2_3/2_3reflections.pdf>.

Vincent, J. (1986), *An Introduction to Community Librarianship* (London: Association of Assistant Librarians).

Vincent, J. (2005), *Libraries and Community Cohesion: A Paper for the South East Museums, Libraries and Archives Council* (Winchester: SEMLAC).

Vincent, J. and Pateman, J. (2006), 'From Equal Opportunities to Tackling Social Exclusion', in J. Bowman (ed.).

Walker, A. and Walker, C. (eds) (1997), *Britain Divided: The Growth of Social Exclusion in the 1980s and 1990s* (London: Child Poverty Action Group).

Woodcraft Folk (2006), 'Prejudice' [Global Village website] <http://www.globalvillage2006.org/en/find_out_about/prejudice/prejudice>.

CHAPTER 7

CUSTOMER SERVICE TRAINING

BERYL MORRIS

INTRODUCTION

This chapter is aimed at people who are involved in library staff training and development or charged with organizing a training activity on customer service. The intention is to provide an overview of customer service training – what it means and what makes it effective, as well as sharing tips and ideas for success. The appendices include sample programmes and a selection of exercises which can be used as part of in-house training activities.

BACKGROUND AND CONTEXT:
THE CUSTOMER SERVICE CHALLENGE

Customer service is essential for libraries in all sectors. According to the Office of the Government Committee (Office of the Government Committee 2005), customers' expectations are rising all the time. Research by MORI for the Institute for Customer Service (Institute for Customer Service 2006) shows that people expect faster responses, have less patience and complain more. People are also much more discriminating and increasingly likely to demand the service they want, as opposed to putting up with what they are given.

Other influences on the demand for customer service include:

- The continuing emphasis on quality developed from the work of Deming and Peters in the 1980s
- Increasing competition from electronic sources, the Internet, and so on
- Higher expectations of customers in all libraries. Examples include the increase in student fees, expecting value for money, comparison with retail, bookshops, and so on
- Quality audits and reviews – Best Value in local authorities, the Quality Assurance Agency in HE, and professional accreditation, for example, the Helicon scheme in health libraries

CUSTOMER SERVICE – DEFINITIONS

Definitions of Good Service

The National Consumer Council published its report, *The Stupid Company*, in 2006 (National Consumer Council 2006). The report suggested that British businesses could increase their profits by paying more attention to customer service and listed the things that consumers hate about service:

1. Broken promises and unrealistic expectations
2. Hard sell
3. Dishonesty including:
    -   Misleading information/being fobbed off
    -   Very small print and exclusions
4. Impersonal:
    -   Call centres/cold calling
    -   Impersonal/inappropriate responses
5. Incompetent:
    -   Mistakes when there is no apology or responsibility
    -   Slow service or poor access
    -   Too technical/patronizing

The Office for Government Commerce (Office for Government Commerce 2005) suggests that a customer-focused service should:

-   Understand its customers
-   Ensure that its structures and operations are geared towards customers
-   Manage its relationships with customers and accept feedback
-   Develop and improve its service based on the knowledge it has of its customers

Barlow's book, *Batteries Included* (Barlow 2001), looks at customer service in the IT era and suggests that good service consists of the following:

1. Reliability:
    -   Accuracy of information, meets expectations and delivers what is promised
    -   Open as advertised and accessible in terms of opening hours, phone enquiries, and so on
2. Assurance:
    -   Users feel confident when using services and facilities
    -   Staff are knowledgeable and courteous and there is a 'Can do' approach – seeing a problem through
    -   Good reception/greeting/direction

   –   Help and advice is available in a variety of forms and at point of use
   –   Staff identification – badges, photographs, and so on and good signs
       and guiding
3. Tangibles:
   –   Good access to facilities and services and a comprehensive range of
       services and resources
   –   Clear standards of service, choice
   –   Safe working environment and attention to cleanliness/tidiness/litter
   –   Consistent approach to service across sites and times
4. Empathy:
   –   Prompt attention. Making people feel that they matter
   –   Individual focus and sees things from the customer's perspective
   –   Willing to help – good listening and questioning skills, knowing when
       (and how) to refer
5. Responsive:
   –   Committed to continuous improvement
   –   Availability of customer feedback and complaints systems
   –   Acts on suggestions, corrects mistakes and provides an apology when
       things go wrong
   –   Follow up if things go wrong

CUSTOMER SERVICE IN LIBRARY AND INFORMATION SERVICES

According to Gates (1990), most library and information staff find themselves
dealing directly with their users in a variety of contexts. This is particularly true
of front line staff that operate counter services or deal directly with users in other
face-to-face situations. Interpersonal skills have therefore become increasingly
important. Many libraries require their staff to attend customer care courses as
part of in-service training, or to undertake qualifications, for example, Customer
Service NVQs.

Gates defines customer service as follows:

> *Attaining the balance between polite but never obsequious on the one hand
> or patronizing on the other, friendly (but always professional) and always
> able to behave in a courteous, patient and tactful manner. This behaviour
> must be able to accommodate the particular requirements of a wide range
> of users (hearing-impaired, sight-impaired, with learning or mental health
> difficulties, wheelchair-bound, elderly, with a poor command of English or
> speech difficulties). This is emphasized by the requirements of the Disability
> Discrimination Act. The amount and level of help given in meeting the needs
> of the user should be precisely that which is required, always bearing in*

mind any inevitable time constraints and the need to balance the needs of the customer with the needs of the organization. Library staff need good body language and the ability to listen actively and ask an appropriate range of questions (Gates 1990).

Good customer service is difficult to define. When is enough enough? Jan Carlzon, former CEO of Scandinavian Air Services and a customer service guru, defined customer care as a 'moment of truth' and emphasized that we never get a second chance to make a first impression! (Carlzon and Peters 1989) On a local level, there are a number of definitions of good service within library and information work. One recent example is that published by the American Library Association (ALA 2007) and aimed at prospective university students and their parents.

A STUDENTS' GUIDE TO EVALUATING LIBRARIES IN COLLEGES AND UNIVERSITIES

Facilities

- Is the library easy to find?
- When you are in the library, is it easy to find your way around?
- Is the library space inviting?
- Is there adequate space for users and collections?
- Are there a variety of study spaces?
- Are the opening hours convenient?
- Is the library sensitive to specific needs, for example, disability?
- Are multimedia production facilities available for your use?

Resources

- Is there a good collection in a variety of formats?
- Is the collection sufficiently up to date?
- Is there a web-based catalogue?
- Are there electronic tools for locating magazine and journal articles?
- Are lecturers' book lists available electronically?
- Are resources available electronically in full-text format?
- Are library resources available remotely, for example, from halls of residence?
- Will the library readily obtain materials for you that are not owned by the library?

Services

- Are there sufficient staff available to help you?
- Are the staff friendly, helpful, knowledgeable, and available when you need them?
- Are there information skills sessions to teach you how to use the library?
- Are computer terminals available and easily accessible?
- Can you access the library from your personal computer?
- Are there fees for services, such as printing? If so, are these reasonable?
- What services are available on a 24-hour basis?
- Can you get help electronically, such as via an e-mail question to a library staff member?
- How does the library support distance learning?
- Does the library support emerging technologies such as laptops, palm pilots and e-books?

Schroer (2003) suggested that librarians face a paradox with customer service; for example, customer expectations may become so high that they are never fulfilled. However, library managers in all sectors are under pressure to maintain the number of users and be seen to respond to changing demands and expectations. As libraries become more 'virtual' there is still a need to maintain the people elements. In fact, Phil Sykes, writing in *SCONUL Newsletter* (2005), suggested that we should put library staff back into libraries. This would support more personal services, for example, roving helpers, subject focus help desks, personalized support through faculty teams and one-to-one support for distance learners.

WHO AND WHAT? ANALYSING TRAINING NEEDS

Many libraries make customer service training mandatory for all staff. This helps to reinforce a corporate commitment to service skills and is vital if the library wishes to apply for the Charter Mark or quality accreditation. It also provides an opportunity to describe customer service in a library context, emphasize why customer care is increasingly important, promote local policies and procedures and explore issues that can inhibit good service.

Customer care training should be incorporated in induction activities for new staff. Such training helps to clarify expectations of staff and emphasize where the priorities lie. Induction training can also help new staff to feel more competent and confident through helping people to deliver to expectations.

More specialized training may arise from a number of factors. For example, the development of new services such as electronic sources or virtual learning environments may necessitate training in IT and related topics. Introducing services for new user groups such as people with disability or young people also benefits from awareness training or the development of specific skills. Recent initiatives such as the roving concept adopted by a number of public and academic libraries may require refresher sessions or training to alleviate anxieties. Roving (or floor walking), defined as pointing with our feet, not our fingers, has been adopted by many libraries to provide 'point of use' help and assistance to users. It also helps to support the 'hidden' customer, for example, those who are reluctant to ask for help. However, it can create anxieties in staff and a reluctance to intrude. Similarly, the introduction of services to new client groups such as distance learning students in Further and Higher Education and Travellers in public libraries may be assisted by training in targeted topics.

Aspects of customer service training might also arise from negative circumstances, for example, poor response in customer surveys, increase in complaints about the service, criticism from quality audits or reviews, or complaints/problems with individual staff. In such cases, training needs to be seen as a constructive response to a problem, not a panacea, and handled with sensitivity.

For example, when the University of Texas Libraries LibQual survey of 2005 indicated that customer service across the library could be enhanced, planning to improve the quality of service for both internal and external customers was instigated immediately. A library-wide customer service training programme was developed. This included discussions of the cultural change required and the important issues to consider when developing customer service in an academic library. The customer service programme was delivered to all staff in the summer of 2005. The programme was successfully completed by 292 members of library staff, with a participation rate of 98 per cent.

Developments such as providing services to users with special needs/social inclusion issues also create demands for customer service training. This aspect is covered in more detail in John Vincent's chapter, but examples include:

- Targeted services for young people
- Children's services
- Support for users with disability
- Visual impairment
- Specialized support for users from ethnic minorities
- Business users
- Housebound services
- The growth of remote access such as services delivered electronically and by telephone/e-mail
- Helping staff to respond to complaints
- Dealing with difficult and sensitive situations such as mobile phone use, noise, eating and drinking, and so on

- Recent initiatives such as roving or virtual reference
- Specialist groups such as student assistants, volunteers or stand-by staff
- Internal customers

OBJECTIVES

Although each organization will have its own reasons for providing customer service training, the following objectives are likely to be important in general customer service training.

- Raising awareness of the importance of customer service and the consequences of getting it wrong
- Promoting recent developments within the sector and library and information work
- Developing relevant skills such as listening and assertiveness
- Providing an opportunity to explore practical ways to defuse or avoid difficult situations

In addition, many sessions stress the importance of exchanging ideas and experience with others and developing plans and priorities for future action.

According to Zennerich (2006), there are other advantages to customer service staff development:

Enhances the new staff experience
A good induction programme helps people to feel they belong. It says to new employees how welcome they are and that they are encouraged to take advantage of training and development opportunities as part of their jobs.

Improves external and internal customer service
Because all staff attend customer service training, everyone understands the service philosophy and expectations of the organization. Paying attention to training helps to ensure good results from customer surveys and other audits.

Increases expectations/decreases anxiety
It helps to build confidence because people know that they will receive training to assist with change.

Improves group communication skills
Over time, staff members gain confidence to communicate well in groups, whether it be work groups, committees, task forces, and so on.

Gives tools for tackling problems creatively
By observation, training and participation, people learn to use tools to help groups reach consensus and decisions. Brainstorming and force field analysis are among the basic techniques staff may acquire.

Empowers individual staff members, makes library staff valuable to their users and instils confidence throughout the organization
By offering training and development in a variety of ways and by making opportunities available, an environment is created in which staff members believe themselves to be valuable to the organization. Consequently, they want to share their opinions, knowledge, and skills.

Invigorates the need for personal improvement
Investing in training and development helps staff to approach problems in a constructive way.

Change over the long term
The impact of a staff development and training programme on a large organization is gradual and will only happen with sustained effort and consistent attention. Patience, persistence and repetition, however, are the keys to engendering change and unlocking the potential within library staff members.

One example of such customer service training is at Dumfries and Galloway Library Service where 150 staff completed the Customer Care Serve Up programme at their local college. The programme focused on customers and their expectations, aspects of good service and how to deal with complaints.

TOPICS AND LEVELS

Most customer service training commences with agreeing definitions of good, and possibly bad, service. An exercise for this is included in the appendices. Most training courses would provide published examples of good and bad service, such as those produced by the National Consumer Council (2006) and the American Library Association. Encouraging the participants to produce their own definition is a good way to foster discussion and provides concrete examples to refer to later on in a session. Trainer's tip – always get people to identify positive experience first!

Interpersonal skills usually form the bulk of customer service training sessions. These often include the use of positive language – translating negative responses such as 'I don't know' into something more constructive and thinking about how what we say can affect the customers' experience. Listening and questioning skills are also particularly important for staff involved with enquiry work and increasingly vital for everyone. Body language is also important. Although less service is provided on a face-to-face basis, paying attention to non-verbal communication is key to making people feel welcome and helps to avoid problems.

More specialised topics can include:

- Problem solving including how to deal with complaints or difficult situations. This could include understanding why such problems occur and the consequences of not handling complaints, and so on, in an effective way. These sessions might also include work on assertiveness skills, non-verbal communication, personal safety and how to refer problems to someone more senior.
- Internal customer service. This aspect is increasingly important as much of the service provided at the front line depends on the support given by colleagues within and outside the library service.
- Product knowledge/technical training, such as the People's Network and ECDL
- Managing and supporting staff to deliver excellent service. The way people are managed and supported helps to determine whether the service to customers is as good as it could be. Many libraries have developed courses for managers on how to support staff to deliver excellent customer service

FORMS AND FORMATS: TRAINING APPROACHES

There are numerous approaches to training. Table 7.1 provides a summary of different training approaches and their appropriateness to customer service training.

Table 7.1 Approaches to training

Method	Advantages and appropriateness
External training courses and conferences	• Opportunity to explore new developments and good practice • Chance to network with colleagues from elsewhere • Often used to 'test' training or trainers before bringing them in-house • Only reaches one person, so can be expensive unless the content is cascaded to other staff • May not be relevant to the organization's needs
Qualifications, e.g. NVQ's and City & Guilds	• Provides evidence of study and may be helpful to career development • May help people to gain promotion or a new post • Credibility and acknowledgement • Can be expensive and takes time and commitment • May not be tailored to library examples

Method	Advantages and appropriateness
Internal staff events, conferences, awaydays, etc.	• Provides an opportunity to explore strategic issues and engage in forward planning • Enables all staff to get together, although this might create tensions with maintaining services • Helps to encourage 'ownership' of problems and threats • However, sessions can be too vague to be practical and frustrations are created if issues and ideas are not followed up • Can be expensive in terms of staff time, logistics, etc., especially if an external venue is used
Interactive workshops One or half day [sample programme appended]	• The interactive workshop is probably the most popular and common form of customer service training. Because these are interactive they aid learning and help to translate theory into practice • Usually delivered as a one or half day event, workshops give an overview of customer service in a library context and provide time to practise relevant skills such as positive language, non verbal communication, listening and questioning skills. • These workshops can also help to reinforce the principles of customer service, whilst providing the chance to practice relevant techniques. • Practical work can include case studies, role plays, watching videos as well as encouraging people to share their ideas and experience. • They can be good for new staff as it enables the service to promote policies and the way we do things here • They can also be tailored for evening or weekend staff • In addition, many libraries provide shorter sessions as part of a training hour or to fit in with service constraints. For example, Edinburgh University provides five short sessions for library staff covering topics such as customer expectations, dealing with difficult situations, communicating effectively, providing a quality service and maintaining a service attitude • However, workshops do not suit everyone and introductory workshops could be regarded as too 'basic' for people who are experienced or who have been in post for some time • They take time and commitment if they are to work well
Staff training 'hour'	• This is a useful adjunct to more formal training as it reinforces learning and enables specific or more targeted concerns to be addressed • It is also good for updating, e.g. new policies and procedures • Maintains a focus on customer service as an important element • However, closing the library for training purposes can create problems with service priorities • Sessions also need to be practical and useful if people do not resent the time they take • One area to consider is how to cover people who work at different times or sites

Method	Advantages and appropriateness

E-learning, e.g. Folio, Open Rose, etc.	• E-learning enables people to learn at their own pace and time
	• It is an approach which is particularly useful where people work in the evenings or weekends
	• Focused and allows specific aspects to be covered
	• Also provides a refresher or a source of regular reminder
	• Does not always work if people like to explore ideas with others and it can make people feel lonely and difficult to maintain motivation
	• How do you assess learning?
	• Interesting examples of e-learning is the FOLIO programme [Facilitated Online Learning as an Interactive Opportunity] developed by the National library of Health for health librarians in the UK. At the time of writing, there are 14 modules covering topics such as management skills, quality, marketing and promotion and customer service. Health librarians can take part in the programmes by registering; others can access the archive material when the programmes are completed.
	• A more focused approach aimed at student assistants in an academic library has been produced by the University of Louisville. The Student Assistant Training Program [sic] is a self teaching programme which takes new staff through a series of presentations and training exercises. These are designed to emphasise the importance of customer service and to reinforce the people skills needed. There is a companion programme for supervisors which includes a checklist and evaluation forms to assist in checking progress.
	• Training in more specific aspects of customer service also lends itself to distance or e-learning. For example, the Open Rose Group, a cooperative group based in Yorkshire have developed a distance learning package on working with students with disability. The pack containing a DVD and support materials covers the following topics:
	  ◦ Dyslexia
	  ◦ Hearing
	  ◦ Mobility
	  ◦ Vision

Shadowing	• This technique provides an opportunity to 'learn from Nelly' • Useful for people who are new to learn about processes • It also helps to build confidence and a sense of belonging • However, its success depends on how good Nelly is at training others! • It can distort good practice and make it difficult to reinforce the correct approach

Method	Advantages and appropriateness
Visits	• Useful for opening people's eyes and for raising awareness of good or interesting practice on other organizations • Helps to rejuvenate interest in customer service • Provides staff with an opportunity to network with other organizations and can assist team building • Does not need to be limited to libraries • However, visits take time and could be regarded as a 'jolly' • They need to be focused, e.g. identify three interesting things done by the visited service/organization which would be of benefit • Time for a debrief is important • May create difficulties for people who work part time or evenings/weekends
Coaching – see also the session on making it stick below	• Personalized – focuses on current individual needs and builds on experience • Content can be tailored and allows sensitive or difficult areas to be addressed • Can be provided on a timely basis and can be short and succinct • Feedback can be given in private • Encourages incidental and self directed learning • However, coaching can be very time consuming and requires proper preparation • Needs privacy • Needs specific goals • Does not work for everyone and not always appropriate • Trainee might feel inhibited or intimidated
Blended learning	• The combination of e-learning with other methods • Enriches the experience and allows different learning styles to be accommodated [see below] • Helps to overcome problems with distance/e-learning and provides reminders and reassurance to participants. • Helps the learner to translate learning into action • However, blended learning needs careful organisation and coordination if it is to be successful • It is also time consuming and could be expensive • There is a useful overview of what is involved at: <http://www.e-learningcentre.co.uk/eclipse/Resources/index.html>.

DISCUSSION

Perhaps the most common form of customer service training is the interactive workshop. Delivered as a one or half-day event, this usually provides an overview of customer service in a library context, and practice in relevant skills such as positive language, non-verbal communication, listening and questioning skills. These workshops can help to reinforce the principles of customer service, whilst providing the chance to practise relevant techniques. Practical work can include case studies, role plays, watching videos or DVDs, as well as encouraging people to share their ideas and observations. Many libraries provide shorter sessions as part of a training hour or to fit in with service constraints.

Other considerations when developing training activities for customer service include whether to use internal or external trainers. Internal trainers have the advantage of knowing the system and being able to talk with authority about users and their specific needs. In addition, using colleagues can help to reinforce management commitment to customer service. Also smaller groups can be covered, which means that there is less need to delay induction training until there are sufficient staff.

External trainers will need careful briefing to ensure that the training is tailored and relevant to participants. They may also be more expensive than internal colleagues. However, they may be able to present the ideas in the context of what is happening elsewhere and may also be able to challenge assumptions and deal with sensitive issues without causing offence or cynicism.

Other factors which are important to the success of all forms of training include ensuring that the environment is conducive, that the sessions conform to good training practice and also that people are informed of the content/approach in advance. Many courses ask people to identify the issues/questions they would like to explore to ensure that the content is as tailored as possible. The SCONUL checklist (SCONUL 2001) provides useful advice and information for people organizing training events.

TRAINING METHODS AND CONTENT

According to Todaro in her recent book on customer service training (Todaro and Smith 2006), today's learner presents quite a challenge. People have short attention spans, need fast-paced activities and 'glitz', and need more results than previously. Training needs to be seen to be relevant and to take account of individual needs and preferences. Also, in choosing training methods, the following is also important:

- I hear and I forget
- I see and I remember
- I do and I understand

LEARNING STYLES

As customer service training is essentially practical, the training methods should reflect this. However, it is also important to pay attention to people's preferred learning styles as this can assist training to become embedded. There are many pieces of work on learning styles. One of the most common is Honey and Mumford's.

Learning style is defined as 'a description of the attitudes and behaviour which determine an individual's preferred way of learning'. Honey and Mumford developed their Learning Styles Questionnaire (Honey and Mumford 1982). The questions identify four types: of learner – activists, reflectors, theorists and pragmatists, and although most people exhibit more than one trait, an understanding of individual preferences helps training to feel more tailored and to be more effective. If people are able to use their natural style, learning becomes much easier and quicker.

Activists

Activists like to be involved in new experiences. They are open minded and enthusiastic about new ideas but get bored with implementation. They enjoy doing things and tend to act first and consider the implications afterwards. They like working with others but there is a danger that they might hog the limelight.

Activists learn best when they:

- Are involved in new experiences, problems and opportunities
- Work with others in business games, team tasks, role playing
- Are thrown in the deep end with a difficult task, especially if they can lead the discussion!

They are less likely to learn by:

- Listening to lectures or long explanations
- Reading, writing or thinking on their own
- Following precise instruction to the letter

Reflectors

Reflectors like to stand back and look at a situation from different perspectives. They enjoy collecting data and think about it carefully before coming to any conclusions. They like observing others and will listen to their views before offering their own.

Reflectors learn best when:

- They can observe others at work
- They have time to review what has happened and think about what they have learned

- They are asked to produce analyses and reports without tight deadlines

They are less likely to learn when:

- Acting as leader or role playing in front of others
- Being thrown in at the deep end or doing things with no time to prepare
- Reing rushed or worried by deadlines

Theorists

Theorists like to integrate their observations into sound theories and models. They think problems through in a logical way and have a tendency to be perfectionists who like to fit things into a rational scheme. They can appear to be detached and analytical in their thinking.

Theorists learn best when:

- They have to use their skills and knowledge in complex situations
- Situations are structured with clear purpose
- Ideas are interesting and challenging
- They have the chance to question and probe ideas

Theorists are less likely to learn when:

- They have to participate in situations which emphasize emotion and feelings
- The activity is unstructured or briefing is poor
- They have to do things without knowing the principles or concepts involved
- They feel they're out of tune with the other participants, for example, with people of very different learning styles

Pragmatists

Pragmatists are keen to try things out. They want concepts that are practical and can be applied to their job. They tend to be impatient with lengthy discussions and will want to get on. They can lose interest very quickly and need variety to stay engaged.

Pragmatists learn best when:

- There is an obvious link between the topic and job
- They have the chance to try out techniques with feedback, for example, role playing

- They are shown techniques that save time or effort
- They are shown different ways to do things

They learn less well when:

- There is no obvious or immediate benefit that they can recognize
- There is no advice on how to do something
- There is no apparent advantage, for example, shorter meetings

TRAINING METHODS

Table 7.2 Training methods

Method	Advantages	Limitations
Lectures/guest speakers/ lunchtime sessions	• Provides an external perspective which can be valuable for new or contentious topics • Provides evidence of good practice/tried and tested • Personalizes the topic • Can be engaging/inspirational if the speaker is credible and relevant • Can cater for large groups and can be recorded for people who were unable to attend	• Passive – does not engage the learner • Does not allow skills or techniques to be practised • Ignores the use of interactive discussion and less collaborative learning • A poor speaker could do more harm than good
Interactive discussion/ small group workshops	• Less intimidating – safety in numbers • Allows everyone to take part leading to collaborative learning • Allows the sharing of ideas and learning with colleagues • Useful in conjunction with other approaches	• Time consuming and not really suitable for large numbers • Needs careful planning and facilitation to keep things on track • One person can dominate or skew the discussion • People may want to be given the solutions to problems rather than discuss them

Method	Advantages	Limitations
Case studies/ scenarios Useful examples in FOLIO, Infopeople	• Enables the discussion of real life examples in a safe environment • Develops analytic and problem solving skills • Allows exploration of complex issues • Fosters the exchange of ideas and approaches. Good for mixed groups • Helps people to apply new knowledge and skills	• People may not see relevance to their own situation • Needs careful preparation if they are to be relevant and practical • Need careful briefing to ensure people keep on track • Solutions can appear to be superficial and glib
Role play/ Drama based training	• Drama is used by commercial companies such as John Lewis to address inter personal skills training • It is also becoming popular to address issues of diversity, etc. through the use of role play	• Expensive • May be too intimidating for some people • People may be too self-conscious • Takes time and not appropriate for large groups
	• Allows people to experience different perspectives and see other points of view • Provides a chance to explore different solutions • Provides a 'real' experience which can help to build skills and confidence • There are many examples of libraries developing role-playing training for reference assistants. These programme has reinforced positive interactions, and given people confidence. A useful list is at web.uflib.ufl.edu/ps/Main/SSQ/ • ssq-biblio.pdf	• Need to define problem and roles clearly • Need to provide clear instructions and respect the learner – no fishbowls!
Quizzes/ observation	• Practical and engaging • Allows people to work by themselves – works for some • Helps to reinforce points made • People like success	• Use sparingly • Keep short and simple • Needs careful preparation to ensure relevance

Method	Advantages	Limitations
Homework/ project work/ guided reading	• Provides time for people to reflect and helps people to translate theory into practice • Acts as a reminder for linked sessions • Useful as a complement to coaching • Flexible • Opportunity to practise relevant skills and techniques	• Needs commitment and dedication on the part of the learner • Needs careful instructions
DVD/video	• Useful as part of a broader session to provide variety • Helps to engage the learner • Illustrates how and how not to • Liked by some	• May need to be contextualized • Keep short and sharp • The how not to may be offensive to some and require careful introduction and debriefing

MAKING IT STICK – IMPLEMENTATION, IMPACT AND EVALUATION

Implementation

In making customer service training happen, there are two issues to be addressed – how to make the training stick and how to ensure that there is follow up at local level to reinforce the training and make it standard practice.

Making Training Stick

As noted before, the more interactive the training, the greater the retention level. For example, it is suggested that people retain:

10% – 30% of what they only read, hear or see
50% of what they both see and hear
70% of what they talk over with others
80% of what they use and do in real life
95% of what they teach someone else to do

Practical ways to aid retention of learning include: encouraging participants to prepare before the session; clarifying questions and concerns in advance; and reading case studies or looking at websites.

The Manager's Role in Embedding Learning

According to Kolb, we all need to view training in a holistic way. His four-stage learning cycle was published in 1984 (Kolb 1984). This sets out four distinct stages and suggests that the concrete experience (or training activity) is only the first step in the process. In order for training to be effective, people need time to reflect on the learning gained. They also need to relate the learning to their existing knowledge or observation which can then inform action or a change in approach.

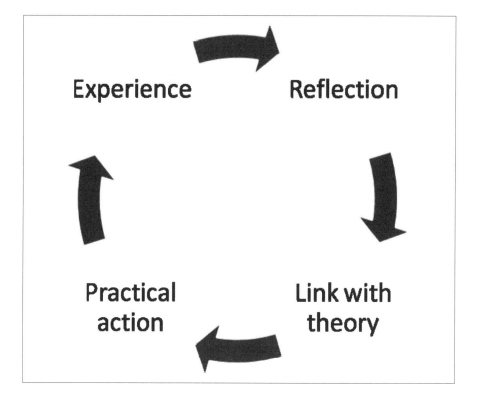

Figure 7.1 Kolb's learning cycle
Source: Adapted from Kolb 1984.

Kolb suggests that this process represents a cycle and the learner should be encouraged to 'touch all bases'. The reflection phase helps us to absorb the learning, while the theory element helps us to link that learning with our existing knowledge and experience. In order to become balanced, integrated learners, we should all gain competence in the four stages.

Managers can help their staff to develop competence in Kolb's model by encouraging them to reflect on courses and other training activities they have attended, to share their ideas and observations with colleagues and to assist them to translate those ideas into practice.

For example, appraisal and regular one-to-one meetings are excellent vehicles for the review of training and learning. Similarly, managers can help their staff to understand why the training is taking place and how the activity will affect what they do and how they work. On return, they can ask whether the activity was successful, what has been learned and how it will impact on the person's work. It is helpful to ascertain what further training might be necessary and whether there are any resource considerations such as access to equipment or time to practise newly learned skills. Finally, establish a date for the review of progress and to consider whether the training would be of interest or benefit to other colleagues. This process helps people to reflect on the learning achieved, provides a reminder of the points learned and also helps to give people confidence to try new techniques.

Other management actions that help to encourage a customer service culture include the development of charters and statements of service. In the UK, charters and statements of service were encouraged by the then Conservative Government in the late 1980s and early 1990s. Charters were intended to clarify customer expectations and foster a culture of quality. The Charter Mark provided a framework for the development of customer service. Many libraries – both academic and public – have attained and retained the Charter Mark. This provides recognition of the library's work in quality and can raise the profile of the library within the parent organization. John Morrow (2005) emphasized the importance of staff training in gaining the award of Charter Mark.

Many organizations also suggest that staff selection is an important part of delivering excellent customer service. Increasingly, libraries are asking for retail or other customer service experience when recruiting staff. Others ask potential employees to carry out a practical test to ascertain their aptitude for customer service. This could be a case study on a specific aspect of the work, designing a service for targeted user groups, planning a promotional event or dealing with difficult situations with colleagues or users.

Standards and Service Level Agreements

Other libraries have developed standards of service or service level agreements. These help to clarify the level of service that users can expect, as well as assisting library staff to prioritize their work. In other cases, considerable use is made of surveys to ascertain users' views.

The advantage of charters and standards is that they help to clarify expectations, such as response to requests, time taken for replies to enquiries, and so on. They can also be used to specify the responsibilities of users, such as acceptable behaviour.

Managing Poor Performance

Poor performance in customer service can be disastrous. Depending on the scale and scope of the problem, it could have severe repercussions for the service and other staff. Training options for poor performance are many. Peter Honey's model below suggests that we should analyse the problem and explore a range of possibilities, rather than leaping to an immediate solution.

Peter Honey's model:

1. Do nothing
2. Alter your perception
3. Modify the situation
4. Persuade the 'problem' person to change (Honey and Mumford 1982)

Often the most effective way of tackling poor performance is to consider coaching. John Whitmore's GROW model is recognized as one of the most effective in helping people to change their behaviour (Whitmore 1992).

Table 7.3 Whitmore's GROW model

Stage	Aspects
Goal	• What does this person need to achieve? • What will be the benefit to them or their team?
Reality	• How easy will it be to get started? • What will help/hinder the person in achieving success? • Can they get the support, resources or time they need?
Options	• What are the possibilities for making this happen? • Are there other options that have not been considered?
Will to change/what next?	• What, exactly, are they going to do next? • On a scale of 1–10, how committed are they? • How will they get the necessary support or time? • How will they know when they have succeeded?

Source: Adapted from Whitmore 1992.

Return on Investment – Impact and Evaluation

Evaluating the effectiveness of training has become more crucial in recent years. This is partly because training represents a considerable investment in terms of money and time. The effectiveness of training is also assessed during Investors in People and other accreditation processes.

Kirkpatrick's model of evaluation (Kirkpatrick 1994) is probably the most heavily used approach at present. It suggests that there are four levels of evaluation:

1. **Reaction**: what participants thought about the training
   – Programme evaluation sheets (happy sheets)
   – One-to-one discussions with line manager
2. **Learning**: what participants have actually learnt from the programme
   – Opportunities to practise what has been learned
   – Observations and feedback by line managers and/or peers
   – Use of, for example, role plays, work-based projects or action learning
3. **Behaviour**: how can the learning be applied to the job?
   – Observations and feedback from others
   – One-to-one discussions
   – Additional responsibilities
4. **Results/impact**: whether that application is achieving results or longer term impact
   – Tangible results include improved productivity, fewer mistakes, reduced turnover, and so on. Observations and feedback from others
   – Less tangible results include better staff motivation, favourable feedback from clients

Determining the impact of training on the individual can be achieved through the observation of their performance and pre- and post-training assessments. More general evaluation can be obtained through the use of surveys, and quality audits and assessments.

One approach has become more prevalent in libraries in recent years. Mystery shoppers provide an objective and confidential review of services and facilities. They are usually given a series of questions to ask as well as specific aspects of the service to explore. *Update*, April 2006, included a series of articles about mystery shoppers in libraries, whilst *SCONUL Newsletter* for Winter 2005 carried a useful article about mystery shoppers in Liverpool.

True evaluation of customer care training is gained through the impact on the users' experience. The University of York Library Service received funding to provide customer service training for all their staff. According to their annual report:

... workshops covering positive language, non-verbal communication, active listening, dealing with difficult situations, and techniques for remaining calm and confident were provided by a consultancy specialising in library staff training. Work has been done to clarify the customer service policy and expectations of users and there is now a shared understanding about what constitutes good customer service.

CONCLUSION

Customer service training is vital if libraries are to survive and thrive. Paying attention to people skills, including non-verbal communication and listening, will help libraries in all sectors to be responsive and to deliver a good service every time. Finally according to Hopson and Scally, good service is not smiling at the customer; it is getting them to smile at you! (Hopson and Scally 2000).

REFERENCES

ALA (American Library Association) (2007), *A Student's Guide to Evaluating Libraries in Colleges and Universities* (ACRL). <http://www.ala.org/ala/acrl/acrlissues/marketingyourlib/studentsguide.htm>.

Barlow, N. (2001), *Batteries Included* (London: Random House).

Beevers, C.J., Burt, S.L. and Conway, P.W. (2004), 'The Open Rose Group: Opening up Access for Disabled Users of Academic Libraries in Yorkshire', *SCONUL Focus*, 32, Summer/Autumn 2004, 55–7. <https://www.sconul.ac.uk/publications/newsletter/32/21.pdf>.

Carlzon, J. and Peters, T. (1989), *Moments of Truth* (Glasgow: HarperCollins).

FOLIO (ongoing), 'Facilitated Online Learning as an Interactive Opportunity'. <http://www.nelh.nhs.uk/folio/>.

Gates, J. (1990), *Introduction to Librarianship*, 3rd edn (New York: Neal Schuman).

HeLicon Scheme (2003), 'The HeLicon scheme'. <http://www.nelh.nhs.uk/librarian/accreditation.asp>, no longer available.

Honey, P. and Mumford, A. (1982), *Manual of Learning Styles* (Berkshire: Peter Honey Publications). <http://www.peterhoney.com/>.

Institute for Customer Service (2006), 'Transforming Front Line Staff'. <http://www.idea-knowledge.gov.uk/idk/core/page.do?pageId=73411>.

Kirkpatrick, D.L. (1994), *Evaluating Training Programs: The Four Levels* (San Francisco, CA: Berrett-Koehler).

Kolb, D. (1984), *Experiential Learning* (New Jersey: Prentice Hall).

Morrow, J. (2005), 'Newcastle University Library and the Charter Mark', *SCONUL Focus*, 35, 17–19. <www.sconul.ac.uk/publications/newsletter/35/6.pdf>.

Murray, S. (2005), 'Mystery Shoppers in Liverpool', *SCONUL Newsletter*, 36, Winter 2005. <https://www.sconul.ac.uk/publications/newsletter/36/8.pdf>.

National Consumer Council (2006), *The Stupid Company* (London: NCC). <http://www.ncc.org.uk/publications/stupid_company.pdf>, no longer available.

Office for Government Commerce (2005), quoted by Stephen Emmett at the *Customers, Suppliers and the Need for Partnerships* conference, 6 June 2005. <www.ukoln.ac.uk/web-focus/events/workshops/webmaster-2005/talks/emmott/emmott.ppt>.

Office of the Government Committee (2005), *Transformational Government* (London: Cabinet Office). <www.cio.gov.uk/documents/pdf/transgov/transgov -strategy.pdf>.

Schroer, W. (2003), 'Too Much Customer Service?' *Library Journal.* <http://www.libraryjournal.com/article/CA317639.html>.

SCONUL (2001), *Organising a Staff Development event: A Briefing Paper* (SCONUL). <http://www.sconul.ac.uk/publications/pubs/Organising_staff_event.doc>.

'Special Report on Mystery Shoppers in Libraries', *Library and Information Update*, April 2006.

Sykes, P. (2005), 'Putting Library Staff Back into Libraries', *SCONUL Focus*, 34. <https://www.sconul.ac.uk/publications/newsletter/34/1.pdf>.

University of Louisville (2003), 'Patron Service Training for Student Assistants' (PowerPoint) (Louisville: University of Louisville). <http://louisville.edu/library/training/>.

Whitmore, J. (1992), *Coaching for Performance* (London: Nicholas Brealey Publishing Limited).

Zennerich, E. (2006), 'The Long Term View of Library Staff Development', *College and Research News* 67:10, November 2006.

OTHER USEFUL SOURCES

Hopson, B. and Scally, M. (2000), *Twelve Steps to Success Through Service* (Cirencester: Management Books 2000 Ltd).

Melling, M. and Little, J. (2002), *Building a Successful Service Culture* (London: Facet).

Todaro, J. and Smith, M. (2006), *Training Library Staff and Volunteers to Provide Extraordinary Customer Service* (London: Facet).

APPENDIX 1

SERVICE SKILLS:
AN INTENSIVE ONE-DAY WORKSHOP

Objectives

- To help participants to feel confident when dealing with a range of internal and external customers
- To give practical help in providing excellent ISS services, including making a good impression, telephone techniques and listening skills
- To consider practical ways to defuse difficult situations
- To allow an exchange of ideas and expertise
- To encourage the preparation of plans for future action

Suggested Programme

09.30   Coffee and registration
09.45   Welcome and introductions
10.00   What would make today useful for us?
         Practical work and feedback in small groups
10.20   In the customers' shoes: a practical session on the principles of 'good' service
         What constitutes good service in an academic library context?
         The changing nature of our customers and their demands
11.00   Coffee/tea
11.15   Service skills. Practical work on:

- Language and listening skills
- Non-verbal communication
- Defining and refining the question

12.45   Lunch
13.30   Dealing with difficult situations 1

Practical work using case studies and participants' own examples

14.45   Tea

15.00   Dealing with difficult situations 2

- Assertiveness techniques
- Modelling authority

16.15   Action summary and workshop review

16.30   End of workshop

APPENDIX 2

IN THE CUSTOMERS' SHOES EXERCISE

Please consider an occasion when **you** are the customer. Think of examples such as:

- Going to a restaurant to celebrate a birthday or other special event
- Buying a present for a friend's wedding
- Going to a travel agent to book a holiday
- Making a significant purchase, such as a computer or new TV

1. What matters when **you** are the customer? Is it the way you are treated, the environment, rectifying a problem or something else?

2. Please identify examples of good service – when you were made to feel important or respected.

3. Now consider examples of poor or unsatisfactory service. Identify the key things that make them poor. What did you do as a result?

Note for trainers: This exercise is useful as an ice breaker. It gets people talking and sharing their experience and observations. The lists generated can be used during the session to reinforce good practice.

APPENDIX 3

'AMBIENCE' CHECKLIST

Aspect	Criteria	Comments
Exterior	Attractive; easy to find?	
	Informative?	
Interior	Clean, tidy and in good repair?	
	Wheelchair/mobility access?	
	Lighting and temperature?	
	Consistency, colour/housestyle?	
	Noisy and unhelpful?	
Signs and guiding	Attractive, clear and informative?	
	Suitable for the visually impaired?	
	Floor plans at key points?	
	Helpful guiding on copiers, and so on?	
Notices	Correct and up to date?	
	Languages other than English?	
	Large print/visual?	
Publications, for example, guides, leaflets, and so on	Attractive and informative?	
	Correct and up to date?	
	Well displayed?	
Furniture/ equipment	Clean and safe?	

	Modern and/or in good repair? Copiers and terminals working? Clear instructions for use?
Staff	Appearance? Identifiable – ID or badges? Helpful and approachable?
Stock	Tidy, clean, attractive, up to date? Materials shelved quickly? Attractive interesting displays?
Miscellaneous	Forum for customer comments? External view/staff work areas? Duty manager/senior staff available?

Note for trainers: This exercise helps to develop empathy by showing staff the library from their users' perspective and could be used as part of diversity awareness training to help staff to understand the library from different perspectives.

MANAGEMENT

CHAPTER 8

SUPPORTING FIRST LINE MANAGERS

BARBARA ALLAN

INTRODUCTION

The aim of this chapter is to consider current training practices that are relevant to first line managers. Many new and aspiring managers require training in specific aspects of their new role and this includes topics such as budgets, project management, performance management and quality management. While much of this training takes place through short courses, blended learning, which combines different approaches to learning and training, is an increasingly common approach to developing managers in the workplace. This chapter is organized around the headings: blended learning; budgets; project management; performance management; and quality management.

BLENDED LEARNING

Training practice for first line managers may involve 100 per cent e-learning and this is particularly useful for topics that are rule-based, for example, accounting and finance, or legislation. Conversely, many training programmes are delivered 100 per cent by face-to-face workshops, and examples given below include accounting and finance, project management and a range of training and development events associated with quality management processes. Increasingly, blended learning is used as a means of tailoring a training solution that meets the needs of the employing organization and the participants. Many people use the term blended learning to mean a combination of e-learning and face-to-face workshops, as illustrated in Figure 8.1.

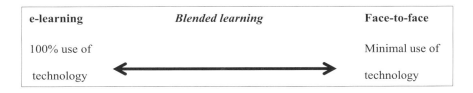

Figure 8.1 Popular conception of blended learning

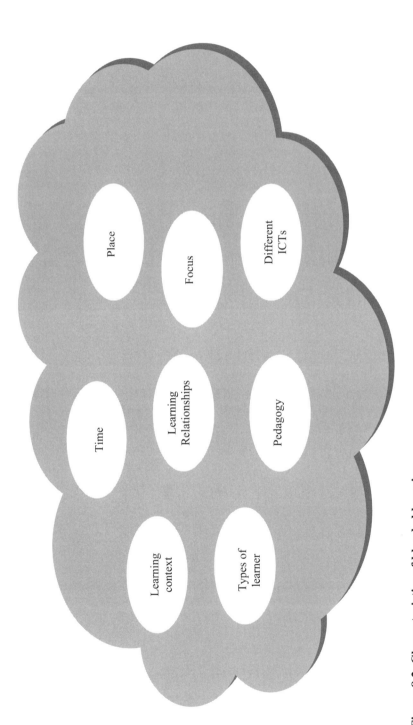

Figure 8.2 Characteristics of blended learning
Source: Allan 2007.

However, blended learning can involve designing a specific training and development process that requires a carefully selected blend of characteristics (Allan 2007). This is illustrated in Figure 8.2 which identifies the different aspects of learning and teaching which may be blended together:

- Time, for example, synchronous or asynchronous learning activities and communications
- Place where learning takes place, for example, on-campus, in workplace, at home
- Different information and communication technologies, for example, CD/DVD, first generation Internet technologies, social networking software or Web 2.0, or new developing technologies
- Context of learning, for example, academic, training provider or workplace
- Pedagogy, for example, tutor- or student-centred, behaviourist or constructivist
- Focus, for example, aims of learning process presented by tutors or aims negotiated and agreed by individuals, groups or communities
- Types of learner, for example, learners with different roles such as student or practitioners, or multi-disciplinary or professional groupings of learners and teachers
- Relationships with others in the learning process, for example, individual learning, group learning, or development of a learning community

The examples given in this chapter include a mixture of 100 per cent e-learning, 100 per cent traditional face-to-face workshops, and blended learning.

BUDGETS

All library and information services operate within a particular financial context and the ability to understand finance is important for all managers. Individual organizations will have their own finance department which manages all aspects of finance including financial policies and procedures, the management of budgets, associated computerized information systems, and also financial planning. In addition to internal budgeting policies and procedures, many library and information workers manage projects that are funded by external sources. This means that they become involved in obtaining external funding and then managing a budget.

For many library and information workers their first experience of budgets and financial management is at library school where this topic is likely to be covered within a general management module. Once in the workplace, they are likely to find that they need to update this knowledge and also develop skills in working with the financial systems of their employing organization. Training practice in the context of budgets commonly involves attending short courses that focus on specific aspects of finance. These courses are commonly provided by:

- Employing organization
- Professional associations and groups
- Funding bodies, for example, for externally funded projects

TFPL[1] provides a good example of a one-day workshop on finance and budgeting that is aimed at library and information professionals 'with responsibility for managing their own budgets, but who have received little financial skills training and who want to increase their confidence in this topic'. Its outline is presented in Box 8.1:

Introduction
Library and information managers are increasingly expected to manage complex financial resources; to develop and interpret budgets and financial statements; to make a case for financial resources and also to negotiate value-for-money contracts with their suppliers.

This intensive one-day workshop recognizes that many people are anxious about managing their budgets. The day will be very practical and participants will be supported to carry out a range of exercises including understanding and interpreting financial statements, using financial information for decision making and planning, and making a case for financial resources.

Outcomes
As a result of attending this course participants will:

- Feel more confident in understanding, interpreting and presenting financial information
- Gain experience in developing and controlling budgets
- Be able to communicate more effectively with finance departments
- Develop services with a sound financial basis
- Exchange ideas and experience

Programme content includes:

- The language of finance
- The role of financial planning in strategic management
- Financial cycles and timescales
- Interpreting financial statements
- Compiling a budget, monitoring and controlling expenditure
- Costing methods and making a case for financial resources
- Financial decision making toolkit
- Dealing with difficult situations with financial managers

Box 8.1 Finance and budgeting for LIS course
Source: TFPL. <http:/./www.tfpl.com>.

ASLIB[2] and the Chartered Institute for Library and Information Professionals (CILIP)[3] also provide one-day workshops, and examples of their courses are shown in Box 8.2, Box 8.3 and Box 8.4.

---

1   TFPL. <http:/./www.tfpl.com>.
2   ASLIB. <http://www.aslib.com>.
3   CILIP. <http://www.cilip.org.uk>.

Programme features:

The budget cycle

The different types of figures/terminology

- Requested budget
- Given budget
- Increase on previous year's spend
- Actual spend
- Savings
- Overspend
- Reforecast
- Quotes vs. estimates
- Recording receipt of invoice vs. actual payment

A practical look at a spreadsheet example

- Percentage formulae
- Recording monthly, periodic and annual payments
- How to record subs with monthly invoices that do not fit in with your same financial year
- Copying contents of cells to a summary sheet
- Working out the rolling reforecast
- How to work out what is overdue
- How to record credits

Why you should attend
What this course intends is to demonstrate how you can use Excel spreadsheets to manage your library budgets. To compare what you estimated you would spend with what you actually spent. To enable you to know at a moment's notice where you are at any point in time with your actual and newly predicted spend and not have to spend ages doing a manual reforecast. Common and more complex Excel formulae will be explored to make your professional life easier and to automate as much as possible. It is not intended to be a book-keeping course, but is aimed at the average library manager who is too busy to spend ages on budget management but for whom it is important that they can lay their hands on vital, up to date information without having to have a major trawl through past invoices and catalogue records to try and work out where they are in the spending stakes.

Who should attend
Anyone who has to manage all or part of a budget, whether this is for work or for a professional association or organization. Only a very basic knowledge of Excel is required; beyond that there is no need to know Excel well.

By the end of the course
You will have gained more knowledge about how you can use the functionality of Excel to not only record the budget but to keep it as a living, useful document throughout the financial year. There will be a focus on the specific vagaries of library budgets but many of the tips could be applied to other arenas. You will be able to take away some formulae and ideas of how you could use Excel to manage your budget.

Box 8.2 Spreadsheet course outline
Source: ASLIB. <http://www.aslib.com/>.

You can only spend it once! With organizations facing tougher competition for funding and resources, and increasing pressure to offer more for less, it is no longer sufficient to be able to present the facts and a well-reasoned argument when submitting a business case. Whether developing a new service, defending an existing one or trying to secure staffing levels, using and presenting financial information effectively can help you secure the desired result.

By the end of the event participants will have:

- Gained an understanding of the key techniques involved in appraising financial information and making a 'Business Case' using financial data
- Examined the processes involved in:
     – Cost comparison
     – Justifying staffing structures and budgets
- Be able to use the techniques learnt to evaluate data and present their case in effective ways, on return to work place

Who should attend?

Senior managers whose role includes responsibility for evaluating the quality of service delivery against the cost of delivering that quality. These senior managers are likely to contribute to service development and service planning decisions, or be seeking imminent promotion to a similar role.

Programme content includes:

Key ground rules for presenting financial information
The 'business' case
Cost comparison
Justifying a staffing structure
Group work: cost comparison justifying staffing requirements scenarios
Group work: evaluating a request for increased resources to extend opening hours
Presentation of group work
Review

Box 8.3 Supporting your case using costing and budgeting data

Source: CILIP. <http://www.cilip.org.uk/>.

Against a background of constrained resources, the challenges in maintaining a modern, fit-for-purpose range of services in the public library sector is immense. This one-day training programme will help library professionals identify where they are spending their library's money and whether that fits with the current strategic plan.

Participants will be provided with a framework to challenge the financial structure of their budget and compare and contrast against published national information, for the purposes of planning continuous improvement measures for the future.

Benefits of attending
By the end of the event participants will have:

- Compared key financial performance indicators of their library service with national averages
- Identified where their library service performs differently to the national average
- Identified further areas for investigation to understand differences in actual performance
- Levied preliminary challenges as to the possible reasons for differences in financial performance and service delivery consequences

Who should attend?
Senior library managers in the academic sector responsible for evaluating the most appropriate budgetary allocation for their service. Understanding of service delivery quality thresholds and staffing structure will be helpful.

Special notes
Participants will need to bring details of the information they provided for the collection of statistics collated by LISU

Programme content includes:
Demonstration of the first template for comparison of LISU statistics
Input and comparison of LISU figures
Good or bad? Alternative use of similar situations
Identification of differences from national averages
Comparison of trends with LISU statistics
Trends in proportions spent on staffing and materials: issues to consider .
Where do we go from here?
Review

Box 8.4 Budget allocation solutions
Source: CILIP. <http://www.cilip.org.uk/>.

These one-day workshops are all clearly located in everyday practice and involve participants working on case studies and examples which are either based on their workplace practices or provided by the course leader.

Many new managers develop their financial skills by attending in-house training courses, provided by their employers, on using their financial systems and procedures. These are extremely useful as not only are they tailor-made to the requirements of the organization but they also provide a networking opportunity with colleagues. One colleague of mine who worked in a private company updated her knowledge of finance through an e-learning course. She found the courses provided by Learndirect suited her needs and enabled her to learn at a time and pace that suited her. Learndirect[4] provides the following short courses (one to nine hours) that are aimed at people with little prior knowledge of finance.

- Budgeting Basics
- Cost-Benefit Analysis
- Finance for Non-Financial Managers
- Financial Environment
- Managing your Budget
- Preparing your Budget
- Understanding Balance Sheets
- Understanding Costs
- Understanding Profit and Loss
- Working to a Budget

In summary, the preferred method of training first line managers in budgets and finance appears to be short courses, and there are a wide range of providers who offer courses that are aimed at library and information managers, as well as courses from general providers that are aimed at people with little prior knowledge of this subject.

PROJECT MANAGEMENT

Project work is common practice in libraries and information services, and typical projects include moving a library, introducing a new system or service, or developing and implementing new technologies. Project work provides opportunities for staff development as it may involve working at the 'cutting edge' of professional practice, working with technological developments and innovations, and also experiencing new and different ways of working. Individual library and information workers may be employed solely on project work, often on a contract basis, or they may be working on a project in addition to their 'full-time' library or information role. In both of these situations it is important that project managers have the appropriate range of skills and expertise required to manage the project.

Training practice in project management tends to focus on the following areas:

- Generic project management skills
- Information technology for project management, for example, MS Project
- Use of specific project methodologies, for example, PRINCE2
- Bidding for projects
- Project management requirements and practices supported by indivdiual organizations, for example, funding bodies

---

4   Learndirect. <http://www.learndirect.co.uk/>.

- Associated training including:
  - Managing finance
  - Time management
  - Leading and supervising teams
  - Working in collaborative teams or partnerships
  - Dealing with challenging situations
  - Report writing
  - Presentation skills

In this chapter, I focus on the main areas of project management, for example, generic project management skills, use of IT, use of specific project methodologies, bidding for projects, and project management in specific contexts. Generic project management skills include knowledge and skills of standard project management practices including:

- The project life cycle – analysis, planning, implementing, evaluation and review
- Using standard project management techniques such as GANTT charts and network, PERT diagrams, risk analysis
- Managing project resources including staff and finance
- Managing project communications including disseminating good practice
- Legal issues: health and safety; data protection; intellectual property, and so on

Typically, these skills are taught through short courses provided by employers, professional associations and groups, colleges or universities. The following example in Box 8.5 shows the typical schedule for a one-day course on project management:

Aim
The aim of this workshop is to equip participants with basic knowledge and skills of project management

Learning outcomes
As a result of attending this workshop, participants will be able to:

- Explain the project management process and cycle
- Use standard project management tools such as GANTT charts and network diagrams to plan, monitor and control a project
- Develop and implement a communications strategy for their project
- Lead and manage the project team
- Ensure that they provide a safe and legal working environment for the project

Indicative programme:
Welcome and introductions
Introduction to projects, project management and different types of projects
The life cycle of the project: initial planning; defining the project
Tools, techniques and methods: GANTT charts; network diagrams; risk assessment; contingency planning
Project management software
Planning resources and estimating finance
Management and reporting
Implementation phase and project completion
People side of projects
The project manager
Action planning
Course evaluation

Box 8.5 Example project management course

Typically, this type of one-day workshop will involve a range of learning and teaching activities including: mini lectures and presentations; videos and DVDs; hands-on activities; practical activities and exercises; group activities; and case studies. Sometimes, participants are asked to bring along one of their work-based projects to use as an example during the workshop. Examples of practical activities include:

- Developing a project plan, for example, GANTT chart and network diagram using Post-it notes and flipchart paper
- Calculating the cost of a project and developing a project budget
- Carrying out a risk assessment for a given project

Increasingly blended learning is used as a means of delivering training including project management programmes. Figure 8.3 illustrates some of the features of a blended learning programme that I have delivered to library and information staff, and university administrators. It involved new and aspiring managers attending three face-to-face workshops (each workshop lasted four hours) which were used to deliver the basic principles of project management and also to introduce MS

Project. In between the face-to-face sessions, the course participants worked together in small learning sets using a virtual learning environment. As course tutor, I supported them using the discussion group and chat-room facilities. This blended programme enabled the face-to-face elements to be kept to a minimum which saved staff travel time and costs as the programme was located in a multi-campus university. Throughout the three-month course, participants worked on a real management project in their workplace, and this meant that they each completed the plans for their individual project and also gained feedback from colleagues. The programme enabled them to combine academic and workplace study, and to gain academic credit for their work.

While generic project management training programmes are likely to mention the use of project management software such as MS Project to support the project process, they are unlikely to provide detailed opportunities for participants to gain hands-on experience. Consequently, many organizations offer specialist workshops that deal with the use of specialist project management packages such as MS Project or with the use of commonly used packages such as spreadsheets which may be used to support a project. These workshops may range from a two-hour introduction through to a five-day intensive workshop.

There are many project management methodologies available which provide detailed rules and guidelines on the processes and procedures involved in project management, and they may be backed up by specialist software and also documentation. Common methodologies include PRINCE2 (UK-based) and PMBoK (a US methodology). PRINCE2 (Projects IN a Controlled Environment) is widely used in public sector organizations in the UK and it was written by the UK Government. A quick Internet search indicates that there are many accredited training organizations that will provide training from basic to advanced user levels of PRINCE2. It is possible to become PRINCE2 accredited at one of three levels. PMBoK (Project Management Body of Knowledge) is published by the Project Management Institute in the USA and is a set of guidelines rather than rules. It is used worldwide and, like PRINCE2, accredited training providers provide an extensive range of courses plus the opportunity to become an accredited trainer.

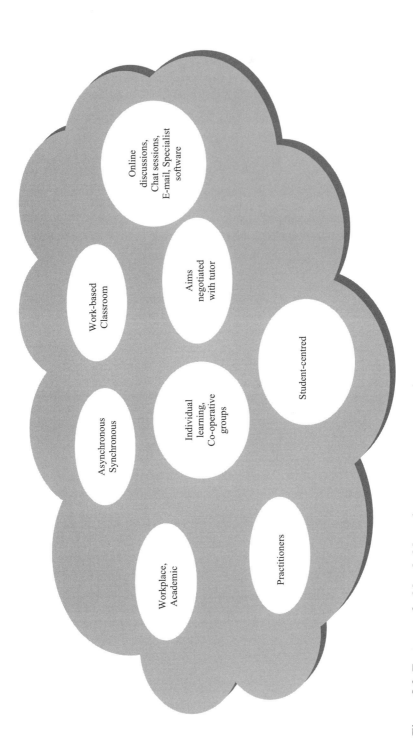

Online discussions, Chat sessions, E-mail, Specialist software

Work-based Classroom

Aims negotiated with tutor

Asynchronous Synchronous

Individual learning, Co-operative groups

Student-centred

Workplace, Academic

Practitioners

Figure 8.3 Features of a blended learning programme on project management
Source: Allan 2007.

In the UK and other countries, the last ten years has seen the rise of a competitive bidding culture in which different organizations bid for public or private sector funds to carry out specific projects. Funding is available from a wide range of sources including international organizations, European Union, central and regional governments, businesses, charitable and other special funds, and individual donors. A review of the contemporary library and information literature provides news of a wide range of projects on themes as varied as: e-learning and e-mentoring; ICT developments; social inclusion needs; improvement of storage to meet standards; extending access; digitization of resources; lifelong learning; information provision; remote services, for example, to rural communities; upgrading and relocating accommodation, for example, developing 'one-stop shops' that provide a wide range of information and learning services. This means that it has become increasingly important for library managers, particularly in the public and voluntary sector, to understand and be able to source funds, and also to write successful bids.

Keeping up to date with possible sources of funding is a challenging task as there is a diverse range of sources of funding, and the types and availability of funds is constantly changing. Examples of funding sources include: central and regional government agencies; European Union funds; international funds; local authorities; National Lottery; trusts and foundations; businesses, for example, as part of their corporate social responsibility activities; and also philanthropic individuals. Funding opportunities change over time as the priorities of funding organizations change, as does their access to funds. This means that anyone who is considering bidding for funding must do extensive research to identify current sources of funding and their up to date detailed requirements. Many information workers make use of specialists who will provide up to date information and advice on funding matters; for example, local authorities typically employ specialist staff with expertise in funding and funding applications in their economic development units, while universities often have a centralized research and development department that provides access to this type of specialist information. These services often provide short workshops that either give an overview of sources of funding and/or update colleagues with information about specific funding streams. Attendance at this type of workshop is sometimes the first step in the bidding process.

The bidding process involves a number of steps, as listed below:

1. Identifying a potential project and starting work on project brief
2. Identifying a potential source of funding
3. Obtaining the necessary documentation
4. Checking funders' requirements and criteria
5. Checking with parent organization that this meets their aims
6. Identifying a senior manager who will support the funding application

7. Identifying a single individual who will be responsible for the project
8. Carrying out research within the sector
9. Carrying out research within the bidding organization
10. Setting up or calling together a bidding team
11. Producing a draft funding application
12. Checking out queries with the funding organization
13. Obtaining feedback and guidance from colleagues
14. Editing and re-drafting the funding application
15. Obtaining approval to send off the funding application from own organization
16. Submitting the funding application within the timescale identified by the funding organization
17. Receiving outcome of selection process
18. If successful, then rejoicing and starting project; and if unsuccessful, then obtaining feedback from the funding organization and using it to help you become successful in your next application (Allan 2004)

These steps often form the structure of workshops on 'bidding for funds' that may be organized by employing organizations or the funding agencies themselves. Typically, these workshops provide an opportunity for individuals to learn about the bidding process and often involve working on a 'live' bid. For newcomers to this field, they offer a useful and often reassuring introduction to the process of bidding for funding, and they often clarify the specific language that is associated with external funding. In addition, they provide an important opportunity for networking and creating relationships with staff in the funding organizations.

Organizations that provide funding for projects, such as Joint Information Services Committee (JISC) in the UK, often demand that a condition of gaining funding is that the project is managed in line with their own project management standards, policies, procedures and documentation. Consequently, these funding bodies often provide training on their project management requirements and practices. Typically, these training events tend to be face-to-face workshops supported by detailed documentation. Further information about this type of workshop is normally available from the funding body's website.

In summary, the preferred method of training first line managers in project management appears to be short courses which may be delivered face-to-face or through blended learning. Project management is a very specialist field and provision ranges from general courses to very specific courses.

PERFORMANCE MANAGEMENT

Performance management is a powerful tool that may be used to review, motivate, develop and retain staff. The aims of this process are normally to ensure that the organization and department develop and manage their staff in line with their overall strategy and objectives. In other words, this process provides a link between strategic planning and human resource management, and it helps to ensure that staff performance and development is in line with the requirements of the organization.

Different organizations use different terms for performance management and it is sometimes referred to as an appraisal process. The objectives of performance management or appraisal processes are likely to involve some or all of the following:

- To improve staff performance
- To provide feedback on individual performance
- To identify training needs
- To consider individual career development

This means that it is important to be clear about the main emphasis of the system that you are involved in. This is one of the reasons that attending relevant training events is important.

The performance management or appraisal process involves the formal assessment of an individual's performance against specific targets, and then setting new targets to be achieved during the next appraisal process. This process normally involves a meeting between the team leader and the member of staff and it provides both parties with the opportunity to give and discuss feedback. Many appraisal processes run on an annual cycle. Different organizations will structure and organize their performance management or appraisal processes in a manner that meets their needs. Some processes are extremely lengthy; for example, the 360 degree appraisal process involves gaining feedback from a number of colleagues, and may require lengthy documents to be completed. In contrast, other schemes are less formal and may only require the completion of one sheet of A4 paper by the team leader and member of staff. Some performance management schemes are linked with reward systems; for example, staff may be scored during the appraisal process and those staff achieving a score above a certain level may be given a pay rise or bonus.

Most organizations provide specialist training to their supervisors, managers and leaders who are involved in the appraisal process. These are well worthwhile attending as they provide valuable information and assistance on this process. An example outline for a training event on the performance management system for library staff at Purdue University (see <www.purdue.edu>) is presented in Box 8.6:

Overview Session

Overview
This session will review the concepts of the LPMS. You will learn how to determine job responsibilities, identify expectations, give and receive constructive feedback, and learn how the LPMS fits within the performance appraisal process in the libraries.

Session Objective(s)
At the end of this training session, you will be able to:

- Describe how LPMS can assist supervisors and employees in the performance management process
- Identify the six elements of the LPMS
- Describe the overall goals of the LPMS
- Identify and define the four strategic directions of the libraries
- Define your current job responsibilities
- Identify and define the eight performance competencies
- Establish three or four performance competencies to work on next year
- Document progress towards meeting expectations
- Document all training/education that you receive through the training plan
- Identify and define the five performance ratings
- Identify areas in the performance appraisal time period in which the employee has met or exceeded expectations or needs to improve
- List specific examples that support the overall rating
- List specific areas in which the supervisor can assist the employee to improve performance as it relates to organizational needs

---

Box 8.6 Libraries performance management system
Source: Purdue University. <http://www.purdue.edu/>.

Although this training event has a large number of learning objectives, it indicates the typical content of this type of event. One area where training practice in this arena varies is the emphasis that is placed on the specific performance management and appraisal process, or the interpersonal skills that are required to carry out successful performance management meetings. Training workshops that focus on the interpersonal skills cover topics such as:

- Listening skills
- Giving constructive feedback
- Dealing with difficult situations
- Learning from reflection
- Action planning.

An example of a one-day workshop on performance management is provided by CILIP in the UK and is outlined in Box 8.7:

Often staff are out of touch with the aims and objectives of their organizations and, even though they might be running what they deem to be effective services, many staff fail to be motivated. There is often a mismatch between delivery of local services and the organizational goals. This one-day course will examine the relationship between organizational and individual goals, staff development and motivational values and techniques.

Objectives
By the end of the event participants will have:

- Identified different motivations in the workplace
- Learned how to engage with employees
- Examined different styles of leadership
- Explored different delegation techniques
- Looked at ways to translate organization strategies into specific work-plans
- Learned how to support staff when implementing change

Who should attend?
Middle to senior managers in any sector who want to get the best performance from their staff.

Programme content includes:
From organizational goals to individual development plans
The role of job design
Motivational theories and team dynamics
Motivational practice: from organizational culture to personal engagement
The people aspects of change management
Monitoring performance: what infrastructure needs to be in place?
Leadership styles
Situational leadership and delegation

Box 8.7 Project management course
Source: CILIP. <http://www.cilip.org.uk/>.

In summary, the preferred method of training first line managers in performance management appears to be in-house short courses which are tailor-made for the management processes used in the organization. Individual managers may augment their development experiences in this area by taking part in generic interpersonal skills courses that are offered by a wide range of training providers.

QUALITY MANAGEMENT

Quality management is defined by Roberts and Rowley as: '… all of the processes, activities and measures that contribute to the management of the quality of the products, service or other outputs from the organisation. Quality management then involves: processes, to measure or improve quality; measures, to set targets and monitor progress' (Roberts and Rowley 2004).

Many libraries and information services work within a quality management environment that is specific to their context; for example, libraries in the Higher Education sector respond to the quality management processes of the Quality

Assurance Agency and Ofsted, Further Education colleges follow those of Ofsted and the Learning Skills Council, and public libraries follow those of the Department of Culture, Media and Sport. Private sector organizations may follow the quality management procedures of the ISO 9000 provided by the British Standards Institute. An extensive range of additional standards exist, including the Business Excellence Model of the European Foundation for Quality Management, Charter Mark, Investors in People, Customer First. Each standard has its own special characteristics and focus; for example, Investors in People focuses on the human resource aspects of an organization while Customer First focuses on customer services. Many library and information services strive to achieve these quality management awards and proudly display their logos when they are successful.

New and aspiring line managers develop their knowledge and skills of quality management in a number of ways. Quality management is normally studied as part of library and information qualifications where they are included in general management modules. Individual assignments or dissertations provide an opportunity for students to focus on this topic. Once in work, day-to-day library operations provide an opportunity for on-the-job development about working within a specific quality management environment. Many libraries and information services provide training in their policies and procedures as part of their induction and ongoing staff development activities. Specialist training is normally provided when a library or information service becomes involved in working towards a new quality standard and, in addition, it is possible to take short courses in quality management.

Implementing a quality management process and achieving a quality award normally requires a development process which typically involves the following steps: becoming familiar with the quality standard; understanding the detailed standard; self-assessment activities; development activities; mock assessment; assessment; celebration or progress towards achieving the required standards; maintenance and continuous development. Typically when a library or information service is working towards a quality standard, then they will be supported by an experienced manager or consultant who is familiar with the detailed requirements of that particular standard. Many library and information services establish small working parties to manage and operationalize the work required to achieve the standard. This may involve a series of training and development events as follows:

- Introductory briefing sessions to all staff to provide an introduction to the performance management process and the quality standard. This is aimed at raising awareness and understanding of the quality management process and standard. Sometimes a guest speaker will be invited along, for example, someone representing a library which has already achieved the quality standard.

- Introductory workshops which focus on the general requirements of the standard, and these may be used to start the self-assessment process.
- Self-assessment workshops in which participants work at a detailed level on the quality standard and its requirements. These workshops may involve identifying potential sources of evidence of the library's working practices and procedures.
- Action planning sessions which enable teams within the library to develop an action plan as a result of the initial self-assessment. This action plan will identify gaps or areas for improvement.
- Additional staff development sessions may be introduced to help fill gaps identified in the previous stages.
- A mock assessment session is often held as a means of preparing staff for the external assessment process.

In addition, the quality management process may be supported by an online communications process, for example, using a virtual learning environment such as Blackboard or computer conferencing software such as iCohere. This enables presentations and briefing notes to be made available to all staff online. It also provides access to discussions and question and answer sessions. Using an online environment means that individual managers can work and learn together in private and also at a time and place that suits their work schedule.

An example of a quality management training programme is the Six Sigma programme provided by the University of Delaware[5] which is aimed at newly promoted or aspiring quality managers, new or experienced quality professionals, managers, and teams and leaders who want to continuously improve their work processes. It has proved useful in library training as shown by the following quotation:

> *Over twenty Delaware library staff participated in the Performance Management Certificate, which is key to our quality initiatives. We were able to apply what we had learned to real world situations in our organization, and due in part to the training in this program, the Delaware Division of Libraries received the Delaware Quality Commitment Award in 2004 and the Delaware Quality Award of Merit for 2005. When we are managing our resources and services effectively, we are increasing the value of libraries to the public* (Annie Norman, State Librarian and Director, Delaware Division of Libraries 2006).

This Certificate programme takes place over a four-month period and it consists of 14 three-hour sessions. It is a validated programme and successful participants

---

5   University of Delaware. <http://www.continuingstudies.udel.edu/business/perform ance/program.shtml>.

achieve a Certificate plus academic credit. The Certificate programme includes the following modules:

Roadmap to Excellence

This introductory seminar provides an overview of the key components for developing a quality system that fits your organization and can deliver positive results. The workshop focuses on proven methods and current research in exploring the use of the PDSA (Plan, Do, Study, Act) cycle, the Malcolm Baldrige National Quality Award Criteria, Six Sigma, ISO 9000, and Lean Manufacturing. It provides a foundation for understanding how standards of excellence support quality systems.

Continuous Improvement Methods

The core module focuses on models of continuous improvement and problem solving, and on how to apply them in the real world. The Six Sigma DMAIC (Define, Measure, Analyze, Implement, Control) methodology is used as a framework. Participants will use the DMAIC model to initiate a process improvement project during this phase of the programme.

Implementation and Project Presentations

During the final module, the focus is on applying management techniques in the workplace. Participants will present the results of their process improvement projects and the class will celebrate the completion of the programme.

In summary, the preferred method of training first line managers in quality management appears to be through on-the-job training; for example, the manager learns about the quality management process as they use it. When new quality management processes are introduced into a library or information service, then they are likely to involve a staff development process aimed at all staff.

REFERENCES

Allan, B. (2004), *Project Management: Tools and Techniques for Today's ILS Professional* (London: Facet).
Allan, B. (2007), *Blended Learning* (London: Facet).
Roberts, S. and Rowley, J. (2004), *Managing Information Services* (London: Facet).

CHAPTER 9

TRAINING AND CONTINUING PROFESSIONAL DEVELOPMENT (RECRUITMENT, SELECTION AND INTERVIEWING, AND INDUCTION)

CAROL BROOKS

INTRODUCTION

This chapter aims to outline some of the needs of individuals and current good practice available within the library and information services (LIS) profession in the areas of recruitment and selection. These are skills which new managers need in order to form an effective basis of practice for years to come. However, they are also areas which need regular updating and up-skilling throughout a manager's career to ensure that best practice is always maintained. The skills are critical to the future of our profession – one poor selection can damage an organization and leave a service under-performing for years. In addition they are skills which are embedded in law and it is vital for all those involved to understand the legal requirements surrounding the subject.

BASIC RECRUITMENT AND SELECTION SKILLS

The fundamental boundaries of good recruitment and selection are set through national standards hosted by the Management Standards Centre. These are supported by, and meet the requirements of, the Chartered Institute of Personnel and Development (CIPD). All staff involved in the recruitment and selection process need to be properly trained.

A good training package on recruitment and selection will cover the following aspects:

- Job analysis
- Job descriptions
- Person specifications
- Marketing the post – attracting the right applicants, including advertising and the use of agencies
- Managing the applications and process

- Information to be provided to applicants
- Short-listing
- Interview questions
- Interview techniques
- Making the appointment – follow up processes including references
- Induction training

This chapter will cover each of these areas in more detail.

STARTING THE PROCESS

Recruitment procedures start considerably before the advertisement goes out and training needs to cover the entire process. In fact the process starts from the exit interview of the previous job holder. This will, however, differ from organization to organization. It may well be that first line managers are not heavily involved in the early process of discussing the needs, the job description and the person specification, but they should, as a minimum, understand the process which is undertaken to ensure that the post is still required and that all the necessary details about it are updated. There is a definite case to be made for all staff undertaking the selection process to be involved in the early elements of drafting or updating job descriptions and person specifications. With detailed knowledge of post requirements, those interviewing are much more aware of the real skills needed in the post-holder and able to make sound and valid judgements on suitability. In most workplaces, this element of knowledge building will be provided in-house, by personnel officers or local managers. It will be covered in principle within any effective recruitment and selection package provided through training agencies.

At this stage, you need to consider whether the process is being undertaken entirely internally, linked with a recruitment agency, or given over entirely to a recruitment agency. There are pros and cons to all options and only you can decide which is best for your organization or the post which is vacant.

APPLICATIONS AND SHORT-LISTING

Actual applications can vary widely. Some organizations will ask for a CV, whilst others will insist on the completion of an application form and a CV will not be acceptable. It is critical that advertisements are clear about these requirements and about what additional information is available for the candidate upon request. Do not underestimate the importance of the advertisement. This is the place in which you will not only market the post but your whole organization. The advertisement will give the first taste of the organization to the potential applicant; it can be the moment when they decide they do or do not want to work for you. Spend time to ensure that you are not only making clear what the role of the post is, but what you can offer successful candidates and what characteristics and skills you will need from them.

It is also important to have a policy on what additional information can be supplied to potential applicants – and if you do supply further information on request, are you supplying it to all applicants? Bear in mind how important it is to ensure that the information makes it clear to internal applicants that they must give full information and not assume your knowledge of them.

Ideally the team should set short-listing and interview dates prior to advertising so that they can be included in the advert. Not all organizations can manage this as the gap from sending an advert to a central team, such as a shared services centre or Human Resources section, and it appearing may be unpredictable, but where possible it is helpful to the applicant and it speeds up the entire process. Where dates are pre-set, organizations may choose not to offer flexibility for people unable to attend – however, this is worth careful consideration if you do not wish to exclude potentially excellent candidates.

The next line in the development of recruitment and selection tools are those which cover the processes involved in short-listing candidates. Often overlooked as a skill, this is an area which can make or break the effective selection of staff. The ability to critically read applications against the specification of requirements is too often skimmed over, at the risk of missing excellent candidates or misjudging prolific descriptions for real evidence of performance. Good short-listing procedures will include the scoring of applications against a clear structure such as that shown below:

Table 9.1 Sample scoring for shortlisting

Score	Evidence shown
0	No evidence or mention made
1	Assumption might be made from previous positions held but no mention is made
2	A statement is made without evidence: for example, 'I have undertaken daily banking procedures'
3	Work undertaken is described, with evidence of the impact of performance

Organizations differ in practice as to whether they score and how many people they will interview. Where a limit on interviews is set, usually 6–7 per post, scoring becomes more vital to ensure that the very best people are being seen.

In setting up the process for short-listing there are two main schools of thought. The first is that all 'essential' elements to a role are measured through the application process. This leads to long applications and needs some very lateral thinking to assist in providing the evidence. The other, and for me preferred, practice is to identify within the person specification which elements will be judged through the application form and which by other methods, such as questioning, tests or presentations. This allows the candidate to focus thoroughly on the main elements being tested at application stage, keeping the application shorter and more specific. For instance, if one essential criteria is presentation skills, you need to consider whether the skill can be thoroughly evidenced through words on paper or whether it would be better evidenced through the delivery of a presentation. Likewise, numeracy skills are hard to evidence in writing, but can be very effectively judged through a test or exercise incorporated into the interview process. Many a good candidate has failed to make it to an interview because they have found it hard to fully evidence a skill which is better judged through questioning or practice. Whichever method you opt for, the process of short-listing needs careful thinking through and training to ensure that the interviewing panel is well prepared for effective selection of interview candidates. Finally, as part of the short-listing process, consider whether you are prepared to offer feedback to unsuccessful applicants. If you are serious about helping people prepare for new roles, then offering feedback at this stage can be immensely valuable – it might take up some of your time but it might also help you get better applicants in the future and bring in some valuable new people to the profession.

INTERVIEW TECHNIQUES

You need to be aware that there are a number of techniques used in interviews, which can lead to severe limitations in the selection process:

- Stereotyping: assuming that particular characteristics are typical of members of a particular group, for example, race, sex, sexual orientation, religion, marital status, ex-offenders. Decisions made on such assumptions are illegal and all interviewers should be well briefed in the legalities of discrimination laws
- Self-fulfilling prophecy: asking questions which seek to confirm impressions of the candidate based on prior knowledge or information gained prior to or in early stages of the interview
- Contrasting: letting a previous experience of interviewing one candidate influence the way you see others
- Looking for someone similar to me: giving preference to candidates who seem to have a similar background, attitude or personality
- Personal liking: selecting candidates because of a personal feeling of liking or disliking them

- Using the 'good guy'/'bad guy' technique: where two interviewers take different approaches in questioning, which can lead to very unbalanced decision making and very confused responses from candidates

Interviews can be held in a number of different formats. Many private sector organizations and small businesses will focus on one-to-one interviewing. The obvious advantage of this is that it tends to be relatively relaxed; however, alone it is more difficult for the interviewer to be able to fully consider responses and much easier for personal bias to affect the outcome.

Using two interviewers gives a second opinion and different approaches, and allows the pair to identify follow-up needed to get more detail. However, it is more formal, often makes the candidate feel less at ease, and there is also the danger that there will be diametrically opposed views at the end. This danger exists in any panel using exact numbers of interviewers, so a decision-making process using a casting vote needs to be agreed, although the effective use of scoring each stage of the interview including questions can alleviate any such conflicts.

Many larger organizations, especially local government, traditionally use panels of three. In these situations the panel all need to be highly involved in the whole process and all fully part of it. I would also caution that questions be asked in batches by each interviewer so that the candidate can face one person at a time and does not go through the whole interview feeling like a 'nodding donkey', flipping backwards and forwards from one person to another.

Finally, in cases for which a large number of posts are available, it is possible to run a number of panels each interviewing different people. This approach has many inherent problems and needs an immense amount of organization and structure, and a tight scoring system, so that the best people from across the whole spectrum are selected. Some organizations will also include informal elements, such as tours and lunches, although since this is not formally structured, the opinions of people involved in this process should only be used with great caution, not least because people involved informally will not have assessed every applicant equally, or indeed have talked with each one. Applicants should always be advised of all aspects of the interview process against which they are being assessed. However, the use of informal elements including site visits can be immensely valuable to sell your organization to potential staff in a positive way – remember, the interview should be a two-way process which allows the candidate to decide if you are an organization they want to work with, as well as for you to decide if they are best for you.

Telephone interviewing can also be used as a screening tool to find a smaller number of people for face-to-face interviews or when it is not possible to undertake a face-to-face interview. The questions still need to be carefully structured and measured.

INTERVIEW QUESTIONS

An important part of the process is setting the interview questions. If you have opted to identify with the person specification as the method of assessing evidence then you will already have identified which areas you need to focus questions on. Setting questions effectively is critical if you want to get the best out of your candidates and if you want to be able to properly identify the best person for the job. It is easy to write a question without being clear about the response you may receive or indeed the response you are looking for. To each question you can identify key words or phrases, which you expect to hear in an appropriate answer. Having identified this will help you as a panel to be sure whether the candidate has really got to the point of the question. Whilst equity requires each candidate to be asked the range of questions, there are limitations in interviews being too highly structured, and you need to avoid the danger of failing to ask appropriate supplementary questions and ensure that the candidate feels at ease and does not feel as though there is only one answer. As necessary it is also acceptable to ask appropriate questions which reflect something from the application form, which the panel feel needs follow-up or amplification.

There are some obvious basics in setting questions:

- Avoid closed questions, which can be answered with a simple 'yes' or 'no'
- Use open questions starting with 'what', 'where', 'when', 'how', 'why', or which ask the candidate to illustrate a situation or experience they have been involved in
- Avoid questions which include the answer you are looking for
- Ask one question at a time – avoid asking multiple questions which will confuse the candidate

Although all questions will not fit into a category, there are a few different types of question styles from the chatty to the more formal, which are illustrated below:

- Examples of experience – a good opening question is to ask what experience the candidate has which makes them suitable for the role. This helps the candidate relax and refresh their experience in their own mind.
- Behavioural – focusing on past events will enable the candidate to demonstrate the abilities and behaviours relevant to the job. For instance, 'Tell us about a time when you had to make a particularly difficult decision' Bear in mind that these types of questions must match the criteria of the person specification and can link to any competencies which are matched against the role. Behavioural questions can also include elements about working style, such as 'What actions would you take to ensure that you are working effectively with team colleagues?'

- Hypothetical – asking how candidates would react or behave in specific circumstances or situations. For example, 'How would you deal with a customer who is unhappy about the levels of noise in the library from a children's activity?' Beware that this type of question can lead to the candidate giving the 'ideal' or 'expected' answer, rather than one which illustrates reality.

Be careful that questions are not repetitive and do not require very similar answers. The aim of the interview is to find out as much as you can about the suitability of the candidate for this post.

SETTING UP THE INTERVIEW

The actual setting up of interviews will be undertaken in different ways according to the structure of your organization. In some it will be done centrally and in some it will all be down to the interview panel. Whichever methodology is used, it is still essential that the candidate is clearly advised of some basic information:

- Location, including a map and information about transport and parking
- Date and time of interview
- Whether there is a test/exercise to be undertaken
- Whether there is a presentation to be made
- The likely length of the interview
- The names and post titles of the interview panel
- Documents required (for example, proof of qualifications, driving licence, passport, proof of right to work in the UK)
- Requirement for candidate to confirm their intention to attend
- Specific contact details so that the candidate can contact someone if they have any queries

Whether at this stage, or during the application process, candidates should be asked if they have any objections to references being taken up. Many people who work for small or highly competitive organizations fear being penalized if their employers are aware that they are seeking alternative employment and thus choose not to have their employers know unless they have been offered the post.

PREPARING THE PANEL FOR THE INTERVIEW

In addition to the setting of questions, which we have discussed earlier, the panel needs to have thought through a number of issues:

- Where are the interviews to be held – are you setting a table between you and the candidate, or are you using an informal layout of chairs? Think about the implications of non-verbal communication – are you wanting to imply a strict hierarchy or an environment where discussions are open and equal?
- Can you shut off telephone interruptions?
- Where will the candidates wait on arrival?
- Are you allowing sufficient time for the candidate to ask questions of the panel? Make sure one of the panel has sufficient knowledge about the job and organization to answer questions.
- How will you assess the information you gather at interview – do you have a scoring system; how will this match against other activities such as tests and exercises?
- Take brief notes during the interview; allow time to write more detailed notes immediately after, before you see the next candidate.
- When will you be making a decision? Inform the candidate of the process following the interview.
- Are all interviewers aware of the legal implications such as discrimination laws, the use of notes and the rights of candidates not appointed to see notes written about them in appeal or discrimination cases.

MAKING THE APPOINTMENT

After the choice is made, various processes need to be undertaken such as medical checks, Criminal Records Bureau checks and references. A variety of options exist for the taking up of references. In some organizations they are requested prior to the interview for all short-listed candidates, whilst in others, the process is only activated after a selection is made. Likewise, some organizations will ask for a general reference whilst others will ask specific questions linked to the job description, person specification and possibly the application.

As with the short-listing stage, the offer of feedback is an important tool in both supporting individuals and guiding them as to where they need to improve their skills or knowledge, and in helping us to develop good people for the profession. It can be hard to be honest but in terms of fairness and equity, it is a role we should all be prepared to undertake and we owe it to the individuals who have put their all into applying and preparing for an interview to support them. It is equally important to give feedback on the interview to successful candidates to assist their further development.

In the final appointment letter, various details need to be covered, such as:

- Start date, place, time and contact name

- Salary; when and how it will be paid
- Conditions of service including pension, annual leave arrangements and allowances
- Working hours
- Induction arrangements
- Any documents you require such as P45 or P60
- Options for a pre-start visit

A checklist covering the stages of the recruitment and selection process covered above can be found in Appendix 1 at the end of this chapter. This gives the reader a ready-made aid to be used to support them.

TRAINING RESOURCES

Most organizations have their own training programmes for the recruitment and selection process; however, if you need a training course, 'About Recruitment and Selection Skills' is available through CIPD, as are other advanced training courses for specific recruitment problems, such as 'About Effective Recruitment, Selection and Retention – Building an Effective Team'. There are also various resources available for e-learning through the Internet such as the Open University's Open Learn LearningSpace[1] and the free access Nottingham University Staff and Educational Development Unit[2] packages.

Should you be in the position of needing to train others in the recruitment and selection process, there is a useful toolkit available through Trainer Active[3] from which you can purchase downloadable activities and exercises as well as information about the process.

INDUCTION TRAINING

It is impossible to overestimate the importance of good induction. The point at which an employee joins an organization is described by many management gurus as a 'golden moment' where opportunities exist to guide a new employee into the organization in the way you want to. If you neglect it, others will offer their own, perhaps less helpful, form of induction! No new member of staff, no matter how skilled, can slot into a new organization, or even a new department or role,

---

1   Open University's Open Learn LearningSpace. <http://openlearn.open.ac.uk>.
2   Nottingham University Staff and Educational Development Unit. <http://www.nottingham.ac.uk/sedu/recruitment>.
3   Trainer Active. <http://www.fenman.co.uk/traineractive>.

and become fully effective without receiving adequate briefing and introduction to appropriate people, policies and procedures.

Induction starts, of course, before the person walks through the door on the first day. It starts when the last post-holder leaves when, with the information gained from their exit interview or other means, you will have assessed or reassessed what the post entails and what skills you are looking for.

As they start, employees will need information about the team and site they will be working in. All employees need to have an understanding of the organization's aims and the team's tasks, and how their job fits into the overall picture. This will obviously need to be tailored to each individual role. Induction programmes must be reviewed for each new post-holder – using a standard programme without reviewing it and tailoring it to the individual's needs is poor management and setting up yourself and the individual concerned for failure. The secret to good induction is taking the time to plan and supervise – even if that means other work needs to be put aside for a while. Induction also includes a handover of work from the previous post-holder. You need to identify the best method for this – by that person, if available, by other colleagues or by the line manager.

It is equally important that employees moving between departments and teams, or returning after a secondment or extensive break, get an appropriate re-induction. If it is not offered, it may be even harder for people in these situations to make their needs known as it may be assumed that they know what they are doing. These are excellent opportunities to reinforce the aims of the organization and the expectations you have of them, especially since in the current world of work things change very quickly and a great deal can develop even in the few months of maternity leave.

Induction training needs to be structured to take into account both the needs of the organization and the individual. At the start you need to be clear how quickly and how much you need the new employee to be able to undertake. For instance, in the case of a library assistant, you might like to think through how soon they need to be able to answer most normal enquiries and cope if they are the only permanent member of staff on duty. Once you have worked this out, you can plan exactly what they need to know and how you can programme it in. If the organization has competencies linked to posts, then these also need to be included and measured within the induction process. You also need to be sure to build in very thorough reviews to check how they are getting on and what gaps have been identified, so that the plan can be adapted. No training plan should ever be set in concrete – you will always need flexibility if you are going to ensure that new staff members gain all the knowledge and experience they need. Reviews apply for all levels of staff – be sure you know what you are reviewing:

- Knowledge – specific to role, organization and of policies
- Skills
- Attitudes
- Understanding of vision, priorities

Effective probation periods are reliant on good reviewing, remedial training programmes and good planning. Poor induction programmes and reviewing processes lead to poor performance of both individuals and organizations and ultimately to low morale and weak teams. You can make the difference by spending time and effort in ensuring that all new staff into your team are properly inducted and supported.

Quality induction programmes can also be linked to qualifications such as the National Open College Network (NOCN) or City and Guilds certificates, further details of which can be discovered in Chapter 12.

Qualifications available:

- City and Guilds NVQ level 2 Information & Library Services. Scheme Number 7372
- City and Guilds NVQ level 3 Information & Library Services. Scheme Number 7372
- City and Guilds Information and Library Services Progression Award. Scheme Number 7371

To find your nearest provider, please contact The City and Guilds of London Institute[4] directly, quoting the Scheme Number.

- NOCN Level 1 Award in Information, Advice and Guidance Awareness 100/3587/4 PS3FAQ0004
- NOCN Intermediate Award in Developing Information, Advice and Guidance Skills 100/2451/7 PS3IAQ0002
- NOCN Advanced Certificate in Information, Advice and Guidance 100/2406/2 PS3ACQ0001

For more details, contact the National Open College Network[5]. Warwickshire libraries sucessfully link their training to the OCN programmes using 29 accredited learning units which can be delivered at level 2 or level 3 (see <http://www.warwickshire.gov.uk/web/corporate/pages.nsf/(DisplayLinks)/A0D6F8C7D5DA19E780257124002DFE9D>).

---

4   The City and Guilds of London Institute. <http://www.city-and-guilds.co.uk>.
5   National Open College Network. <http://www.nocn.org.uk>.

This linking to qualifications benefits both the staff and the organization in setting and raising standards and opening up a career structure for individuals alongside a sense of achievement in gaining a qualification. The time and effort taken in offering such a structure can only improve the service delivery, and at the end of the day, all training in LIS is about our customers and effective service delivery.

FURTHER READING

Billsberry, J. (2007), *Experiencing Recruitment and Selection* (London: Wiley and Sons).

Roberts, G. (2005), *Recruitment and Selection* (London: CIPD).

Taylor, D. and Fox, G. (2000), *The Complete Recruitment and Selection Toolkit* (London: CIPD).

APPENDIX 1: RECRUITMENT AND SELECTION CHECKLIST

Below is a sample checklist, which you can adapt to ensure all the necessary elements of recruitment are covered:

Task	By whom	By when
Exit interview of previous post-holder		
Select and brief interview panel		
Review need for post		
Review job description		
Review person specification		
Check against competencies		
Check grading		
Decide whether to use recruitment agency		
Consider most appropriate place to advertise		
Draft advertisement to ensure post is attractive to the right people		
Produce all support material to go out to applicants		
Decide on interview process – questions, tests, presentations, site visits, and so on		
Set dates for advertisement, short-listing and interviews		
Receive applications		
Shortlist		
Advise applicants		
If required, send for references		
Re-read applications of interviewees, check interview questions and review if specifics are needed for individuals		
Plan room layout and ensure support is available from other staff		
Interview		
Advise successful candidate pending personnel checks		

Task	By whom	By when
Advise unsuccessful candidates – offer feedback		
Undertake personnel checks as appropriate		
Send out final confirmation of appointment and agree start date		
Plan induction programme including reviews		
Carefully plan welcome and first day		
Undertake reviews and probationary checks		

CHAPTER 10

STRATEGIC DEVELOPMENT

SHEILA CORRALL

INTRODUCTION

This chapter covers the education, training and development of library and information workers in relation to the area of work commonly described as strategic management. This term is generally preferred to the narrower traditional label of strategic planning, as it helps to convey the need for a holistic view of the strategy process which encompasses implementation and evaluation, in addition to the development of a plan. It is also consistent with the view that the process of planning and strategy making can take place without the production of a document labelled in this way. The concept of strategic thinking underpins this whole area of activity and the construct of strategic change is typically its desired outcome.

The title 'Strategic Development' has been chosen as it usefully separates these important concepts from the formal management hierarchy and flags up the desirability of engaging staff at every level and in all parts of the organization in the strategy process. Many students of library and information science need to be persuaded that topics such as strategic planning and managing change are relevant to the sorts of jobs and roles they envisage in their early careers. Some heads of library and information services also seem reluctant to acknowledge that all members of their workforce can be strategists in their own spheres of operation. Everyone should be involved to some extent in continuously reviewing the current profile and performance of the organization and thinking about its future development and design. Strategies will only work if those charged with implementation at an operational level are committed to them, and the best way of achieving this is to encourage their contribution to the process. There is plenty of evidence from both the library domain and other sectors that service organizations adopting this participative style have experienced significant benefits.

This chapter begins by defining and scoping the subject in general terms, before identifying its key elements and the topics around which the rest of the discussion is structured. Additional contextualization is provided by a short summary of development needs in strategic management identified by academics and practitioners, followed by a brief review of the main methods of development available. The chapter then takes a thematic approach to the subject, dealing with each identified topic in turn, defining the area, explaining its significance and suggesting methods of development, illustrated by examples from practice as available. The discussion draws on related published literature throughout and is complemented by appendices containing additional examples and an annotated list of publications recommended as learning resources.

DEFINITION AND SCOPE

The terminology of the strategy arena can be daunting and confusing as a result of the multiplicity of terms and the different interpretations and nuances given to them as thinking and practice have advanced and shifted over time. For example, strategic planning was defined by Drucker more than 30 years ago as a 'continuous process of making present entrepreneurial (risk-taking) decisions systematically and with the greatest knowledge of their futurity; organizing systematically the efforts needed to carry out these decisions; and measuring the results of these decisions against the expectations through organized feedback' (Drucker 1973).

However, today many commentators favour a narrower interpretation of strategic planning, concentrated on the planning which translates the strategy developed by strategic thinking into a plan that can be implemented. They regard other aspects, such as organizing efforts and measuring results, as part of strategic management, as shown by this definition from a leading contemporary textbook: 'Strategic management includes understanding *the strategic position* of an organisation, making *strategic choices* for the future and managing *strategy in action*' (Johnson, Scholes and Whittington 2008).

The term 'strategy' is also problematic as it can be used to cover what an organization wants to do, where it wishes to go, and how it intends to get there. Chandler's widely cited definition from his classic text combines these dimensions as follows: '... the determination of the basic long-term goals and objectives of an enterprise, and the adoption of courses of action and the allocation of resources necessary for carrying out those goals' (Chandler 1962).

The leading contemporary textbook takes a similarly broad view, but puts more emphasis on the environmental context, stakeholder demands and organizational competencies, reflecting present-day concerns: 'Strategy is the *direction* and *scope* of an organisation over the *long term*, which achieves *advantage* in a changing *environment* through its configuration of *resources and competences* with the aim of fulfilling *stakeholder* expectations' (Johnson, Scholes and Whittington 2008). The highlighted words indicate issues typically associated with strategic decisions.

Some writers equate the 'what' and 'how' components with strategy and tactics respectively, but such distinctions overlook an important point, that there are different levels of strategy to consider. Strategy can exist at several levels, from the individual to the organization and beyond. Johnson, Scholes and Whittington identify three levels of strategy: corporate-level, business-level and operational (Johnson, Scholes and Whittington 2008). De Wit and Meyer identify four levels: functional, business, corporate and network (De Wit and Meyer 2005). White introduces the notion of a community strategy as an alternative to a network strategy and adds two further levels: an industry strategy and a country (that is, national) strategy (White 2004). The multi-level nature of strategy is particularly relevant to library and information services where library strategy generally needs to be related to the strategy of a parent organization (corporate-level strategy) and often also to those of partner organizations (network-level strategies) and government (national-level strategies). Similarly, there may be several levels of strategy within or associated with a library or information service organization, for example, a library human resources strategy, a collection development strategy or an information literacy strategy.

Another key point to note is that strategies are not necessarily articulated in a plan or even captured in a document. Mintzberg and Waters helpfully define strategy as 'a pattern in a stream of decisions' and then usefully distinguish both between intended and realized strategies, and between deliberate and emergent strategies (Mintzberg and Waters 1985). Figure 10.1 displays the relationships between these concepts.

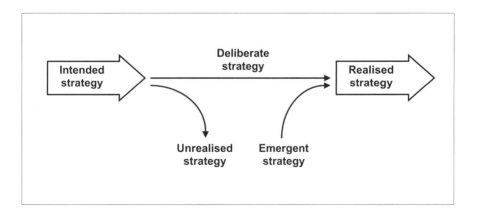

Figure 10.1 Types of strategies

Despite differences in terminology and presentation, there is more consensus on what strategic planning and management cover. In general terms, strategy making is about having a vision, knowing your resources, understanding the business arena and asking the right questions. It is basically about shaping the future for an organization (or other entity) and many writers stress that developing strategy is essentially concerned with asking a series of questions about the future of an organization and its products or services, including questions about the environment in which it operates and the resources available to it. Strategic management can thus be conceptualized as a set of fundamental questions:

- Why are we here? What business are we in? (purpose/mission)
- Where are we now? How did we get here (situation audit)
- What factors will impact our future? (environmental appraisal)
- What do we want to be? Where do we want to go? (vision and goals)
- How can we get there? What are the implications? (strategic options)
- What needs to be done? Who will do it? When? (action plans)
- How will we track progress and measure success? (performance indicators)

Commentators also stress the need to bring a range of perspectives to such questions, which is most effectively done by engaging a large number of people in the process, including staff who would not generally see themselves as strategists. Staff in 'boundary-spanning roles' who interact with customers, suppliers and technologies have the potential to make a significant strategic contribution (Floyd and Wooldridge 1994). Similarly, people with a youthful perspective, new to the organization or working at its geographical periphery (for example, in outlying branches) can inject fresh, even revolutionary, thinking (Hamel 1996). The notion of 'planning as learning' (De Geus 1988) is well established, and adopting the diagonal-slice approach of involving staff from all parts of the organization and different levels of the management hierarchy can have benefits beyond the development of strategy to its implementation and ongoing enactment, as observed by White:

> *Strategy making is simultaneously a learning process and a learned skill. If done well, it promotes learning in every significant area of organizational activity. Where strategy is regarded as important, it assists the staff of the organization to confront positively a series of changing problems, both external and internal* (White 2004).

Although White argues that 'strategy is best made by everyone in a process which is integrated into all the core activities of the organization', he recognizes that while it is desirable for all staff to engage in strategic thinking, the level of involvement in strategic planning will vary according to their roles.

The nature of the questions set out above in turn suggest that strategic development requires engagement in four key types of activity, which should be seen as interdependent elements of the strategy process, rather than sequential steps:

- Environmental appraisal – researching and analysing external forces, and auditing the internal situation, using tools such as STEP analysis, stakeholder mapping, competitive benchmarking, SWOT analysis and scenario development
- Strategic focus – discussing the scope, purpose, functions and principles of the organization and taking decisions about high-level objectives, future aspirations and goals, using tools such as critical success factors or key result areas
- Strategy development – evaluating alternative options, considering supporting strategies, specifying performance indicators and developing action plans, using tools such as portfolio matrices, cost–benefit analysis and the 7S framework
- Programme management – implementing the development/change strategy, typically via a portfolio of projects, and evaluating progress against targets, using tools such as GANTT charts, responsibility matrices, milestone plans and scorecards.

In common with other areas of management, effective strategic performance requires a mix of conceptual, interpersonal and technical abilities. The technical aspect is represented by the many analytical tools that have been produced to support the strategy development process, but which also have an acknowledged role in developing strategic capabilities and therefore merit special consideration here. The conceptual understanding needed includes areas already indicated, such as change management and performance evaluation, but also extends to two key aspects of organizations frequently affected by strategy, which often form a central component of strategic development, namely organizational structure and organizational culture. Interpersonal competences are necessary to complement other abilities, but are particularly important in engaging staff and other stakeholders in strategy development and implementation. Johnson, Scholes and Whittington (2008) point out that the strategist is typically not only making strategy, but also helping others to develop their own capabilities in strategy, and so needs to be able to communicate clearly to various audiences and to work well with teams, in addition to possessing strategic thinking and analytical skills. White lists seven characteristics of a good strategist as follows:

- the desire to identify and describe alternative directions for the future development of the enterprise and to take new approaches, all consistent with likely scenarios of the future which are relevant to the organization

- an entrepreneurial vision embracing action which creates competitive advantage and articulates at least part, if not the whole, of the strategic intent and tries to realize it
- a willingness to consider the long-term interests of all stakeholders, not just shareholders
- an ability to provide the kind of leadership which empowers all employees to act freely without hindrance within their own domains but coherently within the framework of a generally accepted strategy
- the drive to build an organization designed and structured in a way that fits the vision and which makes full use of the existing corporate identity and corporate culture
- the ability to integrate strategy with corporate identity and corporate culture
- the ability to ride luck, that is, to recognize and take unexpected opportunities and avoid unexpected threats (White 2004).

DEVELOPMENT NEEDS AND METHODS

A series of skills foresight and related studies conducted with employers by the Information Services National Training Organisation during 2000 to 2003 identified a striking need for more highly developed 'strategic skills' among information professionals, including skills in managing change, and significantly also for a shift in mindset from the service focus of a support function to that of a strategic player and equal partner in the organization (Corrall 2005). Other UK research confirms this picture: 'strategic management' emerged among the most wanted capabilities from an analysis of more than 150 job advertisements from different sectors, and many person specifications listed 'strategic thinking' among the essential criteria (Fisher, Hallam and Partridge 2005). This echoes the need identified in Australia for 'strategic thinkers, people who see and understand the big picture and the environment within which their library operates' (reported by Missingham 2006).

It is also interesting to note that the need for strategic competency is increasingly mentioned in relation to other technical and professional abilities. Thorhauge discusses the challenge of IT upskilling for an ageing public library workforce in Denmark and identifies a requirement for staff to handle strategic development, including cultural change (Thorhauge 2004). Similarly, in the context of information literacy development, Peacock identifies strategic (interpersonal and organizational) competencies among those needed for staff to move from 'librarians who teach' to educators and learning facilitators (Peacock 2001), while Booth and Fabian (2002, 139) advocate a 'strategic, forward-looking, entrepreneurial approach' and Doskatsch emphasizes the need for practitioners to 'think and act strategically' (Doskatsch 2003).

Explicit descriptions of strategic competencies are surprisingly rare in the strategy literature and most library-related discussions do not move beyond rather general comments on strategic skills, or slightly more specific references to strategic thinking. Further guidance on what the phrase 'strategic skills' could include can be found in the syllabus for the Executive Diploma in Strategic Management offered by the Chartered Management Institute, which lists a total of 36 skills needed by practitioners (Chartered Management Institute 2005). Twelve skills are common to all three of the required study units, as shown in Figure 10.2.

Analysing	Thinking systematically	Information management
Benchmarking	Thinking strategically	Presenting information
Evaluating	Decision making	Communicating
Reviewing	Risk management	Networking

Figure 10.2 Key strategic skills

The term 'strategic thinking' is often simply interpreted to mean all thinking about strategy, but is also used more specifically to differentiate the synthesizing, creative processes of strategy making which complement the analytical, information-based processes of strategic planning. A widely cited article by Liedtka defines five characteristics of strategic thinking, which can be summarized thus:

- *a systems perspective* – understanding internal and external contexts and linkages;
- *intent-focused* – providing energy and direction for activities;
- *intelligent opportunism* – being continuously open to alternative strategies;
- *thinking in time* – relating the future to the present and past;
- *hypothesis-driven* – generating 'what if' questions and testing them (Liedtka 1998).

Bonn offers a simpler definition of strategic thinking, which is consistent with the above, identifying three main elements at the individual level: a holistic understanding of the organization and its environment; creativity; and a vision for the future. In addition, she specifies two requirements at the organizational level: fostering ongoing strategic dialogue among the top team, and taking advantage of the ingenuity and creativity of every employee (Bonn 2001). Liedtka also argues for planning to be seen as a developmental dialogue or inquiry and a democratic process, which also requires questioning and listening skills. In addition, she points out that the frameworks, concepts and techniques typically used to manage the strategic issues agenda can simultaneously help to develop the different strategic thinking capabilities (Liedtka 1998).

Professional Education

Within the UK, the official subject benchmark statement for educational programmes in librarianship and information management specifies the following areas of understanding in the section on management and organizational behaviour:

- Understanding of the organizational context of service operations, including the significance of organizational mission, strategy, systems, structures and cultures.
- Understanding of the concepts, principles and techniques of strategic management and their application in directing and leading service organizations (Quality Assurance Agency 2007).

As there are 35 specific areas of subject and generic knowledge, understanding and skills listed in the statement, most programmes can probably devote no more than a few teaching sessions specifically to these topics, although aspects of strategic management are likely to feature in discussions related to other parts of the curriculum, for example, sessions covering the design, development and delivery of library and information services in different sectors.

At the University of Sheffield, the module on Management for Library and Information Services includes a set of four two-hour sessions, supported by guided reading and tailored handouts, which aim to help students think and act strategically and to prepare them for strategic engagement in the workplace. These sessions focus respectively on: Organizational Structure and Culture, Strategic Planning and Management, Managing Change and Project Management. In each case they provide an overview of the topic, including the key concepts and terminology; an introduction to models and tools relevant to library and information services; examples of best practice and successful applications in the sector; and opportunities to use selected techniques in practical exercises. However, unless students choose to do extensive reading, assessed coursework and/or a dissertation in this area, they graduate with only a rudimentary understanding of the areas specified, which it is assumed will be enhanced by workplace learning and continuing professional development.

Workplace Learning

As suggested earlier, strategic management abilities can be developed through direct involvement in strategic planning and related activities in the workplace, by learning 'on the job' (that is, learning by doing), which generally includes participation in workshops or 'awaydays' that combine practical work on strategy-related tasks with expert guidance on the use of tools and techniques and instruction in their application. Such events can be led or facilitated by in-house experts or external consultants from the library or organization development domains. Many public, academic and special libraries report the successful employment of consultants to guide the planning process and assist with strategy tasks, but often also comment on the developmental aspects of the experience and the educational benefits for staff (Dougherty 2002; Higa-Moore et al. 2002; Kuntz et al. 2003). Appendix 1 provides sample outlines of strategic development workshops designed by the author for an academic library.

Library managers may also turn to published literature for guidance and inspiration, consulting general management and/or library-specific textbooks and case studies for planning models and lessons learned. Bryson's model for non-profit organizations (Bryson 2004) is popular with academic libraries (McClamroch, Byrd and Sowell 2001; Ladwig 2005), while Kaplan and Norton's balanced scorecard and strategy maps (Kaplan and Norton 1992; 2004) have been adopted in both university and industrial information and knowledge services (Pienaar and Penzhorn 2000; Jacobson and Sparks 2001). Textbooks, manuals, case studies and classic articles by leading thinkers in the field all offer valuable guidance on the conceptual, procedural and technical aspects of the subject and can be used to complement and inform practical work, and also to substitute for expert input where a self-managed process is the preferred option (McClamroch, Byrd and Sowell 2001). Additional resources at the end of this chapter provides a selected sample of materials suitable for independent study or as background reading prior to a training event or development workshop.

The need for strategists to understand their operating environment has already been mentioned: professional literature, research reports, official publications and social commentary should also be included among the sources of information regularly scanned by practitioners aiming to bring a strategic perspective to their work. Professional networks, e-mail discussion lists, current awareness services, news feeds and blogs can all help people to track developments and spot trends in the field; for example, the Information Literacy Weblog (Webber and Boon 2003–present) is an excellent authoritative source of news and reports of information literacy developments around the world, and Open Access News (Suber 2002–present) performs a similar function for the open access movement in scholarly communication.

Short Courses

Both professional organizations and specialist training providers have recognized the need to develop strategic capability in the library and information profession. One-day courses on different aspects of strategic management are available, including generic and sector-specific offerings, pitched at various levels. Figure

10.3 outlines the content of an advanced-level course with a particular focus on the use of strategy development tools, while Figures 10.4, 10.5 and 10.6 show details of courses aimed at senior/middle managers in workplace, school and academic libraries respectively. Figure 10.7 outlines a course covering the technical and interpersonal aspects of identifying and managing stakeholders.

Such courses typically use an interactive style combining short presentations with group activities and often provide opportunities for participants to work on their own strategic agenda. They offer a useful means of gaining an overview and introduction to the subject quickly, but require commitment from individual participants to follow through and act on the learning gained. Many course providers are willing to deliver similar on-site events for individual organizations, which can often be more cost-effective and have added benefits from team learning and group work on shared agenda.

**Breakthrough Thinking and Communications in
Knowledge and Information Strategy**

Introduction:

This advanced one day course is designed for information and knowledge managers who want to make an impact at the highest levels in their organisation. The course will provide delegates with an advanced information and knowledge strategy toolbox that will enable them to design and plan radical effective programmes. These tools are transferable outside the information and knowledge domain and will allow delegates to participate in the wider strategic debate in their organisations.

Outcomes:
- an understanding of the principles of knowledge and information strategy development
- an ability to use six advanced strategy development tools
- membership of a community of practice of information and knowledge managers
- an understanding of business strategy development
- electronic copy of the information and knowledge strategy toolbox

Programme:
- the role of information and knowledge services in organisational strategy
- advanced techniques for verbal and non-verbal communication
- scenario planning tools
- knowledge strategy analysis
- building the knowledge value matrix
- exploring the business technology matrix
- strategic skills analysis tools

Speaker: Adrian Dale, Senior Advisor, TFPL

Teaching style: course/presentations/group work

Level: 3

Who should attend?

This programme is designed for information and knowledge centre managers who are ready to make a big impact in their organisations. An open mind and a willingness to accept radical change are essential.

Course fee:

£495.00 + VAT (£581.63) includes buffet lunch and refreshments and an electronic version of the toolbox.

| 04 Mar 08, London | 27 Nov 08, London |

Figure 10.3 Example of an advanced-level course on knowledge strategy

Source: TFPL Training and Learning. <http://www.tfpl.com/skills_development/training_learning.cfm>.

**Strategic Planning and Thinking for
Workplace Library and Information Staff**
24 September 2008, London

It is often much easier to attend to operational tasks, meeting short term goals than trying to think and plan strategically, setting long term goals, especially if you are a solo worker. This one-day course will provide you with appropriate tools and techniques to help you set a direction and to think and work more strategically.

Benefits of attending:
The day will outline how to create a strategic plan for your service and how to execute this plan, including overcoming barriers. It focuses on how to work more efficiently and productively as an individual and within a team.

By the end of the event participants will have:
- identified their work values
- gained an understanding of how these need to inform decisions and strategic planning
- created a vision and mission for their service
- set result-driven and purposeful goals to achieve their vision and mission
- discovered a strategic time management model
- overcome barriers to delegation

Who should attend?
Middle to senior managers who are solo workers and those who are deputising or leading a team.

Special notes: participants are asked to bring work objectives/goals and their work diaries.

Programme:
- Course outcomes and objectives
- Laying the foundations for your strategy
- Understanding your work values and how these can be used to inform decisions and strategy
- Visioning your strategy
- Creating a vision of where you want your service to be in the short, medium and long-term
- Creating a mission which encapsulates your vision
- Executing your strategy
- Result-driven and purposeful planning
- Overcoming barriers to delegation
- Managing time strategically
- Putting your strategy into action

Places are limited to: 20
9.15 Registration & coffee – 12.45 Lunch – 5.00 Close

Course leader: Candy Janetta

Fees:
CILIP personal members: £220 plus VAT **£258.50**
CILIP organisation members: £265 plus VAT **£311.38**
Non members: £310 plus VAT **£364.25**

Figure 10.4 Example of a course on strategic planning for workplace libraries
Source: CILIP Training and Development. <http://www.cilip.org.uk/training/training>.

School Library Policy-making and Planning
6 May 2008, London

'CILIP recommends that the school should have a library policy and a development plan that reflects the needs of the school, its students and its teachers.'

Good school library policies and plans are set within the context of whole school aims. They articulate the role, aims and objectives of the library and are important means to achieving them.

Many school librarians and library coordinators are unsure about suitable components for practical and realistic policy and planning documents, and need guidance on how to construct and implement them.

Benefits of attending:
This new course will explore the role and value of policy making and development planning for the school library and will identify the constituents of effective policies and plans. Participants will have the opportunity to start to devise policies and plans appropriate for their own libraries.

The course is suitable for staff working in both the primary and secondary sectors.

By the end of the event participants will have:
- increased their understanding of the importance of a school library policy and plan
- identified the areas a policy and plan should cover
- begun to formulate a library policy and development plan
- explored ideas for linking library policy to other school policies
- discussed the library self-evaluation toolkit and strategies for exploiting it
- considered monitoring and evaluation
- developed more confidence in managing and developing the school library.

Who should attend?
School librarians and library coordinators and others with responsibility for the school library in the primary or secondary sector in state or independent schools.

Programme:
- The role of library policy and plans
- Library policy-making
- Development planning
- Putting policy into practice

Places are limited to: 16
9.15 Registration & coffee – 12.45 Lunch – 4.30 Close

Course Leader: Anne Harding

Fees:
CILIP personal members: £200 plus VAT **£235**
CILIP organisation members: £235 plus VAT **£276.13**
Non members: £275 plus VAT **£323.13**

Figure 10.5 Example of a course on strategic planning for school libraries
Source: CILIP Training and Development. <http://www.cilip.org.uk/training/training>.

Planning & Managing Services
Middle Management Theme

19/05/2006
10:00–16:30

Tutor: Sheila Corrall

Aim:
To provide an opportunity for middle managers who aspire to senior management to share experience, exchange ideas and explore approaches to strategy and planning.

Outline:
Short inputs from the workshop leader on
- Trends and developments in corporate strategy
- Tools and techniques for strategic planning

Group work on practical activities such as
- Identifying environmental forces and change drivers
- Articulating strategic issues facing academic libraries
- Relating library strategies to institutional strategies
- Involving stakeholders in planning and implementation
- Presenting and communicating academic library strategies

Who should attend?
This course is part of the NoWAL Middle Management Theme. The NoWAL middle management theme is aimed at staff working within library and information services at middle/intermediate management level and above.

Figure 10.6 Example of a course on strategic planning for middle managers
Source: NoWAL – The North West Academic Libraries. <http://www.nowal.ac.uk/middle_management.php>.

Influencing Stakeholders and Personal Impact

Introduction:
Knowledge and information professionals are working with an ever diverse range of stakeholders and have daily opportunities to either make positive, negative or unintended impacts. It is important for these professionals to plan an approach for working with, and influencing stakeholders, and to be able to communicate the benefits of knowledge and information management activities with impact

This workshop will offer a number of techniques and approaches to help delegates segment, manage and influence stakeholders. Delegates will also have the opportunity to consider the ways in which they impact on others and the personal brand they communicate.

Outcomes:
- be able to map and segment key stakeholders
- understand stakeholder influencing strategies
- know how to communicate the benefits of knowledge and information management activities
- learn about the ways we impact on others
- understand interpersonal (verbal and non-verbal) communication
- know how to create a personal brand

Programme
Topics covered include:
- stakeholder mapping
- influencing strategies
- how we see ourselves and how others see us
- positive, negative or unintended impacts
- verbal and non-verbal communication
- communication channels

Speaker: Ian Wooler, Senior Associate, TFPL

Teaching style: Workshop/presentations/group work

Level: 2

Who should attend?
This workshop is for those delegates who wish to communicate the benefits of knowledge and information management to stakeholders and influence them through strategies and personal impact.

Course fee:
£395 + VAT (**£464.13**) including refreshments and a buffet lunch

27 Feb 08, London   22 Oct 08, London

Figure 10.7 Example of a course on influencing stakeholders
Source: TFPL Training and Learning. <http://www.tfpl.com/skills_development/training_learning.cfm>.

Extended Programmes

There are several alternative options available to practitioners wanting a deeper learning experience than can be gained from a one-day event, ranging from two-day events or three-day residential programmes to e-learning and credit-bearing courses, including general management degrees, such as the Master of Business Administration (MBA) and related qualifications. Most offerings here are not library-specific, but professionals who have followed this path generally argue that the loss of professional context is more than compensated for by the broader perspectives gained from interacting with managers from different backgrounds. However, the fees for such courses are frequently much higher than those aimed at the library market. Figure 10.8 gives details of a two-day generic course on strategic thinking and business planning, while Figures 10.9 and 10.10 provide examples of short residential programmes offering more intensive development experiences, which link strategy and change with political agenda and cultural issues, in the second example through the use of action learning sets.

Strategic Thinking and Business Planning – 2 Days

This wide-ranging programme provides an opportunity for participants to develop their understanding of the concepts of strategic management and review the strategic direction of their organisations/departments. It also places particular emphasis on planning and provides practical guidance on how to draw up (and monitor) business plans so that strategic goals can be turned into practical achievement.

Course membership:
All Managers and professionals who need to adopt a 'strategic mindset' and particularly those who have to draw up and implement business plans for their departments and sections.

Course objectives
By the end of the course participants will:
- appreciate what 'strategy' means especially in today's turbulent environment
- have explored the 'strategic tool-kit' of models and processes and learnt how to apply them to their own organisational context
- be able to analyse and respond to the forces of change working on, and within, their organisations
- be able to draft practical and realistic business plans
- be able to assess the difficulties of implementation and identify means of overcoming them

Course outline
Topics covered include:
- strategy – definition and terms
- the full strategic planning process
- preparing a business plan
- environmental and industry analysis – PESTLE
- competitor analysis
- SWOT and capability analysis
- competitive advantage
- implementation issues
- strategic management of change

Course methods:
This is an exciting and practical course. It makes extensive use of case studies giving participants the opportunity to learn from the successes and failures of other organisations and from examples of good and bad practice. An opportunity is also given for participants to work on drafting their business plans.

Course Leader: Jean Pousson

Maximum number of participants: 12

10–11 Mar 2008, Regus Monument, 68 King William St., London EC4N 7DZ
8–9 Jul 2008, Regus Monument, 68 King William St., London EC4N 7DZ

Fee: £885 + VAT

This course is also available on an in-company basis – date and location to meet your convenience.

Figure 10.8 Example of a two-day generic course on strategic planning
Source: Chartered Management Institute. <http://www.managers.org.uk>.

Delivering Strategy and Change

Understanding the role of the manager in delivering strategy and implementing change

In a fast-paced modern organisation, managers need to play an enhanced central role in delivering business success. In addition to planning, monitoring what happens and responding to difficulties, managers are increasingly expected to help top management by modifying strategies to fit changing conditions, by adapting central initiatives to meet local requirements and by feeding back up the line their own perspectives on strategy.

This programme focuses on this enhanced management role and will enable participants to explore the link they provide between strategy and operations and the organisation's internal and external world.

Participant profile:
You are an experienced manager seeking to enhance your role and add further value to the organisation by understanding and participating more fully in strategic and change initiatives.

Benefits:
- Improved understanding of your organisation's strategy, the operating reality and top management's perspective
- Greater ability to engage in, and contribute to, strategic discussions from your position in the organisation
- Better equipped to engage more in the entire change process in addition to the implementation of strategy
- Able to demonstrate a degree of political acumen and understand its key role in ensuring success
- Increase your effectiveness and confidence in your central role as the link between strategy and operations

Programme content:
- Understanding the language of strategy and change and its use in your organisation
- Explore strategic and change management models and compare with your own organisation's approach
- Explore examples of specific strategic choices and consider their implications for change in organisations, including your own
- Enhance your role as a manager in understanding the need for change, preparing for it, stimulating and managing the process
- Developing further your political and interpersonal skills

Programme Director:
David Cleeton-Watkins MSc, BSc, FCIPD

Fees for 2008:
£2200 + VAT inclusive all tuition fees, materials, meals and accommodation

Dates for 2008:
7–9 May 2008
10–12 September 2008

Figure 10.9 Example of a residential generic course on strategic development
Source: Roffey Park Institute. <http://www.roffeypark.com/>.

Strategic Leadership

Developing ways to turn strategy into reality

There is a marked difference between thinking and acting operationally and thinking and acting strategically. Moving from the former to the latter can be a complex and isolating experience.

This innovative programme develops strategic leadership skills in a confidential, privileged environment. It strengthens participants' ability to lead by pooling their expertise with that of their peers. Each participant benefits from the group's on-going feedback and support over the problematic issues facing them and their organisations.

Participant profile:
You are a director, senior manager or strategic leader looking to develop your leadership skills with a group of like-minded peers. You want a more in-depth understanding of strategy and leadership as well as ideas about how to move your division or organisation forward.

Benefits:
- Increased awareness of your impact as a strategic leader and the opportunity to identify what leadership means for you and your organisation
- Enhanced ability to lead with purpose and be better able to turn strategy into reality
- Access to a range of strategic frameworks that can benefit your organisation
- Ongoing support and challenge in peer learning sets

Programme content:
- Contrasting approaches to strategy
- Strategic dilemmas and current thinking
- Influencing strategy
- Linking strategic direction with corporate culture and people management
- Leading change and its associated barriers
- Leadership demands on senior managers
- Developing your leadership style

Programme Director:
Margi Gordon MSc, BA, AMCIPD

Fees for 2008:
£5500 + VAT inclusive all tuition fees, materials, meals and accommodation

Dates for 2008:
31 Mar–3 Apr 2008
7 Jul–10 Jul 2008
13 Oct–16 Oct 2008

Duration:
Part 1: 3 days + 1 evening
Part 2: 4 separate days over 6–9 months in action learning sets

Figure 10.10 Example of a residential generic course on strategic leadership
Source: Roffey Park Institute. <http://www.roffeypark.com/>.

MBA programmes cover several other topics in addition to strategic management, but strategy is central to the curriculum and this qualification is often considered the way to achieve a step-change in management development. Many library and information professionals have successfully used this method of developing their strategic abilities, some choosing part-time study via the Open University, others opting for the convenience of studying at their own institutions (if working in an academic library) and a few attending full-time at mainstream business schools (Morgan 1996; Noon 1994; Robinson 1999). A less demanding alternative now available is the Chartered Management Institute's Executive Diploma in Strategic Management, which takes an estimated 125 guided learning hours (including both study and assessment), typically spread over six to twelve months of part-time study. This qualification includes three units – Strategic Positioning, Strategic Planning and Strategic Implementation – and a dissertation (10,000 words) and is offered by many colleges in the UK via traditional and distance learning modes (Chartered Management Institute 2005).

Other distance learning options include e-learning programmes offered by the SLA (the former Special Libraries Association) via its Click University. Figure 10.11 shows an example of a three-week course on strategic planning for knowledge management, where the cost is comparable to a conventional one-day short course. Another option, attractive for busy professionals, is the free online course in strategic management offered by the Open University via its OpenLearn initiative to make learning materials available as 'open content' via its website. Figure 10.12 provides an outline of the course content, which can be completed in an estimated four hours of independent study time.

KMKS05. Strategic Planning for Knowledge Management
19 May–5 June 2008 [3 weeks]

Instructor: Guy St. Clair

CEU Credit: 1   **Cost:** USD 495.00

This course provides guidelines for developing the vision, mission, and values statements for aligning knowledge management and knowledge services with organizational priorities and identifies critical steps—including change management and change implementation—for launching or enhancing service delivery for the benefit of the larger organization.

Topics covered include:
- strategic planning basics (definitions/applications/organizational role)—"strategy" vs. "strategic"
- organizational structure and the environment for knowledge
- management/knowledge services
- visioning vs. planning
- determining strategic direction
- change management/change implementation
- infrastructure and planning for future needs

Course learning objectives:
At the end of this course, participants will recognize the role and value of "planning to plan," survey the service sphere and choosing survey methods, and interpret financials and the impact of financial information on planning. Participants will also relate to the life cycle of the strategic plan.

Specific learning outcomes:
1. Establish terms of reference for strategic planning for knowledge management/ knowledge services
2. Identify the survey/census methodology
3. Identify participants and establish the value of their potential participation
4. Develop conclusions and establish findings
5. Report findings and communicate recommendations
6. Determine future follow-up activities

At the conclusion of the course, participants will design an action plan for first steps in implementing a strategic plan for addressing a specific situation with respect to knowledge management/knowledge services delivery in their parent organization. Using learning outcomes from the course and based on their understanding of the current or potential planning environment in the parent organization, the exercise will enable participants to return to the workplace with a product that can be incorporated into their work in their area of responsibility.

Performance measure:
Course assessment, exercises and discussions will measure and evaluate the degree of understanding that participants achieve over the learning process.

Prerequisites:
While the primary goal in developing these programs is to allow SLA members to earn one or more certificates, each of these courses has inherent value and any course may be taken à la carte. KMSKS01 is recommended but not required.

Figure 10.11 Example of an e-learning course on strategic planning
Source: SLA Click University Course Catalog. <http://www.clickuniversity.com>.

Strategic View of Performance (B700_3)

Strategic management and planning are no longer the preserve of senior executives. This unit looks at three different approaches to strategy before analysing the direction that strategic management may take now that it has become an accumulation of small tactical decisions rather than a top-down process. If you are interested in 'how' a business 'ticks', this unit could provide some of the answers.

Unit outline:
Introduction

1. What do we mean by strategy? Activity 1
    1.1. Organizational purposes
    1.2. Stakeholders
2. Market-based approach to strategy. The 'near environment'
    2.1. Porter's five forces framework
    2.2. Applying the five forces model
    2.3. Strategy as fit between organization and environment
3. Resource-based approach to strategy
    3.1. Understanding organizational capabilities
    3.2. Building capabilities and relationships
    3.3. Understanding the value chain
4. Strategy as rational planning
    4.1. Emergent strategy
5. Summary
    References
    Acknowledgements

Time: 4 Hours

Topic: Business and Management

Level: Advanced

Figure 10.12 Example of a free online generic course on strategic management
Source: Open University OpenLearn LearningSpace. <http://openlearn.open.ac.uk/>.

STRATEGY TOOLS

A striking feature of the strategic management arena is the proliferation of models, methods and techniques devised to support the process of analysis which underpins the development and formulation of strategy. The large number of tools arises from the cumulative nature of work in this area, which has meant that new models have been added to the toolkit each decade, but have not replaced established methods, which continue to be valued and used. Such tools can be very useful in helping managers and other practitioners to identify crucial questions that must be answered and relevant variables to consider at different stages of the strategy process. They offer frameworks that can stimulate discussion and highlight issues that might otherwise be overlooked.

At a more general level, as previously mentioned, the use of strategic analysis tools can play an important role in developing the capacity for strategic thinking by prompting people to think about things in new ways. Some tools, such as the PEST and SWOT analysis frameworks, have been around for a long time and are already reasonably well established in the library world; but other tools, such as stakeholder mapping and portfolio matrices, are less extensively used and/or could be exploited more effectively.

Examples of strategy tools include the following:

- PEST analysis (also known as STEP analysis and as PESTLE or STEEPLE analysis in an extended variant)
- SWOT analysis (also known as TOWS or WOTS UP analysis)
- Scenario development
- Stakeholder influence grid
- Directional policy matrix
- Life-cycle portfolio matrix
- Product-market matrix (also known as growth vector analysis)
- Seven S framework
- Force field analysis
- Balanced scorecard

The best way to learn how to use such tools is arguably in a workshop situation where practitioners can apply the tools to real issues under the guidance of an expert instructor. In-house development events and external short courses may both offer such opportunities, as shown by several of the examples given previously (see Appendix 1 and Figures 10.3, 10.6, 10.7 and 10.8). In addition, there are a few courses for library and information professionals that focus specifically on the use of particular models and techniques: Figures 10.13 and 10.14 give details of courses dealing with scenario analysis and the balanced scorecard respectively.

However, time constraints often limit the number of tools that can be introduced and used to one or two per event. An alternative method, which can also be a useful way of supplementing learning gained from workshops, is to seek guidance from one or more of the handbooks/workbooks devoted to this subject and specifically designed for this purpose. Some of the established planning and strategy textbooks (Bryson 2004; Johnson, Scholes and Whittington 2008) are now supported by complementary manuals (Bryson and Alston 2005; Ambrosini, Johnson and Scholes 1998) that expand the coverage of tools and techniques provided in the main volume at a more practical level, offering fuller explanations illustrated by worked examples. Such manuals are obviously intended to be used in tandem with the related textbook, but some work well as stand-alone resources (for example, Bryson and Alston 2005) and there are also several self-contained books, designed as guides and reference sources for students and professionals (Coyle 2004; Fleisher and Bensoussan 2003; Turner 2002).

CIC12. Scenarios Analysis and Futures Techniques
Date and Location TBD

Instructor: Cynthia Cheng Correia

CEU Credit: 1   **Cost:** USD 495.00

How can I anticipate and understand scenarios, events, and developments that can impact my organization?

Anticipating future conditions, trends, and actions is fundamental to generating effective competitive intelligence. While there is no crystal ball that can predict the future, CI employs a range of tools and techniques to develop an understanding of future developments, as well as possible and likely scenarios that can impact our organization's competitiveness. This live, hands-on course presents common futures models and techniques that are used to support strategic development. Participants will learn how to choose and apply the appropriate techniques, how to develop scenarios, and how to combine futures techniques with other, complementary intelligence models.

Prerequisite: Participants enrolled for the "Core" and Dual Competitive Intelligence Certificates are recommended to complete courses CIC-08 and CIC-09 [Competitive Intelligence Analysis: Fundamental Frameworks and Competitive Intelligence Analysis: Intermediate Frameworks].

Course level: Advanced

Course Learning Objectives:
At the end of this course, participants will understand key fundamental techniques that can help them and their organizations better anticipate and understand future events and conditions that can impact their competitiveness. When presented with relevant questions, issues and problems, participants will be able to support intelligence needs and outline possible solutions and recommendations.

Specific learning outcomes:
1. Distinguish common models and techniques used to anticipate future developments and now to address uncertainty.
2. Evaluate and apply common models and techniques for intelligence questions and concerns.
3. Prepare and participate in a scenario planning exercise.
4. Combine futures techniques and scenario analysis with other techniques to identify key drivers and possible outcomes, as well as discern signals, wild cards, and other indicators.
5. Demonstrate how futures techniques and scenario analysis support strategic development, can address changes, and enhance an organization's competitive intelligence efforts.

Participants will develop skills and abilities according to professional competencies outlined by Knowledge inForm.

Performance measure: Exercises and discussions will measure and evaluate the degree of understanding that participants achieve over the learning process.

Figure 10.13 Example of a course on scenario development
Source: SLA Click University. <http://www.clickuniversity.com>.

Balanced Scorecard: Practical Approaches
7 February 2008, London

Performance measurement and management is an essential library management activity to ensure effective and efficient use of resources. There are many tools and techniques available to help the library manager undertake this process. Increasingly, the balanced scorecard is being employed by libraries as a key tool to support this activity.

Benefits of attending:
This brand new course will give attendees an understanding of the balanced scorecard and its application to their performance measurement and management activities.

By the end of the course participants will have:
- a thorough understanding, with examples, of the balanced scorecard and its associated strategy mapping activity
- considered the application of the tools and techniques to their library context
- devised a basic balanced scorecard process for their own library service

Who should attend?
Senior library and information staff from any sector of the profession who have responsibility for performance measurement and management

Special notes: participants should expect to contribute to a number of practical exercises during the day.

Programme:
- What is the balanced scorecard and why is it useful?
- The Strategy Map
- Managing the Scorecard
- Creating your own library balanced scorecard template

9.15 Registration & coffee – 12.30 Lunch – 4.30 Close

Workshop leader: Terry Kendrick

Fees:
CILIP personal members: £240 plus VAT **£282.00**
CILIP organization members: £290 plus VAT **£340.75**
Non members: £310 plus VAT **£364.25**

Figure 10.14 Example of a course on the balanced scorecard
Source: CILIP Training and Development. <http://www.cilip.org.uk/training/training>.

ORGANIZATIONAL STRUCTURE

There is general consensus that strategy and structure need to be compatible and the significance of this point is evidenced by the discussion of organizational structure in many strategy texts (Chandler 1962; Johnson, Scholes and Whittington 2008; White 2004). The classic view (Chandler 1962) is that 'unless structure follows strategy, inefficiency results'. However, Mintzberg (1990) argues for a more nuanced approach, on the basis that strategy and structure have a reciprocal – rather than unidirectional – relationship. Similarly, White sees the formal structure of an organization as 'an important input into strategy making' (White 2004). Strategy and structure need to be considered together to ensure that existing structures do not constrain strategic thinking or undermine strategy implementation. If an organization develops a new vision which shifts its priorities, it may need to redesign or adjust its structure to support the new strategy. Many libraries have created new structures, including new specialist posts, to deal with the electronic resources and digital collections which are now central to their vision and future direction (Higa et al. 2005). Other libraries have experienced radical structural change as a result of higher-level decisions to merge them with other parts of their organization, such as a computer centre (Renaud 2006).

Organizational structure has been defined as 'the sum total of the ways in which its labor is divided into distinct tasks and then its coordination is achieved among these tasks' (Mintzberg 1993). This widely cited definition highlights two significant aspects of organizational design which are difficult to balance, namely the division of labour to enable specialization and the co-ordination of effort to achieve integration of activities. A key question here is on what basis tasks are organized as jobs and people grouped into teams, sections, departments, and so on. In addition to considering the basis for specialization, organizational designers need to think about the degree of specialization, that is, whether roles and units are tightly specified and self-contained or loosely defined and overlapping, with fuzzy boundaries; there is a trade-off here between expertise and flexibility. Other important components of organization include the number of levels or layers ('tall' versus 'flat' structures), the distribution of authority (centralized versus decentralized decision making) and reporting lines (single versus multiple bosses, known as matrix management).

Traditional conceptions of organizational structure suggest two main organizing principles: the functional approach, where specialization is based on the nature of the task, equipment, technology or skills involved (a focus on means); and the divisional or market approach, where specialization is based on product, service, region/territory or customer/client group (a focus on ends). Application of these principles results in four basic organizational types: the pure functional structure; the pure divisional or market structure; the mixed or hybrid structure, which applies different principles of division for different parts of the organization; and the matrix or grid structure, which combines the functional and market focus simultaneously. Mixed structures are common in library organizations, with circulation and other generic provision typically organized on a functional basis, but specialist services and liaison activities organized on a market (geographical/client) basis.

Dissatisfaction with traditional structures combined with dramatic changes in the business environment has led to new organizational forms, which often emphasize a *process* orientation, cross-functional teamworking and strategic alliances with business partners. Child identifies five key influences on contemporary organizational design: globalization, new technologies, the knowledge-based economy, hypercompetition and demands for social accountability (Child 2005). The new organizational vocabulary includes terms such as the boundaryless organization, bull's eye organization, cluster or federal organization, inverted organization, network organization, spider's web organization, star organization, starburst organization and virtual organization (Child 2005; Goold and Campbell 2002; Pugh 2007; White 2004).

Organizational structure is generally covered at a rudimentary level in professional education programmes. Structure is often mentioned as an important contextual factor in strategic management training, and courses on leading and managing change can help with the process aspects of restructuring. Many practitioners learn about structural design by researching what others have done in similar circumstances, by using their peer networks and reading published case studies. Further guidance on the underlying principles can be found in the management and organizational behaviour literature, including library management textbooks (see Additional Resources at the end of this chapter for recommended books and articles).

ORGANIZATIONAL CULTURE

The importance of harmony between an organization's strategy and culture is shown by the emphasis placed on this issue in the strategy literature (for example, Johnson, Scholes and Whittington 2008; Kono 1990). The organizational culture of libraries has also been described as a 'strategic resource' influencing organizational effectiveness (Kaarst-Brown et al. 2004). Strategists need to understand the culture of their organization because it affects all aspects of organizational life: it shapes the thoughts and actions of organizational members and thus pervades decision making and problem solving. Culture can impact on strategy in several ways: for example, by influencing how people scan the environment and interpret trends identified; and, more fundamentally, by determining the values which (explicitly or implicitly) inform an organization's mission and vision. Culture affects how people filter and exchange information and can be a powerful driver or constraint on organizational development and change (for example, in forming strategic alliances or managing service convergence).

Organizational culture is a nebulous concept, which can be defined in many ways. Brown lists 15 of the most widely cited definitions, which he classifies into two main categories that interpret culture as a metaphor and objective entity respectively (Brown 1998). The latter category includes both behavioural (how people do things) and cognitive (how people think) characteristics. One of the most frequently quoted definitions is that of Schein, who describes culture in rather abstract terms as 'the sum total of all the shared taken-for-granted assumptions that a group has learned throughout its history' (Schein 1999). Brown expands on this as follows:

'Organisational culture refers to the pattern of beliefs, values and learned ways of coping with experience that have developed during the course of an organisation's history, and which tend to be manifested in its material arrangements and in the behaviour of its members' (Brown 1998, 9).

The situation is complicated by the fact that organizational culture is rarely unitary, as most organizations contain identifiable subcultures that typically form around different managerial levels, professional groups, service points, and so on. Such subcultures may be in conflict with the overall culture and/or each other. Another significant issue in a global environment is the cultural diversity represented by different countries and the need for intercultural co-operation and understanding in the workplace: this is obviously particularly important for service organizations, especially those with a culturally diverse clientele. Research in this area suggests the basic requirement for surviving in a multicultural world is first an understanding of one's own cultural values and next the cultural values of those with whom one has to co-operate (Hofstede and Hofstede 2005).

Several authors have developed typologies or classifications of types of cultures to help people understand their organizations and how they work (for example, Harrison 1972). Methods used to discover and examine culture include observation, facilitated workshops, interviews and questionnaires, details of which can be found in several books (for example, Brown 1998; Handy 1993; Schein 1999). Johnson (1998) uses the concept of a multi-faceted 'cultural web' to explain how culture mapping and re-mapping can be used to compare an existing culture with a desired culture associated with an intended strategy to flag up potential problems with implementation and stimulate thinking about solutions. A similar exercise in a university library revealed discrepancies between management and staff views of service strategies (Davies, Kirkpatrick and Oliver 1992).

No open courses dealing specifically with organizational culture have been identified. Experience suggests that a combination of reading, reflection and discussion with colleagues can be a fruitful way to gain insights into prevailing culture(s), preferably including the use of some of the methods outlined above (for example, facilitated workshops).

MANAGING CHANGE

Change management is a central part of strategic development. At one level, planning and managing change can be seen as the implementation phase of strategic planning; at another level, the term change management can be used in relation to the introduction of any new process, structure, technology, and so on, and can thus range from small-scale local adaptation to large-scale global transformation. The term organization development (OD) is properly used for formal behaviour-related organization-level change interventions, aimed at improving organizational effectiveness, but is sometimes used simply as a low-key alternative to organizational change. In addition to categorizing change according to its obvious characteristics of scale, scope and speed, commentators have differentiated types of change as reactive or anticipatory, as incremental or discontinuous, and also as planned and emergent (Hayes 2002).

The change management literature offers various theories and models of change, including both process and diagnostic models. Popular diagnostic tools include: the McKinsey 7S framework of seven interrelated factors whose alignment determines the effectiveness of an organization; and Lewin's force field analysis technique, which identifies and quantifies forces that are respectively driving/pushing and restraining/resisting change (Corrall 2000; Hayes 2002). Another commonly used model is the *transition curve* or coping cycle, which identifies the seven stages or phases that people experiencing change typically go through, irrespective of whether the change is voluntary or imposed, desirable or undesirable (Gallacher 1999; Hayes 2002). Experience has shown that an understanding of this cycle of emotional and cognitive states can help both managers and individuals to work through the transition process.

The roles, skills and identities of change agents are all important areas, but it is particularly important to recognize that change agents can exist at all levels of an organization:

> *Good change agents are central to the process of managing change effectively: people who can take the change forward; people who can provide the right blend of support and pressure to motivate staff; people who can maintain momentum. Potential change agents can be found anywhere in your library service. They may be managers – but not necessarily* (Information Management Associates 2004).

According to the literature, change managers require – and can be helped to acquire – conceptual understanding, personal characteristics and interpersonal skills, with particular emphasis placed on interpersonal skills. *The People's Network Change Management Toolkit* provides a checklist of 33 'interpersonal skills needed to manage change effectively' (Information Management Associates 2004, 35–9). Pugh (2007, 203) lists trust, empathy, self-awareness, openness, listening and dialogue skills as 'universal requirements in change management', and the *Change Management infoKit* identifies 'seven winning characteristics of the successful change agent': they have a sense of purpose, have the capacity to act, sell success, are strategically connected, are critically reflective, build supporting structures and are opportunistic (JISC infoNet n.d.).

Change is now recognized as a constant feature of the library environment; change management is frequently mentioned as a required competence in job advertisements and has also been identified as a priority development need in several reports on sector skills needs (Corrall 2005; Fisher, Hallam and Partridge 2005; Thorhauge 2004). Change management is also listed among the generic management and organizational behaviour abilities and competencies specified in the UK subject benchmark statement for librarianship and information management: 'Understanding of the concepts, principles and techniques underpinning key aspects of planning, managing and leading services, including financial management, human resource management, project management, marketing, service quality, customer relationship management and change management' (Quality Assurance Agency 2007). The theory and practice of managing change is typically covered in management modules of professional education programmes, but the changing nature of the library environment is likely to be a recurring theme across all specialist modules.

Many short courses for the profession on strategic planning include change management/change implementation among the topics covered (for example, see Figure 10.11). There are also short courses specifically on leading and managing change offered at both senior and middle management level, by organizations within and outside the library and information sector. Such courses typically focus particularly on issues such as dealing with resistance to change and helping people through the transition process. Figures 10.15 and 10.16 give details of two library-specific courses of this type.

Further guidance can be found in both general management and library management textbooks and case studies. In addition, the Joint Information Systems Committee (JISC) and the Museums Libraries and Archives Council (MLA) have both sponsored the production of web-based downloadable change management toolkits (JISC infoNet n.d.; Information Management Associates 2004) which offer an alternative type of learning and reference resource on this topic.

PERFORMANCE EVALUATION

Performance measurement is an essential element of strategic management. Practitioners working in fast-moving environments need continually to evaluate and review what they are doing to ensure relevance and effectiveness. At a more specific level, performance measurement can make a particular, crucial contribution at successive stages of the planning process. Collecting baseline information to establish the present position of a service is a necessary first step in analysing the current situation as part of environmental appraisal. This enables comparison with peers and identification of targets for improvement or development when setting objectives to articulate strategic focus. It also makes it possible to measure progress towards strategy goals and assess success in implementing strategy and managing change.

Leading others through Change
24 June 2008, London

A one-day practical course on the main areas of management relevant to change in library and information work, with emphasis on managing staff and teams. This course is ideal for senior professionals or managers planning or implementing change.

Benefits of attending:
Participants will gain a good understanding of the nature of change and how to implement it with minimal workplace resistance. Participants will have the opportunity to review their own situations and present alternative approaches to handling change.

By the end of the course participants will be able to:
- distinguish the features and stages of the change process
- identify responses to change in yourself and your staff and appreciate how resistance can be minimised
- review their own responses to situations of change and establish how they might alter their own approach

Who should attend?
Those facing or undergoing strategic change in their team or organisation and have leadership responsibility.

Special notes: all sessions require a high level of involvement and participation. You will be asked to bring notes on your current job and organisation with you.

Programme:
- Change in organisations: now and in the future; participants' work and issues of interest; objectives for the day
- How change affects individuals and teams
- Myths and reality: how change is managed
- at strategic and operational levels
- Making purposive and effective changes which affect your staff and others

Places are limited to: 15

9.30 Registration and coffee – 12.30 Lunch – 5.00 Close

Course leader: Sheila Ritchie

Fees:
CILIP personal members: £240 plus VAT **£282.00**
CILIP organization members: £290 plus VAT **£340.75**
Non members: £340 plus VAT **£399.50**

Figure 10.15 Example of a course on leading change

Source: CILIP Training and Development. <http://www.cilip.org.uk/training/training>.

Managing Change
Middle Managment Theme

25/05/2008
10:00–16:30

Tutor: Deborah Dalley

Charges:
NoWAL Members: £90
External Delegates: £135

Aim:
This workshop is designed for managers who are responsible for achieving results in a climate of continuous change. It will help participants to identify the key components of managing change effectively.

Objectives
By the end participants should be able to:
- Analyse the factors involved in a change situation.
- Identify and use techniques available to help manage the situational aspects of change.
- Outline ways to help people through personal transition during the change cycle.

Who should attend?
The NoWAL middle management theme is aimed at staff working within library and information services at middle/intermediate management level and above.

Figure 10.16 Example of a course on managing change
Source: NoWAL – The North West Academic Libraries. <http://www.nowal.ac.uk/middle_management.php>.

This vital link between performance measurement and strategic objectives is frequently neglected. Traditional approaches to performance measurement – in both the business world and the library profession – have often concentrated on operational and financial data, with an internal and historical perspective, rather than being outward-facing and forward-looking. Recent trends have broadened the framework, placing more emphasis on qualitative data gathered through customer surveys and intangible/intellectual assets, represented by staff expertise. The best known and most widely used example of this shift in thinking is Kaplan and Norton's balanced scorecard model, which combines financial measures of past performance with operational measures of internal processes, customer-related measures and an organization development perspective, reflected in measures of innovation, learning and growth (Kaplan and Norton 1992; 1996).

Properly interpreted, the balanced scorecard involves translating an organization's mission and strategic objectives into a coherent set of measures reflecting specific goals and targets, and then cascading this approach throughout the organization.

On this basis, a well-designed scorecard should enable the observer to deduce an organization's strategy at a glance. Kaplan and Norton subsequently developed their model into a more comprehensive strategic management system, by introducing the concept of strategy maps to articulate the cause-and-effect relationships between objectives specified across the four scorecard perspectives and extending the original framework to improve its capacity for describing, measuring and aligning human, intellectual and organizational capital to strategic objectives (Kaplan and Norton 2000; 2004).

Performance measurement in libraries has similarly recognized the need to move beyond conventional input and output measures to evaluating higher-order outcomes or impacts (Markless and Streatfield 2001; Town 2004; Usherwood 2002). Approaches adopted from other domains include the use of social audit methodology to show how a library contributes strategically to the objectives of its parent organization (Usherwood 2002) and using the balanced scorecard model to support transformational change and to link a library's strategic plan with that of the university (Pienaar and Penzhorn 2000; Cribb and Hogan 2003). The most sustained and well-documented current work in this area is Markless and Streatfield's impact evaluation model, which has been developed and tested with more than 700 library and information service managers in numerous different settings (Markless and Streatfield 2006). The model advocates the generation of impact and performance indicators derived from the library's overall purpose and objectives as a means of articulating a workable development plan and integrating the collection of evidence into the planning cycle.

There are fewer courses on performance evaluation than on other topics covered here, but the Chartered Institute of Library and Information Professionals (CILIP) has recently extended its provision in this area, with the introduction of courses on the balanced scorecard and on impact evaluation, as shown in Figures 10.14 and 10.17. However, the main source of guidance on this topic remains published literature – books, articles and published case studies – from both the general management and library domains (see Additional Resources at the end of this chapter for recommended materials).

Evaluating the Impact of your Library
29 April 2008, London

How good is your library? How can you measure the impact you make?

Designed for library services managers, this one-day course will help you move beyond performance indicators to see the effectiveness of your library or information service. The day will help participants get to grips with evaluating service impact, incorporating this effort into the overall service monitoring and evaluation process, and learn how to put the evidence of success across in convincing ways.

Benefits of attending
By the end of the course participants will have:

- considered the main differences between monitoring efficiency and evaluating impact and their consequences for evidence gathering
- explored the main stages in evaluating service impact examined how to incorporate impact evaluation into their ways of working
- focused on issues in presenting impact evidence effectively for different purposes.

Who should attend?
Library and information service managers in any work environment who are responsible for evaluating services or considering how to do so.

Programme:
- What is impact? Impact as a slippery concept
- What impact can the library or information service have? Impact on what? (How far can you reach?) Frameworks from recent research
- Some issues in evaluating impact. What is really changing? How do you know?
- How can you tell that you are making a difference? Finding useful impact indicators. Why are you doing it? Collecting the evidence
- Building impact into what we do Where to start? The planning cycle
- Getting the messages across. Organising the evidence. Bringing the recipients on board

Places are limited to: 24

9.30 Registration and coffee – 12.45 Lunch – 4.30 Close

Course leader: Sharon Markless

Fees:
CILIP personal members: £220 plus VAT **£258.50**
CILIP organisation members: £265 plus VAT **£311.38**
Non members: £310 plus VAT **£364.25**

Figure 10.17 Example of a course on impact evaluation
Source: CILIP Training and Development. <http://www.cilip.org.uk/training/training>.

CONCLUSION

Strategic development has been interpreted here to include the processes of strategic thinking, strategic planning, managing change and evaluating performance, alongside consideration of the associated concepts of organizational structure and organizational culture. The discussion has flagged the significant contribution of strategic analysis tools in both supporting planning activities and developing organizational capabilities in strategic thinking, which has been identified as an important development need for the library and information services workforce – a need that is relevant to all categories of library and information workers, and not limited to managerial or professional-level staff. The suggested methods for developing strategic competencies are in-house workshops, external short courses, extended education programmes and guided reading, drawing on both general management and library/information resources. Practical activity should ideally be complemented by suitable reading to provide the conceptual underpinning for the tasks undertaken, and for some aspects of the subject this is the main development method generally available.

REFERENCES

Ambrosini, V., Johnson, G. and Scholes, K. (eds) (1998), *Exploring Techniques of Analysis and Evaluation in Strategic Management* (London: Prentice Hall Europe).

Bonn, I. (2001), 'Developing Strategic Thinking as a Core Competency', *Management Decision*, 39:1, 63–70.

Booth, A. and Fabian, C.A. (2002), 'Collaborating to Advance Curriculum-based Information Literacy Initiatives', *Journal of Library Administration* 36:1/2, 123–42.

Brown, A.D. (1998), *Organisational Culture* (Harlow: Financial Times Prentice Hall).

Bryson, J.M. (2004), *Strategic Planning for Public and Nonprofit Organizations: A Guide to Strengthening and Sustaining Organizational Achievement*, 3rd edn (San Francisco: Jossey-Bass).

Bryson, J.M. and Alston, F.K. (2005), *Creating and Implementing your Strategic Plan: A Workbook for Public and Nonprofit Organizations*, 2nd edn (San Francisco: Jossey-Bass).

Chandler, A.D. (1962), *Strategy and Structure: Chapters in the History of Industrial Enterprise* (Cambridge, MA: MIT Press).

Chartered Management Institute (2005), *Executive Diploma in Strategic Management* [Syllabus], Valid from September 2005 (Corby: Chartered Management Institute). <http://www.managers.org.uk/client_files/user_files/Rattigan_8/Syllabuses/7EDSM.pdf>.

Child, J. (2005), *Organization: Contemporary Principles and Practice* (Oxford: Blackwell).

Corrall, S. (2000), *Strategic Management of Information Services: A Planning Handbook* (London: Aslib/IMI).

Corrall, S. (2005), 'Developing Models of Professional Competence to Enhance Employability in the Network World' in P. Genoni and G. Walton (eds).

Coyle, G. (2004), *Practical Strategy: Structured Tools and Techniques* (Harlow: Financial Times Prentice Hall).

Cribb, G. and Hogan, C. (2003), 'Balanced Scorecard: Linking Strategic Planning to Measurement and Communication', 24th Annual Conference of the International Association of Technological University Libraries, 2–5 June 2003, Ankara, Turkey. <http://epublications.bond.edu.au/library_pubs/8/>.

Davies, A., Kirkpatrick, I. and Oliver, N. (1992), 'The Organisational Culture of an Academic Library: Implications for Library Strategy', *British Journal of Academic Librarianship* 7:2, 69–89.

De Geus, A.P. (1988), 'Planning as Learning', *Harvard Business Review* 66:2, 70–74.

De Wit, B. and Meyer, R. (2005), *Strategy Synthesis: Resolving Strategy Paradoxes to Create Competitive Advantage: Text and Readings*, 2nd edn (London: Thomson Learning).

Doskatsch, I. (2003), 'Perceptions and Perplexities of the Faculty-Librarian Partnership: An Australian Perspective', *Reference Services Review*, 31:2, 111–21.

Dougherty, R.M. (2002), 'Planning for New Library Futures,' *Library Journal*, 127:9, 38–41.

Drucker, P.F. (1973), *Management: Tasks, Responsibilities, Practice* (New York: Harper & Row).

Fisher, B., Hallam, G. and Partridge, H. (2005) 'Different Approaches: Common Conclusion', *New Review of Academic Librarianship*, 11:1, 13–29.

Fleisher, C.S. and Bensoussan, B.E. (2003), *Strategic and Competitive Analysis: Methods and Techniques for Analyzing Business Competition* (Upper Saddle River, NJ: Prentice Hall).

Floyd, S.W. and Wooldridge, B. (1994), 'Dinosaurs or Dynamos? Recognizing Middle Management's Strategic Role', *Academy of Management Executive* 8:4, 47–57.

Gallacher, C. (1999), *Managing Change in Libraries and Information Services* (London: Aslib).

Genoni, P. and Walton, G. (eds) (2005), *Continuing Professional Development – Preparing For New Roles in Libraries: A Voyage Of Discovery*, Sixth World Conference on Continuing Professional Development and Workplace Learning for the Library and Information Professions (Munich: KG Saur).

Goold, M. and Campbell, A. (2002), *Designing Effective Organisations: How to Create Structured Networks* (San Francisco: Jossey-Bass).

Hamel, G. (1996), 'Strategy as Revolution', *Harvard Business Review* 74:4, 69–82.

Handy, C.B. (1993), *Understanding Organizations*, 4th edn (London: Penguin).

Harrison, R. (1972), 'Understanding your Organization's Character', *Harvard Business Review* 50:3, 119–28.

Hayes, J. (2002), *The Theory and Practice of Change Management* (Basingstoke: Palgrave Macmillan).

Higa, M.L., Bunnett, B., Maina, B., Perkins, J., Ramos, T., Thompson, L. and Wayne, R. (2005), 'Redesigning a Library's Organizational Structure', *College and Research Libraries* 66:1, 41–58.

Higa-Moore, M.L., Bunnett, B., Mayo, H.G. and Olney, C.A. (2002), 'Use of Focus Groups in a Library's Strategic Planning Process', *Journal of the Medical Library Association* 90:1, 86–92.

Hofstede, G. and Hofstede, G.J. (2005), *Cultures and Organizations: Software of the Mind*, 2nd rev. edn (New York: McGraw-Hill).

Information Management Associates (2004), *The People's Network Change Management Toolkit*, rev. edn (London: Museums, Libraries and Archives Council). <http://www.mla.gov.uk/programmes/peoples_network/peoples_network_archive/change>.

Jacobson, A.L. and Sparks, J.L. (2001), 'Creating Value: Building the Strategy-Focused Library', *Information Outlook* 5:9, 14–15, 17–18, 20.

JISC infoNet (n.d.), *Change Management infoKit* (Newcastle: Northumbria University/Joint Information Systems Committee). <http://www.jiscinfonet.ac.uk/infokits/change-management>.

Johnson, G. (1998), 'Mapping and Re-mapping Organisational Culture' in V. Ambrosini, G. Johnson and K. Scholes (eds).

Johnson, G., Scholes, K. and Whittington, R. (2008), *Exploring Corporate Strategy: Text and Cases*, 8th edn (Harlow: Financial Times Prentice Hall).

Kaarst-Brown, M.L., Nicholson, S., von Dran, G.M. and Stanton, J.M. (2004), 'Organizational Culture of Libraries as a Strategic Resource', *Library Trends* 53:1, 33–53.

Kaplan, R.S. and Norton, D.P. (1992), 'The Balanced Scorecard – Measures that Drive Performance', *Harvard Business Review* 70:1, 71–9.

Kaplan, R.S. and Norton, D.P. (1996), 'Using the Balanced Scorecard as a Strategic Management System', *Harvard Business Review* 74:1, 75–85.

Kaplan, R.S. and Norton, D.P. (2000), 'Having Trouble with Your Strategy? Then Map It', *Harvard Business Review* 78:5, 167–76.

Kaplan, R.S. and Norton, D.P. (2004), *Strategy Maps: Converting Intangible Assets into Tangible Outcomes* (Boston: Harvard Business School Press).

Kono, T. (1990), 'Corporate Culture and Long Range Planning', *Long Range Planning* 23:4, 9–19.

Kuntz, J.J., Tennant, M.R., Case, A.C. and Meakin, F.A. (2003), 'Staff-Driven Strategic Planning: Learning from the Past, Embracing the Future', *Journal of the Medical Library Association* 91:1, 79–83.

Ladwig, J.P. (2005), 'Assess the State of Your Strategic Plan', *Library Administration and Management* 19:2, 90–93.

Liedtka, J.M. (1998), 'Strategic Thinking: Can It be Taught?', *Long Range Planning* 31:1, 120–29.

Markless, S. and Streatfield, D. (2001), 'Developing Performance and Impact Indicators and Targets in Public and Education Libraries', *International Journal of Information Management* 21:2, 167–79.

Markless, S. and Streatfield, D. (2006), *Evaluating the Impact of Your Library* (London: Facet).

McClamroch, J., Byrd, J.J. and Sowell, S.L. (2001), 'Strategic Planning: Politics, Leadership, and Learning', *Journal of Academic Librarianship* 27:5, 372–8.

Mintzberg, H. (1990), 'The Design School: Reconsidering the Basic Premises of Strategic Management', *Strategic Management Journal* 11, 171–95.

Mintzberg, H. (1993), *Structure in Fives: Designing Effective Organizations* (Englewood Cliffs: Prentice Hall).

Mintzberg, H. and Waters, J.A. (1985), 'Of Strategies, Deliberate and Emergent', *Strategic Management Journal* 6:3, 257–72.

Missingham, R. (2006), 'Library and Information Science: Skills for Twenty-First Century Professionals', *Library Management* 27:4/5, 257–68.

Morgan, S. (1996), 'A Personal View of Personal Development', *Managing Information* 3:9, 41–3.

Noon, P. (1994), 'Managing to Build a Career', *Librarian Career Development* 2:3, 22–25.

Peacock, J. (2001), 'Teaching Skills for Teaching Librarians: Postcards from the Edge of the Educational Paradigm', *Australian Academic and Research Libraries* 32:1, 26–42. <http://www.alia.org.au/publishing/aarl/32.1/full.text/jpeacock.html>.

Pienaar, H. and Penzhorn, C. (2000), 'Using the Balanced Scorecard to Facilitate Strategic Management at an Academic Information Service', *Libri* 50:3, 202–9.

Pugh, L. (2007), *Change Management in Information Services*, 2nd edn (Aldershot: Ashgate).

Quality Assurance Agency (2007), *Subject Benchmark Statement: Librarianship and Information Management*, QAA 201 12/07, rev. edn (Mansfield: Quality Assurance Agency for Higher Education). <http://www.qaa.ac.uk/academicinfrastructure/benchmark/statements/Librarianship07.pd>.

Renaud, R.E. (2006), 'Shaping a New Profession: The Role of Librarians when the Library and Computer Center Merge', *Library Administration and Management* 20:2, 65–74.

Robinson, L. (1999), 'Feel the Fear and Do It Anyway', *Business Information Review* 16:2, 65–70.

Schein, E.H. (1999), *The Corporate Culture Survival Guide: Sense and Nonsense about Culture Change* (San Francisco: Jossey-Bass).

Suber, P. (2002–present), Open Access News [Blog]. <http://www.earlham.edu/~peters/fos/fosblog.html>.

Thorhauge, J. (2004), 'New Demands: Old Skills', World Library and Information Congress: 70th IFLA General Conference and Council, 2004. <http://www.ifla.org/IV/ifla70/papers/053e-Thorhauge.pdf>.

Town, S. (2004), 'E-measures: A Comprehensive Waste of Time?', *VINE* 34:4, 190–95.

Turner, S. (2002), *Tools for Success: A Manager's Guide* (London: McGraw-Hill).

Usherwood, B. (2002), 'Demonstrating Impact Through Qualitative Research', *Performance Measurement and Metrics* 3:3, 117–22.

Webber, S. and Boon, S. (2003–present), Information Literacy Weblog [Blog]. <http://informationliteracy.blogspot.com/>.

White, C. (2004), *Strategic Management* (Basingstoke: Palgrave Macmillan).

ADDITIONAL RESOURCES

This annotated resource list provides information on books, articles and case studies selected as recommended reading to support the development of competency in strategic management. The resources are arranged in the following sections and sub-sections:

Strategy and Planning
Tools and Techniques
> Balanced Scorecard and Strategy Maps
> Environmental Scanning
> Scenario Development
> Mission, Vision and Critical Success Factors
Organizational Structure
Organizational Culture
Managing Change
Performance Evaluation

Within each section, entries are arranged alphabetically, but with items from general management literature placed before those from the library literature (where available).

STRATEGY AND PLANNING

Bryson, J.M. (2004), *Strategic Planning for Public and Nonprofit Organizations: A Guide to Strengthening and Sustaining Organizational Achieve*ment, 3rd edn (San Francisco: Jossey-Bass). Classic text for public sector and non-profit organizations, which is widely cited in the library literature and valued for its emphasis on the political dimensions of strategy. Appendix presents 13 stakeholder analysis techniques and explains how to use them.

Johnson, G., Scholes, K. and Whittington, R. (2008), *Exploring Corporate Strategy: Text and Cases*, 8th edn (Harlow: Financial Times Prentice Hall). Leading textbook in the field, which includes chapters on 'Culture and Strategy', 'Organising for Success', 'Resourcing Strategies' and 'Managing Strategic Change'. Provides explanations of key terms in page margins in addition to a seven-page glossary, which gives page numbers linking definitions to discussion in the text.

Liedtka, J.M. (1998), 'Strategic Thinking: Can It be Taught?', *Long Range Planning* 31:1, 120–29. Widely cited article identifies and explains five aspects of strategic thinking, then gives examples of frameworks and techniques which utilize and develop these abilities, presenting planning as an inclusive learning process.

Mintzberg, H. and Waters, J.A. (1985), 'Of Strategies, Deliberate and Emergent', *Strategic Management Journal* 6:3, 257–72. Seminal article, which explains the concepts of deliberate and emergent strategies, and describes how these basic concepts give rise to a continuum of different types of strategies, labelled respectively as planned, entrepreneurial, ideological, umbrella, process, unconnected, consensus and imposed.

Sutherland, J. and Canwell, D. (2004), *Key Concepts in Strategic Management* (Basingstoke: Palgrave Macmillan). Compact A–Z glossary of strategic management terminology, providing brief descriptions, with illustrations of models, cross-references to related terms and references to books and articles for further study.

Burkhardt, J.M., MacDonald, M.C. and Rathemacher, A.J. (2005), *Creating a Comprehensive Information Literacy Plan: A How-To-Do-It Manual and CD-ROM for Librarians* (New York: Neal-Schuman). Practical guide covering all aspects of the planning process in addition to advice on content and structure. Includes planning worksheets; bibliographies on needs assessment, peer institution comparisons and marketing; and screenshots and URLs for plans produced by college and university libraries. CD-ROM enables customization of worksheets for local use.

Corrall, S. (2000), *Strategic Management of Information Services: A Planning Handbook* (London: Aslib/IMI). Still the most comprehensive treatment of the application of strategic management theory to information services practice. Offers practical guidance on all aspects of strategy development and implementation, supported by references to management and library literature. Chapters include 'Planning Paradigms', 'Environmental Appraisal', 'Strategic Focus', 'Strategy Formation' and 'Achieving Change'.

Corrall, S. (2002), 'Planning and Policy Making', in: M. Melling and J. Little (eds), *Building a Successful Customer-Service Culture: A Guide for Library and Information Managers*, 27–52 (London: Facet). Presents key messages from the author's book (cited above), illustrated with a new set of real-world examples drawn from public, national and academic libraries. Explains concepts and terminology, then considers different aspects of strategy formulation, including mission, values, vision and goal statements, in addition to discussing planning processes and strategy documents.

Jones, R. (2000), 'Business Plans: Roadmaps for Growth and Success', *Information Outlook* 4:12, 22–7. Provides a concise overview of a strategic planning process based on the Direction Planning Framework of five strategic questions, concluding with useful advice on presentation and communication.

McClamroch, J., Byrd, J.J. and Sowell, S.L. (2001), 'Strategic Planning: Politics, Leadership, and Learning', *Journal of Academic Librarianship* 27:5, 372–8. Discusses the application of Bryson's not-for-profit planning model at Indiana University Bloomington Libraries. Explains the main elements of the model, describes the participative process used and evaluates its success.

MacDonald, M.C., Rathemacher, A.J. and Burkhardt, J.M. (2000), 'Challenges in Building an Incremental, Multi-Year Information Literacy Plan', *Reference Services Review* 28:3, 240–47. Discusses the process used to develop an information literacy plan at the University of Rhode Island-Providence, which is discussed more fully in the authors' book (Burkhardt, MacDonald, M.C. and Rathemacher 2005) cited above.

Nelson, S.S. (2001), *The New Planning for Results: A Streamlined Approach* (Chicago: American Library Association). Latest version of the US Public Library Association strategic planning manual, revised to provide a more compact guidebook with a reduced planning timeline. Six chapters offer step-by-step guidance on 12 planning tasks, supported by examples. Part 2 articulates 13 'service responses' to help libraries determine their distinctive approaches to serving their clientele. Parts 3 and 4 comprise a toolkit and workforms to support group work processes and compilation of planning data.

Orna, E. (2004), *Information Strategy in Practice* (Aldershot: Gower). Concise updated version of the author's classic text, *Practical Information Policies*, aimed at newcomers to the field. Provides a step-by-step guide to developing and using an information strategy, starting with conduct of an information audit, prior to formulating an organizational information policy and translating this into a practical information strategy. Includes useful checklists, tables, diagrams and references. New material offers insights from recent fieldwork.

TOOLS AND TECHNIQUES

Ambrosini, V., Johnson, G. and Scholes, K. (eds) (1998), *Exploring Techniques of Analysis and Evaluation in Strategic Management* (London: Prentice Hall Europe). Companion to Johnson, Scholes and Whittington's (2008) book listed above, offering expanded practical guidance with worked examples of 17 tools and techniques featured in the main text, including core competences, benchmarking, scenarios, SWOT analysis, stakeholder mapping and portfolio matrices.

Bryson, J.M. and Alston, F.K. (2005), *Creating and Implementing your Strategic Plan: A Workbook for Public and Nonprofit Organizations*, 2nd edn (San Francisco: Jossey Bass). Companion to Bryson's 2004 book (listed above), but can also be used as a stand-alone resource. Part 1 provides a concise overview of strategic planning, offering several ways of looking at the different phases and tasks of the planning process. Part 2 contains more than 30 worksheets and instructions related to ten key steps in the process.

Fleisher, C.S. and Bensoussan, B.E. (2003), *Strategic and Competitive Analysis: Methods and Techniques for Analyzing Business Competition* (Upper Saddle River, NJ: Prentice Hall). Stand-alone compendium covering 24 widely used techniques, presented in a standard format that explains the background, strategic rationale, advantages and limitations for each tool, in addition to instructions and references. Tools covered include portfolio matrices, SWOT analysis, customer segmentation, issue analysis, macroenvironmental (STEEP) analysis, scenarios, stakeholder analysis and product life cycle analysis.

Burwell, B. and Jones, R. (2005), 'Libraries and their Service Portfolios: Getting the Right Mix', *Searcher* 13:6, 32–7. Discusses the potential value of portfolio planning for libraries and information services, arguing the need for regular critical appraisal of services offered. Explores the application of portfolio analysis techniques, outlining a seven-step process (using the Boston Consulting Group matrix).

Claggett, L. and Eklund, B. (2005), 'Create, Organize and Expedite a Strategic Plan: How to Use the Balanced Scorecard and the Stage-Gate Funnel', *Information Outlook* 9:3, 21–3. Shows how the scorecard can be used with the stage-gate funnel tool to develop and manage a library strategic plan, by moving project ideas through a structured process from initiation to implementation and review.

Balanced Scorecard and Strategy Maps

Kaplan, R.S. and Norton, D.P. (1992), 'The Balanced Scorecard – Measures that Drive Performance', *Harvard Business Review* 70:1, 71–9. Introduces the authors' groundbreaking approach to performance measurement, which encourages strategists to define goals and measures in four areas offering financial, customer, internal and learning perspectives.

Kaplan, R.S. and Norton, D.P. (1996), 'Using the Balanced Scorecard as a Strategic Management System', *Harvard Business Review* 74:1, 75–85. Explains how scorecards can be used as the foundation of an integrated strategic management system, through the four key processes of translating the vision, communicating and linking, business planning, and feedback and learning.

Kaplan, R.S. and Norton, D.P. (2000), 'Having Trouble with Your Strategy? Then Map It', *Harvard Business Review* 78:5, 167–76. Extends the authors' previous system through the introduction of strategy maps, articulating the cause-and-effect relationships that link objectives specified across the four balanced scorecard perspectives.

Kaplan, R.S. and Norton, D.P. (2004), *Strategy Maps: Converting Intangible Assets into Tangible Outcomes* (Boston: Harvard Business School Press). Provides comprehensive guidance on the development and application of strategy maps, extending the authors' previous work on balanced scorecards with a new framework for describing, measuring and aligning human, intellectual and organizational capital to strategic objectives.

Cribb, G. and Hogan, C. (2003), 'Balanced Scorecard: Linking Strategic Planning to Measurement and Communication', 24th Annual Conference of the International Association of Technological University Libraries, 2–5 June 2003, Ankara, Turkey. Available at <http://epublications.bond.edu.au/library_pubs/8/>. Case study of Bond University, Australia, which discusses how use of the balanced scorecard helped the library to link its strategic plan with that of the university, and explore cause-and-effect relationships between performance measures.

Jacobson, A.L. and Sparks, J.L. (2001), 'Creating Value: Building the Strategy-Focused Library', *Information Outlook* 5:9, 14–15, 17–18, 20. Describes the development of a strategic plan for the Knowledge Integration Resources group at Bristol-Myers Squibb, based on defining the value proposition, opportunity assessment, strategy mapping and the balanced scorecard.

Pienaar, H. and Penzhorn, C. (2000), 'Using the Balanced Scorecard to Facilitate Strategic Management at an Academic Information Service', *Libri* 50:3, 202–9. Explains the balanced scorecard concept and then describes how it has been used to implement organizational transformation measures at the University of Pretoria.

Environmental Scanning

Choo, C.W. (2001), 'Environmental Scanning as Information Seeking and Organizational Learning', *Information Research* 7:1. <http://InformationR.net/ir/7-1/paper112.html>. Reviews research on environmental scanning and develops a model showing four different modes of scanning observed in practice. Discusses the information behaviours and learning processes associated with each mode of scanning and their implications for management action.

Morrison, J.L. (1992), 'Environmental Scanning' in M.A. Whitely, J.D. Porter and R.H. Fenske (eds), *A Primer for New Institutional Researchers*, 86–99 (Tallahassee, Florida: The Association for Institutional Research). Available at <http://horizon.unc.edu/courses/papers/enviroscan/>. Explains the concept of environmental scanning, reviews several models and discusses the use of scanning in Higher Education. Also provides suggestions on establishing an environmental scanning process (including training for scanners) and a list of resources.

ACRL Research Committee (2008), *Environmental Scan 2007* (Chicago: American Library Association, Association of College and Research Libraries). Available at: <http://www.ala.org/ala/mgrps/divs/acrl/publications/whitepapers/Environ mental_Scan_2.pdf>. Explains the purpose and methodology used for the scan and identifies emergent issues discovered during the process, before presenting and discussing the top ten assumptions for the future of academic libraries and librarians. Includes selected sources.

Scenario Development

Schoemaker, P.J.H. (1995), 'Scenario Planning: A Tool for Strategic Thinking', *Sloan Management Review* 36:2, 25–40. Explains the rationale and process of scenario development. Describes a ten-step methodology, using two case studies to illustrate techniques for addressing interrelations among uncertainties. Includes examples of trends and uncertainties identified, scenarios developed and extensive bibliography.

Schwartz, P. (1997), *The Art of the Long View: Planning for the Future in an Uncertain World*, new edn (Chichester: John Wiley). Accessible guide by one of the gurus in the field. Explains the purpose and process of scenario building, illustrated with business examples and personal anecdotes. Finishes with eight steps for developing scenarios.

Giesecke, J. (ed.) (1998), *Scenario Planning for Libraries* (Chicago: American Library Association). Explains the purpose and nature of scenarios, describes an eight-step process, and provides guidance on writing plots with examples of common story lines. Includes three extensive case studies of scenario planning in libraries, and concludes with suggested reading and website resources.

Mission, Vision and Critical Success Factors

Campbell, A., Devine, M. and Young, D. (1990), *A Sense of Mission* (London: Pitman Publishing). Defines the concepts of mission and 'sense of mission' and examines the use and misuse of mission statements. Provides ten questions to test effectiveness of mission statements, concluding with advice on mission planning and mission thinking.

David, F.R. (1989), 'How Companies Define their Mission', *Long Range Planning* 22:1, 90–97. Classic article which reviews published literature and survey findings on the contents and functions of mission statements, noting that service firms had shorter and less comprehensive statements than manufacturing firms. Concludes by advocating list of nine basic components as a practical framework for evaluating and writing mission statements.

Finlay, J.S. (1994), 'The Strategic Visioning Process', *Public Administration Quarterly* 18:1, 64–74. Provides a step-by-step account of the visioning process advocated by Peter Senge, covering guided imaging, brainstorming, affinity diagrams, cause-and-effect (fishbone) diagrams and interrelationship diagraphs, concluding with the relationship between the organizational vision and statements of mission, and of principles and values.

Hardaker, M. and Ward, B.K. (1987) 'How to Make a Team Work', *Harvard Business Review* 65:6, 112–17. Covers the development of mission statements and identification of critical success factors (CSFs). Defines criteria for CSFs and then outlines method to identify most critical business processes, decide nature of improvement needed and establish relevant measurements.

Wilson, I. (1992), 'Realizing the Power of Strategic Vision', *Long Range Planning* 25:5, 18–28. Defines the concept of strategic vision, identifies six interlocking elements, and provides guidelines for a visioning process based on eight key steps. Discusses the pros and cons of individual versus collective approaches and the benefits of involving informed outsiders. Concludes with five characteristics of successful visions and seven pitfalls to avoid.

ORGANIZATIONAL STRUCTURE

Child, J. (2005), *Organization: Contemporary Principles and Practice* (Oxford: Blackwell). Authoritative text by one of the key figures in the field combines scholarship with tables and checklists, highlighting key points for managers to consider. Good coverage of symptoms of organizational deficiencies, the impact of ICT, differences between conventional and new organizational forms, and the use of cross-functional teams.

Goold, M. and Campbell, A. (2002), *Designing Effective Organisations: How to Create Structured Networks* (San Francisco: Jossey-Bass). Practical guide to contemporary organizational structure and design issues, which offers a new taxonomy of different kinds of organizational units and provides nine design tests to help managers assess the fitness for purpose of different structural solutions.

Goold, M. and Campbell, A. (2002), 'Do You Have a Well-designed Organisation?' *Harvard Business Review* 80:3, 117–224. Introduces the key ideas from the authors' book (cited above).

Davis, S.M. and Lawrence, P.R. (1978), 'Problems of Matrix Organizations', *Harvard Business Review* 56:3, 131–42. Summarizes distinguishing features of a matrix organization and then identifies nine types of problem (characterized as 'pathologies') associated with matrix management arrangements and how to resolve them. Issues discussed include confused relationships, power struggles, internal distractions and decision blight.

Mintzberg, H. (1981), 'Organization Design: Fashion or Fit?', *Harvard Business Review* 59:1, 103–16. Classic article which provides a useful introduction to key structural concepts. Defines five basic parts of an organization (strategic apex, middle line, operating core, technostructure and support staff) and then shows how these fit together in five natural configurations (simple structure, professional bureaucracy, machine bureaucracy, divisionalized form and adhocracy). Explains the need to ensure that elements of structural designs are internally consistent and fit the organization's particular situation.

Higa, M.L., Bunnett, B., Maina, B., Perkins, J., Ramos, T., Thompson, L. and Wayne, R. (2005), 'Redesigning a Library's Organizational Structure', *College and Research Libraries* 66:1, 41–58. Case study of the systematic evidence-based approach taken to reorganization at the University of Texas Southwestern Medical Center at Dallas. Describes the project methodology, changes introduced, strategies adopted and lessons learned.

Savenije, B. (2002), 'An Organisational Model for University Libraries in Transition', *LIBER Quarterly* 12:2/3, 245–59. Available at: <http://webdoc. gwdg.de/edoc/aw/liber/lq-2-02/245-259.pdf>. Identifies technological and managerial trends affecting library structures and suggests design criteria and a possible model for the development of a new structure suitable for the hybrid library, advancing towards the vision of a digital library.

ORGANIZATIONAL CULTURE

Brown, A.D. (1998), *Organisational Culture* (Harlow: Financial Times Prentice Hall). Accessible overview of the subject, which includes a chapter on 'Organisational Culture, Strategy and Performance', and tools for diagnosing organizational culture and measuring its strength, in addition to discussing the main cultural typologies, subculture and multiculturalism, and understanding and managing cultural change.

Harrison, R. (1972), 'Understanding your Organization's Character', *Harvard Business Review* 50:3, 119–28. Introduces the author's theory of organizational culture as four distinct and competing 'ideologies' (representing power, role, task and person orientations) and discusses their strengths and weaknesses in relation to external and internal pressures. Includes table showing how well each type serves six key organizational and individual interests.

Johnson, G. (1992), 'Managing Strategic Change: Strategy, Culture and Action', *Long Range Planning* 25:1, 28–36. Discusses the links between strategy and culture, using the 'cultural web' model.

Davies, A., Kirkpatrick, I. and Oliver, N. (1992), 'The Organisational Culture of an Academic Library: Implications for Library Strategy', *British Journal of Academic Librarianship* 7:2, 69–89. Describes mapping the culture of a multi-site university library by identifying and investigating staff views of management philosophy, and formal and informal rules of behaviour. Justifies time required by pointing to insights gained into mismatches between management and staff preferences and interpretations of service strategies.

MANAGING CHANGE

Hayes, J. (2002), *The Theory and Practice of Change Management* (Basingstoke: Palgrave Macmillan). Concise textbook which presents theories and models of change management in an accessible style. Provides good coverage of motivating and supporting staff and other stakeholders through change.

Curzon, S.C. (2005), *Managing Change: A How-To-Do-It Manual for Librarians*, rev. edn (New York: Neal-Schuman). Contains ten chapters dealing with different aspects of change, each with a 'Quick Check' list of key steps and questions, followed by 15 'change scenarios' with questions intended as discussion points or coaching prompts. Offers good advice on forming a change task force, analysing resistance and evaluating progress, but neglects technological change and omits references to the literature.

Gallacher, C. (1999), *Managing Change in Libraries and Information Services* (London: Aslib). Excellent pocket-sized guide designed to help managers and supervisors understand, plan and manage change. Covers pressures for change, effects on people, the strategic context, structures and cultures, generating and selecting strategies, planning and implementing projects, with examples of a decision matrix, stakeholder map and communication chart. Concludes with summary of knowledge, skills and qualities needed.

Pugh, L. (2007), *Change Management in Information Services*, 2nd edn (Aldershot: Ashgate). Provides insights on change processes and guidance on implementing change, drawing on contemporary theory and real-world practices from organizational studies and information services. Topics covered include: change theories, strategies and models; organizational metaphors and structures; teams and leadership in change management; the psychology of change; and skills of change management.

PERFORMANCE EVALUATION

Brophy, P. (2006), *Measuring Library Performance: Principles and Techniques* (London: Facet). Authoritative guide to current thinking and practice, drawing on literature from the library and business management domains. Covers staff surveys, infrastructure assessment, benchmarking and standards, in addition to user satisfaction and input, throughput, output and impact measures. Appendices include a 40-page guide to data collection methods, followed by shorter sections on analysis of data and presentation of results.

Hiller, S. and Self, J. (2004), 'From Measurement to Management: Using Data Wisely for Planning and Decision-Making', *Library Trends* 53:1, 129–55. Reviews the development of performance measurement in libraries, from the traditional use of operational statistics to contemporary application of SERVQUAL/LIBQUAL, benchmarking and the balanced scorecard, illustrated through university library case studies.

Markless, S. and Streatfield, D. (2001), 'Developing Performance and Impact Indicators and Targets in Public and Education Libraries', *International Journal of Information Management* 21:2, 167–79. Discusses issues surrounding performance evaluation in public and education libraries, identifying an 'activity fixation' while neglecting impact assessment. Reports initial work on the development and testing of the authors' process model for generating impact indicators and related development planning model (subsequently presented in their book cited below).

Markless, S. and Streatfield, D. (2006), *Evaluating the Impact of Your Library* (London: Facet). Based on a model which explicitly links evaluation to overall purpose/mission, aims to 'put the impact back into planning' by offering a framework for strategic and service-level development planning. Provides detailed guidance on formulating success criteria, defining impact indicators, and methods for collecting, analysing, interpreting and presenting evidence. Companion website provides downloadable evaluation tools and materials. Available at: <http://www.facetpublishing.co.uk/evaluatingimpact/>.

APPENDIX 1: STRATEGY DEVELOPMENT WORKSHOPS

These workshop outlines show examples of practical activities that contribute to the development of a service strategy, while also facilitating the development of strategic skills among participants. The workshops were designed for a mixed group of 25–30 staff, drawn from all areas and levels of an academic library. The two workshops focus on:

Environmental Challenges and Stakeholder Concerns
Strategic Vision and Key Result Areas

WORKSHOP ON ENVIRONMENTAL CHALLENGES AND STAKEHOLDER CONCERNS

Which are the key environmental influences and how will they affect the library's services?

The environment in which libraries currently operate is dynamic and complex. Our appraisal needs to cover external forces in the global 'macro-environment', trends in relevant sectors (for example, Higher Education, scholarly publishing) and internal institutional issues (specific to the university).

1. Discussion in small groups to identify key drivers. Groups are asked to focus on different areas:

    Group 1 Societal/Global *General Environment* (for example, social, economic, political, legal, technological)

    Group 2 Operating/Sectoral *Market Environment* (for example, Higher Education, research, knowledge transfer)

    Group 3 Library/Information *Professional Environment* (for example, information resources, services, facilities, systems)

    Group 4 Local/Institutional *Internal Environment* (for example, mission, values, vision, strategic priorities)

Groups are asked to generate long lists initially and then to reduce their lists to the ten most significant issues. Groups follow a set process:

- Identify and capture key drivers individually
- Share, compare and collate drivers as a group
- Debate, evaluate and agree your top ten drivers

Results are then captured on flipcharts and shared with other groups.

2. Discussion in small groups to analyse each of the ten drivers/forces identified in turn. Groups consider two questions:

    – What is the level of its impact on the library – high, medium or low?
    – How much uncertainty surround this force – high, medium or low?

Results are then recorded in an Issues Priorities Matrix on flipcharts , shared and discussed with other groups.

Who are our stakeholders and what are their expectations of and ambitions for the library?

A stakeholder is any individual or group with an involvement or interest in the organization, actual or potential, in the past, present or future. According to Bryson and Alston (1996, 43):

> *A stakeholder is any person, group or organization that can place a claim on an organization's resources, attention or output, or is affected by its output.*

3. Discussion in small groups to identify exactly who the library's stakeholders are. Groups are asked to concentrate on particular stakeholder categories:

    Group 1   Taught and research students
    Group 2   Academic and research staff
    Group 3   External library users/customers
    Group 4   Library funders and sponsors

Groups are asked to identify the key sub-groups within their stakeholder group and to consider each sub-group in turn. Groups consider two questions:

    – How important is this group – high or low?
    – How much influence to they have – high or low?

4. For important and/or influential sub-groups, groups consider two more questions:

- – Are they single- or multi-issue stakeholders?
- – What *really* matters to them, in terms of their needs/wants/expectations of the library?

Results are then recorded in Stakeholder Tables on flipcharts, shared and discussed with other groups.

REFERENCE

Bryson, J.M. and Alston, F.K. (1996), *Creating and Implementing Your Strategic Plan: A Workbook for Public and Non-Profit Organizations* (San Francisco: Jossey-Bass).

WORKSHOP ON STRATEGIC VISION AND KEY RESULT AREAS

In the light of your analysis of environmental influences and stakeholder issues, what or where should the library aspire to be in five/ten years from now?

The final vision statement should be a coherent description of the desired future state of the library, showing how it is realizing its capacity to anticipate, determine, stimulate and satisfy the needs of existing and potential users for access to information in an ethical manner.

What will the library look like five/ten years from now?
How will people behave when seeking and using information?
How would you be working if you were optimally meetings their needs?
What is your desired position in the institution and in the wider library community?

1. Discussion in small groups to identify the key words, phrases or images that capture the essence of where the library is going in the future. Groups are asked to reflect on a set of questions individually, to write down their ideas and then produce a shared list.

Questions to help reflection

How will things be different from the present in terms of:

- • Scope – range and mix of collections and services?

- Scale – size of the organization and extent of the user base?
- Focus – particular products, services and facilities?
- Competition – basis of your distinctive/niche offerings?
- Relationships – internal and external partnerships?
- Organization – management structure and systems, staff specialisms and categories, organizational culture and climate of the library and university?

Participants are asked to choose the clearest, crispest, most informative and inspirational words that capture their vision. Groups follow a set process:

- Start by writing down thoughts individually
- Share, compare and discuss in your group
- Produce a list on a flipchart reflecting your collective vision, aiming for around six to eight points in total

2. First round of consolidation by larger groups to reduce the multiple lists of key messages to a single list that can be used to create a vision statement. Groups 1–2 and 3–4 are asked to work together. The new larger groups follow a set process:

- Bring the two lists together and debate key messages
- Distil down into a new list, again aiming for six to eight points in total
- Combine concepts, accept trade-offs and/or substitute words as necessary

3. Second round of consolidation. All groups work together, gathering around one flipchart and bringing the two new lists of key points together as before, distilling down again, this time aiming for a shared list of no more than ten points in total.

What strategic initiatives, developments, enhancements or changes to the library and its services are needed to enable it to move towards realizing the aspirations of the vision?

The vision provides a high-level picture of the directions in which the library intends to go, which then needs to be translated into actionable goals or medium-term strategic objectives, often referred to as key result areas, key performance areas or similar.

4. Discussion in small groups to clarify the messages of the vision, if necessary translating the points into more specific descriptions, which can be compared with the current situation. Groups consider two questions:

- Is it clear what each point means in terms of the practices, activities, facilities, and so on, envisaged?
- Are the messages sufficiently specific to compare what is envisaged with what exists?

5. Discussion in small groups to identify gaps between the current situation and desired future state, and the actions or resources needed to close the gaps. Groups develop statements in the form:

   In order to ... [the desired state or activity], the service/unit needs to ... [become/do/have/and so on]

The process then continues to consider at a more specific level what exactly needs to be done in terms of practical strategies or action steps and the likely resource implications, such as whether the change would require a significant or substantial increase in budget.

CHAPTER 11

MENTORING

JANE WALTON

INTRODUCTION

Mentoring as a concept has existed for centuries and originates in Greek mythology when Odysseus, before setting out on an epic voyage, entrusted his son to his friend Mentor. Mentoring in current practice takes many forms and is used in a range of contexts.

For the purposes of this book, mentoring is defined as 'supporting the professional development of others in the library and information services sector in order to maximize their potential, develop their skills and develop the profession to meet the needs of service users now and in the future'.

The author advocates the use of mentoring within and across the profession. The chapter advocates the use of mentors who are external to the mentees' own organizations. It takes as its basis the good practice developed by CILIP's mentoring programme.

In writing this chapter, the author acknowledges the work of David Clutterbuck and Eric Parsloe, who have provided both a theoretical and practical approach to mentoring which has influenced the development of the thoughts, ideas and recommendations developed during this work.

The author also acknowledges the experiences of both mentors and mentees in the Museums Association and CILIP's professional accreditation scheme and members of the museum, library and archive sector who have offered their advice.

DEFINITIONS OF MENTORING

There are many different definitions of mentoring and this has created a range of interpretations and practice. Later in the chapter the range of interpretations will be explored. In the context of current practice advocated by CILIP, the approach to mentoring which has been adopted is informed by the work of Eric Parsloe and David Clutterbuck:

To help and support people to manage their own learning in order to maximise their potential, develop their skills, improve their performance and become the person they want to be (Parsloe 1992).

Mentoring includes coaching, facilitating, counselling and networking. It is not necessary to dazzle the protégé with knowledge and experience. The mentor just has to provide encouragement by sharing his enthusiasm for his job (Clutterbuck 1991).

The key component of CILIP's mentoring scheme is based on the requirement for qualification candidates to develop continuing professional development (CPD) plans and records. Mentors are trained and supported to ensure that candidates are able to identify their development needs, to identify development activities and to reflect on the learning outcomes and benefits of these activities. The following information will provide support for those who are considering becoming a mentor or developing a mentoring scheme in their own organization where mentors will be sought externally.

THE BENEFITS OF MENTORING

In order to inform this chapter, the author examined the statements of 200 mentees and 50 mentors who had recently completed a mentoring relationship as part of the Museums Association AMA programme. Four key beneficiaries were identified but there are many more.

The Mentee

The mentee benefits from the opportunity to develop a planned approach to their professional development. The mentee is expected to produce a personal development plan as a result of reflecting on their current needs and future aspirations. In examining the CPD statements of museum professionals, all highlighted the focus that the mentoring process had brought to their personal, professional and career development. Many mentees have achieved promotion and recognition as a result of developing themselves in a coherent and consistent way. The opportunity to discuss issues and needs with someone outside their own organization was identified as significant in their development.

The Mentor

Those who have become mentors list a number of reasons for doing so; professional status, the opportunity to give something back, talent spotting and the development of interpersonal skills are some. Many mentors have had a positive experience of mentoring themselves. The mentoring experience provides an opportunity to support the development of the profession and yourself at the same time. The skills involved in mentoring are transferable to managing people generally. The ability to develop networks, contacts and sources of information in order for the mentor to contribute to the mentee's professional development will also support their own development.

The Organization

Organizations within the sector have still to realize the benefits of mentoring. The organization can benefit from mentoring if it is able to manage it. Effective mentoring needs the support of line managers, colleagues and organizational policies and procedures. If the mentee is required to take annual leave in order to be mentored, if the mentee does not feel able to share their CPD plans with their line manager or even keeps the mentoring relationship secret, then this will undermine the benefits to the organization. Mentoring offers an opportunity for staff to receive personal, professional and career development advice from someone who has a range of networks, contacts and sources of information which may not be accessible to the organization. The mentor is helping the mentee to have a planned and coherent approach to their development which should make better use of the organization's resources, increase motivation and improve performance. The ultimate outcome might be that the mentee leaves the organization in order to pursue their career; this has been stated as a drawback of mentoring. It is suggested that it is better to lose an employee who has a positive view of the organization as a supportive employer than one who leaves and is only too happy to tell the world about the lack of support they received.

The Profession

The aim of this chapter is to provide advice and support in implementing mentoring. The benefits that mentoring can bring are illustrated by the number of professional bodies that endorse it. A professional mentoring programme which aims to develop people in the sector also aims to enhance the professional standing of the sector. This chapter provides advice on mentoring but there is also an underlying aim of communicating the professional standards which have been developed by the sector. Mentoring provides a framework for professional development which includes the communication and implementation of professional standards. Those standards which inform how members of the sector carry out their roles from an ethical standpoint are an integral part of the mentoring process. Other beneficiaries of the mentoring process include line managers, colleagues, service users, friends and families.

ROLES AND RESPONSIBILITIES

As described above the mentoring process has key beneficiaries; in order for the process to work effectively, each of the roles and associated responsibilities need to be made clear.

The mentee	The mentor
Focused career development	Personal development
Imporved self-confidence	Job satisfaction
Advice and guidance	Developed interpersonal skills
Access to networks and contacts	Discovering talent
Management development	Professional status
The organization	**The profession**
Development of skills bank	Improved networks
Focused employees	Managed career development
Planned work programmes	Focused individuals
Increased efficiency	Communicated standards
Improved staff morale	Status
Low cost career development	

Figure 11.1 The benefits of mentoring

WHAT IS MENTORING?

Mentoring is a way of developing individuals to achieve their potential. Usually it is associated with a senior or 'expert' person adopting a protégé. Informally, it is characterized by a mentor helping the person they are mentoring to discover something new about themselves and their capabilities.

MENTORING FOR CPD IN THE CONTEXT OF PROFESSIONAL QUALIFICATIONS

CPD is about being responsible for your own career-long development. In the library and information services sector, candidates are expected to develop a personal and professional development plan and to keep a reflective account of their development. Mentoring assists people undertaking professional qualifications to plan their professional development and evaluate their achievements.

Mentors

- Will be people with considerable experience working in or for the sector. They often hold a professional qualification themselves
- Will be prepared to commit time to helping another member of the profession to develop their potential – around four meetings a year
- Are unlikely to be in the same workplace as the mentee

How CPD Mentoring Differs from Tutoring, Managing and Appraising Staff, and NVQ/SVQ Assessing

The tutor/student relationship is a familiar one, particularly in the context of guiding students through a professional qualification route. Tutoring differs from mentoring in that it centres on a syllabus which students are expected to follow. In the traditional qualification routes, the focus was primarily on the students producing an academic outcome and developing their skills and knowledge to perform effectively in a practical exam. The tutor usually took the lead, whether new skills were to be taught or new areas of knowledge imparted.

Within a CPD mentoring relationship, the development needs of each mentee will vary; it is the mentor's role to guide, to offer advice, and to act as a sounding board, encouraging the mentee to be ultimately responsible for their own personal and professional development. A manager/employee relationship is primarily task-orientated; the manager is in control and responsible for the outcomes of the relationship. Although a good manager plays a significant role in developing and guiding their staff and in appraising their progress, the main concern is to ensure that organizational objectives are achieved within the resources available.

In a CPD mentoring relationship, the mentor is likely to be an objective outsider. Although organizational objectives are a consideration in establishing the mentee's development needs, the primary concern of the mentor is to encourage the mentee to examine broader professional issues and to explore a range of development possibilities.

The NVQ/SVQ assessor/candidate relationship has also been compared with that of the mentor and mentee. The role of the NVQ/SVQ assessor is rather different from that of CPD mentor as the outcomes or competencies required are specified within the NVQ/SVQ standards of competence; although the assessor may help to guide the candidate's development, the outcome, or level of competence to be achieved, is prescribed already.

Although the exact nature of the relationships vary, many of the skills needed in these roles are also a requirement of the CPD mentor.

ROLES OF A MENTOR

A range of situations may occur in the mentor/mentee relationship requiring the mentor to move between different roles. Clutterbuck identifies a mentor as a coach, co-ordinator, supporter, monitor, and organizer (Clutterbuck 1991).

The following is adapted from Holloway, Whyte and Kennington (1994):

Table 11.1 The role of the mentor

The role of the mentor is to:	To encourage the mentee to:
• Listen • Question, find out facts • Pass on information and knowledge • Give guidance on career development • Offer different perspectives on an issue • Offer support; be encouraging • Take the lead and make decisions, at least in the early stages of the relationship • Describe own experience (if appropriate) • Confront difficult issues	• Listen • Check their understanding • Share their thoughts • Review and reflect on own learning • Be open to new perspectives • Get the most from the relationship • Take responsibility for their own development

The importance of having a mentor is characterized by the comment of one mentee who said: 'Without a mentor you feel very much on your own and it's quite daunting' (Mentee).

IMPLEMENTING AN ORGANIZATIONAL MENTORING SCHEME

This section outlines the process for establishing an organizational mentoring scheme. It is recommended that this would be based on the premise that mentors will come from outside the organization and that internal staff could mentor those outside the organization. The implementation of this model will require the organization to accept that mentoring is beneficial to organizational as well as individual development. To implement an organizational scheme, there are a number of steps in the process which are as follows.

Justifying the Need for Mentoring

Organizations that are already committed to training and developing their staff will see mentoring as a natural progression which provides the organizational benefits as described above. For those that do not work in this way, mentoring may seem difficult to justify in terms of the time staff will need to spend away from their place of work.

Developing a Mentoring Policy

Mentoring needs to be established as part of the staff development policy of the organization. The following sample policy in Box 11.1 gives an indication as to how this can be incorporated.

Mentoring forms an integral part of the organization's training and development policy. Mentoring is defined as 'the provision of external one-to-one support for an employee's development which operates outwith the performance review process and is linked to career development'.

The following outlines the organization's approach to mentoring:

- All staff are entitled to request support via mentoring.
- Staff will be advised on the process involved in identifying and approaching a suitable mentor.
- Mentors will be sourced externally and the organization will ensure that they understand the role of mentoring as defined by the organization by providing access to appropriate training/briefing.
- Staff will be fully briefed on their role and expectations as mentees.
- The mentoring process will be supported by a mentoring agreement agreed by both parties.
- The mentee is entitled to request to change their mentor on discussion with their line manager or HR officer.
- The verbal or written accounts of mentor meetings will remain confidential between both parties.
- Mentoring arrangements and procedures will be kept under review and amended as appropriate.

Box 11.1 Model mentoring policy

Developing Mentoring Procedures

In order to ensure consistency in how staff implement the mentoring policy, procedures should be developed and staff offered training in using them. The key procedures should cover:

How to register as a mentor/mentee (see Appendix 1 and 2 at the end of this chapter)
How to develop a mentoring agreement
How to record the outcomes of a mentoring meeting
How to evaluate the mentoring relationship
How to seek advice and information should issues arise
How to develop a personal and professional development plan
How to develop a development record

THE SUCCESSFUL MENTORING RELATIONSHIP

The quality of people's working and professional relationships directly affects their motivation and learning capacity. This is true of the relationship between the mentor and their mentee. Holloway identifies a number of factors which influence an effective mentoring relationship (Holloway, Whyte and Kennington 1994). She suggests that these need to be present in both mentor and mentee to facilitate the development process.

1. *Rapport*

   This enables communication between people and without rapport there can be no relationship. People become hostile and isolated and the development process is blocked. You can develop rapport by:

   - Having respect for others
   - Actively demonstrating empathy
   - Being genuine

2. *Respect*

   Valuing the other person for who they are and respecting their uniqueness and individuality. By offering respect you help to create a climate of trust and openness. Respect is an attitude – it can be acquired through practice.

3. *Empathy*

   Empathy is the ability to see things from the other's point of view and communicate to them that understanding. Empathy is a skill and can be learnt.

4. *Genuineness or sincerity*

   This is a quality in your personality. It is the capacity to be yourself, to communicate to others that you are open and want to help. If you are not committed to the mentoring relationship it will be immediately apparent to your mentee. At the same time, if the mentee sees no potential value, you will very quickly become aware of this.

   It is important that you actively enter into the relationship and seek to develop a positive attitude from the start. One mentee has said: 'My mentor is a very charismatic and inspirational person – a role model. It's a pity I've only seen him once!' (Mentee)

THE MENTORING RELATIONSHIP

As mentioned at the beginning of this chapter, there are many different roles which relate to mentoring. In examining the evidence from mentors and mentees, the author identified a number of related roles and has developed a way of capturing the dynamics of the relationships (see Figure 11.2).

The experience of mentors suggests that they manage the mentoring relationship within a framework of approaches which extend from coaching to nurturing and from networking to counselling. The characteristic which seems to determine the nature of the mentoring role is whether a directive or non-directive approach is required and whether the mentee needs to be supported or challenged. The author would suggest that the mentor needs to remain aware of the status and nature of the relationship to ensure that they are not stepping outside the mentoring role and into a role which may require additional skills, knowledge and expertise. This awareness will also help to identify when the mentoring relationship is being effective.

In order to illustrate the dynamic of the mentoring relationship the author has developed the following scenarios:

Context: mentor as guardian – the mentee appears to expect that the mentor will undertake all of the actions agreed on the mentee's behalf including contacting the mentee's line manager.

Action: the mentor should ensure that the mentee understands that it is their responsibility to undertake actions which relate to their own development; the mentor may need to support the mentee to have the confidence to action this.

Context: mentor as coach – the mentee has identified that they require some skills development; the mentor has identified that they have these skills.

Action: the mentor should decide if it would be appropriate to offer to coach the mentee outside the mentoring relationship.

Context: mentor as networker – the mentee has identified the need to become a member of relevant networks; the mentor is a member of these networks.

Action: the mentor acts as a referee for the mentee and introduces the mentee to the network before enabling the mentee to sustain this activity independently.

Context: mentor as counsellor – the mentee has shared personal information with the mentor which suggests that they need some counselling support.

Action: the mentor makes appropriate referrals to relevant support organizations.

The mentoring relationship can constantly change in its nature even within the period of an hour long meeting.

Mentors must be aware that they need to maintain a balance between facilitating and supporting development. It is all too easy to be the answer to all the mentee's problems.

Directive	
Coaching Stretching	Guardian Nurturing
Challenging Networking	Supporting Counselling
Non-directive	

Figure 11.2 The mentoring relationship

Are You the Right Mentor?

It is recommended that the mentee is encouraged to select their own mentor and will want to talk to them about how they see the relationship before a commitment is made on either side. There are many definitions and views of the role of a mentor but all include the need to support, guide and facilitate. Although each mentee will be seeking different things from their mentors, all the following are important general qualities:

- A good track record of achievement within the sector which may or may not relate directly to the individual's chosen career path
- An informed and current overview of the sector, and of the challenges and opportunities the sector faces
- Experience of developing people and the skills which accompany this
- Specific personal qualities and interpersonal skills
- A real desire to help
- The willingness to commit time to the process (around four meetings a year)

Potential mentors should consider their potential contribution as a mentor in relation to the above general points and the questions below.

- Are you able to discuss openly what you think you can offer?
- Can you be honest about areas where you feel that you cannot help?

The perfect mentor does not exist and potential mentors should try to regard this as a learning process for both themselves and the mentee. Before starting out as a mentor, individuals should take some time to consider their position. Figure 11.3 provides a checklist that can aid their decision.

	Question	Self-Assessment	Action Plan
1	Do you understand how mentoring differs from other roles?		
2	Are you willing/able to make the necessary time available?		
3	Are you comfortable about creating your own CPD action plan?		
4	Do you have the knowledge to be able to advise/refer the mentee?		
5	Have you got the skills – questioning, supporting, challenging?		
6	Are you aware of the ethical considerations regarding relationships and confidentiality?		
7	Are you able to act as a sounding board?		
8	Can you give clear, honest and constructive feedback?		
9	Will you be able to end the relationship positively?		
10	Do you still want to be a mentor?		

Figure 11.3 Mentoring checklist

Benefits to the Mentor

From the mentee's point of view, mentors are giving their time and sharing their experiences, but there will be a number of additional benefits for the mentor:

- Skills development, for example, interpersonal skills, objective setting, counselling, and so on
- Satisfaction – of giving help
- Network expansion
- Better understanding of career development needs of more junior members of the profession
- Changing your own behaviour as a result
- Peer recognition within the profession
- Good for your own CPD

THE MENTORING PROCESS

The AMA strategy is about defining direction and it has been particularly timely for me. What has been most beneficial is having a wonderful mentor who encouraged me to think long-term – strategically and in the broader scale – he boosted my confidence and provided professional support that was lacking at work. He believed that I could do it which was really important (Mentee).

This quotes one mentee who states the importance of the mentoring process. The following four stages act as a guide:

1. Getting to know each other and drawing up a mentoring agreement
2. Planning
3. Providing support to achieve CPD goals
4. Final stages: planning for the future; evaluating and summarizing CPD

1. Getting to know each other and drawing up a mentoring agreement

Establishing expectations
If both mentor and mentee have different expectations of the relationship, it is inevitable that misunderstandings will arise. Although the mentor is likely to have more experience, it should not be seen as a relationship between the inexperienced and the expert. An effective mentoring relationship should be regarded as one of sharing and mutual learning. Although some initial discussion will have taken place, probably on the telephone, it is a useful exercise for both the mentor and the mentee to think about what they expect before the first meeting and then

discuss expectations frankly. Time invested at the first meeting will pay long-term dividends.

Confidentiality

The mentee will need to feel comfortable in openly discussing their development needs, and weaknesses, with the mentor. They will require reassurance that aspects of these will not be discussed outside the mentoring situation. If there is uncertainty, then barriers may be created which could inhibit the development of the mentoring relationship and hence its effectiveness. It is likely that the mentor will be asked to act as a referee for the mentee and is able to comment on their commitment to CPD. For this reason it is important to agree what will remain confidential and perhaps to make a brief record of each meeting in the form of action notes, which can be used when drafting the reference. As part of this process, a mentoring action plan should be drawn up and the following questions can be used as a framework for this purpose:

- What would you like to have achieved by (date)?
- What are your critical success factors – the things you will have to do to make your plan come true?
- What could hinder you in taking these actions?
- How will you overcome these hindrances?
- Who or what can help you to achieve your vision?
- What is the very first thing you will do?
- When will you do it?
- How will you be sure to keep your resolutions – to prevent the telephone, the e-mail and the in-tray from swamping your plan?
- When we meet again, what will we celebrate?

The mentoring agreement or contract

Findings from the research mentioned earlier in the chapter identified that both mentors and mentees would find an informal contract or agreement helpful in clarifying processes and expectations. A discussion based on the mentoring agreement checklist below would help you formulate such an agreement:

- Confidentiality and trust – checking out what this means to each of you
- Number and frequency of meetings
- Where will the meetings take place and how long will they be?
- Who initiates meetings?
- What will be the mentee's access to the mentor; for example, can the mentor be contacted at home or not?
- What areas are legitimate to discuss and what are not?
- Clarifying the expectations of your mentee in respect of your role and your input to their development
- What are your own expectations of them?

- Determining boundaries within the relationship
- What if something goes wrong, such as personality difficulties?
- How and what will you evaluate at the end of the two years?

2. Planning

> *I have found the plan format useful as it links career aims to actual activities and means you have to justify your plans and activities. It means that some things that would be nice to do but don't really fit are obvious* (Mentee).

As one mentee says above, using a planning tool helps to support and guide their choices. The most effective way to structure the mentoring process is to agree a CPD personal and professional development plan with the mentee, setting out their goals and resulting needs and the activities that they intend to undertake to achieve these goals.

Mentees will have different requirements of their mentors in terms of the support they require at this stage, and the process of identifying needs, reviewing progress and adapting CPD goals will be a continuous one during the mentoring relationship.

A personal SWOT analysis
The mentee may seek the mentor's help in undertaking their own personal SWOT analysis, which is the starting point for analysing their CPD needs. It is an audit of their:

- Personal and professional strengths
- Weaknesses that should be addressed
- Opportunities for development
- Threats to achieving their goals

However, the mentor should encourage them to undertake this self-analysis, perhaps in consultation with their line manager, prior to any involvement you may have. Some mentors have found themselves closely involved at this stage and others less so. Your role is as a sounding board. You will need to listen actively, clarify and guide the mentee, essentially helping them to 'think out loud'. It is not your role to tell the mentee what they should do.

CPD goals
These should be focused on the main priorities or the main changes or areas of development that the mentee identifies. These relate to:

- Short term job-related development needs
- Long-term career plans

The proforma CPD personal action plan is divided into these two categories. The mentee may seek your guidance in determining which goals are a priority within their plan. Although the professional CPD scheme places emphasis on the individual's professional aspirations and development, the organizational implications and value of particular goals should be discussed by the mentee with their manager.

CPD needs

It is important to encourage the mentee to look for a reasonable spread when identifying their CPD needs. For example, a personal and professional development plan that only deals with the development of a specialism would be inadequate. The following list provides guidance on what areas of professional skills and knowledge should be included:

- Personal competence, incorporating interpersonal skills
- Management of both resources and people
- Professional: for example, improving knowledge of new approaches to user education or development of other specialism; involvement in and contribution to the wider profession
- Specialist skills (including information technology)

Area of activity	Development Needs	Proposed Activities
Present role Future role Personal priorities	Aim Timescale SMART	Mentoring Shadowing Courses Work based projects

Figure 11.4 Personal and professional development plan (PPDP) template

Identifying activities

In addition, the mentee must identify a range of activities which will help them to meet these needs. For example, a personal and professional development plan with activities entirely reliant on work-based learning would be neither balanced nor acceptable.

Remember, CPD activities can fall into one of three categories:

- Professional work-based activities including involvement in professional activities outside work
- Formal learning – courses, seminars, conferences
- Informal or self-directed learning

3. Providing support to achieve CPD goals

At the planning stage, and beyond, it is important that the mentor recognizes and articulates their own limitations in relation to the mentee's development needs. Unlike a tutoring role, the mentor is not expected to be a teacher. They may, however, be in a position to guide the mentee about where to go for help or suggest what they might do to develop their competence or know-how.

Developing the mentee's confidence

A key objective at this stage is to develop the confidence of the mentee to question and challenge their own and your assumptions and to evaluate their own learning experiences. Some mentees have said that their mentors have not been sufficiently challenging. Others have found the reverse. One mentee recently interviewed said: 'My mentor is constantly challenging and always seems to be ten years ahead of me in what I'm thinking.' This approach works well if the mentor is also prepared to listen to what the mentee wants.

It is likely that the mentee's manager will also be closely involved in helping to create development opportunities within the workplace and in giving the mentee feedback on their progress.

Impartiality

As an independent figure, the mentor is in a position to offer impartial support by helping the mentee to review their work experience in the context of other learning activities they are engaged in.

Giving information and providing guidance

The mentee is likely to draw on the mentor's experience and knowledge and it may be appropriate for the mentor to give the mentee an insight into their own work. Any information, knowledge or experience the mentor gives should not be biased or prejudiced in any way – it should be designed to help the mentee explore the options that may be open to them and to see things from a new or different perspective. One mentee quoted below indicates how their view was influenced:

> *I asked her why she wanted to be a mentor which was interesting and about how she'd got where she was. In some ways it made me feel quite uncomfortable because she was saying that her job as a registrar is very different to mine. I saw what being a registrar elsewhere might involve which was really useful. It broadened my perspective and helped planning for future jobs* (Mentee).

4. Final stages

Having established a supportive relationship within which the mentee can explore their own development, the mentor's ultimate goal is to encourage them to be responsible for their own CPD. The mentor should not wish to foster an ongoing dependency and should be moving towards a position where the formal relationship will come to an end.

Planning for the future
At this stage it is likely that the feedback the mentor gives and the questions that they ask their mentee will become more challenging and demanding. The mentor will help them to identify areas for their ongoing development and explore options available for continuing support if this is considered necessary. Whether the mentee is completing a professional qualification or applying for a promotion or new job, they will be expected to talk about their future plans and CPD needs, so these discussions are an important element of their preparation.

Evaluating and summarizing CPD
The mentor has an important role throughout in helping their mentee evaluate their learning so they are able to complete their ongoing CPD record, and some may also wish to build up a portfolio to demonstrate what they have learnt.

It is recommended that mentees are encouraged to summarize their CPD on an annual basis. This can then be used as evidence for work-based development reviews and appraisals, professional reviews and when preparing job applications. It also encourages the mentee to reflect on the past year, to recognize their achievements and identify those areas requiring further development.

Record of activity	Outcomes	Benefits
What When Where Who Resources	What did you learn?	How have you benefited from the activity?

Figure 11.5 Personal development log template

The CPD summary should ask the mentee to describe their learning under the following headings:

- Personal competence incorporating interpersonal skills
- Management of both resources and people
- Professional: for example, improving knowledge of new approaches to user education or development of other specialism; involvement in and contribution to the wider profession
- Specialist skills (including information technology)

They should also be asked to summarize the impact of CPD on their current job and to comment on the impact this has made on their future plans.

> *The mentor provides an objective view to make you think about what you have learnt and question if it was the right thing. That kind of self-analysis is not always easy to do on your own* (Mentee).

UNDERSTANDING HOW WE LEARN

Learning is a continuous process. Many opportunities for learning occur during structured learning events, training courses and the like, but perhaps the majority arise from informal opportunities or may be facilitated by new experiences or activities. CPD acknowledges that all these experiences are valuable, as long as one takes the time to recognize, review and learn from them. When mentees complete their CPD records, they will need to identify not only relevant activities that have contributed to their learning, but also what they have learnt and what impact this has had on their work. The mentor's role is to help them with this process.

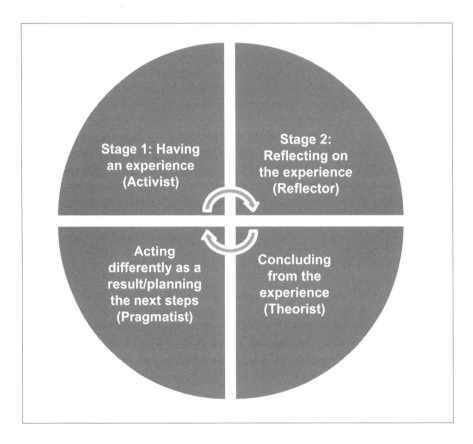

Figure 11.6 Kolb's learning cycle model

The learning cycle model, developed by David Kolb, identifies four stages of learning as noted in Figure 11.6 (Kolb 1984). In terms of the mentoring relationship, it is important to understand that people learn and develop in different ways and that each stage in the cycle requires them to adopt a different approach. Peter Honey and Alan Mumford (1982) connected each stage in this learning cycle with a preferred learning style as noted below:

Table 11.2 Learning stages and styles

Learning Stages	Learning Styles
Having an experience	Activist Learns best from activities where they can throw themselves into a task
Reflect on the experience	Reflector Learns best when they can review what has happened
Conclude from the experience	Theorist Learns best when they can understand what they have learned as part of a wider picture
Plan the next steps	Pragmatist Learns best when an opportunity presents itself to learn on the job

Mentors will most likely be working with the mentee at the second and third stages, helping them reflect on their experiences and to draw conclusions from these, although they will probably get involved at the fourth stage in planning the next steps for learning. Part of the role will also be to help the mentee identify how they learn most effectively and develop their capacity to progress smoothly through the four stages in the learning cycle.

> *My mentor helped me draw out more from each activity. She said 'you can be negative and critical as well', which I wasn't sure about before* (Mentee).

THE MENTORING PROCESS

Figure 11.7 graphically depicts the stages in the mentoring process that the mentor will go through when supporting a mentee. From the inception of the CPD action plan they will continue to encourage the individual to help themselves while providing support and assistance during evaluation.

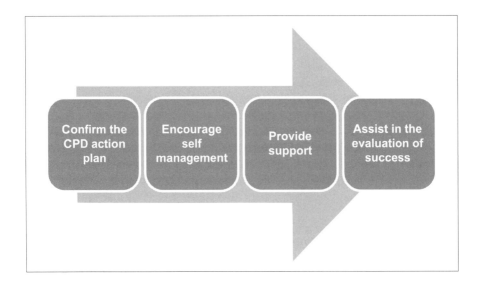

Figure 11.7 The mentoring process

SKILLS OF MENTORING

The ability to provide guidance to mentees will depend on how the mentor uses their interpersonal skills. In the mentoring relationship they will need to draw on a number of core skills. Here are some of the most important ones.

Attending and Active Listening

Communication is a two-way process. It is not just about giving others information; it is also about attending to what people are saying and responding appropriately. Active listening is an important skill in the mentoring relationship and in counselling generally. People like and feel warm towards those who listen to them. A mentee is more likely to open up and discuss their needs with the mentor if they listen carefully. Attending means actively listening, paying attention to the speaker and looking at him or her. It takes enormous concentration to do it well.

We ARE NOT attending when:

- We say we understand before the mentee has finished talking
- We have an answer before the mentee has finished speaking
- We finish sentences for the mentee
- We are dying to say something we think is important and interrupt
- We tell them about our experience, at an inappropriate time, making theirs seem less important

- We are clearly thinking about something else
- We are not making eye contact with the mentee and are using our body language to tell them that we are not listening

We ARE attending when:

- We really do try to understand
- We hold back our desire to tell the mentee what to do or give 'good' advice
- We use silence constructively
- We smile and look encouraging
- We encourage the mentee to describe their ideas and opinions freely by using prompts such as 'Hmm', 'I see', 'So what happened then?'
- We are able to paraphrase what has been said which indicates our careful listening
- We encourage them to find their own solutions by asking them questions and helping them to explore alternatives

Drawing Out and Probing

Open and closed questions can be used to encourage the mentee to express themselves more fully as well as to probe more deeply into what they are saying. Using expressions such as 'I see', and reflecting back what the mentee has said will encourage them to go on talking and to explore their own thoughts and ideas. In problem solving with the mentee, the mentor will be encouraging them to find their own answers rather than to give them their solutions. It is not easy asking questions when you think you know the logical course of action, and this requires practice and self-control. The following tips will help.

- Try to ask clear, concise and specific questions
- Always acknowledge responses fully and positively
- Probe for extra information using phrases such as, 'Is that all?' 'Have you covered everything?'
- Give answers real consideration before responding – use pauses and silence
- The following questions are particularly helpful in a mentoring situation; they encourage self-awareness of the mentee:
    'How did you feel when that happened?'
    'Why do you think you got that response?'
    'What else could you have considered?'
- Stay focused and use questions to bring the discussion back on track
- Do not ask leading questions
- Do not use the question 'why' too frequently as this may become irritating
- Use closed questions to establish specific information or facts

- Use open questions to establish rapport, explore opinions, attitudes and feelings and to find out more information
- Use questions to challenge and stimulate fresh creative approaches to problem solving

Giving and Receiving Feedback

Feedback is a vital skill within a mentoring relationship; it helps increase self-awareness in the mentee and builds their confidence. It is important to handle feedback sensitively and constructively and to ensure that negative feedback is balanced with positive. The idea is to build confidence and commitment in the mentee, not to set them back or to discourage. Equally, to encourage the development of trust and openness within the relationship, mentors should be prepared to disclose their own ideas and feelings and be prepared to receive feedback on how they are handling the mentoring process.

Helpful feedback is achieved if:

- It matters
- It is asked for
- It is specific
- It fits into context
- It focuses on behaviour or actions, not personality
- It is constructive and offers alternatives and suggestions
- The benefits to the receiver are clear

FINAL THOUGHTS

Mentoring is now accepted as a key component of the majority of professional and organizational development schemes. The benefits which have been outlined above enable individuals both as mentees and mentors to develop skills which are transferable into general people management and to move forward professionally and personally. Professional organizations that have adopted mentoring have recognized the value of training mentors who can then ensure that standards are maintained and that a culture of CPD is passed from generation to generation. Organizations which accept that staff should engage in mentoring and are able to support employees by allowing meetings during work time will realize the motivational role of mentoring.

A successful mentoring scheme is dependent on the skills of the mentor, the willingness of the mentee to take ownership in the process and the support provided by professional bodies and employers. Mentoring will not be effective or will at worst have a negative impact if these key elements are not present.

The processes outlined in this chapter aim to ensure that any mentoring scheme is effective and contributes to the continuous improvement of those who work in the library and information sector and to the success of the sector itself.

REFERENCES

Clutterbuck, D. (1991), *Everyone Needs a Mentor* (London: Institute of Personnel Management).

Holloway, A., Whyte, C. and Kennington, R. (1994), *Mentoring: The Definitive Workbook* (Manchester: Development Processes Ltd.)

Honey, P. and Mumford, A. (1982), *Manual of Learning Styles* (London: Peter Honey).

Kolb, D.A. (1984), *Experiential Learning: Experience as the Source of Learning and Development* (New Jersey: Prentice-Hall).

Parsloe, E. (1992), *Coaching, Mentoring and Assessing: A Practical Guide to Developing Competence* (London: Kogan Page).

WHERE TO LOOK FOR FURTHER INFORMATION

Websites

Museums Association. <www.museumsassociation.org>.

Chartered Institute of Library and Information Professionals (CILIP). <www.cilip.org.uk>.

Society of Archivists. <www.archives.org.uk>.

Professional Accreditation of Conservators-Restorers (PACR). <www.pacr.org.uk>.

European Mentoring Centre. <www.mentoringcentre.co.uk>.

International Mentoring Association. <www.wmich.edu/conferences/mentoring/ima.html>.

National Mentoring Consortium. <www.uel.ac.uk/nmc/>.

National Mentoring Network. <www.nmn.org.uk>.

Oxford School of Coaching and Mentoring. <www.oscm.co.uk>.

The Coaching Network. <www.coachingnetwork.org.uk>.

Amazon Books – search under mentoring. <www.amazon.co.uk>.

Reading List

The majority of texts on mentoring explore the topic in the context of workplace mentoring. However, the skills and techniques are highly relevant to those mentoring in a professional membership scheme and the following were useful in developing this training package.

Parsloe, E. (1999), *The Manager as Coach and Mentor*, Training Extras Series (CIPD). Cheap and short, this is a helpful starting point. Contains a limited amount of guidance on mentoring skills.

Clutterbuck, D. (2004), *Everyone Needs a Mentor* (CIPD). A succinct and useful book. It explores some of the problems that can occur in mentoring relationships with a useful section on gender-related mentoring issues.

Various authors (1995), *Create and Maintain a Learning Environment*, Number 7 in the series HRD route to Competence (Development Processes Ltd.). A comprehensive guide to the range of techniques and skills that can be used to optimize learning including mentoring, coaching and counselling. An all-round extremely useful text for any mentor, trainer or manager.

Holloway, A. (1994), *Mentoring – The Definitive Workbook* (Development Processes Ltd.). This explores the mentoring process, relationships and interpersonal skills in some depth and includes helpful exercises and checklists that can be used by the mentor to assess his or her own development needs and evaluate progress. Pricey and detailed.

This is a small selection; many more are available.

APPENDIX 1

MENTOR REGISTRATION FORM

Name:

Organization:

Contact Address:

Daytime Phone: Fax:

E-mail:

1. How long have you been working in the library and information sector?

2. Please summarize your career details starting with your current or most recent work.

Occupation/Job Title	Organization	Dates

3. What LIS qualifications do you hold?

4. Please specify other relevant training or qualifications.

5. Please specify the skills, qualities and experience which you can offer as a mentor.

   Skills and Qualities

   Particular experience relevant to mentoring

6. Do you have any particular requirements or preferences which you would like potential mentees to be aware of (for example, specialism, geographical location, and so on)?

The information on this form will be made available to potential mentees.

I confirm that I would like to attend an Introduction to Mentoring workshop.

(please tick the box)

Signed: ....   Date: ....

APPENDIX 2

MENTEE REGISTRATION FORM

Name:

Organization:

Contact Address:

Daytime Phone: Fax:

E-mail:

1. Do you have any particular requirements or preferences which you would like potential mentors to be aware of (for example, geographical location, specialism, organization type/size)?

2. If you are able at this stage, what CPD needs have you identified?

3. What qualifications do you currently hold, if any?

4. Are you intending to undertake any qualifications?

5. If yes, when?

The information on this form will be made available to potential mentors.

I confirm that I would like to attend an Introduction to CPD workshop.

(please tick the box)

Signed: ....   Date: ....

PROFESSIONAL DEVELOPMENT

CHAPTER 12

NATIONAL AND VOCATIONAL QUALIFICATIONS

KATH OWEN

INTRODUCTION

National and vocational qualifications in the library and information world seem to have been in a continuous state of review and change in the last 20 years. A relatively straightforward offering of the Library and Information Certificate for Library Assistants and Chartership for Librarians has been shaken up and developed to enable it to keep up with other developments in qualifications. This has led to greater choice for employees and greater challenges for providers if they want to keep up with developments and ensure that the profession which is probably not known for its innovation stays in the forefront of development and offers relevant qualifications for the twenty-first century.

NATIONAL OCCUPATIONAL STANDARDS

Lifelong Learning UK (LLUK) was established in 2005 as the new sector skills council whose five constituencies include libraries, archives and information services. With a strategic role for leading workforce development in the lifelong learning sector, LLUK is responsible for the National Occupational Standards (NOS) which underpin vocational qualifications such as NVQ Information and Library Services (7372) and the Level 3 Progression Award in Library and Information Services (7371), both awarded by City and Guilds. They will also provide a benchmark for foundation degrees, should these be developed.

In 2007 LLUK embarked on a period of consultation on the framework for the new generation of National Occupational Standards for Information and Library Services, Archive Services and Records Management. The previous standards published by the Information Services National Training Organisation in 2000 have been reviewed and out of date content has been removed. The new standards relate to four generic roles:

- Operational
- Practitioner

- Manager
- Senior Manager

They are organized in eight areas of activity:

- A – Planning and developing and evaluating services
- B – Governance and ethics
- C – Identifying, evaluating and acquiring content and collections
- D – Managing knowledge
- E – Managing content and collections
- F – Enabling access to and use of content and collections
- G – Facilitating lifelong learning
- H – Managing people to deliver services

[…] and are intended to focus on specialist skills. The standards framework, when published in the approved version, will be available for users to decide which ones are relevant to their own organization. The National Occupational Standards for libraries, archives and records management were approved in 2008 and are available on the Lifelong Learning UK web site (http://www.lluk.org).

LEVEL 3 PROGRESSION AWARD IN LIBRARY AND INFORMATION SERVICES (7371)

This award replaced the longstanding 7370 Library and Information Assistants Certificate in 2001. It can be undertaken as a stand-alone qualification. Delivery may be traditional classroom teaching or distance learning or any other method which is convenient. Recommended 'classroom' time is 160 hours and a minimum of 50 hours is required in the workplace completing practical assignments. Candidates therefore need to be in employment or on a work placement. The award aims to provide a basic qualification in library practice providing underlying theory which will complement workplace training and experience. However, it also contributes to the knowledge and understanding required for the National Vocational Qualifications in Information and Library Services Levels 2 and 3 (see below). Some colleges run both qualifications in parallel to make this link.

The award is made up of four core units and one (of a choice of two) optional unit. The core units are:

- The organization of library and information services
- The selection, organization and physical usage of materials

- Assisting users to locate and find information
- The library and information services environment

In addition the candidate must choose between the two optional units:

- Supporting learning for users
- Promoting library and information systems

Assessment is by written test set for each core unit and designed to test knowledge and understanding. The written tests are graded pass, credit and distinction. Assignments are set (one for each unit) which assess practical activities; these have externally set marking criteria and are externally verified for quality assurance.

City and Guilds have also identified where candidates may develop and demonstrate key skills in communication, application of number, information technology, working with others, improving own learning and performance and problem solving whilst following this scheme.

The award is also offered by distance learning, an option which makes it available to those who are unable to attend a college-based course. One disadvantage identified by candidates is the lack of opportunity to network on a regular basis with candidates from other workplaces and sectors. For many candidates taking a college course, this has proved to be a rare opportunity which has been enjoyed and which has provided additional knowledge and understanding of their work context.

NATIONAL VOCATIONAL QUALIFICATIONS (NVQ) INFORMATION AND LIBRARY SERVICES LEVELS 2 AND 3

An NVQ is a nationally recognized, vocationally based qualification. It assesses a candidate's competence, that is, the skills, knowledge and understanding they have, in a work situation. NVQs are based on national occupational standards (see above) which describe the performance expected of someone working in information and library services. The current awarding body in England is City and Guilds; the same standards are used for Scottish National Vocational Qualifications (SNVQs).

Introduced at levels 2, 3 and 4 in 1995, the award offered a qualification for library assistants which could be gained in the workplace without having to take an examination or do a written test. The awarding body was OCR and many organizations set up programmes to support candidates, some working through local colleges and others gaining the status of an approved centre themselves with their own centre co-ordinator and qualified assessors and internal verifiers. OCR arranged regular visits to externally verify procedures and assure quality.

The levels reflecting the type of work carried out by the candidates are generally accepted to be:

- *ILS/NVQ Level 2 for recognising competence of library assistants or for use as an induction programme for newly appointed library assistants.*
- *ILS/NVQ Level 3 for senior library assistants who have considerable experience in a range of library activities usually including some management responsibility*
- *ILS/NVQ Level 4 suitable for candidates who have considerable experience of a range of library activities usually including some management responsibility.*

These levels provide a career path for library assistants even though they are somewhat limited (Blyth 2003).

Candidates are required to present a portfolio of evidence which demonstrates skills and knowledge required to do their job in a range of circumstances. The advantages as perceived by many are that the award recognizes competence rather than academic ability, it is relevant and work-based, it helps to identify training needs and therefore increase skills whilst building confidence, and it requires no formal entry requirements, thus opening up a qualification path to many people who had not had such an opportunity before. For organizations with a culture of offering NVQs, links are also made with awards in areas such as information technology, customer service and management, offering wider opportunities for personal and professional development. The disadvantages for some candidates were feelings that they were only proving what they could do without substantial development, and a lack of recognition of the value of an NVQ by their organization or by senior staff with traditional qualifications. Some organizations found the process time-consuming and had difficulties in attracting staff to take on and continue the role of assessor in addition to their 'day job' when it meant going through their own award programme and assessment. Nevertheless NVQs have become an accepted opportunity for career progression in a number of organizations including Lincolnshire Library Service, University of Leicester and Lancashire Library and Information Service.

In 2002 City and Guilds took over as the awarding body offering levels 2 and 3, and the standards were updated soon afterwards. Current requirements are:

INFORMATION AND LIBRARY SERVICES LEVEL 2

Mandatory Units:

IL2/1 Maintain the arrangement of material to facilitate retrieval
IL2/2 Indentify and provide information and material required by users
IL2/3 Solve problems for customers (CSLB Unit 4 Level 2)

Optional Units (select one from each option group, plus one other)

Group 1: User Services

IL2/4 Direct users
IL2/5 Issue and recover loan material
IL2/6 Enable the use of information technology (ITNTO 201)
IL2/7 Provide and maintain information for clients (CAMPAG A10)
IL2/8 Process payments for purchases (DNTO 2/19)

Group 2: Activities

IL2/9 Process and secure information and material
IL2/10 Contribute to the maintenance of a supportive environment for users
IL2/11 Display stock to specification to attract customer interest and promote sales (DNTO 2/1)
IL2/12 Produce documents using word processing software (ITNTO 202)

Candidates must achieve a total of six units.

INFORMATION AND LIBRARY SERVICES LEVEL 3 – REVISED QUALIFICATION STRUCTURE

Mandatory Units:

IL3/1 Provide information and material to users
IL3/2 Identify information and material required by user and its availability
IL3/3 Solve problems on behalf of customers (CSLB Level 3 Unit 4)
IL3/4 Manage yourself (MCI C1)

Optional Units (select one from each group)

Group 1: Organising Information

IL3/5 Organise information and material

IL3/6 Index information
IL3/7 Create new material to preserve information
IL3/8 Design and produce spreadsheets (ITNTO 306)
IL3/9 Control the use of electronic communication (ITNTO 327)

Group 2: User Services

IL3/10 Provide displays
IL3/11 Maintain a supportive environment for users
IL3/12 Evaluate and monitor receipt of payments from customers for the purchase of goods and services (DNTO 3/7)
IL3/13 Provide induction and orientation activities for users
IL3/14 Collect and process information for use with clients (CAMPAG A8)
IL3/15 Enable clients to access and use information (CAMPAG B1)
IL3/16 Store and display information and material
IL3/17 Provide customers with information technology support (ITNTO 317)

Group 3: Supervising Activities

IL3/18 Support the efficient use of resources (MCI B1)
IL3/19 Maintain activities to meet requirement (MCI A1)
IL3/20 Create effective working relationships (MCI C4)
IL3/21 Assess candidate performance (ENTO D32)
IL3/22 Assess candidate using differing sources of evidence (ENTO D33)

Candidates must achieve a total of eight units. (Codes in brackets after units denote units borrowed from other NVQs.)

The units are intended to be used in all types of information and library work and may therefore appear vague. However, with specified performance criteria and required knowledge and understanding, they can be applied in all situations and made relevant to individual candidates.

NVQs are one application of the National Occupational Standards (see above). When the new NOS are complete they will form a basis for a new generation of vocational qualifications.

FOUNDATION DEGREES

Foundation degrees were launched in 2001 as work-based Higher Education qualifications. They involve two years' full-time or more usually four years' part-time study, they are designed with employers and with the Sector Skills Council and they may, if appropriate, be a pathway to an honours degree. Time and place of delivery may be negotiable between provider and employer; the course may involve work-based learning, college/university learning and/or distance learning. Students are supported through mentors and tutors. Although a number of institutions have talked about developing an information and library service-based foundation degree, nothing is available at the present time.

CHARTERED INSTITUTE OF LIBRARY AND INFORMATION PROFESSIONALS (CILIP) FRAMEWORK OF QUALIFICATIONS

CILIP introduced its Framework of Qualifications in April 2005. Awards of chartership and fellowship had been available for many years but the introduction of an opportunity for voluntary revalidation and for certification at a para-professional level were new departures which aimed to underline the importance of continued professional development and to provide new opportunities for access to chartership. 'A chartered profession is defined by its knowledge base and has standards for professional conduct, performance standards, accredited education and a voice with which to represent its professional community' (Martin 2007).

All the qualifications require the submission of a portfolio of evidence and demonstration of the ability to evaluate personal experience and professional development. Candidates are offered a range of support through mentors, volunteers from CILIP membership, through the Career Development Group and its network of Candidate Support Officers, and through the Personnel Training and Education Group (PTEG) and its network of Mentor Support Officers, as well as from CILIP's own Qualifications and Professional Development team.

The CILIP website is used to provide proformas, information, forms and sample applications for candidates. Candidates also have access to the assessment forms used for each award so that they can check their own applications for the required content. All the awards are underpinned by the Body of Professional Knowledge which helps candidates to relate application to core knowledge.

ACLIP: CERTIFICATED MEMBER OF CILIP

This totally new award recognizes the work of library assistants and senior assistants who do not have a degree level qualification in librarianship or information services and have therefore been prevented from progressing to chartership. It enables para-professionals to prove to themselves and to their employers that they are skilled and knowledgeable workers; in many organizations it makes them eligible to apply for professional posts and with appropriate experience to apply for chartership. Experience has shown that motivation for undertaking accreditation covers all these areas and that candidates have clear ideas of what they wish to achieve.

Applicants must have been working in library and information work for two years (full time equivalent) or longer.

To apply for Certification all candidates must demonstrate:

1. An ability to evaluate personal performance and service performance
2. An understanding of the ways in which their personal, technical and professional skills have developed through training and development activities and/or practice
3. An appreciation of the role of library and information services in the wider community

Candidates are provided with proformas available on the CILIP website which they are required to use to structure their application, and all candidates have to include a letter of recommendation, normally from a Chartered Librarian, with their application.

Certification was piloted in the East of England and the South East where CILIP Assessment Panels (CAPs) were set up with part-time CPD officers appointed to support the work of the panels. Further regional CAPs were established in the East Midlands, London, North East, West Midlands and Scotland, comprising a range of volunteers from all sectors of library and information work. In all over 100 people took part in the work of the panels; many of them had had little involvement in CILIP activities before but felt that this structure gave them an opportunity to support the development of others whilst contributing to their own CPD and networking. A training programme was established and each CAP was assigned a member of Chartership Board to act as Moderator. In 2006–07, 151 applications were considered.

The existence of panels in this form was short lived due to financial constraints at CILIP and some joint panel meetings took place in 2007. A national panel with members drawn from across the country meets in London four times a year.

Employers' attitudes to this new qualification vary considerably in enthusiasm and willingness to support candidates. Many organizations are proactive in encouraging staff to undertake the award and offer support programmes, networking opportunities and public recognition of achievement. Hertfordshire Public Libraries, who took part in the pilot, have made their support documentation available to all candidates through the CILIP website. Candidates come from all sectors and show massive enthusiasm to take this opportunity for development and to prove themselves. By the end of 2007 the first ACLIP candidates who went on to work towards chartership had gained that award, an achievement in itself considering the requirement to complete two further years of appropriate experience before submitting their application.

MCLIP – CHARTERED MEMBERSHIP OF CILIP

Chartership is a rigorous test of professionalism. It is also inclusive as it welcomes skills, knowledge and learning from all areas that contribute to personal development and improvements to library and information services (Martin 2007).

The Framework of Qualifications took chartership away from the previous forms of submission which at their most basic involved a year's experience and a form signed by a manager who was also chartered, and at their most complicated involved a choice of formats, one of which included an interview. It established the portfolio as the sole format for applications, with a requirement to demonstrate:

- An ability to reflect critically on personal performance and evaluate service performance
- Active commitment to CPD
- An ability to analyse personal and professional development and progression with reference to experiential and developmental activities
- Breadth of professional knowledge and understanding of the wider professional context

Applicants who have a qualification accredited by CILIP are required to have completed one year (full-time equivalent) of professional practice and experience (Pathway 1). Pathway 2 is for candidates with:

- CILIP certification (ACLIP) and sufficient professional level experience to put together a suitable training plan and portfolio
- Acceptable qualifications from overseas
- A degree or equivalent in another subject and professional level experience

Pathway 2 candidates are required to have two years' (full-time equivalent) professional practice and experience.

Pathway 2 has opened up opportunities to gain CILIP professional qualifications to a much wider range of people who have the skills and knowledge to make a substantial contribution to the profession. Candidates are required to submit a Personal Professional Development Plan which they should then evaluate as part of their completed application. They have to show evidence of meetings with a mentor and to have attended an approved CILIP chartership course.

The portfolio takes the form of a personal evaluative statement and supporting evidence which demonstrates the candidate's ability to meet the assessment criteria. Applications are assessed by the Chartership Board which is made up of

20 chartered members drawn from all regions of the UK and from all sectors of the profession. Their work is moderated by two external examiners.

Employers' attitudes towards the need for chartership vary from those who actively encourage employees to charter, offering time, modular programmes, financial incentives and support, to others who no longer recognize chartership as advantageous. Many, however, do recognize the value of chartership in nurturing knowledgeable professionals, and some such as Salford University are 'using CILIP's chartership programme as an integral part of its staff development and change management programme' (Lewis and Jolly 2007).

Many candidates, whilst finding the process of putting together a portfolio to be a challenge, acknowledge that they find that the experience of stepping back from their day to day work and reflecting on their own performance and development and evaluating the performance of their organization gives them confidence and a huge sense of achievement.

FCLIP – CHARTERED FELLOW OF CILIP

This is CILIP's highest award and recognizes a chartered member's continued professional development and significant contribution to the profession. Fellowship is normally awarded only to members who have been on the Register for at least six years or have completed two cycles of revalidation.

Candidates are required to demonstrate the following:

- Evidence of substantial achievement in professional practice
- Evidence of significant contribution to all or part of the profession (this may be in a broad area of professional work or in a very specific and specialized context)
- Evidence of active commitment to CPD

Applications take the form of a personal statement with supporting evidence, a curriculum vitae and at least two letters of support. The presentation of fellowship certificates takes place at CILIP Members' Day with a citation for each person. Assessment is by members of the Chartership Board.

REVALIDATION

Chartered members and fellows may seek assessment of their continued professional development every three years. There are three assessment criteria:

- Critical evaluation of personal learning outcomes from a range of training and development activities
- Increased competence in a range of professional and management skills developed through professional practice
- Evidence of continuous professional development through reading, participation in professional affairs and contribution to or attendance at courses/conferences, and so on

Applications take the form of a portfolio containing a curriculum vitae, a record of CPD and a personal statement. Revalidation applications are assessed by the CAPs.

After much debate it was decided to make this a voluntary commitment, a decision which has perhaps led to relatively low take-up and some questioning of its value. Recorded and monitored CPD is a requirement in many professions but it is not clear that this is widely recognized in the world of library and information services.

CONCLUSION

At a time when many academic institutions are reviewing the content of their information and library programmes, frequently strengthening those elements which relate to business studies or computing, it is perhaps right that all areas of professional and vocational qualifications should also be under scrutiny. The launch of new National Occupational Standards will lead to a review of National Vocational Qualifications, and CILIP is also undertaking a review of its Framework of Qualifications.

National and vocational qualifications in the information and library profession have progressed substantially in recent years. The progress is not going to stop now, particularly at a time when many employers are questioning the role of library and information specialists and the need for traditional qualifications. The profession will have to move forward and prove the unique offer provided by the information professional.

REFERENCES

Blyth, K. (2003), Education and Training Opportunities for Para-professional Staff: Dunn and Wilson Scholarship. <http://alia.org.au/~kblyth/uk.htm>.
CILIP (2008), Framework of Qualifications. <http://www.cilip.org.uk/qualifcationschartership/FrameworkofQualifications/>.

City and Guilds (2003), *A Centre's Guide to NVQs in Information and Library Services 7372* (London: The City and Guild of London Institute).

Lewis, T. and Jolly, L. (2007), 'Chartership: A Firm Basis for Change Management', *Library and Information Update* 6:7–8 (July/August).

Lifelong Learning UK (2008), LLUK. <http://www.lluk.org>.

Martin, M. (2007), 'CILIP Framework of Qualifications', *Library and Information Update* 6:7–8 (July/August).

University of Leicester (2007), Staff Development Centre: The NVQ's National Vocational Qualifications. <http://www.le.ac.uk/staffdev/qualifications/nvq.html>.

Woodburn, S. and Carruthers, C. (2007), 'NVQ: A Key to the Future?', *Public Library Journal* 22:2 (Summer).

CHAPTER 13

COMMUNITIES OF PRACTICE

BARBARA ALLAN

INTRODUCTION

The aim of this chapter is to provide an overview for librarians and information workers of approaches to personal and organizational development mediated by communities of practice. The concept of a 'community of practice' is a new approach to thinking and talking about a very traditional activity within the library community; for example, collaborative working and networking both within the profession and also in multi-professional groups.

Traditionally membership of professional groups and networks provides access to information, help and support as well as informal mentoring and professional development. For many library and information workers, membership of these groups or communities is an important aspect of their development as a professional practitioner. They often provide a vehicle for development and also opportunities to enhance a wide range of skills including management and leadership.

In addition to the communities associated with the profession, individual libraries or groups of libraries may establish and nurture a community of practice as part of their development strategy or as one of their services (this aspect of communities of practice is not specifically explored in this chapter). The use of managed communities as an approach to organizational and personal development helps to promote change both in individuals and across teams.

COMMUNITIES OF PRACTICE AND COMMUNITIES OF INTEREST

There is a large and developing academic literature on communities of practice and Andrew Cox (2005) provides a helpful comparison and summary of four seminal works on this subject (Lave and Wenger 1991; Brown and Duguid 2001; Wenger 2003; and Wenger, McDermott and Snyder 2002). Ideas presented in this chapter focus on those introduced by Wenger, McDermott and Snyder who developed the concept of communities of practice by linking it with professional or work-based communities.

Wenger coined the phrase 'communities of practice' which he defined as: 'groups of people who share a concern, a set of problems, or a passion about a topic, and who deepen their knowledge and expertise in this area by interacting on an ongoing basis' (Wenger 2003).

This definition is a helpful one as it enables us to distinguish between communities of practice and communities of interest. Anyone reading the literature on communities of practice is likely to come across the term 'communities of interest' and these are large groups or networks, perhaps involving hundreds of people, which support the dissemination and exchange of information but do not necessarily support collaborative learning processes. They emerge when people come together to exchange news or information about a specific topic. Examples include groups that cluster together around their interests in hobbies, technology, education, research fields and specialist work-related practices. E-mail discussion lists are a good example of communities of interest and sometimes a sub-group of such a community may evolve into a community of practice.

The rise in Web 2.0 tools such as weblogs, wikis and social networking sites also act as a focus for many communities of interest. It is worth noting that the term 'community of practice' is frequently used loosely to describe what are actually communities of interest and Table 13.1 illustrates the differences between communities of interest and practice.

Table 13.1 Comparison of communities of interest and communities of practice

Characteristics	Community of Interest	Community of Practice
Purpose	To share ideas and expertise To create, expand, and share knowledge. To develop individual's professional practice.	To create, expand, and share knowledge. To develop individual's professional practice.
Membership	People who become subscribers or members of a particular group e.g. mail list, wiki, social networking site. Membership may be very large e.g. 12–1000.	People who share a particular interest or passion in a topic. People who become subscribers or members of a particular group e.g. special interest group supported by a website. This may be self-selected or by invitation. Membership is likely to be relatively small e.g. 6–24.
What holds them together	Access to information and sense of community.	Passion, commitment, identity with group. Personal relationships within the group.
Examples in the library and information profession	Some discussion groups Newsgroups.	Some groups involved in collaborative project work. Professional groups supported by professional organizations. Managed groups supported by an organization or project.

Source: Adapted from Lewis and Allan 2005.

CHARACTERISTICS OF COMMUNITIES OF PRACTICE

What are the features of communities of practice in the library and information profession? Communities of practice are normally focused around a particular group of information and library workers such as law librarians or business information workers, or they may focus on specific workplace issues and problems such as e-learning or training skills. Membership is normally open to individual practitioners whose interests and professional practice map those of the community; for example, they share a common goal or purpose. Members may be at the same or different stages in their professional life and they develop their professional practice by sharing information and ideas, shared learning and through knowledge construction. Learning is an integral part of the process of participation in a community and it cannot be separated from the social situation and interactions through which it occurs.

Wenger, McDermott and Snyder identify different levels of participation by individual members within a community of practice and this is represented in Figure 13.1 (Wenger, McDermott and Snyder 2002). They identify three levels: peripheral members who rarely participate but are on the sidelines observing discussions; active members who join in with discussions when they feel they have something to say; and core members who introduce new topics or projects, and help shape and lead the community. They suggest that there is a development route from being peripheral through to becoming an active or core member. Many information workers will be familiar with this model even if they had not previously conceptualized it in these terms. It is a model that appears to operate in traditional face-to-face professional groups; for example, special interest groups of associations such as the Chartered Institute of Library and Information Practitioners (CILIP), the American Library Association (ALA) and the Association of Australian Librarians (AAL). In virtual groups, as in more traditional professional groups, the presence of a co-ordinator or facilitator may help to integrate new members into the community and this will enable them to become active or core members. Again like the face-to-face support groups, in virtual environments the use of e-buddies or mentors can be a useful means of providing support and encouragement to new community members.

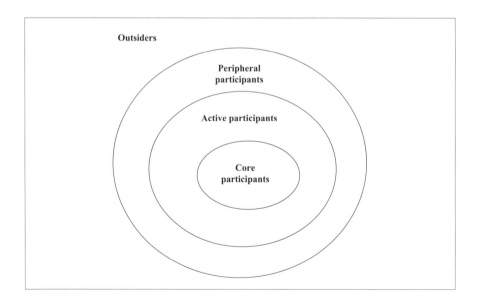

Figure 13.1 Membership of a community of practice

BENEFITS OF COMMUNITIES OF PRACTICE

What are the benefits of establishing or participating in a community of practice? The benefits of membership of a community of practice can be divided into three groups: task-specific; social; and career benefits:

Task-specific benefits include:

- Access to information and expertise
- Wider perspective on problems and issues
- Opportunities for sharing resources
- Opportunities to share workload
- Opportunities to find innovative solutions to complex problems

Social benefits include:

- Access to like-minded individuals
- Support and friendship
- Sense of identity and group membership
- Opportunity to 'let off steam' in a safe environment

Career benefits include:

- Confidence building
- Development of professional expertise
- Continuing professional development

An increasing number of library and information services are supporting communities of practice as they may be used to support staff development; for example, a university-based community established to enable members to enhance their knowledge and understanding of e-learning (see later in this chapter). Using a community of practice rather than one-off workshops or staff development events means that the learning that takes place within the community is grounded in workplace practices and may be readily transferred into practice. One of the advantages of using a community of practice for staff development is that it also helps to build a community who then may champion change within their department or unit. Additional benefits of communities of practice in the workplace include:

Service improvements:

- Forum for 'benchmarking' against other information or library units
- Ability to establish long-term relationships with colleagues and other ILS services
- Ability to act as a pressure group

- Opportunities for collaboration on projects
- Opportunities to share resources
- Ability to take advantage of emerging opportunities
- Emergence of unplanned capabilities and opportunities

Evaluations of communities of practice demonstrate that they are particularly helpful for three groups (Lewis and Allan 2005):

- New entrants to a profession who are managing the challenges of establishing their own professional credibility and translating and applying academic theory into practice. Communities of practice can provide newly qualified professionals with ready access to established practitioner's knowledge and experience, offering a safe environment in which to model and observe professional practice
- Individuals who are moving into situations that are new to them, for example, as a result of a change in employment in which they want to quickly develop relevant knowledge and expertise
- Individuals who are working at the forefront of specialist knowledge and tackling new problems and unique situations; communities of practice provide them with access to experienced colleagues with whom they can discuss and construct knowledge and develop new approaches to practice

Wenger, McDermott and Snyder suggest that many communities of practice are spontaneous, free-flowing and develop out of existing communities of interest and networks (Wenger, McDermott and Snyder 2002). The concept of a managed community of practice has become increasingly important, for example (Swan, Scarborough and Robertson 2002; Lewis and Allan 2005). Managed communities of practice are established by an host organization or project and they frequently employ facilitators to enable the community to work towards goals that match the organizational ones. This type of managed community is often established with a specific membership in mind and members are recruited by invitation only. In contrast, some communities are established as open communities.

Many communities of practice operate through face-to-face meetings and e-mail, and a typical example of this is a community established within an organization with a particular remit. In contrast, some communities spring up over the Internet and enable library and information workers working in different regions or countries to work together. Virtual communities of practice provide an opportunity for individuals with a common purpose to come together across barriers in time and space. Many communities of practice operate using a blended mixture of face-to-face and virtual communications. Some of the benefits of membership of a virtual community of practice are expressed by Hyams and Mezey who write:

... virtual communities offer much richer opportunities to share best practice and know-how in an active sense. They can stimulate the sharing of intelligence, and make it possible to harvest, organise and share 'knowledge' for preservation and re-use. They provide common ground for solving problems and sharing insights ... Communities offer much more than mere email discussion lists to members, too, because they can share access to resources (including multimedia and datasets), and communicate in real time using facilities such as live chat (Hyams and Mezey 2003).

Virtual communities use a variety of online communication tools to support their interactions and this means that busy professionals and individuals who are geographically isolated from their peers can access a community of those peers at a time and place that suits them. Virtual communities of practice may be mediated in a number of different ways:

- Using a virtual learning environment such as Blackboard or WebCT[1]
- Using collaborative communications software such as iCohere[2]
- Using a website that provides access to communications tools such as discussion groups and chat software
- Using Web 2.0 tools such as weblogs, wiki, or social networking software such as Facebook or MySpace

Many communities combine a range of approaches including online, face-to-face, facilitator-led and resource-based activities. Data gathered from research into communities of practice has shown that the participants rate a blended approach more highly than 'pure' online communications (Lewis and Allan 2005).

EXAMPLES OF COMMUNITIES OF PRACTICE

The library and information profession supports a huge number of communities of practice. Individuals may be members of a number of different communities representing their professional interests, the interests of their library or information service, and also their membership of professional associations. In addition, they may be members of multi-professional communities involving individuals from other professions; for example, health communities of practice may involve librarians and other knowledge workers, doctors, nurses and representatives from other healthcare specialities.

Professional associations such as CILIP, ALA and AAL all support a wide range of communities of practice through their websites and also through face-to-face

---

1   WebCT. <http://www.webct.com>.
2   iCohere. <http://www.iCohere.com>.

activities. These communities may be open to all members or to a specific group of members; for example, those involved in a particular type of information service such as school libraries, a particular issue such as digitization, or a particular type of member such as those working towards a librarianship qualification. The communities may be moderated or facilitated by members. One example of a community supported by a professional association is the *Emerging Leaders* community designed to enable new librarians 'to get on the fast track to ALA and professional leadership'. Each year a new community is established with 120 new librarians (60 open and 60 sponsored candidates) (see <http://wikis.ala.org/ emergingleaders/>). This scheme provides a structured approach to engaging new librarians in the professional association and also supporting their personal and professional development.

Some communities represent a particular group of librarians, for example, International Association of Music Librarians[3] and the British and Irish Association of Law Librarians,[4] and these provide a wide range of activities and resources for members. They frequently offer training courses, and these may be organized through the community and then run at appropriate venues. One of the advantages of this approach to the design and delivery of training programmes is that it is firmly embedded in the needs of the librarians or information workers. In addition, these professional associations often support specialist sub-groups which provide an opportunity for members to work together on specific issues or problems.

Communities may be established around a particular theme. An example of a community of practice is the CSG Information Literacy Group which is a special interest group supported by CILIP. This group supports a diverse range of activities including an annual conference (LILAC) and their own website (see <http://www.informationliteracy.org.uk/>). Similarly another information literacy community of practice is the Library and Information Management Employability Skills (LIMES) project (see <http://www.ics.heacademy.ac.uk/limes/>) and this has supported activities that include: academics and practitioners sharing their knowledge of information literacy resources; identifying useful teaching materials; a virtual space for community communications; and the production of bids for the development of teaching materials.

Managed communities of practice may be established by organizations or projects as a means of achieving a particular goal. Later in this chapter (in the section on evaluation) there is an extended case study of a managed community of practice which was established to enable participants to develop their knowledge and skills

---

3   International Association of Music Librarians. <http://www.iaml.info>.
4   British and Irish Association of Law Librarians. <http://www.biall.org.uk/>.

of e-learning, and to play a major role in implementing e-learning within their university (Allan, Hunter and Lewis 2006).

DEVELOPING A COMMUNITY OF PRACTICE

As with other training practices and staff development processes, implementing and supporting a community of practice involves a series of stages or phases. Different researchers offer differing approaches to their description of the stages in the development of a community of practice. The following approach is based on the work of Lewis and Allan and involves six phases which are outlined below:

- Foundation
- Induction
- Incubation
- Improving performance
- Implementation
- Community closure or change (Lewis and Allan 2005)

Phase 1. Foundation

The community may be initiated for a number of different reasons and the starting point may be an individual, a group of practitioners, a sponsor, or employing organization. The idea of a community of practice may be a particular issue or problem, the need to enable practitioners to share good practice and exchange ideas, to help implement the organization's strategic plan, or the need to overcome issues of time and/or geography. Conversely, some communities evolve organically, for example, from a group of colleagues working together on a new project, and some may be created as part of a professional or strategic workforce development activity. Sometimes communities of practice evolve out of communities of interest, conferences, training events or other professional activities.

Sometimes communities are sponsored, for example, by an employer, professional association or other agency, and in these cases it is likely that there will be a 'formal' foundation phase. This is likely to involve the sponsor, facilitator(s), and library and information workers spending time planning and working out how the community will come together and interact. It means establishing the key parameters that will enable the community to achieve its goals; for example, identify community participants and (if required) the facilitator(s), communication methods, administrative support, and the technical infrastructure to support the community. The following questions, based on the work of Lewis and Allan, need to be addressed at this stage:

- What is the purpose of the community?

- What is the structure of the community?
- Who are the potential community members?
- How will members work and learn together?
- What ICT infrastructure is required?
- What administrative support is required?
- What type of design is required for the virtual learning environment? (Lewis and Allan 2005)

Phase 2. Induction

This is the stage when the community facilitator introduces members to the community and enables them to get to grips with the technical infrastructure. In some respects this is rather like the process of taking part in ice-breaking activities in a face-to-face workshop. Sometimes this process will take place in a workshop where members and facilitator(s) are in the same room. However, it will often take place online. The facilitator will be extremely active throughout this phase, reassuring participants and creating a safe and comfortable community environment. Much of the facilitator's work will be online, although they may also be involved in face-to-face sessions and telephone conversations with members. The following activities are helpful during the induction phase:

- Personal introductions
- Ice-breaker activities
- Technical introduction to the ICT infrastructure
- Establishment of community ground rules
- Surfacing and discussing hopes and fears of community members

These activities can be facilitated online or face-to-face, depending on the circumstances of the community and facilitator.

Personal introductions by participants and facilitator(s) help the community to become established and they enable members to begin to know each other and develop a sense of each other's identity and professional interests. Photographs also help participants and facilitators to get to know each other, and some collaborative software systems attach a photograph of the author of each message as it is posted in the community. However, some participants are reluctant to make their photograph available online. The following example in Boxes 13.1 and 13.2 provides an insight into the style of a typical online introduction.

Hello everyone,

I am really looking forward to this opportunity to work with you in this new Information Skills in Higher Education community of practice.

A little about myself. I am the Information Skills Librarian at the Esk University and part of my brief is to enable the business school students to develop their skills and move beyond Google. It means that I'm always busy.

In my spare time I enjoy the rigours of family life (we've two kids approaching independence), travel (without offspring) and walking in the Yorkshire Dales.

I'm excited about this new project and the chance of establishing a community of practice. I know that many of us have worked together in previous lives and also met at conferences. In addition, there are new members who have recently moved into the region. I'm sure that we will be able to work together in this way and develop new approaches to teaching information skills.

In addition to the VLE online community I can be contacted on:

J.Smith@esk.ac.uk or phone 0123 456789

I look forward to working with you.

All the best,

Jane

Box 13.1 Example of facilitator's introduction

Hi folks!

I'm Project Information Skills Development worker for the University of Ambridge Learning Development Unit. My previous background has included working a further education college library and I've also spent a few years in government libraries. I have been at Ambridge for just over three years and really enjoy my work. I currently support information skills teaching in two faculties: science and engineering; and health.

About me. I enjoy socializing, don't do any sport although I should, and LOVE food, any time/ type/amount (I also love McDonalds!) I have two cats, one of which weighs 7.1 kilos and lost his first tooth recently, the other is neurotic and a pain in the butt! I am really enjoying being involved in this learning community and find it great to be learning again.

Finally, my biggest fear about being in this community is a worry about my technical skills. I'm not a technology person!!!

Cheers

Sam

Box 13.2 Example of participant's introduction

Many facilitators and participants have mixed feelings about the value of online ice-breakers or social games used to encourage the group to get to know each other. If you are considering using an ice-breaker with your community, then it is worthwhile using the following list of questions to help ensure that it is an effective activity. Questions for facilitators when using ice-breakers:

- Is this activity appropriate for my group?
- Is it work-related?
- Will this activity encourage participation and collaborative learning?
- Will my group enjoy this activity?
- Are the instructions clear and easy to follow?
- Will the group feel comfortable doing this activity?
- How can I encourage them to extend their comfort zones?

During the induction phase, it is important to provide a technical induction to the ICT facilities. If there is a face-to-face induction session, then it may be helpful to invite a technician or an IT trainer to deliver a short practical session on using the virtual communication site in a workshop. Participants definitely benefit from a hands-on exploration of the functions and facilities of the ICT infrastructure. Sometimes one session is not enough and it may be necessary to arrange for a follow-up session within a week or two, so that any technical difficulties that arise can be resolved quickly and effectively. However, this is not always possible, and for those groups that are inducted online it is helpful to provide basic guidance and online interactive guides to software facilities. Step by step instructions available in hardcopy are also very useful.

Establishing ground rules is a useful way of enabling individual members to start to take ownership of the community, as they can explicitly identify and agree expectations in terms of community behaviour. Ground rules also enable variations in expectations between individual members to be raised and explored; for example, one member may anticipate accessing an online community once or twice a month while another member may expect interactions on a daily basis. Identifying and resolving these differences is an important precursor to successful community development.

Facilitators of communities of practice will find that some time spent exploring the ground rules of the community will help the induction process. There are generic topics that are relevant to most communities and the facilitator can offer helpful prompts on the following topics:

- Confidentiality
- Frequency of online participation
- Respect for others

The following examples illustrate the type of posting a facilitator may use to initiate a discussion, and also examples of typical sets of ground rules.

Hello everyone

At the beginning of a new virtual learning community it is helpful to agree a set of ground rules for group participation. At this stage it is usually helpful for members to make explicit and agree their expectations for online participation. Examples of ground rules that you might find helpful are:

a) For the group to agree a minimum frequency of participation; with a learning set such as this it is important that the group agrees to participate regularly

b) Confidentiality – anything discussed within this area is confidential to the group.

Please make your own suggestions for ground rules for participation in this learning community and also comment on each other's suggestions.

Thanks very much

Dina

Box 13.3 Example of a facilitator's initial posting

If the behaviour of individual members later becomes a problem, participants can be reminded of the original ground rules agreed by each member and this can help to restore standards of behaviour, for example, in the use of inappropriate language or the need for all views to be accepted and considered. The following set of ground rules was developed in a learning community involving healthcare knowledge workers and trainers (Lewis and Allan 2005).

- We all agree to check out the Blackboard site at least twice a week and most of us will aim for three times a week. (Any less than this and you will be in danger of missing out on activities)
- Confidentiality is an agreed underpinning principle
- We will encourage succinct written contributions
- We will aim to be focused and avoid procrastination
- Speling is not an issue and we will not make judgements about typoss and speling errers
- We recognize and respect the differing levels of experience and technical competence within the group
- We will avoid gossip and encourage and support less confident and verbal members of the group
- All opinions will be valued equally; we aim to nurture tolerance
- Humour is to be encouraged; we want the experience to be enjoyable
- Members will be encourage to ask for and offer help
- We want to encourage the whole community to grow and thrive; sub-communities should be discouraged
- Everyone agrees to contribute to every activity whenever possible

Box 13.4 Examples of ground rules for health professionals

During the induction phase it is helpful to encourage participants to surface their expectations of the community; this often involves participants in voicing their hopes and fears. It is surprising how many 'fears' participants voice if given the opportunity. Common fears or concerns include:

- Fear of not being able to keep up with other members
- Fear of not having the same levels of expertise as other practitioners in the community
- Fear of technical skills letting them down
- Fear of being embarrassed by poor spelling or grammar

The facilitator will need to encourage openness in discussing any issues that arise. A discussion around different types and levels of participation may be useful at this stage. During the community closure phase it is useful to return to the original hopes and fears lists, and discussion around the induction hopes and fears of the community can make a valuable contribution to the community evaluation process.

Fears associated with technical difficulties need to be addressed during the early stages of community formation and the need for technical support is discussed earlier in this chapter. It is helpful to provide a discussion thread or forum within the virtual discussion area specifically for technical queries. Facilitators will need to respond to technical queries very quickly in order to maintain ICT confidence within the group, and sometimes it will be necessary to refer participants to other sources of technical help.

Phase 3. Incubation

The incubation phase is an important phase in the life cycle of a learning community as the foundations of good practice are established and the conditions for healthy growth are embedded. During the incubation phase community members start to communicate, develop confidence in their online voice and start to work together. The group begins to develop trust and often disclose and discuss their concerns. The incubation phase is an important stepping stone in the life cycle of the community as, unless members develop trust and share their real concerns, then these may lie at the heart of many barriers to constructive development later on. The facilitator will need to take a proactive role, supporting and encouraging members to engage actively in open discussions and guided activities. Paired activities that require members to share information and experience and begin to tackle work-related problems can work well at this stage in the life of the community. Facilitators need to incubate their communities during the early phase, taking care to respect comfort zones and not to challenge members too much too quickly. The incubation phase is about comfort and confidence, and encouraging the community to grow and develop through mutually supportive ways of working.

Phase 4. Improving Performance

This is the phase when the serious business of the community starts to happen. Group members are likely to be working on real work-based problems and sharing resources, knowledge and understanding. The learning community is performing at its full potential as real-life issues are tackled and the members work collaboratively to develop practical solutions. The speed of work at this phase may be very fast with messages posted on a daily and sometimes hourly basis. Group members are likely to be engrossed in collaborative work practices and there is often a sense of excitement as individuals and the learning community are working on the boundaries of current practice.

This stage may include examples of:

- The whole group brainstorming, pooling ideas and resources
- Developing and agreeing an action plan
- Individuals testing out ideas and asking for feedback
- Whole group synchronous discussions, for example, face-to-face or in a virtual conference room
- Production of draft ideas, reports and products
- Creating new knowledge and understanding
- Developing innovative work practices
- Developing solutions to work-based problems
- Production of new products and by-products
- Collaborative project outcomes

There is often a sense of hard work and a real commitment to achieving community goals. The group is likely to work constructively to share ideas, resources and solutions. There is likely to be evidence of the trust, openness and honesty, and good humour that has been established during the incubation phase. At this stage the group is going to be involved in both sharing and managing information and resources. They may be exchanging information based on their own knowledge and experiences, and there is often a real need for this information to be managed. This is particularly important in very active communities when large numbers of postings can lead to information overload. The provision of summaries, outline reports, action plans, and so on, can all help to manage the information that is generated during the improving performance phase. At this stage, the levels of intervention by the facilitator will drop as the community is self-managing and, to a certain extent, self-sufficient.

Phase 5. Implementation

The purpose of most work-based learning communities is to support improvement practices in the workplace; communities that are successful lead to improvements in the workplace and changes to the participants' professional identities. The implementation phase involves transferring learning from the community to the work situation. This can be in the form of a product or outcome, or it can be in the form of changed work practices, for example, implementation of personal transferable skills and practitioner expertise. Some communities work towards implementing a single project or improvement practice, whereas other communities have a much more strategic and dispersed impact on the workplace.

Phase 6. Community Closure or Change

The learning community may come to the end of its natural life, for example, as a result of achieving their initial goals, and this may result in community closure or it may evolve into a new community with a new goal. If the learning community ends, then it may go through the traditional rituals of closure, for example, reflection on the life of the learning community, celebration of achievements, party (face-to-face or virtual), exchange of personal contact details. These enable the community and its members to complete their business and say their 'goodbyes'.

At this stage the facilitator may be required to become more active than during the previous two phases (improving performance and implementation). The facilitator may be involved in initiating and supporting closure activities; or in helping members move to a new community. In one learning community facilitated by Lewis and Allan (2005) the community had come to the end of its life cycle – it had achieved its goals, and members indicated that they wanted the community to continue. Agreement was made to e-mail all community members after four weeks to re-establish the community but when the time came there were no replies to this e-mail – the community had closed and individual members had moved onto new activities.

If the learning community evolves into a new community then it will start the life cycle again with the initiation process. This may be extremely brief and take place over a few days as members discuss the 'new community' and re-establish themselves with a new goal and direction. Alternatively it may involve a series of discussions and negotiations with the employing organization. The new community may involve different members, for example, a mixture of people from the 'old' community and also new members. In this type of situation the induction and incubation periods are vitally important if the 'new' community is to work effectively and not break down into a series of cliques. The facilitator is likely to be very active in the establishment of the new community and supporting it through the community life cycle.

The ending of a virtual learning community needs careful management to make sure that a variety of processes takes place. It is important to ensure that the learning process is consolidated and members often find it helpful to spend time reflecting on their development process. The group process needs to be completed and this often involves reflecting on the life of the community, celebrating strengths and successes, acknowledging weaknesses, and discussing the end of the community and the need for individuals to leave it and move onto the next stage. In some organizations the transactions and transcripts produced by the community will be harvested for new knowledge and archived. It is up to the facilitator to ensure that community members have a sense of reaching an ending, that they have no unfinished business and that there is time to complete the closure process in an unhurried way.

EVALUATION

Two aspects of evaluation of communities of practice are considered here. The first is the evaluation of the impact of individual membership of communities of practice, for example, their engagement with communities of practice associated with professional bodies. The second is the evaluation of facilitated communities of practice established to support a specific organizational need.

How do you evaluate the impact of membership of a community of practice on individual practitioners? If library and information services are supporting their staff in their engagement with professional communities of practice, for example, through the provision of time to access online communities or to attend conferences and other events, or through financial support, then they may want to evaluate the impact of this activity on both the individual and the service. Common approaches to evaluating the impact of engagement with professional communities of practice include: identifying and discussing their impact at annual appraisal meetings; asking the individual to report on their activities and their impact on their professional practice and the service, for example, through a written report. In addition, these activities may be used within personal development portfolios or as a means of supporting an application for promotion or an award. They may also be used by the library and information service as a means of demonstrating their engagement with the broader community and profession.

How do you evaluate the impact of a facilitated community of practice? In many respects, this involves the same process that is used in evaluating training programmes or staff development processes; for example, generating feedback from participants and other stakeholders such as team leaders and managers, using data collection methods such as questionnaires and interviews. Typically, the evaluation process needs to be built into the community design and implementation process so that each stage is evaluated and the project manager or community facilitator can then adapt the community process in response to the feedback. The actual evaluation process may be designed and managed by community members. The evaluation process may be quite simple and involve asking questions such as:

1. What have you liked about participating in the community?
2. What could be improved about this community?
3. What have you learnt from your involvement in the community?
4. How has membership of this community affected your professional practice?

There are relatively few longitudinal studies on the long-term impact of a managed community of practice. The following case study is an edited version of a paper (Allan, Hunter and Lewis 2006) and it is concerned with the long-term impact of membership of a blended community of practice established in 2001 by a development unit within a UK university. The purpose of the community was to enable staff to develop knowledge and understanding of e-learning pedagogy, and to equip them with the skills to support e-learning within their role at the university. The programme was validated by the university at M level and also accredited by the Institute for Learning and Teaching (now the Higher Education Academy). There were 16 community members representing a multi-professional group: academic staff, information and library staff, ICT support staff and administrative staff, and the community was facilitated by two external facilitators using an underlying pedagogic framework of socio-cultural theories of learning. The community members participated in a series of face-to-face workshops (induction, mid-life, and end-of-community) and also structured collaborative and co-operative online activities designed to develop their understanding of e-learning theories and constructs, and to highlight implementation issues from a learner's perspective. The participants were also encouraged to reflect on their learning experiences. The sponsoring UK university and original members of the learning community were revisited in 2005 in order to research the long-term impact on the individuals and their workplace.

The programme was evaluated through a series of standard questionnaires that were distributed online. In addition, data was collected via the community discussion board messages and also in-depth interviews (held four years after the inception of the community) with six participants, two facilitators, and the manager of the development unit. Narrative analysis of both the discussion board messages and also the interview transcripts was used to identify significant themes and issues.

Impact on Individuals

The findings from the study suggest that community membership had long-term impact on the work-based performance of many of the members and enabled some to change and develop their professional identity. The analysis of the interviews indicated that, as would be expected, membership of the virtual learning community impacted differently on different members. An analysis of the findings suggests that the community provided a continuing professional development programme for members to develop their knowledge and skills, and also their careers. Two members of the community went on to facilitate new communities within the university. The role and skills of e-learning facilitators and the differences between the approaches of online facilitators and face-to-face tutors were explored within the community discussion groups and online activities. In particular, the importance of working in a supportive community was mentioned by all the interviewees. For some members, their experiences within the community had a transformational impact and led to them moving on to part-time study on a degree programme and/or promotion within the university. One member stated that she had changed her role within the university, received a substantial salary increase and was now speaking at professional conferences. She directly attributed her newly adopted professional identity to the confidence she developed through provisional role experimentation during her community of practice experiences.

Impact on Workplace Practices

The interviews also illuminated how this experience had an impact on the workplace practices of individuals. Specific examples showed that community members had developed in the following ways:

- The confidence to present papers at conferences
- A new appreciation of students' experiences at the start of their university careers
- An understanding of the importance of social aspects of the student learning experience and the need to develop learning communities within both full- and part-time student groups
- Approaches to working with groups online
- Development of e-learning facilitation skills
- Development of innovative teaching and learning activities, materials and programmes

The development of the community provided opportunities for members to improve their workplace practices. Once members became established within the community and had overcome their initial anxieties, then the community appeared to provide a 'comfort zone' from which they could develop and improve their workplace practices. The emergence of the comfort zone appeared dependent on individual members honestly acknowledging their feelings, both positive and negative, within the virtual environment. A visual image of the comfort zone and associated learning trajectories is presented in Figure 13.2. It appeared that once a comfort zone had been established, then members used it as a launching pad, retreating to the security and comfort of being with like-minded professionals when the going was too tough. Members used the community comfort zone to gain the strength and confidence to initiate new learning trajectories, work practices, and innovations and solutions outside the community in the 'real' world of their work and professional lives; these activities took them way beyond the secure boundaries of the community. This process of bursting out into innovation and improved performance and then returning to the community was a recurrent pattern for those individuals who were fully engaged with the life of the community. During their interviews, many members stated that they still felt part of this community and were in regular contact with each other via e-mail, phone and face-to-face meetings. However, individuals who were less engaged or negative about their community experiences did not appear to experience this process within this community.

Impact on the Organization

The interview with the manager of the development unit highlighted that the community was part of a wider change process which was concerned with developing and integrating e-learning into learning and teaching within the university. The use of a blended learning community provided an environment which appeared to support change and innovation, and this appeared to be as effective as one that was established involving only face-to-face meetings. The community of practice played a significant role in the university's broader change process as it addressed and changed people's perceptions of the uses of information technology in learning and teaching. It enabled the development of a group of people who developed their understanding of what was required to change and that facilitated the changes. In addition, community members networked with each other and also key stakeholders within the university. An evaluation of the programme identified that there were time issues associated with the programme and this realization led to the development of two approaches to e-learning development: a ten-credit module facilitated by their department for lifelong learning; and a number of short e-learning programmes which were delivered through the development unit.

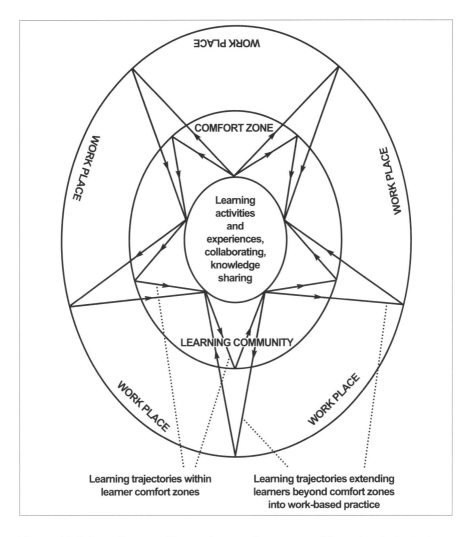

Figure 13.2 Star diagram illustrating comfort zone and learning trajectories
Source: Lewis and Allan 2005.

SUMMARY

The chapter introduces the concept of communities of practice and explains their difference from communities of interest. This is followed by an outline of the characteristics of communities of practice and these are illustrated with a number of practical examples of library and information communities of practice. This is followed by an outline of the processes involved in establishing and facilitating a work-based community of practice. This involves the following six-phase process:

foundation; induction; incubation; improving performance; implementation; community closure or change. This chapter concludes with a brief consideration of two approaches to the evaluation of communities of practice. Finally, a case study illustrates the value of membership of a multi-professional community of practice for individuals and their workplace.

ACKNOWLEDGEMENTS

I would like to acknowledge the work of Dina Lewis as our book, *Facilitating Virtual Learning Communities* (Maidenhead: Open University Press, 2005), helped to inform the content of this chapter. In addition, some of the ideas presented in this chapter were also developed while I was working on the book *Blended Learning* (London: Facet Publishing, 2007). I would like to acknowledge all colleagues who have shared their experiences with me about learning in communities of practice.

REFERENCES

Allan, B., Hunter, B. and Lewis, D. (2006), 'Four Years On: A Longitudinal Study Assessing the Impact of Membership of a Virtual Community of Practice', *Networked Learning Conference 2006*, University of Lancaster.

Brown, J.S. and Duguid, P. (2001), 'Structure and Spontaneity: Knowledge and Organization' in I. Nonaka and D. Teece (eds).

Cox, A. (2005), 'What Are Communities of Practice? A Comparative Review of Four Seminal Works', *Journal of Information Science* 31:6, 527–40.

Harrison, R. et al. (eds), *Supporting Lifelong Learning: Volume 1. Perspectives on Learning* (London: Routledge).

Headlam-Wells, J. (2004), 'E-mentoring for Aspiring Women Managers', *Women in Management Review* 19:4, 212–18.

Hyams, E. and Mezey, M. (2003), 'Virtuous Virtual: Weblogs: The New Internet Community?', *Information Update*, 2, 36–7.

Lave, J. and Wenger, E. (1991), *Situated Learning: Legitimate Peripheral Participation* (Cambridge: Cambridge University Press).

Lave, J. and Wenger, E. (2002), 'Legitimate Peripheral Participation in Communities of Practice' in R. Harrison et al. (eds).

Lewis, D. and Allan, B. (2005), *Facilitating Virtual Learning Communities* (Maidenhead: Open University Press).

Nonaka, I. and Teece, D. (eds) (2001), *Managing Industrial Knowledge* (London: Sage).

Salmon, G. (2000), *E-moderating* (London: Kogan Page).

Swan, J., Scarborough, H. and Robertson, M. (2002), 'The Construction of Communities of Practice in the Management of Innovation', *Management Learning* 33:4, 477.

Wenger, E. (2003), *Communities of Practice: Learning, Meaning, and Identity* (Cambridge: Cambridge University Press).

Wenger, E., McDermott, R. and Snyder, W.M. (2002), *Cultivating Communities of Practice* (Boston: Harvard Business School Press).

CHAPTER 14

EVIDENCE BASED PRACTICE

ANDREW BOOTH

INTRODUCTION

Evidence based practice is a model for ongoing professional development that has enjoyed increasing prominence since 1994 (McKibbon 1998). From its early origins in medicine and associated healthcare disciplines its influence has extended to such fields as social care, education and management (Trinder and Reynolds 2000). Those benefiting from evidence based practice share certain characteristics – they occupy professions with a focus on practical day-to-day decision-making, they face increasing pressure to justify expenditure on their activities or services and they need to remain engaged with an ever-changing body of knowledge – an 'evidence base' (Ford et al. 1999). Library and information practice not only shares these characteristics but also has a further unique role in not only requiring that its own professionals practise this process but also that they are able to support these activities in other professions (Bexon and Falzon 2003). This can lead to 'an inevitable confusion between librarians *supporting* evidence based practice and librarians *practising* evidence based practice' (Booth 2006a).

Fortuitously for the purposes of this book, skills and training required for both roles share a generic skills base. In this chapter the emphasis is on skills for evidence based practice in general, but this is illustrated with examples taken from evidence based library and information practice.

DEFINITIONS

Reference is frequently made within evidence based practice to the Confucian saying: 'Give a man a fish you feed a man for one day, teach him to fish and you feed him for life'. While this saying has been appropriated by others within the teaching and training community, it particularly resonates with the lifelong model of learning espoused by the evidence based practice movement. Medical students were perhaps the most extreme example of learning by rote, with five or more years of formal medical education characterized by a succession of lectures by which, as Mark Twain wrote, 'a professor's lecture notes go straight to the students' lecture notes, without passing through the brains of either'. As a consequence knowledge acquired by students becomes increasingly obsolescent from the moment they graduate from medical school (Ramsey et al. 1991). Evidence based practice seeks to address this acknowledged deficiency by equipping practitioners with strategies for lifelong learning and continual periodic refreshment of knowledge (Lewis 2006).

A librarian who was heavily involved in development of the paradigm defines evidence based practice as 'an approach to health care that promotes the collection, interpretation and integration of valid, important and applicable patient-reported, clinician-observed and research-derived evidence. The best available evidence, moderated by patient circumstances and preferences, is applied to improve the quality of clinical judgements' (McKibbon 1998).

This three-fold juxtaposition of knowledge derived from practitioner experience, knowledge from user perception and knowledge from formal information sources underpins all aspects of evidence based practice. Although attention has centred on 'research-derived evidence', principally to redress a previous imbalance, this definition is sufficiently encompassing to acknowledge other important sources of knowledge that library practitioners hold dear. From here it is natural to consider evidence based library and information practice thus:

> *Evidence Based Library and Information Practice (EBLIP) seeks to improve library and information services and practice by bringing together the best available evidence and insights derived from working experience, moderated by user needs and preferences. EBLIP involves asking answerable questions, finding, critically appraising and then utilising research evidence from relevant disciplines in daily practice. It thus attempts to integrate user-reported, practitioner-observed and research-derived evidence as an explicit basis for decision-making* (Booth 2006a).

This definition introduces the key stages of the evidence based practice process sometimes codified as the 5 As (Ask, Acquire, Appraise, Apply, and Assess) (Straus et al. 2004) but itemized less alliteratively by Eldredge as:

1. Formulate a clearly defined, answerable question that addresses an important issue in librarianship
2. Search the published and unpublished literature, plus any other authoritative resources for the best-available evidence with relevance to the posed question
3. Evaluate the validity (closeness to the truth) and relevance of the evidence
4. Assess the relative value of expected benefits and costs of any decided upon action plan
5. Evaluate the effectiveness of the action plan (Eldredge 2000)

ANALYSIS OF TRAINING NEEDS

It will be noted from the above that the first three steps of the evidence based practice process require specific technical training. In contrast, steps 4 and 5 necessitate more experiential skills in implementation and evaluation. Even here a difference may be observed when comparing librarians and other information professionals with other professions in that they typically possess skills in finding the evidence, although not necessarily within their own knowledge base (Scherrer and Dorsch 1999). Any consideration of generic evidence based practice-related training needs of health, social care or education staff must recognize that librarians are less likely to require skills in finding, and more likely to require skills in appraising, the evidence (McKibbon and Bayley 2004).

In 1999 the Library and Information Statistics Unit (LISU) at Loughborough University conducted the first systematic Training Needs Census of NHS Library Staff (Maynard 2002), achieving a 53 per cent response rate. This survey attempted to distinguish between 'General librarianship and information work training' and 'Health sciences training'. Significantly training associated with evidence based practice is prominent in both lists and features in both training received and training required. Although general librarianship training was understandably dominated by such areas as database searching (received by 88.4 per cent; required by 13.6 per cent); information retrieval techniques (85.1 per cent; 7.1 per cent); document delivery/interlending services (77.6 per cent; 13 per cent); and Internet searching (76 per cent; 15.9 per cent), critical appraisal/synthesis of information attracted 42.7 per cent and 13.5 per cent of the nominations respectively. Critical appraisal training was thus the fourth placed training need behind knowledge management (18.3 per cent), CD-ROM and online database searching and Internet searching. Perhaps more significantly 'Evidence-based decision making' appeared at the top of the Health Sciences training received list, having been received by just over a third of respondents (36.3 per cent). It also appeared at the top of the training requirements still required by one in every eight respondents (12.9 per cent).

At this point it is worth recording that it is particularly complex to assess training needs associated with critical appraisal, the third step of the evidence based process. Surveys of training need are rarely able to distinguish between levels of training required. As Urquhart and colleagues observe more generally: 'Another of the problems in making comparisons is that the level of expertise in most of the frameworks is not clear' (Urquhart et al. 2005).

Critical appraisal training may be designed simply to equip participants with technical skills in basic research design and statistical concepts or it may seek more ambitiously to assist participants in actually facilitating small group processes (Scherrer et al. 2006). Basic critical appraisal training often seeks to model the appraisal process, choosing perhaps randomized controlled trials, qualitative research or systematic review articles for assessment. However, such study designs are simply exemplars of the process and a full list of subjects for appraisal must include diagnosis studies, causation studies, prognosis studies, economic evaluations, clinical practice guidelines, and so on. It is not unusual to find participants, having reached a comfort zone in respect to one type of article, becoming anxious when they realize that detailed knowledge is also required for other types of study design. Training thus reduces, rather than enhances, self-efficacy, by making them aware of complexity and making them feel less competent and confident. As Urquhart and colleagues observe, 'critical appraisal, and research skills may need practice to build not just competence but the necessary confidence in quantitative data analysis' (Urquhart et al. 2005).

This may explain an almost insatiable demand for critical appraisal from health librarians and why individuals often return for refresher or 'top up' critical appraisal training. Interestingly the census (Maynard 2002) revealed that few participants believed they needed training in quantitative and qualitative research methods (2.3 per cent and 3.3 per cent respectively), suggesting a clear distinction in participants' minds between skills required to 'consume' research studies and skills required to 'produce' research (Booth 2002) – embodied in the critical appraisal mantra 'you don't need to be able to build a car in order to drive one!'

The findings of the first census have been subsequently confirmed by other training needs analyses. In 2004, the Department of Information Studies, University of Wales Aberystwyth undertook a training needs analysis of health library staff in the South Yorkshire area. It found that 'numerical and analytical skills [are] required to support interpretation of the evidence in more advanced critical appraisal' (Urquhart et al. 2004). This particular survey did attempt to get participants to identify their own skills levels but this was subjectively and not against actual benchmarks of competence: 'just under 20% had no experience of research methods, ... and just over 20% considered their skills to be level 3 or 4. Nearly 30% had no experience of ... appraising information, including statistics. Fewer than 10% considered themselves experts in critical appraisal ...' (Urquhart et al. 2004).

In the following year the same team confirmed their earlier experience when conducting an overview survey of the training needs of health library staff in England for the National Library for Health (Urquhart et al. 2005). A report from Lacey and Booth similarly found that critical appraisal and health-specific advanced searching featured strongly (36.5 per cent) amongst training course provision to NHS librarians (Lacey and Booth 2003). The Continuing Professional Development Working Group (CPDWG) of the Irish Health Sciences Librarians Group similarly found that evidence based practice figured high in the list of training needs, coming a close second to electronic resource management (Irish Health Sciences Librarians Group 2004).

OBJECTIVES OF SUGGESTED TRAINING PROGRAMMES

Concern within the evidence based practice community about the use of the phrase as a flag of convenience, under which many poor quality enterprises might sail, led to production of the so-called 'Sicily Statement' to which this author contributed (Dawes et al. 2005). This statement thus accommodates the role of librarians in supporting the evidence based practice of others and also, with the substitution of the more apposite 'practical' for 'clinical', covers objectives for librarians themselves as evidence based practitioners. The Sicily Statement suggests generic objectives for training programmes as well as providing the basis for examples of methods of teaching and examples of methods of assessment as discussed in the following sections.

1. Translation of Uncertainty into an Answerable Question

The student identifies knowledge gaps during the course of practice and asks foreground questions to fill these gaps (Dawes et al. 2005).

The concept of foreground and background questions acknowledges the difference between situations where a practitioner is seeking to make a foreground decision between two or more courses of action and situations where they seek further background information before being able to identify their available options (Richardson and Wilson 1997). As practitioners grow in knowledge and experience they identify more foreground questions and have less need for background knowledge (Green 2000). 'The student should ask focused questions that lead to effective search and appraisal strategies' (Dawes et al. 2005). Within healthcare such focused questions are characterized by having three or more of the following four elements – *P*opulation, *I*ntervention, *C*omparison, *O*utcomes (the PICO 'anatomy') – corresponding to Who? What? Compared With? and How Measured? (Richardson et al. 1995). Work undertaken within evidence based library and information practice (EBLIP) has identified corresponding elements according to the SPICE framework – *S*etting, *P*erspective, *I*ntervention, *C*omparison, *E*valuation (Booth 2006b).

2. Search for and Retrieval of Evidence

The student can design and conduct a search strategy to answer questions. The strategy should be effective and comprehensive: likely to retrieve all relevant evidence (Dawes et al. 2005).

Work within evidence based practice has concentrated on sensitive searching – that is, searching that minimizes the risk of missing relevant material. To compensate for the consequent loss in precision, information specialists have developed filters or methodological hedges to prioritize retrieval of high quality research designs

(Jenkins 2004). Work on corresponding hedges within EBLIP is still in its infancy but is intended to facilitate translation of this competency to the information discipline (Perryman and Lu, in press).

> *The student understands the strengths and weaknesses of the different sources of evidence* (Dawes et al. 2005).

This additional competency statement clearly falls within the traditional domain of library and information science but is enhanced by what research has shown us about the limitations of textbooks and research articles as a source of material for practical decision-making.

3. Critical Appraisal of Evidence for Validity and Practical (Clinical) Importance

> *The student can appraise the validity of a study. The appraisal will include: the suitability of the type of study to the type of question asked, the design of the study and sources of bias, the reliability of outcome measures chosen, and the suitability and robustness of the analysis employed* (Dawes et al. 2005).

Within healthcare a series of user guides or checklists was devised to enable teaching of this particular skill (Guyatt and Rennie 2002). Corresponding checklists have been developed with EBLIP to cover the main types of studies such as user studies, information needs analyses (Booth and Brice 2003) (See Box 14.1 and Box 14.2) and descriptions of educational interventions (Koufogiannakis et al. 2006).

A. Is the study a close representation of the truth?

1.　　Does the study address a closely focused issue?

2.　　Does the study position itself in the context of other studies?

3.　　Is there a direct comparison that provides an additional frame of reference?

4.　　Were those involved in collection of data also involved in delivering a service to the user group?

5.　　Were the methods used in selecting the users appropriate and clearly described?

6.　　Was the planned sample of users representative of all users (actual and eligible) who might be included in the study?

B. Are the results credible and repeatable?

7.　　What was the response rate and how representative was it of the population under study?

8.　　Are the results complete and have they been analysed in an easily interpretable way?

9.　　Are any limitations in the methodology (that might have influenced results) identified and discussed?

C. Will the results help you in your own practice?

10.　　Can the results be applied to your local population?

11.　　What are the implications of the study for your practice?

　　　　　　　– in terms of current deployment of services?

　　　　　　　– in terms of cost?

　　　　　　　–in terms of the expectations or needs of your users?

12.　　What additional information do you need to obtain locally to assist you in responding to the findings of this study?

Other questions to ask:

13.　　Does the research design appear to fit the topic of the study?

14.　　What, if any, potential bias could be present?

15.　　Does the author discuss and account for weaknesses of the study?

16.　　Are methods discussed in a transparent fashion, so that the study can be evaluated on that basis?

Box 14.1 12 questions to help you make sense of a user study

A. Is the study a close representation of the truth?

1. Does the study address a closely focused issue?

2. Does the study position itself in the context of other studies?

3. Is there a direct comparison that provides an additional frame of reference?

4. Were those involved in collection of data also involved in delivering a service to the user group?

5. Were the methods used in selecting the users appropriate and clearly described?

6. Was the planned sample of users representative of all users (actual and eligible) who might be included in the study?

B. Are the results credible and repeatable?

7. What was the response rate and how representative was it of the population under study?

8. Are the results complete and have they been analysed in an easily interpretable way?

9. What attempts have been made to ensure reliability of responses?

C. Will the results help you in your own practice?

10. Can the results be applied to your local population?

11. What are the implications of the study for your practice?

       – in terms of current deployment of services?

       – in terms of cost?

       – in terms of the expectations or needs of your users?

12. What additional information do you need to obtain locally to assist you in responding to the findings of this study?

Box 14.2 12 questions to help you make sense of a needs analysis

An evaluation, conducted within the context of a workshop for health librarians, showed that checklists 'helped participants improve their understanding of research methods and their ability to use research to aid their decision making' (Booth and Brice 2003). 'The student can appraise the importance of the outcomes and translate them into clinically meaningful summary statistics, such as number needed to treat (NNT)' (Dawes et al. 2005).

Work on translating results into a format that is of relevance to the information practitioner is very much under development. Nevertheless there have been attempts to derive meaningful measures such as the 'number needed to retrieve' for evaluating literature searching decisions (Booth 2006c).

4. Application of Appraised Evidence to Practice

The student can assess the relevance of the appraised evidence to the need that prompted the question. The student can explore the patient's values and the acceptability of the answer (Dawes et al. 2005).

Little attention has been paid to the practical implications of applying evidence into practice, although an increasing number of case studies are appearing to exemplify implementation issues (Koufogiannakis and Crumley 2004).

5. Evaluation of Performance

The student asks focused questions, searches sources of evidence, appraises or uses pre-appraised evidence and applies these in practice (Dawes et al. 2005).

Along with others, Booth (2004) recognizes two main aspects to evaluation of performance – first, evaluation of the decision made and whether it led to the desired outcome, and secondly, within a professional development context, 'the student reflects on how well these activities are performed' (Dawes et al. 2005).

The trainer in evidence based practice should bear this in mind when constructing an evaluative framework – the objective is not simply to reach the correct final destination but for the participant to grow and develop along the course of the journey. Key to the process is an increasing preoccupation within the literature with Schön's concept of reflective practice (Schön 1983). The intention is thus that the library and information professional of the future will have 'the ability to critically analyse [and] make informed judgements' (Booth 2003). In doing so they will draw upon a range of catalysts of which research evidence is simply one source. Thus 'ultimately evidence based practice will contribute to a tool box from which the reflective practitioner will occasionally draw' (Booth 2003). The rationale for this is powerfully stated by Todd: '... a profession without reflective practitioners willing to learn about the advances in research in the field is a blinkered profession, one that is disconnected from best practice and best thinking, and one which, by default, often resorts to advocacy and position as a bid for survival' (Todd 2002). While use of reflective diaries and log books and other vehicles for reflective practice is by no means commonplace within the library profession it is possible that the current trend towards increased portfolio learning will see more widespread adoption and utilization.

METHODS OF TRAINING AND MEANS OF IMPLEMENTATION WITH EXAMPLES

A key component of training for evidence based practice is problem-based learning (Miller 2001). As evidence based practice focuses on practical day-to-day decision-making, it is important that it is carried out in conjunction with real, or at the very least, realistic scenarios (see Example Scenario below). Trainers either devise a realistic situation within which an evidence based decision is framed or, optimally, encourage participants to identify such a question to be subsequently explored through the evidence based practice process. This leads naturally to practical sessions where students frame a focused answerable question. Theoretical instruction in searching is usually accompanied by a supervised practical session involving real-time searches of a variety of databases (Cochrane Library, MEDLINE, CINAHL, Evidence-Based Medicine, SumSearch, tripdatabase.com for healthcare; LISA, LISTA (EBSCO) for library and information science). A tension when training is whether to use manufactured pre-prepared questions to increase the likelihood of success or whether to attempt 'live' searching to provide a more realistic impression of the process. Research has shown that students appreciate questions that are located within a real-life context (Coomarasamy and Khan 2004). An acceptable mid-point might be to collect several real questions from participants and then for the trainer to select one from which to model the process with a high likelihood of success.

Critical appraisal is probably the most widely taught skill for evidence based practice (Green 2000). The Critical Appraisal Skills Programme[1] in the United Kingdom has done much to promote such teaching. Educational methods are based on those from McMaster University in Canada with key features including self-directed learning, small group teaching methods and the importance of grounding education within day-to-day decision-making. Workshop objectives include being able to critically appraise a published review article, to understand the terms 'systematic review' and 'meta-analysis', to explain why critical appraisal skills are important and to have greater confidence in the ability to make sense of the research evidence (Taylor et al. 2004).

---

1   The Critical Appraisal Skills Programme. <http://www.phru.nhs.uk/casp/casp.htm>.

Example Scenario – 'I don't want to talk about it'

Over recent years your library has been experimenting with an 'Ask the Librarian' e-mail reference service.

Response to this initiative has been so positive that one of your colleagues suggests that the library offer a chat reference service. Not everyone is in favour of the idea, however, with concerns expressed about the capacity to provide this as part of the standard library service. You decide to examine published research to see if it might throw light on the potential for this approach.

You form your question as follows:

'In a university library (SETTING) what are the benefits and drawbacks (EVALUATION) from a user's viewpoint (PERSPECTIVE) with regard to a chat reference service (INTERVENTION) when compared with e-mail and/or traditional services (COMPARISON).'

You conduct a search of LISA (Library and Information Science Abstracts Database) and you find the following article:

Ruppel, M. and Fagan, J.C., 'Instant Messaging Reference: Users' Evaluation of Library Chat', *RSR: Reference Services Review*, 30, no. 3 (August 2002): 183–97.

Read it and, using the questions on the User Studies Checklist, decide:

1. Does this evidence suggest that it is worthwhile to introduce a chat reference service into university libraries?

YES   NO   DON'T KNOW

2. Should your university library introduce a chat reference service?

YES   NO   DON'T KNOW

3. If your answer to either Questions 1 or 2 is NO or DON'T KNOW, what other evidence would you need to assist you in making your decision?

Box 14.3   Example appraisal scenario

Critical appraisal workshops typically last for three hours (excluding preparation time for reading the article to be appraised and for addressing a written scenario) (Taylor et al. 2005). Each workshop starts with an introductory talk: overview of the importance of evidence based practice, the theoretical basis of appraisal, and orientation to the appraisal checklist (approximately 60 minutes). This is followed by small group work involving appraisal of a published study (again of approximately 60 minutes' duration). Workshops are typically run by three to four individuals – each with formal training in research methods and experience in delivering workshops. Accompanying materials include an orientation guide and a glossary. Optimally a post-workshop pack is sent out one to two weeks after the workshop. Booth and Brice have demonstrated that such methods can be translated with very little modification to workshops on evidence based library and information practice for librarian audiences (Booth and Brice 2003). However, they have found it useful to augment the sessions with additional contextual information on barriers to implementation and how these might be resolved, and with technical sessions on interpreting research designs and statistics (see Box 14.4).

"Don't give up your day job!"
Using EBL in Practice

This workshop aims to increase librarian skills in selecting, interpreting and applying their professional research literature. It will introduce such concepts as focusing your questions, selecting the right research study for your particular question, and using statistics to clarify rather than confuse. Practical sessions will include identifying evidence in support of service improvements and will cover methods for finding out more about the needs of your users and the services that they use.

Aims:

To provide a practical introduction to evidence based information practice. To equip participants with the skills required to practise evidence based practice in their workplace.

Objectives:

As a result of attending this course, participants will:

• Be able to identify key areas of their practice that can be informed by reflective practice, grounded in research evidence.

• Be able to articulate questions from common library practice which are answerable either from the literature or from good practice.

• Understand the main types of research design and their contribution to addressing questions from professional practice.

• Be able to work in teams to appraise and implement evidence from the research literature within their workplace.

• Be aware of the importance of reflective practice for the ongoing improvement of information services and systems.

Timetable

9:15 What is Evidence Based Information Practice?
9:35 Identifying meaningful questions
10:00 Appraising a research study
10:30-10:45 Break
10:45 Appraising a research study (..cont)
11:20 Using research in practice
12:10 Barriers to development & implementation
12:30 Reflection
12:45 Evaluation
13:00 Close

Box 14.4 A sample evidence based practice course programme

Following detailed appraisal of a research study, the group typically discusses issues that relate to applying the evidence. The challenge is to apply a generic item of identified evidence to the specific context that stimulated the originating question. Participants thus discuss generalizability of the evidence to the specific scenario. However, there is also particular value in discussing possible reasons why applying this evidence may differ according to the specific type of library. For example, findings from the evidence may be mediated by the effects of organizational culture, financial constraints or issues of available skill mix or equipment. The final 60 minutes of a CASP three-hour appraisal session includes a concluding plenary session requiring feedback from the small group, general discussion of the relevance of the appraisal to the scenario and canvassing of opinions on the scenario.

Evidence based teachers (more properly called facilitators) usually encourage participants to evaluate and reflect on training sessions. Most participants are more familiar with pedagogic rather than adult learning styles. Facilitators therefore encourage use of adult learning styles, utilizing structured feedback such as that developed by Pendleton (1984). Groups are typically no larger than 8–10 so that the facilitator can concentrate on the learning process and attempt to secure participation and ownership by all members within the group.

A frequent mechanism for developing the entire portfolio of evidence based practice skills is the journal club. Journal clubs facilitate such development through goals that typically include acquisition of skills and knowledge, socialization, personal growth, critical thinking and attempting to keep up with the current literature (Grant 2003). Such journal clubs have a long pedigree within healthcare, predating evidence based practice, and healthcare librarians frequently support and participate in such activities. The rise of EBLIP has coincided with adoption of journal clubs by information professionals as a means for their own continuing development (Hickman and Allen 2005). Typically such journal clubs are established by like-minded individuals with a desire and enthusiasm to develop local practice against a backdrop of colleagues' experiences and published literature.

Participants at a journal club will usually assemble at lunchtime or during a scheduled professional development session. They will typically be expected to have read the article for that session in advance, allowing maximal time for discussion. Often they will also have been given a relevant checklist that matches the article, eliciting structured replies as the group progresses through the article. In some cases an individual may have been assigned beforehand to describe the study. Their role will be to focus only on the study design, leaving the group to arrive at a collective judgement of study quality. The group focuses firstly on the methods, then the results and, finally, concludes with discussing the applicability of the study to their practice. All participants are encouraged to have a share in the discussion and the facilitator's role is to optimize the group process and ensure that the available time is used judiciously. Five minutes may be set aside at the end of the session to agree an agenda and a target study for the next meeting. Optionally one member of the club may be assigned to write up the notes from the meeting and these may be disseminated more widely. The development of e-mail and discussion board facilities has seen some of these activities migrate to a shared online environment – the so-called 'virtual' journal club.

Examples of non-virtual journal clubs from Nottingham, UK (Doney and Stanton 2003) and Edmonton, Canada (Koufogiannakis and Crumley 2003) share common features. Both recognize the importance of nominating a chair to structure and summarize discussions, and of keeping a record of action and learning points. In contrast to clinical journal clubs, neither group employs a formal appraisal tool such as those developed by the CriSTAL project (Booth and Brice 2003). Instead they prefer to utilize a more flexible structure that alternates structured discussion of research articles with more general consideration of professional issues. In purposely keeping attendance relatively small they are able to pay attention to the small group dynamics. A contrasting model is provided by a team at the Karolinska Institute, Sweden, who report in a personal communication how they have taken their journal club forward to more objective discussion by using CriSTAL checklists, and writing the meeting notes to resemble an evidence summary. Perceived benefits from journal clubs lie in facilitating opportunities for continued professional development and lifelong learning, in broadening individual or organizational outlooks, meeting with co-professionals within or beyond their own organizations, or simply keeping up-to-date with current thinking (Grant 2003). Effective journal clubs typically have one person responsible for the club, while longevity and high levels of attendance are associated with provision of food, mandatory attendance and enthusiastic management support (Swift 2004; Phillips and Glasziou 2004) (see Box 14.5).

1.	Focus on burning professional issues of most interest to the group
2.	Create a supportive environment to which participants bring questions, a sense of humour and good food
3.	Publicize repeatedly the time, venue, topics and roles
4.	Bring enough copies for all participants of usually a research article and a topical article
5.	Keep a plentiful supply of, and range of, quick appraisal tools
6.	Keep a record of questions asked and answered
7.	Finish with the group's bottom line (the take-home message from the article), and any follow up actions (for example, additional tools required, evaluation, and further information needs that require subsequent searches)

Box 14.5 Principles for running a successful journal club
Source: Adapted from Phillips and Glasziou 2004.

MONITORING AND EVALUATION OF TRAINING

Within a paradigm for lifelong learning that has been in existence for little over a decade, it is perhaps unsurprising to discover that assessment of evidence based practice skills is still very much in its infancy (Leung and Johnston 2006; Straus et al. 2004; Green 2006). Approaches can be characterized in two main ways:

1. As much evidence based practice teaching originates from within medical education, there is widespread use of the objective structured clinical examination, candidly described by one former student as 'the most barbaric examination ever invented since Madame Guillotine had her apprentices testing the equipment on each other to check their technique' (Mottram 2000). The standard format requires participants to make a circuit of a number of stations, each comprising a task to be attempted in a set period of time, usually five minutes. Skills assessed in this way include the abilities of framing questions, searching and retrieving appropriate evidence (Fliegel et al. 2002). Participants may also be required to interact with a patient, reading and applying evidence to their clinical condition (Bradley and Humphris 1999).
2. More commonly within a non-medical teaching context, assessment is conducted by test or questionnaire. For example, skills in question formulation may be assessed by presenting a scenario and asking the student to form a focused, answerable question. A tool specifically developed to assess

competencies related to the evidence based practice process (the Fresno test) (Ramos et al. 2003) may be used to assess learning. Questionnaires can be employed to assess the key domains of knowledge, attitude and behaviour (Johnston et al. 2003), while tests for critical appraisal include the Berlin questionnaire (Fritsche et al. 2002) and the Fresno test (Ramos et al. 2003).

Identified benefits from journal clubs often focus on intangibles such as opportunities for networking and professional communication. Where effectiveness is concerned, the evidence is not very strong. A Cochrane review concluded that journal clubs probably do improve knowledge of statistics and research design but this was based on a small number of studies with varying 'doses' of critical appraisal (Parkes et al. 2001). There is conflicting evidence on whether journal clubs improve critical appraisal skills. Where skills are measured objectively, participants show lesser gains than where participants self-assess their own improvement (Linzer et al. 1988; Alguire 1998). Attempts to get participants to read more are unlikely to prove successful – the intention should be to get them to read smarter. No well-designed study appears to have investigated the impact of journal clubs on patient outcomes and it is likely that proving direct benefits for library practice would prove similarly elusive. Pearce-Smith evaluated an evidence based librarianship journal club six months after participation (Pearce-Smith 2006). All five respondents agreed that attending the journal club helped them develop appraisal skills, write a critically appraised topic (evidence summary) and be more critical of research. Where principles of adult learning (as listed in Box 14.6) are utilized, sessions are more likely to impact not only on knowledge but also on skills and behaviour.

- •   Relate the task to personal goals or to the immediate environment
- •   Present learning objectives as practical problems
- •   Use problem-solving techniques
- •   Vary teaching approaches to suit different learning styles
- •   Use active learner participation
- •   Provide frequent constructive feedback

Box 14.6 Principles of adult learning
Source: Adapted from Swift 2004.

Within EBLIP there has, as yet, been no attempt to administer standardized evaluation tools to assess learning. Some interest has been shown in developing rigorous instruments by which the acquisition of literature retrieval skills might be gauged (Rosenberg et al. 1998; Grant and Brettle 2006). However, evaluation of EBLIP workshops themselves is typically by Likert scales, measuring immediate post-event satisfaction. Booth and Brice, for example, used Likert scales to evaluate their CriSTAL workshops and found that 23 of the 25 participants were happy with the workshop format (Booth and Brice 2003). Nine felt that the workshop had been an excellent use of their time, 14 that it had been a good use of their time and two a fair use of their time. An overwhelming majority agreed that they had met the workshop objectives, which included learning how to critically appraise a piece of library research, increasing understanding of research issues, contributing to general continuing professional development programmes and gaining expertise to pass on to colleagues.

CONCLUSION

Wider evidence based practice has continued to capitalize on having started earlier and having developed further than EBLIP, with much more effort and resources having been invested in its delivery and evaluation. EBLIP has chosen to adopt, adapt and imitate to create a model that is 'similar enough' to aid dissemination and increase uptake. The reader wishing to gain a basic understanding of the evidence based practice process can thus benefit from considering books from the Bibliography on the paradigm in general (Trinder and Reynolds 2000), or on individual stages of the process, such as finding the evidence (Brettle and Grant 2003) or appraising the literature (Greenhalgh 2006). For the reader wishing to focus on the specific application of the evidence based practice model to librarianship, there are two cited volumes on EBLIP (Booth and Brice 2004; Connor 2007).

Although there have been sporadic attempts to populate the library and information domain with the tools of evidence based practice, much remains to be done. Partridge and Hallam optimistically state that such a model of lifelong learning is congruent with the preferred learning style of the 'millenial generation' (Partridge and Hallam 2006). However, they are also quick to caution that 'the current student cohort is not comprised solely of Millennials, but also includes older students such as Generation X – and even Baby Boomers'. A corresponding challenge is thus for EBLIP to provide 'remedial' education for generations of practitioners who have received little or no formal training in interpreting or using research. In seeking to meet such a challenge we can hope that a future training handbook will chronicle the further development of evidence based practice and testify to its integration within mainstream library continuing education activities.

REFERENCES

Alguire, P.C. (1998), 'A Review of Journal Clubs in Postgraduate Medical Education', *Journal of General Internal Medicine* 13, 347–53.

Bexon, N. and Falzon, L. (2003), 'Personal Reflections on the Role of Librarians in the Teaching of Evidence-based Healthcare', *Health Information and Libraries Journal* 20:2, 112–15.

Booth, A. (2002), 'Evidence-based Librarianship: One Small Step', *Health Information and Libraries Journal* 19:2, 116–19.

Booth, A. (2003), 'Where Systems Meet Services: Towards Evidence Based Information Practice', *Vine* 33:2, 65–71.

Booth, A. (2004), 'Evaluating your Performance', in A. Booth and A. Brice (eds).

Booth, A. (2006a), 'Counting What Counts: Performance Measurement and Evidence Based Practice', *Performance Measurement and Metrics* 7:2, 63–74.

Booth, A. (2006b), 'Clear and Present Questions: Formulating Questions for Evidence Based Practice', *Library Hi Tech*, 24:3, 355–68.

Booth, A. (2006c), 'The Number Needed to Retrieve: A Practically Useful Measure of Information Retrieval?', *Health Information and Libraries Journal* 23:3, 229–32.

Booth, A. and Brice, A. (2003), 'Clear-cut?: Facilitating Health Librarians to Use Information Research in Practice', *Health Libraries Review* 20:Supplement 1, 45–52.

Booth, A. and Brice, A. (eds) (2004), *Evidence-based Practice for Information Professionals: A Handbook* (London: Facet Publishing).

Bradley, P. and Humphris, G. (1999), 'Assessing the Ability of Medical Students to Apply Evidence in Practice: The Potential of the OSCE', *Medical Education* 33, 815–17.

Coomarasamy, A. and Khan K.S. (2004), 'What Is the Evidence that Postgraduate Teaching in Evidence Based Medicine Changes Anything? A Systematic Review', *British Medical Journal* 329, 1017.

Crumley, E. and Koufogiannakis, D. (2004), 'Disseminating the Lessons of Evidence-based Practice', in A. Booth and A. Brice (eds).

Dawes, M. et al. (2005), 'Sicily Statement on Evidence-based Practice', *BMC Medical Education* 5:1, 1.

Doney, L. and Stanton, W. (2003), 'Facilitating Evidence-based Librarianship: A UK Experience', *Health Information and Libraries Journal* 20: Supplement 1, 76–8.

Eldredge, J.D. (2000), 'Evidence-based Librarianship: An Overview', *Bulletin of the Medical Library Association* 88:4, 289–302.

Fliegel, J.E., Frohna, J.G. and Mangrulkar, R.S. (2002), 'A Computer-based OSCE Station to Measure Competence in Evidence-based Medicine Skills in Medical Students', *Academic Medicine* 77, 1157–8.

Ford, N. et al. (1999), 'Information Retrieval for Evidence-based Decision Making', *Journal of Documentation* 55:4, 385–401.

Fritsche, L. et al. (2002), 'Do Short Courses in Evidence Based Medicine Improve Knowledge and Skills? Validation of Berlin Questionnaire and Before and After Study of Courses in Evidence Based Medicine', *British Medical Journal* 325, 1338—41.

Grant, M.J. (2003), 'Journal Clubs for Continued Professional Development', *Health Libraries Review* 20: Supplement 1, 72–3.

Grant, M.J. and Brettle A.J. (2006), 'Developing and Evaluating an Interactive Information Skills Tutorial', *Health Information and Libraries Journal* 23:2, 79–86.

Green, M.L. (2000), 'Evidence-based Medicine Training in Graduate Medical Education: Past, Present and Future', *Journal of Evaluation in Clinical Practice* 6:2, 121–38.

Green, M.L. (2006), 'Evaluating Evidence-based Practice Performance', *Evidence Based Medicine* 11, 99–101.

Guyatt, G. and Rennie D. (eds) (2002), *Users' Guides to the Medical Literature. A Manual for Evidence-Based Clinical Practice* (Chicago: AMA Press).

Hickman, T. and Allen, L. (2005), 'A Librarians' Journal Club: A Forum for Sharing Ideas and Experiences', *College and Research Libraries News* 66:9, 642–4.

Hider, P. and Pymm, B. (eds) (2006), *Education for Library and Information Services: A Festschrift to Celebrate Thirty Years of Library Education at Charles Sturt University*, Occasional Publications, number 2 (Centre for Information Studies, Charles Sturt University). <http://www.csu.edu.au/faculty/sciagr/sis/CIS/epubs/LibEduc/Fschrift_Lifelong_Learn.pdf>.

Irish Health Sciences Librarians Group (2004), 'Continuing Professional Development: Results of 2004 Survey'. <http://www.hslg.ie/files/CPD%20Results%20of%202004%20survey.pdf>.

Jenkins, M. (2004), 'Evaluation of Methodological Search Filters: A Review', *Health Information and Libraries Journal* 21:3, 148–63.

Johnston, J.M. et al. (2003), 'The Development and Validation of a Knowledge, Attitude and Behaviour Questionnaire to Assess Undergraduate Evidence-based Practice Teaching and Learning', *Medical Education* 37, 992–1000.

Koufogiannakis, D. and Crumley E. (2003), 'Facilitating Evidence-based Librarianship: A Canadian Experience', *Health Information and Libraries Journal* 20: Supplement 1, 73–5.

Koufogiannakis, D. and Crumley E. (2004), 'Applying Evidence to Your Everyday Practice', in A. Booth and A. Brice (eds).

Koufogiannakis, D., Booth, A. and Brettle, A. (2006), 'ReLIANT: Reader's Guide to the Literature on Interventions Addressing the Need for Education and Training', *Library and Information Research News* 94, 44–51.

Lacey, T. and Booth, A. (2003), Education, Training and Development for NHS Librarians: Supporting E-learning. A Review Commissioned by the National Electronic Library for Health Librarian Development Programme (Sheffield: University of Sheffield, School of Health and Related Research).

Leung, G.M. and Johnston, J.M. (2006), 'Evidence-based Medical Education – Quo Vadis?', *Journal of Evaluation in Clinical Practice* 12:3, 353–64.

Lewis, S. (2006), 'Creating and Sharing Opportunities for Lifelong Learning' in P. Hider and B. Pymm (eds).

Linzer, M. et al. (1988), 'Impact of a Medical Journal Club on House-staff Reading Habits, Knowledge and Critical Appraisal Skills: A Randomised, Controlled Trial', *JAMA (Journal of the American Medical Association)* 260, 2537–41.

Maynard, S. (2002), 'The Knowledge Workout for Health: A Report of a Training Needs Census of NHS Library Staff', *Journal of Librarianship and Information Science* 34, 17–32.

McKibbon, K.A. (1998), 'Evidence-based Practice', *Bulletin of the Medical Library Association* 86:3, 396–401.

McKibbon, K.A. and Bayley, L. (2004), 'Health Professional Education, Evidence-based Health Care, and Health Sciences Librarians', *Reference Services Review* 32:1, 50–53.

Miller, J.M. (2001), 'A Framework for the Multiple Roles of Librarians in Problem-based Learning', *Medical Reference Services Quarterly* 20:3, 23–30.

Mottram, V. (2000), 'Objective Structured Clinical Examination', *studentBMJ* 8, 81 (March).

Parkes, J. et al. (2001), 'Teaching Critical Appraisal Skills in Health Care Settings', *Cochrane Library*, issue 3 (Oxford: Update Software).

Partridge, H. and Hallam, G. (2006), 'Educating the Millennial Generation for Evidence Based Information Practice', *Library Hi Tech* 24:3, 400–419.

Pearce-Smith, N. (2006), 'A Journal Club is an Effective Tool for Assisting Librarians in the Practice of Evidence-based Librarianship: A Case Study', *Health Information and Libraries Journal* 23:1, 32–40.

Pendleton, D. et al. (1984), *The Consultation: An Approach to Learning and Teaching* (Oxford: Oxford University Press).

Perryman, C. and Lu, D. (forthcoming), 'Finding our Foundation: Analysis of the LISA Database for Research Retrievability', *JASIST*.

Phillips, R.S. and Glasziou, P. (2004), 'EBM Notebook: What Makes Evidence-based Journal Clubs Succeed?', *Evidence Based Medicine* 9, 36–7.

Ramos, K.D., Schafer, S. and Tracz, S.M. (2003), 'Validation of the Fresno Test of Competence in Evidence Based Medicine', *British Medical Journal* 326, 319–21.

Ramsey, P.G. et al. (1991), 'Changes Over Time in the Knowledge Base of Practicing Internists', *JAMA* 266:8, 1103–7.

Richardson, W.S. et al. (1995), 'The Well-built Clinical Question: A Key to Evidence-based Decisions', *ACP Journal Club* 123:Supplement 3, A12–A13.

Richardson, W.S. and Wilson M.C. (1997), 'On Questions, Background and Foreground', *Evidence-Based Healthcare Newsletter*, November 6.

Rosenberg, W.M., et al. (1998), 'Improving Searching Skills and Evidence Retrieval', *Journal of the Royal College of Physicians, London* 32:6, 557–63.

Scherrer, C.S. and Dorsch, J.L. (1999), 'The Evolving Role of the Librarian in Evidence-based Medicine', *Bulletin of the Medical Library Association* 87:3, 322–8.

Scherrer, C.S., Dorsch, J.L. and Weller, A.C. (2006), 'An Evaluation of a Collaborative Model for Preparing Evidence-based Medicine Teachers', *Journal of the Medical Library Association* 94:2, 159–65.

Schön, D. (1983), *The Reflective Practitioner: How Professionals Think in Action* (New York: Basic Books).

Straus, S.E. et al. (2004), 'Evaluating the Teaching of Evidence Based Medicine: Conceptual Framework', *British Medical Journal* 329, 7473, 1029–32.

Swift, G. (2004), 'How to Make Journal Clubs Interesting', *Advances in Psychiatric Treatment* 10, 67–72.

Taylor, R.S. et al. (2004), 'Critical Appraisal Skills Training for Health Care Professionals: A Randomized Controlled Trial [ISRCTN46272378]', *BMC Medical Education* 4:1, 30.

Todd, R. (2002), 'Learning in the Information Age School: Opportunities, Outcomes and Options', paper presented at the International Association of School Librarianship (IASL) 2003 Annual Conference, Durban, 7–11 July. <http://www.iasl-slo-org/conference2003-virtualpap.html>.

Trinder, L. and Reynolds, S. (eds) (2000), *Evidence-based Practice* (Oxford: Blackwell Publishing).

Urquhart, C., Durbin, J. and Spink, S. (2004), *Training Needs Analysis of Healthcare Library Staff, Undertaken for South Yorkshire Workforce Development Confederation* (Aberystwyth: Department of Information Studies, University of Wales Aberystwyth).

Urquhart, C., Spink, S. and Thomas, J. (2005), *Assessing Training and Professional Development Needs of Library Staff. Report for National Library of Health* (Aberystwyth: Department of Information Studies, University of Wales Aberystwyth).

BIBLIOGRAPHY

Booth, A. and Brice, A. (2004), *Evidence-Based Practice for Information Professionals: A Handbook* (London: Facet Publishing).

Brettle, A. and Grant, M.J. (2003), *Finding the Evidence for Practice: A Workbook for Health Professionals* (Edinburgh: Churchill Livingstone).

Connor, E. (2007), *Evidence-based Librarianship: Case Studies and Active Learning Exercises* (Oxford: Chandos Publishing).

Greenhalgh, T. (2006), *How to Read a Paper: The Basics of Evidence-based Medicine*, 3rd edn (London: Blackwell Publishing).

Trinder, L. and Reynolds, S. (eds) (2000), *Evidence-based Practice* (London: Blackwell Publishing).

RESOURCE GUIDE

Critical Skills Appraisal Programme website. <http://www.phru.nhs.uk/casp/casp.htm>.

Evidence Based Library and Information Practice [online journal]. <http://ejournals.library.ualberta.ca/index.php/EBLIP>.

Evidence Based Librarianship. <http://www.eblib.net/>.

Libraries Using Evidence EBLIP Toolkit. <http://www.newcastle.edu.au/service/library/gosford/ebl/toolkit/evidencesummaries.htm>.

Libraries Using Evidence EBLIP Toolkit – Evidence Summaries. <http://www.newcastle.edu.au/service/library/gosford/ebl/toolkit/evidencesummaries.html>.

Libraries Using Evidence – The Hub [blog]. <http://librariesusingevidence.blogspot.com/>.

INTERNATIONAL DEVELOPMENTS

CHAPTER 15

THE AUSTRALIAN TRAINING SCENE

ROSS HARVEY AND RICHARD SAYERS

OVERVIEW

The number of people employed in the library and information services (LIS) sector in Australia was estimated in 2006 at 28,000, of whom 13,000 (46 per cent) were librarians, 5,000 (18 per cent) library technicians, 7,000 (25 per cent) library assistants, and 3,000 (11 per cent) archivists or allied professionals (Hallam 2007a). The number of students and recent graduates in LIS is better quantified. Hallam, using data supplied annually to the Australian Library and Information Association (ALIA) by Australian LIS schools during the course recognition requirements that ALIA uses as part of its quality assurance of education programmes, indicates that in 2005 there were around 1,550 students enrolled in LIS and Teacher Librarianship graduate programmes and about 950 students enrolled in undergraduate programmes (Hallam 2006, 5). All of these groups comprise a potential market for professional development (PD) courses in LIS – of current clients in the case of employees already working in the industry, and of future clients in the case of currently enrolled students not yet working in the industry. They will be seeking to acquire or update information and communications technology skills, behavioural skills such as communication, teamwork and interpersonal proficiencies (Marion et al. 2005; Kennan, Willard and Wilson 2006), and information organization skills such as cataloguing and metadata (Willard, Wilson and Cole 2003). Increasingly too, management and leadership competencies are being sought by LIS professionals and their organizations. In addition, they may have special learning needs as older students, with almost 70 per cent of all Australian librarians in the 35–54 age group (a significantly higher percentage than the 46 per cent which is the average in this age bracket across all occupations in Australia (Australian Bureau of Statistics 2005)).

It is not only the nature of the students that influences the Australian LIS training scene. The nature and form of LIS education in Australia, which has been shaped in large part by ALIA, also have a significant impact. While the LIS profession provides no strong financial incentives to its members to upgrade qualifications, the dominant delivery mode of LIS education is distance education, one that encourages self-motivated study. Three principal factors about the nature and form of Australian LIS education are noteworthy. The first is that there are multiple routes to gaining professional membership of ALIA: while the dominant professional qualification has been, and continues to be, the graduate diploma (attained by a full year's study of librarianship following a Bachelors level qualification in any discipline), professional membership of ALIA can also be attained by holding a recognized Bachelors degree in LIS or a Masters qualification in LIS, and ALIA also allows professional membership for suitably qualified library technicians. The second is that because professionally recognized Bachelors qualifications are accorded the same professional status as graduate diplomas or Masters degrees, pay scales are similar for all first professional qualifications and there is, therefore, no financial incentive to attain higher awards. A lack of clear distinction between technician-level qualifications and university-level qualifications, in the view of ALIA and also of employers who are able to hire technicians at lower salaries than professional librarians, exacerbates this position. The third is that, for most Australian students studying LIS, distance education is a way of life, not a new venture. Currently the largest distance education provider of university-level professionally recognized LIS qualifications in Australia is Charles Sturt University's School of Information Studies, whose graduates in 1998 accounted for about 30 per cent of all graduates from Australian university-level LIS schools; in 2000 this had risen to over 40 per cent, and in 2005 to around 47 per cent. All of these graduates studied part time by distance (Harvey and Higgins 2003; Hallam 2006).

It is, of course, not only the university-based LIS schools that play a role in training and education. Other providers of formal qualifications such as the Technical and Further Education (TAFE) colleges also play an important role by training paraprofessionals, such as library technicians, and providing post-qualification professional development opportunities to professional and paraprofessional LIS workers. ALIA currently recognizes seven TAFE colleges, five universities with attached TAFE divisions and one private organization providing library technician courses. Recognition by ALIA acknowledges that courses contain sufficient of the body of professional knowledge to allow a graduate to seek professional membership of the association without further examination. In 2006, ALIA data based on course returns from TAFE colleges and other providers indicated just over 2000 enrolments in library technician courses, another potential market for PD courses in LIS.

Also playing a significant role in PD are employers and in-house providers who develop and make available training and development opportunities tailored to the specific needs of their staff and organizations. The Local Government Associations in each Australian state routinely provide training and development to public library staff in workplace health and safety, business competencies and customer service. Similarly, professional associations such as ALIA, the Australian Society of Archivists (ASA) and the Records Management Association of Australasia (RMAA) participate as providers, either through directly developing and offering training courses or by accrediting training courses offered by others through their continuing professional development (CPD) schemes. Training and professional development providers are also significant players in the Australian training scene, offering generic programmes (such as the Australian Institute of Management (AIM)) and programmes specific to the LIS industry (most notably CAVAL).

Responsibilities of Employers in Training

An ongoing debate in Australian LIS circles is the role that employers should play in providing training opportunities for employees. Employers can participate in a number of ways: developing and offering programmes tailored to the needs of the organization using staff employed by the organization (for example, a training officer); employing a training organization to develop and offer programmes, either generic or tailored to the needs of the organization; encouraging staff to participate in PD opportunities, activities and events (for example, by providing leave and/or funding to do so); and encouraging staff to enrol in degree courses (for example, by providing study leave and/or subsidizing fees). The size of the organization is a major factor influencing the provision of training by employers; generally speaking, the larger the organization, the better equipped it is to offer training. Australian libraries are now providing fewer training opportunities, one reason being an industrial relations climate which is increasingly hostile to what are perceived as perks of the job, such as study leave, and in which award agreements negotiated on an industry or worksite basis are being replaced by individual contracts.

The Council of Australian University Libraries (CAUL) website notes some of the training opportunities its members find relevant (CAUL 2006). They include generic courses for managers in the tertiary education sector offered by Universities Australia (formerly the Australian Vice-Chancellors' Committee) and by the Association for Tertiary Education Management (ATEM), as well as activities specific to the LIS sector, such as those offered by CAVAL, the QULOC (the Queensland University Libraries Office of Cooperation) consortium, and ALIA. In addition to these Australian offerings, CAUL refers to US offering from the Association of Research Libraries through its ARL/OLMS Online Lyceum courses, and from the Frye Leadership Institute.

Professional Associations and PD Schemes

One aim of professional associations is to maintain and improve the standards of services and personnel in the sector they represent. In common with many other professional associations ALIA takes a specific interest in the standard of qualifications leading to professional awards in LIS, for example, through its course recognition process. It also supports professional development of its members, indicated in one of its objectives: 'To ensure the high standard of personnel engaged in information provision and foster their professional interests and aspirations' (ALIA 2005).

ALIA's professional development policy (provided in full in Appendix 1) articulates the joint responsibilities of LIS personnel, employers and the professional association:

> *Library and information professionals have a responsibility to commit to professional development and career-long learning. Similarly, their employers and the Australian Library and Information Association have a responsibility to provide opportunities which enable library and information professionals to maintain excellent service delivery.*

ALIA meets it responsibilities in five ways:

- Providing mechanisms which enable members to plan and undertake learning and other development activities
- Offering a mentoring programme to assist members in their ongoing professional development
- Organizing partnerships with other professional and training organizations to make available learning activities and opportunities in library and information management and other disciplinary studies
- Formally recognizing members who participate in ALIA's professional development certification scheme
- Facilitating forums where knowledge can be created, shared and disseminated to enable members to better understand the dynamic environment in which they, as library and information professionals, and their clients operate (ALIA 2005)

ALIA's professional development scheme (ALIA 2007) was developed to provide opportunities for its members to undertake training opportunities leading to a recognized award. Membership of the scheme is voluntary and is not a prerequisite for professional practice in Australia. ALIA members who participate in the scheme receive a career development kit, assistance with formally recording participation in the scheme, and the right to use a post-nominal CP (indicating Certified Practitioner), to apply for a Certified Practitioner certificate, and, if they meet the requirements, to become an Associate Fellow (AFALIA or AFALIATec) of ALIA. The career development kit, in the form of a workbook and worksheets available only to members of ALIA, assists with analysing the professional development needs of an individual and setting objectives that allow these needs to be met, as well as providing a mechanism for input from other professionals and mentors and for recording PD activities undertaken.

As the information economy in Australia matures and professional boundaries blur, library professionals are increasingly moving, through choice or circumstances, into allied areas of information practice, including records and information management and knowledge management. A range of specialized organizations and networks exists in Australia to represent their professional interests, promote and maintain standards of practice, and provide ongoing training and development. Relevant bodies include:

- The Records Management Association of Australasia (RMAA)
- The Institute for Information Management (IIM)
- The Australian Computer Society (ACS)
- The Australian Capital Territories Knowledge Management network (ACT-KM)
- The Special Libraries Association (Australia and New Zealand Chapter)

A small but growing number of librarians are choosing to become affiliates or full professional members of RMAA, a dynamic organization with the stated vision to become: 'The recognised leader in professional development, research and networking for the benefit of records management professionals' (RMAA 2007).

An important function of the RMAA is to facilitate the delivery of training courses, workshops and conferences across Australia and New Zealand at national, state and local levels. In concert with this, the RMAA also administers a compulsory CPD scheme for its three levels of professional membership: Associate, Member and Fellow. In common with ALIA's PD scheme, the RMAA CPD scheme operates over a three-year period (triennium) beginning on 1 July each year. Professional members are required to maintain a log of professional development undertaken and lodge this with the RMAA on an annual basis. Points are awarded for different types of professional development, and a Professional Membership Certificate is awarded at the end of the triennium to those who have attained the required point score. The certificate remains valid for three years.

Training and Professional Development Providers

The post-qualification library training and development market in Australia is serviced by a very small number of dedicated niche providers, and a wider range of generic soft-skills providers exemplified by the Australian Institute of Management (AIM) and the Institute of Public Administration Australia (IPAA). Also participating are professional associations such as ALIA, the ACS and the RMAA, their state- and sector-based groups and chapters, member organizations such as CAUL, universities and large institutional libraries. Entering the market via the Internet are overseas library schools, based primarily in North America, and professional associations offering online programmes. Also starting to make its presence felt is the Australia and New Zealand Chapter of the Special Libraries

Association (SLA), formed in 2004. Many SLA members in Australia are now turning to that organization's *Click University* for web-based seminars and courses presented by high-calibre international speakers such as Lesley Ellen Harris and Guy St Clair.

Competition within the Australian library training and development marketplace is thus robust and strong. This strength is not, however, always to the advantage of information professionals, their employers or standards of practice. Considerable variation exists within the market with regard to pricing, availability of training and quality of delivery and content. There are not, as yet, any national quality standards in place to guide course development, or an organization charged with the task of ensuring minimum quality standards for post-qualification library training and development in Australia.

Dedicated library training and development providers in Australia include CAVAL Training, a service of CAVAL, with a national scope, and Information Enterprises Australia (IEA), based in Perth, Western Australia. Other commercial providers with overlap in this area include the Ark Group Australia, which specializes in hosting short conferences on topics relating to knowledge and information management, and a new player in the market in 2007, Key Forums Australia.

Until 2001, AIMA Training and Consultancy Services also provided highly-regarded library leadership and management development from its offices at the National Library of Australia. Many of Australia's current generation of senior library leaders completed management programmes presented by AIMA in the 1990s. In 2004 much of AIMA's intellectual property was transferred to CAVAL and now contributes to courses and programmes presented by that organisation. AIMA also presented the ground-breaking Aurora Library Leadership Institute biennially from 1995 to 2001. This programme is now presented annually by the Aurora Foundation and still targets relatively new members of the profession with identified leadership potential at frontline and middle management levels. (An evaluation of the 2003 Aurora Leadership Institute is available in Barney 2004.) Until 2008, there were no programmes specifically designed to develop executive leadership talent in Australian library professionals. CAVAL undertook a feasibility study through 2006 and 2007 with the intention of bringing a suitable programme to market in 2008. The inaugural CAVAL Horizon Executive Leadership Programme for Senior Library Managers was presented from October 2008 to February 2009 and comprised two residential workshops in Melbourne and Sydney, individual and group projects and executive coaching provided by selected Industry Leaders.

Operating across a range of professions and markets are the so-called generic training providers that offer a veritable smorgasbord of courses, prices and delivery options. Generic providers vary in size from sole operators with specialist expertise – for example, change management, presentation skills or team building – through to large enterprises offering comprehensive training options. Larger providers can include commercial and not-for-profit companies, community organizations, schools, Higher Education institutions, industry organizations and trade unions. Many, but not all, providers are also registered training organizations (RTOs) and thus approved under the Australian Quality Training Framework (AQTF) to 'deliver specified vocational education and training and/or assessment services' (DEST 2007).

With respect to LIS training and development, areas of particular interest to generic providers, large and small, include information and communications technology (ICT), almost all aspects of 'management' (change, front-line, time, project, and so on), customer service, leadership, team working, and communications. A highly regarded management training provider is the Chifley Business School based in Melbourne, an independent initiative of the Association of Professional Engineers, Scientists and Managers Australia (APESMA). The AIM's various state divisions are also important generic training providers, along with the IPAA, and, for public libraries, the Local Government Associations in each state.

Generic training and development providers both complement and compete with niche library training providers operating in Australia. Discrete roles are not always easy to identify, but generally speaking the niche providers focus on traditional library and information management skills sets – for example, cataloguing and metadata – and the generic providers offer complementary management and ICT skills training. This demarcation of training roles is best illustrated by CAVAL's pledge to provide 'specialized training for information professionals'.

In-house Providers

Since 2004 there has been a marked trend towards in-house or onsite training in libraries in Australia. Many training providers offer this service and undertake to provide some level of customization of content for in-house programmes. In practice, customization adds value for clients – the more a programme can be tailored to suit an individual client's needs, the better the learning outcomes for those staff participating and for their organization.

In-house training is of particular benefit to libraries with common professional development needs across a range of staff (for example, customer service), and tight development budgets. The benefits of in-house training include savings on travel costs and course fees for individuals attending external courses, more efficient use of staff time, and course content that is more closely aligned with the organization's needs. Travel costs often represent a significant disincentive to attendance at training in Australia, particularly for library staff in regional and remote areas of the country. Travel from Darwin, for example, to attend training in Adelaide or Brisbane requires a flight of nearly four hours' duration and at least two nights' accommodation, on top of the cost of training itself. Online training delivery can be one solution to the problem but is not always the optimal format for leadership, management or customer skills training.

In Australia, CAVAL Training has pioneered the formation of location- and sector-based library training consortia to leverage buying power and provide greater access to in-house training opportunities for library workers. Since 2004 and the formation of the first Queensland Special Libraries Training Consortium, CAVAL has facilitated the development of training consortia for public libraries in Western Australia, special libraries in South Australia and one-person libraries across New South Wales and Queensland. In 2006, nearly 25 per cent of CAVAL's training revenue was sourced from in-house programmes, and client organizations saved on average up to 50 per cent of the cost of sending the same number of staff to external public programmes; this figure does not include additional savings on travel costs and lost staff time in the workplace.

TRAINING NEEDS IN AUSTRALIA

It is generally agreed that there will be an increasing need for training in Australian libraries in coming years. A study on workforce sustainability for public libraries in Victoria, commissioned by the State Library of Victoria, devotes a section to retaining and developing staff. This study notes that 'the culture within public libraries had changed significantly in the last 10 years or so', but 'staff stagnancy' (Van Wanrooy 2006) was an issue. The importance of training is thus heightened: '... library managers predicted that training will become more of an issue in the future as skill needs are unlikely to be met', with specific training needs relating to technology, customer service, and management and supervision being identified (Van Wanrooy 2006).

Since 2003, CAVAL has undertaken an annual Training Needs Survey for library and information workers in Australia. The most recent survey was conducted over four weeks in August and September 2006 and, as in past years, showed strong representation from special and university libraries. All library sectors were again represented in the 2006 survey, with responses from special and university libraries dominating (see Figure 15.1). In 2006, for the first time, a separate category for records and information managers was added and accounted for 5.2 per cent of responses. The university or academic library sector contributed 27 per cent of responses – up from 20 per cent in 2005 and 22 per cent in 2004 – while national and state libraries were better represented than previous years with 10 per cent of responses. Representation from public libraries dipped marginally to 9 per cent, down from 13 per cent in 2005 and 15 per cent in 2004. In the 2006 survey, special libraries (CAVAL's strongest market sector for training and development in Australia) were again very well represented, contributing 29 per cent of survey responses. Although this figure was proportionately lower than 2005 (36 per cent), there is no reason to conclude that special libraries were less supportive of professional development generally. On the contrary, in 2006 special libraries contributed over a third of all participants attending CAVAL courses in Australia (nearly 500 trainees), followed closely by the academic sector (a little over 400 trainees). Anecdotal feedback and course evaluations received in 2006 and to date in 2007 also indicate a robust market for training and development in special libraries.

As in 2005, the 2006 survey again asked respondents to identify which types of training would be of interest to them and their organizations (Question 8). Four categories of training were indicated: customized in-house (onsite) training, public courses, mediated web-based training, and unmediated (self-paced) web-based training. Data obtained in 2005 showed strong interest in web-based training (71 per cent of responses) and this trend was supported by 2006 figures: mediated web-based training 39 per cent, and unmediated (self-paced) web-based training 32 per cent. Clearly, more library professionals want the flexibility and freedom to access professional development on their own terms, when and where they require it – at home at 3am if necessary. Structured web-based training using an e-learning system such as WebCT or Moodle, whether courses are mediated or unmediated, is one solution. However, the rapid growth and acceptance of social networking (Web 2.0) applications such as blogs, wikis, podcasts and more recently Second Life virtual reality also potentially provide new opportunities for less structured training.

	2004		2005		2006	
		%		%		%
Special Libraries	144	26	201	36	152	29
University Libraries	121	22	113	20	139	27
National / State Libraries	22	4	26	5	50	10
Public Libraries	86	15	70	13	44	9
Polytechnic / TAFE Libraries	36	6	59	11	42	8
Archives, Records Management	49	9	0	0	30	6
Other Sector, including KM	104	19	86	15	27	5
School Libraries	0	0	0	0	18	3
Self-employed, Unemployed, Students	0	0	0	0	18	3
Total (= n)	562	100	555	100	520	100

Figure 15.1 CAVAL Training Needs Survey: Respondents by sector
Source: CAVAL Training Needs Survey 2006.

For the first time the 2006 CAVAL Training Needs Survey introduced a new style of question – one that asked respondents to clarify their own hopes and fears for the library profession in the decade ahead. Respondents were asked to nominate what they believed to be the top three issues or challenges facing libraries and information services through to 2010 (Question 15). By posing this question, CAVAL sought to use the qualitative data obtained to test a range of assumptions about emerging training topics and themes: for example, to what extent are new and emerging technologies actually of interest to library workers? A total of 328 responses were received, representing over half (53 per cent) of those who answered the 2006 survey. Using a simple keyword analysis technique, it was possible to identify at least 50 separate issues or challenges and rank them from highest to lowest by counting the number of individual mentions in responses. Interestingly, the picture that emerges from this analysis suggests a library and information profession in Australia that is proactively seeking the means to resolve, or at least adapt, to some very significant challenges. Looking ahead to 2010, the top 14 challenges (ten mentions or higher) identified by Australian library workers in 2006 include:

- New and emerging technologies impacting on libraries, focusing on Web 2.0 and Library 2.0 applications such as blogs, wikis and podcasts (44)
- Managing budgets and seeking new funding sources for libraries (44)
- Marketing and promoting libraries and information services (32)
- Workforce and succession planning (30)
- Managing e-resources (22)
- Demonstrating the value, relevance and return on investment of libraries (20)
- Library design and space planning – making the most of what we have (14)
- Copyright compliance (12)
- Google! – specifically, staying one step ahead of clients (11)
- Information and digital literacy (11)
- Outsourcing library services (11)
- Understanding users' needs – needs analysis (11)
- Digital rights management (10)
- Institutional repositories – linked in several responses to changes in scholarly publishing (10)

A survey carried out as a scoping study for an Australian LIS school in 2005 documented the then current CPD offerings for professionals in the library sector (excluding school libraries) and investigated future needs. A literature review of CPD needs indicated that online courses are being increasingly favoured by busy information professionals because of their flexibility, and indicated five areas of interest:

1. Information and communication technology (ICT) – such as Internet skills, webpage design, using electronic resources
2. Training and teaching skills, instructional design
3. Subject-specific training for special libraries – such as legal information sources, clinical librarianship, business reference skills
4. Collection management of electronic resources – such as contract management, dealing with vendors
5. Management topics – such as marketing, evaluation, performance management, change management

One characteristic of the LIS Australian training scene noted in this survey is that library professionals appear to be more interested in learning that leads to a qualification. Research by ALIA in the past has elicited wish-lists of training needs, but these have not resulted in high take-up rates when courses intended to satisfy these needs have been offered. ALIA is, therefore, interested in training that leads to qualifications such as a graduate certificate (equivalent to one semester of university-level full-time study). Although graduate certificates are not recognized by ALIA as professional qualifications, they are considered to be valid and desirable qualifications that demonstrate currency of skills or provide refresher courses in specialist areas. Examples of such graduate certificates offered by Australian universities include a Graduate Certificate in Information Organization offered online by Charles Sturt University, and a Graduate Certificate in Information Management (Web Management) offered by Queensland University of Technology.

This survey also asked some senior practitioners around Australia what they considered the professional development needs of their staff to be. The CEO of a large regional public library service indicated a long list: writing skills (reports, policy and procedures, submissions), general HR skills (running effective meetings, minute-taking), library skills at a basic level (cataloguing, advising readers, collection development), performance management, and customer service. It was also suggested that, because public libraries are often responsible for archive collections, some basic training in this area would be useful. A respondent from a state-wide library service also requested readers advisory skills, noting that this was an example of the kind of proactive service desirable in public libraries where training was needed. Other CPD requirements noted were reference skills, collection planning and development, and user education. Marketing and promotion in order to demonstrate the library's value and promote its services was also noted as required, as were (for lower-level desk staff) basic customer service, administrative and library skills; it was noted that these need to be delivered face-to-face in the community.

A 2004 training needs analysis of another large public library service sought the views of staff of that service, not just the CEO. The results indicated a strong preference for face-to-face training (85 per cent), although mentoring, online training and on-the-job training were also noted. For professional-level staff, management training was the most frequently requested area for PD, followed (in descending order) by information technology, personal development and administrative skills. For lower-level staff, the highest demand was for information technology training, then personal development, management and administrative skills. Most frequently requested within information technology training was using online databases.

Hallam's *neXus* survey of the Australian LIS workforce has investigated, amongst other things, the views of LIS workers (both professional and paraprofessional) about education and training (Hallam 2007b). Nearly 40 per cent of respondents attended formal activities (conferences, workshops or training events), 60 per cent felt that their current employment offered them sufficient training opportunities, and 48 per cent indicated that they spent too much time on training activities. The survey data indicates that there is a direct relationship between membership of ALIA and regular participation in both formal training and development activities and informal workplace learning activities. Twenty per cent of respondents expressed interest in completing further academic qualifications, but there was low interest (less than 2 per cent) in Master of Business Administration and Master of Public Policy degrees compared with research degrees in LIS, where 2.5 per cent hoped to pursue PhD studies and 2.9 per cent a research Masters degree.

Respondents to the *neXus* survey considered the areas of training that would be of most benefit to them were information technology skills (53.8 per cent of professionals, 54.6 per cent of paraprofessionals), management training (56.0 per cent of professionals, 40.4 per cent of paraprofessionals) and business training (48 per cent of professionals, 32.9 per cent of paraprofessionals.) By contrast, 75.7 per cent of respondents saw little or no value in participating in leadership training, although the data is not totally clear on this point.

Collectively, these surveys indicate several clear trends. One trend is a strong interest in web-based training, either mediated or self-paced. Another is that ICT skills dominate the areas where training activities are most needed – both current skills such as internet competencies and web design, and those relating to new and emerging technology such as Web 2.0 and Library 2.0 applications. A third is the high interest in management skills; this includes general management skills, such as budgeting, marketing, evaluation, performance management, succession planning and change management, as well as more sector-specific skills such as management of electronic resources. Also in high demand in all surveys were marketing and promoting libraries and information services.

WHO TRAINS AND WHAT DO THEY OFFER?

The training needs in Australian libraries are relatively well articulated, as noted in the preceding section. But how well are they being addressed? Appendix 2 illustrates the range of courses offered by Australian-based providers of LIS training, including CAVAL Training, IEA and Key Forums. (Note that Appendix 2 does not list the courses offered by general providers such as the ACS or the AIM, nor does it list the courses provided as PD by LIS schools in Australia.) This section describes in more detail the activities of several of the major providers.

CAVAL Training

CAVAL has been a significant provider of specialized training to the LIS sector in Australia since the late 1990s, growing from its foundation as one of the first providers of training in the use of the national bibliographic utility, the Australian Bibliographic Network (ABN) for the National Library of Australia in the 1980s. More recently, CAVAL Training has moved into New Zealand and Asia, aiming to complement local providers and meet niche training needs, for example, in web searching and project management. In 2006, CAVAL Training offered 78 discrete courses ranging from LIS specific cataloguing, collection management and Web 2.0 skills, through to library marketing and promotion, customer service and a broad selection of critical management competencies, from hard skills such as budgeting and project management to soft skills such as leading change in the workplace and facilitating group processes. In 2006, CAVAL trainers presented 152 public deliveries, 33 in-house deliveries and one online delivery to over 1,600 LIS workers in the region, the majority of trainees (87 per cent) coming from special, university and public libraries in Australia.

CAVAL Training's emphasis in the past five years has been to develop and strengthen strategic partnerships with other key library consortia, in Australia and overseas, and increase the proportion of customized in-house training as a means of helping the LIS sector to achieve greater returns from diminishing training budgets. Partnerships with organizations such as SOLINET in the south-eastern US have enabled CAVAL Training to bring many high-profile international speakers to Australasia and offer training opportunities in advance of other providers. The flow of expertise is not one way, however, with CAVAL trainers and facilitators adding value to high-profile professional development projects in the US and Asia. In 2006, a successful partnership with UNESCO culminated in a week-long seminar in Colombo, Sri Lanka, followed by the publication of a book (Sayers 2006). Since 2004, CAVAL has also worked with UNESCO on its Information and Communications Technology for Librarians and Information Professionals (ICTLIP) package, and on other LIS projects for librarians in developing countries.

CAVAL Training was until recently an RTO for the Australian Certificate IV in Training and Assessment, a comparatively expensive generic vocational qualification. In response to feedback from libraries, principally in relation to cost, reaccreditation was not sought in 2007 and CAVAL is, instead, presenting a two-day 'Train the Trainer' programme that better aligns with the needs of LIS clients. Market feedback obtained in the annual Training Needs Survey was influential in reaching this decision.

Two significant training initiatives for CAVAL in 2007 were the implementation of the Moodle e-learning system, an open source competitor to Blackboard and WebCT which is quickly gaining popularity in US and European universities, and a scoping study for an executive leadership programme for library and information managers.

Vocational/Technical Training

The Australian Vocational Education and Training (VET) sector offers LIS workers a rich variety of opportunities for nationally recognized training and development, all linked to practical industry-defined competencies described within the AQTF. The majority of VET courses available to LIS workers in Australia are offered by TAFE colleges or institutes and are targeted at library technicians, library assistants and administrative staff. Significant vocational and technical LIS training providers in Australia include the Canberra Institute of Technology (Australian Capital Territory), TAFE New South Wales, Charles Darwin University (Northern Territory), Southbank Institute (Queensland), Box Hill Institute (Victoria), TAFE South Australia and Edith Cowan University (Western Australia). Four qualifications comprise a vocational career path in LIS, from entry level at the Certificate II in Library and Information Services through to Certificates III and IV, and finally a Diploma qualifying the recipient as a library technician. Many degree-qualified librarians working in information literacy and client services roles have also completed the VET qualifications of Australian Certificate IV and Diploma in Training and Assessment. A small but growing number within the university sector are now also being encouraged to build on this qualification with a university-level Graduate Certificate of Tertiary Education, or equivalent.

Online vocational training in Australia is growing in popularity, particularly as more casual and contract workers enter the workplace. Capra Ryan Online Learning is a specialized provider of online VET training to the LIS and education sectors in Australia. Based in Queensland, the company supports nationally accredited courses in library and information services at Certificate II, III, IV and Diploma level. Career paths for those completing the Certificates II to IV include working as a library aide in a school or as a library assistant in a public library. Those progressing to the Diploma of Library and Information Services qualification may be employed as a library technician across all library sectors.

The course is also recognized by ALIA for professional membership as a library technician (AALIATec). Importantly, students undertaking online training such as that offered by Capra Ryan have the flexibility of working at their own pace and have the option to exit at various points and still receive recognition for units of competency completed in the form of a Statement of Attainment. For those LIS workers already holding qualifications, separate units may be undertaken at later points as professional development.

Off-shore Providers

Off-shore providers, usually based in North America, are increasingly making their presence felt in LIS training in Australia. One is the Association of Research Libraries through its Online Lyceum, which it operates under the auspices of its Office of Leadership and Management Services. Participants from 'Asia, Europe, Africa, Australia and North America' have taken its online courses; and it is increasingly collaborating with library associations outside the US and with other organizations (Wetzel 2006).

US LIS schools are increasingly offering online training programmes and Australians participate in them, although the extent to which this is happening is not clear. One example is the University of Wisconsin-Madison's School of Library and Information Studies whose online offerings for (the northern hemisphere) Autumn 2007 included: Library 2.0; Basic Public Library Management; Collection Development; Readers Advisory in the Library; What's New in Childrens Books?; Consumer Health Reference; and Cataloging Web Sites/Integrating Resources (University of Wisconsin School of Library and Information Studies 2007). Increasingly, international communication channels such as e-mail lists are making these training opportunities significantly more obvious to the Australian LIS market. As US LIS schools move increasingly into distance education with online offerings, it can be anticipated that more online PD offerings will be forthcoming from them and more Australians will engage with them.

CONCLUSION

Training and development for the Australian LIS sector is in a healthy state. That this state will continue is assured because of some characteristics peculiar to the LIS sector in Australia. These characteristics, however, also pose challenges. Australia's geographic characteristics of a large land mass and a small, geographically dispersed, population have promoted distance education and training (most recently in online manifestations) as the preferred mode for the delivery of training activities. Some of the demographic characteristics of its LIS workforce, especially the high age profile, mean that there will be an increased need for LIS training, particularly as many new personnel enter the workforce to replace the aging workforce. The strong role of a dominant professional association, ALIA, in standard-setting for LIS education and in promoting a formal PD scheme is also a factor in ensuring that training needs will remain high. Recent surveys of training and development needs for the LIS workforce have also clearly indicated what the requirements will be in the near future. ICT skills will remain in high demand, as also will management competencies and the skills necessary to market and promote libraries and information services effectively.

What is less certain, though, is who will provide the training. Here there are many challenges facing Australian-based training providers servicing the LIS sector. Of foremost concern to providers are the shrinking training budgets of LIS organizations, leading in turn to increasing competition between specialized LIS training providers and generic or internal providers for limited training and development funding. Another outcome of shrinking budgets is the growing popularity of professional development opportunities organized on a largely voluntary basis by members of the profession, and made available to colleagues at a token cost, usually with sponsorship from a library supplier, professional association or large LIS organization. This phenomenon has been described as the 'ten dollar training trap', whereby the quality of learning outcomes is highly variable, ideas and practices are recycled within the profession, and long-term access to quality professional development is made unsustainable. There is also an increasing reluctance on the part of many organizations to release staff to attend training opportunities, such are the pressures on library human resources and budgets. Overall, the prognosis for training and development in the Australian LIS sector is good, but for specialized providers, the future is arguably less clear.

REFERENCES

ALIA (2005), *Policies: Professional Development for Library and Information Professionals.* <http://www.alia.org.au/policies/professional.development.html>.
ALIA (2007), *Education: Professional Development Scheme.* <http://www.alia. org.au/education/pd/scheme/>. accessed 24 July 2007.
Australian Bureau of Statistics (2005), *Labour Force Survey. Catalogue no. 6203.0* (Canberra: ABS).
Australian Bureau of Statistics (2007), *6202.0 – Labour Force, Australia* (Canberra: ABS).
Barney, K. (2004), 'Evaluation of the Impact of the 2003 Aurora Leadership Institute – The Gift that Keeps on Giving', *Australian Library Journal* 53:4, 337–48.
CAUL (2006), *Training and Staff Development Opportunities.* <http://www.caul. edu.au/training&devt.html>.
CAVAL (2004), Training Needs Survey, unpublished.
CAVAL (2005), Training Needs Survey, unpublished.

CAVAL (2006), Training Needs Survey, unpublished.

Ching, H.S., Poon, P.W.T and McNaught, C. (eds) (2006), *eLearning and Digital Publishing* (Dordrecht: Springer).

DEST (2007), *AQTF 2007 – Registration.* <http://www.dest.gov.au/sectors/ training_skills/policy_issues_reviews/key_issues/nts/aqtf/registration.htm>.

Hallam, G. (2006), 'Trends in LIS Education in Australia' in C. Khoo, D. Singh and A.S. Chaudhry (eds).

Hallam, G. (2007a), 'Don't Ever Stop! The Imperative for Career-Long Learning in the Library and Information Profession', *ALIA Information Online Conference 2007.* <http://www.information-online.com.au/>.

Hallam, G. (2007b), 'Library Workforce Planning in Australia: A Focus on Learning, Strengthening and Moving the Profession Forward', *Proceedings of the Librarians: Learning – Strengthening – Moving Forward: Library Association of Singapore Conference 2007* (Singapore: LAS).

Harvey, R. and Higgins, S. (2003), 'Defining Fundamentals and Meeting Expectations: Trends in LIS Education in Australia', *Education for Information* 21:2–3, 149–57.

Kennan, M.A., Willard, P. and Wilson, C.S. (2006), 'What Do They Want? A Study of Changing Employer Expectations of Information Professionals', *Australian Academic and Research Libraries* 37:1, 17–37.

Khoo, C., Singh, D. and Chaudhry, A.S. (eds) (2006), *Preparing Information Professionals for Leadership in the New Age: Proceedings of the Asia-Pacific Conference on Library and Information Education and Practice 2006* (Singapore: School of Communication and Information, Nanyang Technological University).

Marion, L., Kennan, M.A., Willard, P. and Wilson, C.S. (2005), 'A Tale of Two Markets: Employer Expectations of Information Professionals in Australia and the United States of America', *Proceedings of the 71st IFLA General Conference and Council, 'Libraries – A Voyage of Discovery' 14–18 Augus*t *2005, Oslo, Norway.* <http://www.ifla.org/IV/ifla71/papers/056e-Marion.pdf>.

RMAA (2007), *About the RMAA.* <http://www.rmaa.com.au/docs/about/index. cfm>.

Sayers, R. (2006), *Principles of Awareness-Raising: Information Literacy, a Case Study* (Bangkok: UNESCO Bangkok).

University of Wisconsin School of Library and Information Studies (2007), *Current Continuing Education Courses andConferences.* <http://www.slis. wisc.edu/continueed/>.

Van Wanrooy, B. (2006), *Workforce Sustainability and Leadership: Scoping Research*, commissioned by State Library of Victoria (Sydney: Workplace Research Centre).

Wetzel, K.A. (2006), 'Developing and Managing a Professional Development Distance-Learning Programme: The ARL/OLMS Online Lyceum' in H.S. Ching, P.W.T. Poon and C. McNaught (eds).

Willard, P., Wilson, C.S. and Cole, F. (2003), 'Changing Employment Patterns: An Australian Experience', *Education for Information* 21, 209–28.

APPENDIX 1

ALIA POLICY: PROFESSIONAL DEVELOPMENT FOR LIBRARY AND INFORMATION PROFESSIONALS (SOURCE: ALIA 2005)

Professional development for library and information professionals

The phrase 'library and information professionals' refers to those members of the profession who have completed an entry-level qualification in library and information management at either Associate or Library Technician level.

ALIA objects addressed

To promote and improve the services provided by all kinds of library and information agencies.

To ensure the high standard of personnel engaged in information provision and foster their professional interests and aspirations.

Principle

Library and information professionals have a responsibility to commit to professional development and career-long learning. Similarly, their employers and the Australian Library and Information Association have a responsibility to provide opportunities which enable library and information professionals to maintain excellent service delivery.

Statement

Professional development demonstrates the individual practitioner's personal commitment of time and effort to ensure excellence in performance throughout his or her career. The dynamic and changing library and information environment demands that library and information professionals maintain and continue to develop their knowledge and skills so that they can anticipate and serve the information needs of society and their individual clients.

Professional development includes many learning experiences – within and outside the workplace – which aim to increase knowledge, develop library and information skills and attributes and broaden the range of vocational competencies. Learning activities may relate to an extension of general or specialist areas of library and information management education, development of the body of knowledge underlying professional practice, development of the reflective practitioner, development of research expertise, or studies from another discipline which lead to personal and professional development.

The Australian Library and Information Association expects that learning opportunities will be made available in a number of different formats and offered in a variety of different delivery modes. Learning experiences include but are not limited to formal education at advanced (post-first qualification) level, formal training courses, informal learning activities, mentoring, workplace learning, seminars, presentations, research and service activities.

The Association's commitment to its members achieving their career goals is demonstrated by:

- providing mechanisms which enable members to plan and undertake learning and other development activities;
- offering a mentoring program to assist members in their ongoing professional development;
- organising partnerships with other professional and training organisations to make available learning activities and opportunities in library and information management and other disciplinary studies;
- formally recognising members who participate in ALIA's professional development certification scheme;
- facilitating forums where knowledge can be created, shared and disseminated to enable members to better understand the dynamic environment in which they, as library and information professionals, and their clients operate.

Related documents

ALIA's role in education of library and information professionals
Courses in library and information management
The library and information sector: core knowledge, skills and attributes
ALIA core values statement

APPENDIX 2

LIS TRAINING AND DEVELOPMENT COURSES IN AUSTRALIA 2007

* indicates online or distance learning mode of delivery

CAVAL Training

Advanced Presentation Skills
Advanced Web Design and Usability
All Together Now: The Hows and Whys of Library Consortia
Answering Family History Enquiries in Libraries and Information Centres*
Archives and Recordkeeping for Community Organisations
Building Inclusive Websites: A Practical Guide to Web Accessibility for Clients
    with Special Needs
Business Competencies for Information Professionals
Cataloguing Audio-Visual Materials
Cataloguing Books
Cataloguing E-Resources
Cataloguing Non-Book Materials
Cataloguing Resources for Music and Performing Arts
Cataloguing Serials: Print and Electronic
Cataloguing with Dewey: Overview and Application
Change Ability: Mastering Change in Information Services
Consulting Skills for Information Professionals
Customer Service Across Cultures
Deciphering URLs and XML for Beginners
Digital Rights Management for Information Services
Effective Performance Management
EndNote for Information Professionals
Exceptional Customer Service in Libraries and Information Services
Facilitating Effective Group Processes
Fundamental Presentation Skills
General Cataloguing Principles and Practices
Implementing Records and Information Management

Information Architecture for Libraries and Information Services
Introduction to Metadata and the DC Element Set
Introduction to Records and Information Management: Principles and Practice
Introduction to Statistics, Measurement and Performance Indicators
Knowledge Management for Information Professionals
Leading Change in Information Services
Leading in Libraries: A Leadership Program for Libraries and Information Services
Legal Research Basics: Strategies and Sources
Libraries Australia Cataloguing Client
Libraries Australia Document Delivery
Libraries Australia Document Delivery Online*
Libraries Australia Document Delivery Refresher
Libraries Australia Document Delivery Update
Libraries Australia Search Interface
Managing a Disaster Response
Managing Challenging Clients: A Workshop for Libraries and Information Services
Managing Copyright Compliance in Libraries and Information Services
Managing Exceptional Customer Service Teams
MARC 21 for Cataloguers
MARC 21 Format for Authority Data
Marketing for Non-Marketing Professionals
Marketing Information Services: Starting Out and Up
Mentoring for Strategic Staff Development
Moys Classification
Negotiating E-Licences
Negotiation Skills
New and Emerging Internet Technologies: Exploring Web 2.0 and More
Personal Career Development: Planning Your Future
Personal Leadership Planning
Planning an Information Audit
Planning and Managing Technology Projects
Planning for Disaster Preparedness
Practical Book and Journal Repairs
Preserving Digital Information: Challenges and Solutions
Project Management for Information Professionals
Searching the Internet: 'Yahoogle' and Beyond
Spreading the Good Word: Communication Strategies for Libraries and
    Information Services
Stepping up to Supervision: A Program for Libraries and Information Services
Strategic Planning: From Thinking to Creating the Future
Strategic Staff Development: Identifying Needs and Planning Programs
Team Effectiveness: Building Better Teams
The Top 10 Strategies for Library Success – An Expert Forum with Stephen
    Abram

Time Management with Lotus Notes
Time Management with Microsoft Outlook
Train the Trainer for Information Professionals
Web Design and Usability
Web Dewey
Web Resources for Cataloguers
Who Needs to Know? Defining Your Target Audience
Working with Asian Names
Working with Disaster Bins
Writing Business Cases for Information Services
XML for Web Practitioners

Information Enterprises Australia (IEA)

Advanced Internet Searching
Classification and Indexing of Business Records
Developing a Business Classification Scheme
Developing a Retention and Disposal Schedule
Disaster Planning and Risk Management
Email Management
How to Use the Australian Record Retention Manual
How to Write a Collection Management Policy for Your Library
Introduction to Records Management
Retention and Disposal of Business Records
TRIM Context – Administration, Power Users, Desktop Users, Train the Trainer, Archiving and Workflow

Key Forums Australia

Best Practice Library and Knowledge Management
Implementing Library 2.0
Intranet Design and Strategy
Marketing your Library and its Services

CHAPTER 16

LIBRARY TRAINING PRACTICE AND DEVELOPMENT IN THE UNITED STATES

TERRY L. WEECH

INTRODUCTION

A review of the chapters in earlier editions of this book reveals the orientation of the content to be what we term in the US as 'continuing education'. But since the review of library training practice and development in the US has not been included in earlier editions of this series, I have undertaken the task to provide an overall review of education and training for librarianship in the US. Thus this chapter is likely to be much more general than other chapters in this volume.

Libraries and librarianship are in transition in the US as they are elsewhere in the world. Library and information science (LIS) education and training is adapting to stay ahead of the technological and social changes that are driving this transition. A review of journal articles and conference themes confirms that the Internet, and especially web search engines such as Google, have had a significant impact on the role and public perceptions of libraries and librarianship. In academic libraries, the advent of virtual reference for all users and e-reserves for student use, and e-books and e-journals for the use of both students and faculty, is often given as the reason for the decrease in library use and the changes in patterns of services. While the use of public and school libraries may not have been impacted as greatly by changes of user patterns as academic libraries, certainly the web and electronic resources have changed the way services are being provided as well as changing the content and focus of both first professional and continuing education programs in the United States. The Internet has also impacted the delivery of library training practice and development in the US with more and more training programs being delivered in part or in whole by the Internet.

This chapter will summarize national and vocational qualifications for librarians and library support staff in the US, review training practices for some specific topics, and then summarize and draw conclusions about the trends in training for librarianship in the US, including the monitoring and evaluation of the training.

DEFINITIONS

This chapter will not enter into a discussion of the differences between education and training. There is a long history in the literature on this topic, often connecting 'education' to theory and 'training' to practice, and suggesting that library schools must emphasize 'education' over 'training' if they are to maintain a position in academe (Moran 2001). While some may prefer to reserve 'education' for the postgraduate academic degrees and 'training' for the pre-professional and continuing education efforts, in this chapter, the terms 'education' and 'training' are used interchangeably. We will leave the debate to another time as to whether a profession can be based on training or whether it requires education based on theory.

Library job positions in this chapter are defined according to the American Library Association's policy on education and human resource utilization:

> *The title 'Librarian' carries with it the connotation of 'professional' in the sense that professional tasks are those which require a special background and education on the basis of which library needs are identified, problems are analyzed, goals are set, and original and creative solutions are formulated for them, integrating theory into practice, and planning, organizing, communicating, and administering successful programs of service to users of the library's materials and services* (American Library Association 2002).

For purposes of discussing training for professional positions, the training related to the credentialing of professional librarians is the focus. In the US, the primary credentialing program involves graduate degree programs in library and information science at the Masters degree level that are accredited by the American Library Association (ALA). There are also forms of credentialing that involve certification of individuals who wish to assume a position of professional librarian. The most widely applied credentialing based on certification that exists in the US for librarians is for school library personnel. All 50 states in the US have some form of formal certification of school librarians (also called 'school media specialists'). Certification of librarians of other types of libraries is less widely applied in the US. Before we look at specific training examples, we will review the various patterns of credentialing that exist in the US and how these patterns vary from state to state and jurisdiction to jurisdiction.

CREDENTIALING OF PROFESSIONAL LIBRARIANS: ACCREDITATION VERSUS CERTIFICATION

Nationally, the profession of librarianship in the US decided early on to focus on accreditation of professional degree programs instead of certification of individual librarians. Thus there is no national certification of librarians in the United States. Like most educational training and licensing of professionals, the matter of vocational qualifications of professionals is left to each of the 50 states. All states in the US certify school librarians and require continued education and training, as they do of all teachers. Fewer states (less than half) require some form of certification of public and/or academic librarians. In a 2003 report by Christine Hamilton-Pennell, the 24 states with certification were listed as: Arizona, Arkansas, California, Georgia, Idaho, Indiana, Kentucky, Louisiana, Maryland, Massachusetts, Michigan, Montana, Nevada, New Jersey, New Mexico, New York, North Carolina, Pennsylvania, South Carolina, Texas, Utah, Virginia, Washington, and Wisconsin. Hamilton-Pennell notes that there is considerable variation in certification requirements among the states that do have certification for librarians. She reports that Arizona and Texas require certification only for head librarians of county libraries. Indiana certifies library directors at five levels of certification. New Mexico has four levels of certification and Louisiana has two. Kentucky requires certification for all permanent positions (part-time or full-time) for staff who provide library information services as determined by local library policy. New York has similar requirements to those found in Kentucky. Maryland requires two certificates; a Professional Public Librarian Certificate and a Public Library Director Certificate. Every librarian employed by a county public library in Maryland is required to hold a professional certificate issued by the Maryland State Superintendent. In Massachusetts, Certificates of Librarianship based on work experience or education level are required of all Massachusetts public library directors as a prerequisite for municipalities to receive Massachusetts state financial support. Michigan also requires certification of library staff for state financial aid (Hamilton-Pennell 2003).

It should be noted that in many of these states certification is often waived or becomes automatic if an ALA-accredited degree is held. Some local jurisdictions (cities, counties, states, and so on) may require civil service examinations prior to employment as a librarian. These exams may include questions relating to basic library knowledge, but they may also include more general education questions. While the ALA-accredited degree is often preferred, if not required, the applicant may also be required to take the civil service examination to qualify for appointment to the library staff. In many cases certification without the ALA-accredited degree will require the individual to take additional training courses at regular intervals from state-approved continuing education providers.

Thus the typology of qualifications for the position of professional librarian in the US varies considerably from jurisdiction to jurisdiction. Nationally, the ALA-accredited Masters degree is preferred if not required by most organizations that employ professional librarians. But as noted above, in all 50 states, state certification is required for professional school librarians, and in about half of the states in the United States, some form of certification is required for public librarians. Special and academic librarians are less likely to require certification by the state, but the hiring institution may require specialized degrees, such as a subject Masters degree in addition to the ALA-accredited degree. And following the ALA policy on education and human resource utilization, many academic and special libraries may hire staff with advanced training in a special area of expertise without requiring the ALA-accredited degree. With this background, we now turn to trends and patterns of implementing training of library staff in the US.

US LIBRARY TRAINING PRACTICE (PROFESSIONAL NATIONAL AND VOCATIONAL QUALIFICATIONS)

First Professional Level

In the US the first professional level of training for librarians is the Masters degree from an ALA-accredited program. The program of accreditation is administered by the Office of Accreditation and the Committee on Accreditation (COA) within the ALA. The website provides links to the 49 ALA-accredited programs in the US, including the accredited programs in Puerto Rico and Washington DC.[1] The seven accredited programs in Canada are also listed. The names of the members of the Committee on Accreditation are also linked from this site. Volunteers consisting of librarians, interested non-librarians, and library and information science faculty staff teams that conduct on- and off-site evaluations of the programs that apply for accreditation. The Committee on Accreditation reviews the reports of the visiting site teams and provides the final decision on whether the program is to be accredited. All graduates of an accredited program are considered 'credentialed librarians'.

There are guidelines for employment in libraries without having graduated from an ALA-accredited program. These options are outlined in the ALA Library and Information Studies and Human Resource Utilization policy,[2] adopted by the Council of the American Library Association in 2002. This document lists professional and non-professional supportive categories of library personnel. This matrix has not been widely applied in many libraries, but it does supply a structure for identifying professional and support positions in the US.

Job announcements in academic and public libraries usually list the ALA-accredited Masters degree or equivalent as a requirement to be employed as a professional librarian. The 'equivalency' qualification is inserted in part because of court cases

---

1   Office of Accreditation and the Committee on Accreditation. <http://www.ala.org/ala/accreditation/accreditation.htm>.

2   ALA Library and Information Studies and Human Resource Utilization Policy. <http://www.ala.org/ala/hrdr/educprofdev/lepu.pdf>.

in the US that have challenged the requirement of the accredited degree. While court cases have not been consistent in their decisions, most libraries have adopted the 'or equivalent' as a form of legal protection. Such a qualification also provides some flexibility to employers should they decide to make an exception to the required accredited degree.

Advanced Formal Training

The two most common forms of advanced formal training are the Certificate of Advanced Studies (CAS) and the doctorate (PhD). The CAS is also sometimes referred to as a '6th year' degree since it usually requires a Masters degree as a prerequisite. The purpose of the CAS is to provide more specialized education than is possible in the Masters degree program. Sometimes the CAS is also used to provide an update on advances in the field for librarians who may have done their Masters degree work some years earlier. Recent interest in digital librarianship has led a number of schools to establish CAS degree programs to provide specialization in digital librarianship. More details on education for digital librarianship are provided later in this chapter. Other specialized programs offered under the CAS include data curation and biomedical informatics.

The doctorate degree, usually a PhD, but sometimes a Doctorate in Library Science (DLS), is most commonly pursued by those wishing to do research and teaching in the area of library and information science, although some do pursue the doctorate for personal satisfaction or to provide credentials for advancing administratively in a library setting. The PhD in Library and Information Science, since it is not considered a professional degree, is not accredited by the ALA.

A recent form of supplemental education to the basic LIS-accredited Masters degree is the Association of Research Libraries Annual Leadership Institute.[3] Since 2005, the Association of Research Libraries (ARL) has hosted a Leadership Institute for students in Masters of Library and Information Science (MLS) programs. In 2007, it was held in conjunction with the ALA Midwinter Meeting in Seattle, Washington. This institute is open to any MLS student at no cost. It is part of ARL's initiative to Recruit a Diverse Workforce[4] which is an effort to interest more ethnic minorities graduating from library and information science programs to choose academic and research library careers. This effort is unusual in that it is neither an official part of the professional education program nor is it technically continuing education, but is rather a form of supplemental education to establish mentoring and career networking for future academic and research library librarians. Institute topics include Research, Teaching and Learning in the

---

3   Association of Research Libraries Annual Leadership Institute. <http://www.arl.org/diversity/leadinst/index.shtml>.

4   ARL's initiative to Recruit a Diverse Workforce. <http://www.arl.org/diversity/init/>.

21st Century; Library Fund Development; Current Trends in Information Policy/
Federal Relations; and a panel discussion on transitioning into an ARL library.
This effort is especially interesting in that it is a form of training that is designed
as both a recruiting and a supplemental education program to the basic graduate
degree in library and information science. As such, it is unique in the typology of
LIS training in that it is a form of supplemental rather than continuing education
effort, placed during the study for the basic professional degree. Thus, it is placed
in this section rather than in the following section on continuing education.

Other Formal (Pre-professional) Training Programs

There are some undergraduate programs in information studies and a few that
may include training for work in libraries, but since the ALA accreditation is
only at the graduate Masters degree level, these programs are not considered part
of professional training for librarianship except in the case of school librarians.
School librarians (also referred to as School Media Specialists and a variety of
other variants in terminology) may be credentialed as a school librarian with an
undergraduate Bachelors degree with courses specifically proscribed by state
certification agencies. The specific course requirements vary from state to state.

There are also non-accredited undergraduate two-year programs in the community
colleges in the US that have 'associate degrees' training students as 'library
technical assistants'. One example of such a program is that provided by Cuesta
College, a community college in California, that provides an extensive library/
information technology program for all levels of library staff that can result in an
Associate Degree.[5]

The 'library associate' or 'library technical assistant' category of library staff is
somewhat controversial in the US since, with a two-year degree, they are blocked
from advancing to a professional position until they earn the four-year Bachelors
degree required for admission to the ALA-accredited Masters degree programs.

Continuing Education

For those library staff members in the US, continuing education (CE) is delivered
by a widely diverse group of providers. CE training and development programs
are distinguished from the above listed formal education and training programs in
that they do not result in recognized university course credit that can be counted
toward a university degree. Some CE providers do give CE credits that result in
certificates or other papers of recognition. But they do not count toward a formal
degree.

---

5   Cuesta College. <http://library.cuesta.edu/libinf/ for more details>.

Most of the providers can be grouped into three broad categories: 1) professional associations; 2) academic institutions; and 3) libraries themselves. While there are a scattering of other providers, such as individual and private for-profit companies that may provide continuing education to library staff, most of these entities deliver their training through one of the above three categories of providers. The following listings are a selected sample of the groups that exist in each category. No attempt has been made to produce an exhaustive list within each category. But those organizations and institutions listed provide a sense of the scope of the representative organizations and institutions involved.

PROFESSIONAL ASSOCIATIONS

In some respects, professional library associations are the first line of providers of continuing education for library staff in the US since they not only provide educational opportunities as part of their conferences and organizational meetings, but also are providers of specialized workshops and training sessions both on site and through the Internet. As the list of associations below suggests, CE opportunities include a wide spectrum of subjects based on the different specializations of librarians.

National Library Associations

American Library Association. <http://www.ala.org>.
American Association of Law Librarians. <http://www.aallnet.org/>.
American Indian Library Association. <http://aila.library.sd.gov/>.
American Theological Library Association. <http://www.atla.com/atlahome.html>.
Association of Research Libraries. <http://www.arl.org/arl/>.
Medical Library Association. <http://www.mlanet.org/>.
Music Library Association. <http://www.musiclibraryassoc.org/>.
Special Libraries Association. <http://www.sla.org/>.
Theater Library Association. <http://tla.library.unt.edu/>.

Of the national associations, the largest and most involved with continuing education is the American Library Association (ALA). Central to ALA's influence is the Continuing Library Education Network and Exchange (CLENE). This exchange is connected to the membership through the Continuing Library Education Network and Exchange Round Table (CLENERT).[6] It provides a searchable database of CE activities as well as many publications, conference events, and CE workshops. The database is linked from <http://www.ala.org/ce>. It also sponsors the Continuing Education Training Showcase at the annual conference of ALA. CE

---

6   Continuing Library Education Network and Exchange Round Table (CLENERT). <http://www.ala.org/Template.cfm?Section=clenert>.

providers present their programs at the Showcase to inform others of possible CE approaches. The brochure for 2007 can be found at <http://www.ala.org/ala/clenert/trainingshowcase/Showcase_Flyer_2007.pdf>.

Most sections and units of ALA are involved in continuing education. In fact, the annual and mid-winter conferences of ALA are major CE events, as are the conferences of the sections of ALA, held at various intervals. For example, RUSA (Reference and User Services Association), a division of ALA, provides a series of professional development courses online.[7] These courses include: The Reference Interview; Business Reference 101; Readers Advisor 101; and Marketing Basics for Libraries. The course on the reference interview is described as designed for '... support staff, library technicians, newly hired reference librarians, and those librarians who want to brush up on their skills. The topics covered are introductory in nature. Class segments are geared to cover issues of interest to staff in all types of libraries' (RUSA 2007). Costs range from $100 to $190 per course, depending on the status of the student.

In addition to these instructor-led web-based courses, ALA, in co-operation with the Southeast Florida Library Information Network (SEFLIN), has established a contract to make more than 1,500 e-learning courses from Element K, a private provider of web-based courseware available to ALA members at special prices ranging from $75 to $275. The topics are on Office Productivity, Computer Skills, and Business Fundamentals.[8] These learning modules are self-paced online educational opportunities that are available to subscribers for a year.

Another example of professional continuing education is the Public Library Association Certification Courses. In 2006, the Public Library Association, a division of ALA, established a Certified Public Library Administrator (CPLA) program. The program is open only to librarians who are graduates of ALA-accredited LIS programs and have three years or more of administrative experience. Each applicant has five years to complete the program and must take courses in the four core programs,[9] these being:

- Budget and Finance
- Management of Technology
- Organization and Personnel Administration
- Facility Management and Maintenance

---

7   RUSA, professional development online. <http://www.ala.org/ala/rusa/rusaevents/professionaldevelopmentonline/prodevonline.htm>.

8   Element K. <https://www.librarylearning.org/ala/>.

9   Certified Public Library Administrator (CPLA) program. <http://ala-apa.org/certification/cplastandards.htm>.

Three of the following five electives are required:

- Current Issues
- Marketing
- Fundraising/Grantsmanship
- Politics and Networking
- Serving Diverse Populations

The purpose of the program is to enable public library administrators to:

- Further their professional education and development
- Move to a higher level of practical professional experience
- Improve career opportunities through professional expertise
- Demonstrate to colleagues, trustees and board of directors, patrons and the wider information community that the certified person has acquired a nationally and professionally recognized body of knowledge and expertise in public library administration
- Improve the quality of library service through the provision of practical knowledge and skills essential to successful library management

Classes are offered both online and in person.[10] Many of the courses are offered in conjunction with library schools. One example of an announcement for a class in this program is provided in Box 16.1.

---

10 Certified Public Library Administrator (CPLA) classes. <http://ala-apa.org/certification/cplaapplication.html>.

The Graduate School of Library and Information Science at the University of Illinois at Urbana-Champaign is pleased to offer a new continuing education course. This course is ALA-APA approved for Certified Public Library Administrator (CPLA) candidates.

Course title: Politics and Networking

Dates: March 15–April 26, 2007 (No class on April 19)

Times: Online synchronous sessions Thursdays 2:00–4:00 pm Central time

Cost: $300

Instructor: John A. Moorman, PhD Director, Williamsburg Regional Library

Intended audience: Librarians and information professionals needing training in politics and networking; CPLA candidates

Purpose of the course: To provide the student with an understanding of the political process as it relates to public libraries. Topics included are governance and legal structures of Boards and Commissions, how to assess your community, how to assess local political issues, understanding and influencing the local political process, the development and nurturing of library support groups, and how to work effectively with individuals and groups to increase library visibility and support. Upon completion of the course the individual is expected to know how to identify the social, political, and economic issues that affect the library they serve, develop effective relationships with governing boards, library support groups, and influence makers, develop coalitions with groups in the community, and understand the legislative process.

For additional information and to register, please visit http://www.lis.uiuc.edu/programs/cpd/CPLA/fund.html or contact Marianne Steadley, steadley@uiuc.edu or 217-244-2751

Marianne Steadley Continuing Professional Development Program Director, GSLIS

Box 16.1 Course announcement
Note: Description posted 23 February 2007 on JESSE Listserv. Accessed 28 February 2007.

Similar commitments to delivering continuing education can be found in the other national library associations. An exploration of their websites (URLs to the national library associations are provided above) will reveal the extent of their CE involvement.

State and Regional Library Associations

All 50 states have library associations. The size and the nature of their CE activities vary considerably, but at a minimum the state library associations have annual conferences that include programs and workshops that serve to provide delivery of continuing education to library staff. Most states have separate sections within the state association for those interested in a specific type of library or library service, such as public libraries, academic libraries, reference services or government information resources. In these cases the state association mirrors the organizational structure of ALA. These sections, as well as the umbrella association, may provide CE workshops throughout the year to supplement the continuing education provided at their annual conference.

In addition to state associations, there are regional associations that may also provide continuing education through workshops and conferences. Four examples of such regional associations are:

- Pacific Northwest Library Association. <http://www.pnla.org/>.
- Southeastern Library Association. <http://sela.jsu.edu/>.
- New England Library Association. <http://www.nelib.org/>.
- Mountain Plains Library Association. <http://www.mpla.us/>.

There are also regional sections or interest groups of the more specialized associations, such as the Special Libraries Association, the American Association of Law Librarians, and others. These associations often have chapters that cover states or large cities where there is a concentration of their members.

An extensive list of library associations at all levels can be found at the Internet Library for Librarians.[11] ALA also provides a list of state and regional associations.[12]

Other CE Providers

Other CE providers include state library agencies in each of the 50 states, and local and regional library co-operatives (sometimes called 'library systems' or 'library networks'). Most states have some kind of library network or co-operative that helps support local libraries with technical and training activities. These co-operatives are usually affiliated with the state library or state library agency that is concerned with library development in the state. For example, in the State of Illinois there are ten 'library systems' that provide continuing education and other services to libraries in their region. In Illinois these library systems are multi-type, meaning that school, special and academic libraries, as well as public libraries, may take advantage of the training programs offered. The Illinois State Library has a co-ordinating role in the functions of each of these regional library co-operatives. A list of the 50 state library agencies can be found at <http://www.publiclibraries. com/state_library.htm>. This list includes state archive and historical libraries, but at least one of the agencies listed in each state carries out the function of co-ordinating co-operative activities within that state.

There are also regional consortia or groups that respond to CE needs of the participants on a regional basis. One such group is the Western Council of State Libraries (WCSL).[13] WCSL co-ordinates continuing education as well as other

---

11   Internet Library for Librarians. <http://www.itcompany.com/inforetriever/assn_us.htm>.
12   State and regional associations. <http://www.ala.org/ala/ourassociation/chapters/ stateandregional/stateregional.htm>.
13   WCSL. <http://www.westernco.org/>.

activities in the 22 states west of the Mississippi River, working with state library agencies in these states. WCSL has established a Library Practitioners Certificate Program for library staff without an ALA-accredited Masters degree.[14]

Library schools and individual libraries are two other sources of CE activities in the US. Many library schools open their courses, both online and in residence, to librarians for CE credit. Workshops and short courses are also regularly offered by library schools. Larger libraries, both public and academic, often have staff retreats or training days to cover CE topics such as new technology or new services. These are sometimes jointly sponsored by vendors of library equipment or materials. Smaller libraries usually depend on the regional co-operative library systems, noted above, to organize such training events, since they do not have the critical mass to support such training activities that larger libraries have. Library school faculty are often retrained as trainers by larger libraries or library co-operatives to present workshops and training programs independent of the library school offering.

One recent innovative program in continuing education is WebJunction, an online community for library staff. WebJunction is funded in part by the Gates Foundation and has as its mission to establish a co-operative of library staff sharing and using online resources that enable participants to identify and embrace appropriate technologies and apply them to their daily work in libraries. In 2002, the Bill and Melinda Gates Foundation awarded OCLC Online Computer Library Center a three-year grant to build a portal for public libraries and other organizations that provide public access to information. The program builds on the Bill and Melinda Gates Foundation's five-year library program, which has provided over 40,000 computers with Internet access to more than 10,000 libraries across the United States and Canada. WebJunction's programs are not limited to librarians, but they do include programs to assist librarians in sustaining public access computing in libraries and to develop competencies in management of technology.[15]

CASE STUDIES OF TWO ACTIVE LIBRARY TRAINING AND DEVELOPMENT PROGRAMS IN THE US: INFORMATION LITERACY (TEACHING AND TRAINING USERS) AND TRAINING FOR DIGITAL LIBRARIANSHIP

As the above review of the library training and development programs in the US suggests, there is a great variety of excellent and active programs. Two areas are selected for a more in-depth examination. Information literacy was selected because it is one of the best sustained continuing training and development programs in the

---

14   WCSL Library Practitioners Certificate Program. <http://certificate.westernco.org/>.
15   WebJunction. <http://www.webjunction.org/do/Home>.

US. Training for digital librarianship has been selected because it is one of the most recent areas of training interest.

Information Literacy

Information literacy is perhaps the best example of how continuing education has taken the lead in providing education and training for library staff in one specific area of the profession. Information literacy has been taught in LIS schools for many years. But for most students planning to become a librarian in public or academic libraries, exposure to training in information literacy is usually limited to one course and the enrollment in this course often represents a comparatively small proportion of the total students enrolled in an LIS school. Thus information literacy has developed into a sub-discipline in which much of the training is delivered after the initial professional training as a librarian. Part of the reason for this may be the fact that most ALA-accredited library schools offer one-year programs and there is not sufficient time to get the basic professional education and also more specialized training in sub-disciplines such as information literacy.

One of the major providers of information literacy continuing education is LOEX (Library Orientation Exchange).[16] LOEX started in 1971 at Eastern Michigan University as a repository of library instruction material and the hosting of an annual conference. Today it attracts international attention and participation. Members may borrow the materials held in the repository to use to develop their own instruction materials. The LOEX annual conference has become a significant CE event in the area of information literacy training. Annual proceedings are published. LOEX also publishes quarterly and monthly newsletters with articles on training for information literacy.

The other major provider can be grouped as the various sections and divisions of the professional associations that deal with information literacy and library user instruction. For example, within the ALA, a number of sections have groups focusing on information literacy. AASL (American Association of School Librarians), ACRL (Association of College and Research Libraries), LIRT (Library Instruction Round Table), RUSA (Reference and User Services Association) are some of the units in ALA that have specific focus on information literacy and are regularly involved in CE activities on information literacy through conferences and workshops.

ACRL is one of the most active ALA units in the area of continuing education for information literacy. The ACRL Information Literacy Institute Immersion Program is a four and a half-day intensive workshop on how to establish or enhance

---

16   LOEX. <http://www.emich.edu/public/loex/index.html>.

an information literacy instruction program at a library. The annual immersion program consists of two components:

1. The 'Teacher Track' which provides individual development for those who wish to enhance or refresh their individual instructional skills. Classroom techniques, learning theory, leadership skills, and assessment procedures are the subject of the curriculum.
2. The 'Program Track', which focuses on developing, integrating, and managing institutional and programmatic information literacy programs. The description provided by ACRL indicates that:

> Participants selected for the Program Track will develop individual case studies in advance of the Immersion program. Change dynamics, systems thinking, institutional outcomes assessment, scalability, and the integration of teaching, learning, and technology will be brought to bear on analyzing the various programmatic challenges presented in the case studies. Immersion participants will be expected to develop the case studies into an action plan for implementation at the home institution.

Details about both of these programs can be found at: <http://www.ala.org/ala/acrl/acrlissues/acrlinfolit/professactivity/iil/immersion/immersionprograms.htm>.

In some ways, training for information literacy continues to focus on continuing education because it is an interdisciplinary sub-discipline of librarianship. While school librarians are recognized as teachers as well as librarians in elementary and secondary schools in the US, the role of librarians in academic, special, and public libraries has been seen more as conservator, facilitator, and manager rather than that of teacher. This has led to the necessity of those academic, special, and public librarians that wish to become skilled in delivering information literacy to reach out for continuing education in educational delivery skills as well as the other traditional competencies of librarianship.

Digital Librarianship

With the development of digital libraries in the 1990s, more attention has been paid to education and training for the development and maintenance of digital collections. Like information literacy, digital librarianship is an area that is taught in LIS schools, but not all students take the courses and the courses available are limited. Pomerantz et al. found that in 2006, 52 per cent of the ALA-accredited programs in the US and Canada had one or more courses on digital libraries (Pomerantz et al. 2006, 5). The authors observed that there are few certifications and degrees exclusively in digital librarianship and noted the need for digital librarians to ensure the success of digital libraries that are being developed.

Early digital collections were often overseen by staff with computer science background. But as digital collections became more mainstream in libraries at the beginning of the twenty-first century, more staff with traditional library science backgrounds became involved, and thus there was a need for both basic professional education and continuing education on digital librarianship.

Choi and Rasmussen presented a paper at the 2006 Joint Conference on Digital Libraries (JCDL) in North Carolina on a survey they carried out. Digital library professionals in American academic libraries were asked questions about the new knowledge and skills required for digital libraries work. In their paper, Choi and Rasmussen identified three broad categories of digital libraries competencies: technical, library-related, and other managerial competencies. They developed a list of the top three competencies in each category, as ranked by respondents. Technical knowledge competencies that respondents thought important were the 'systems' aspects of digital projects including digital library architecture and software, technical and quality standards, and markup languages. Library-related competencies that respondents considered important included identifying user needs, digital archiving and preservation, and cataloging and classification. Special managerial competencies that were deemed important were communication skills, project management and leadership skills, and the ability to handle legal issues. Although traditional courses may include some of these skills identified as important for digital librarianship, schools of library and information science in the United States are responding to the perceived need to provide course content that specifically focuses on digital libraries by establishing specific programs or concentrations in digital librarianship (Choi and Rasmussen 2006).

Library and Information Science Education's Response to Skills for a Digital Environment

Four schools that have established concentrations or courses of study to educate students to work with digital libraries were selected to examine in detail the content of their concentrations in light of the competencies identified by Choi and Rasmussen. These four schools are:

- University of Illinois – Certificate of Advanced Study (CAS) – Digital Libraries Concentration. <http://www.lis.uiuc.edu/programs/cas-dl.html#coursework>.
- Indiana University – Masters Degree – Digital Libraries Concentration. <http://www-slis.lib.indiana.edu/degrees/joint/dls.php>.
- Rutgers University – Masters Degree – Digital Libraries Concentration online. <http://www.scils.rutgers.edu/programs/lis/OnlineMLIS.jsp>.
- Syracuse University – Certificate of Advanced Study (CAS) – Digital Libraries Concentration. <http://istweb.syr.edu/academics/graduate/mls/digitallibraries/index.asp>.

Note that two of the four programs are for the Masters degree while the University of Illinois' program is for the 6th year (post-Masters degree) certificate of advance study and the Syracuse University program appears to be a post-Bachelors non-degree certificate. The website suggests that in addition to Masters degree students in LIS as well as Masters degree students from other disciplines, the program accepts students with a Bachelors degree as well. It is noted, however, that for those without an LIS degree, 'the certificate by itself provides preparation for working with digital collections outside the institution of the library. In general, a master's degree in library and information science is necessary for professional work in libraries, although there are exceptions.' Also note that the Rutgers program is offered exclusively online. The other programs may have online delivery components, but they are also offered as residential programs on campus.

A review of these four programs of study suggests a variety of skills are seen as appropriate for librarians working with digital libraries. Most have both computer science and LIS course content, although some specify that the courses are to be taken from the Computer Science schools, not LIS. Of the two Masters degree curricula, Rutgers seems to have the most traditional LIS content within their electives, with courses such as Cataloging and Classification, Management of Libraries, and Information Technology for Libraries listed among the electives and two required non-credit LIS 'core' professionalization courses. Indiana University, however, also requires a basic 'core' of professional courses be taken in addition to the more technical electives listed. In both cases, the Masters degree with a digital libraries concentration is based on the foundation of library and information studies.

The CAS degrees, however, are not as clearly based on the LIS foundation and differ greatly from each other. The Syracuse University Degree is not a 6th year degree, requiring only a Bachelors degree for admission. This CAS also indicates that a library background is not a prerequisite for applying to this certificate program, although prior exposure to library work is desirable.

The University of Illinois CAS is a 6th year degree beyond the Masters degree and requires a Masters degree in LIS or a closely related field. While 'closely related field' is likely to be interpreted broadly to include computer science and other technical fields, the Illinois program does suggest a potentially closer tie to the LIS profession than the Syracuse University CAS.

Education for digital librarianship is clearly still in development as these initial programs of study are still in the pilot, if not experimental, stage. But the offering of these programs of study in digital librarianship are providing librarians and employers with options for training. They may serve both as a continuing and an initial professional training in the area. Which approach will become the standard is yet to be determined, but since these efforts are primarily cost-recovery driven, the educational market is likely to be the significant factor in determining which approach and curricula structure becomes the norm.

SUMMARY AND CONCLUSIONS (MONITORING AND EVALUATION OF TRAINING)

The concern over education of professional librarians in the US continues. The monitoring and evaluation of the education and training of professional librarians has been the focus of several meetings at ALA conferences. The past president of ALA, Michael Gorman, focused on the concerns with library education as a central part of his presidential program. In January of 2007, a second joint meet of library educators and practicing librarians was held between the Association of Library and Information Science Education (ALISE) Annual Conference and ALA 2007 mid-winter meetings in Seattle, Washington. This session was attended by several hundred librarians and library educators. The following points are this author's perceptions of some of the more important issues that were raised at the January 2007 meeting at ALA Midwinter:

The importance of connecting LIS education to practice – but at the same time providing balance with theory (Theory versus Practice debate) was the center of much of the discussion. It was noted that many European library schools have emphasized theory to the extent that little practice exists in their curricula. Some expressed the concern that few doctoral students in LIS doctoral programs in the US and Canada have the background or experience to teach the practice of librarianship, and thus theory is being emphasized more than practice.

The role of library education in meeting the needs of employers was a related issue. Some of the librarians present expressed frustration that they were often required to train recent graduates in how to perform as professional librarians on the job because the coursework in library school seemed not to prepare them for professional positions.

Confirming core values and competencies for professional librarians was identified as important for the future of library education and the profession. It was noted by several attendees that the challenge of defining core competencies is a significant barrier to reforming library education. One person cited the fact that for over seven years, an effort to reach agreement on core competencies of LIS professionals has been bottled up in ALA committees, with no evidence of movement toward adoption. Some felt the emphasis of LIS research on issues other than core values and competencies of LIS was part of the reason that little progress had been made in confirming those core values and competencies. Considerable frustration with the lack of forward movement on adopting the draft 'Statement of Core Competencies', which was originally drafted in 2000 but has not moved forward since then, was also expressed at a later meeting of the ALA Education Committee.

Whether certification or accreditation is a better method of quality assurance was discussed by a number of attendees. There was considerable frustration with the way the accreditation standards have evolved over the years from fewer objective and quantitative measures to more subjective and qualitative approaches, which some felt permitted schools to be measured by standards they essentially construct themselves. Some called for a return to the more traditional quantitative measures, with attention to specific core competencies that all LIS programs should focus on. Others opposed such a centralized oversight to LIS professional education programs.

A number of the participants spoke about the division between library science faculty and information science faculty in schools of library and information science. It seemed to some that information science-oriented faculty obtained the larger grants in terms of money and thus information science faculty are valued more than faculty with a library orientation. Some felt that library science faculty are put at a disadvantage. This sense of lack of value for library science sometimes extends to information technology students, who convey a sense of superiority to library science students. At least one participant felt the lack of grounding of some LIS faculty in librarianship might explain the lack of socialization of LIS students in the service orientation and core values of the profession.

In addition to the above stated concerns from the profession of librarianship regarding training of professional librarians in the US, some schools have taken their own initiative to establish a group called 'the I-Schools' or information schools. The formation of this group took place in 2005 when a group of schools interested in research issues related to information formed the I-Schools project. In 2007 there are 19 schools and programs participating. Details on the I-Schools project can be found at: <http://www.ischools.org/oc/>.

In 2005, the I-Schools Caucus established a charter. The following excerpts from the charter, noted in Box 16.2, provide insight to the special characteristics of this group:

I-Schools Charter

Introduction

The I-Schools Project (ISP) consists of schools interested in the relationship between information, technology, and people. This is characterized by a commitment to learning and understanding of the role of information in human endeavors. The I-Schools take it as given that expertise in all forms of information is required for progress in science, business, education, and culture. This expertise must include understanding of the uses and users of information, as well as information technologies and their applications. The I-Schools have organized under the guidelines below to pursue common objectives with a collective commitment of resources.

Guiding Principles

Keep the group small and interactive to promote discussion.

Engage individuals and institutions with strategic skills and vision to find common solutions to the challenges faced by the I-Schools.

Work with existing organizations and activities where issues of interest to I-Schools are already being addressed.

Disseminate opinions and conclusions broadly for all that can benefit from them.

Membership

New members are elected by majority vote of existing members, based on a slate of candidates presented by a Membership Committee appointed by the Steering Committee to represent the different constituencies within the I-Schools Project. Membership will be withdrawn for members that fail to send appropriate representatives to three consecutive meetings, or that fail to pay assessed dues within three months. All members must materially contribute to at least one ISP Agenda activity each year.

Criteria for membership are not rigid, but members are expected to have substantial sponsored research activity (an average of $1 million in research expenditures per year over three years), engagement in the training of future researchers (usually through an active, research-oriented doctoral program), and a commitment to progress in the information field.

The full charter can be found at: <http://www.ischools.org/oc/charter.html>.

Box 16.2 I-schools charter

It is clear from these excerpts from the charter that the I-Schools project has a very different purpose than the ALA accreditation program. The I-Schools project is not focused on education of professional librarians, but rather on training future researchers, usually in doctoral programs. The membership requirement of an average of $1 million in research expenditures per year over a period of three years makes the group a somewhat exclusive club. Of the 19 I-Schools project member schools, only 14 have accredited programs of LIS. It is unlikely that many of the other ALA-accredited programs would qualify with the $1 million dollar in research expenditures per year. But the establishment of the I-Schools project group does relate to the concerns expressed at the joint ALISE-ALA discussions.

Clearly there is evolving in the US two cultures dealing with training of information specialists. One culture focuses on training of professional librarians for work in libraries and related organizations. The other culture has the focus of training researchers to become engaged in information-related research projects. The first culture includes an emphasis on service and the second culture emphasizes the skills needed in academic and scientific research projects usually funded by external financial sources. In the 14 I-Schools that also maintain ALA-accredited professional training programs, the potential for tension between the two goals would seem to reflect some of the comments made at the ALISE-ALA meetings regarding the disparity between those involved in professional library research and training and those who are involved with information science-based research and training. It is likely that we are at the edge of a potential fault in the landscape of LIS training in the US. The question that has yet to be answered is whether those I-Schools with ALA-accredited professional training programs will emphasize the funded information research not specifically related to the library profession over research more directly related to professional librarian interests and concerns. We already see hiring patterns that suggest fewer faculty are being hired in I-Schools who have professional library training or experience, thus leaving the instruction in some of the professional training program coursework to adjunct and/or part-time faculty who do not have the research credentials of those working on so called 'information' research. With the penetration of the Internet and digital information resources in our personal and professional worlds, we may soon see significant changes in the nature and direction of LIS training in the US that will mirror some of the changes that have taken place in Europe in the past decade. We may see more mergers and closing of formal LIS professional training programs, and more reliance on continuing education to support the training needs of library staff in all types of libraries.

REFERENCES

American Library Association (2002), *Library and Information Studies Education and Human Resource Utilization, a Statement of Policy*. <http://www.ala.org/ala/hrdr/educprofdev/lepu.pdf>.

Choi, Y. and Rasmussen, E. (2006), 'What Do Digital Librarians Do?' JCDL '06, *Proceedings of the 6th ACM/IEEE-CS Joint Conference*, 187–8.

Hamilton-Pennell, C. (2003), *A Review of Standards and Guidelines from the 50 States of the U.S. for the Colorado, Mississippi and Hawaii State Libraries*, Mosaic Knowledge Works, April 2003. <http://www.tsl.state.tx.us/plstandards/minstand.html>.

Moran, B. (2001), 'Practitioners vs. LIS Educators: A Time to Reconnect', *Library Journal* 126 (November), 52–5.

Pomerantz, J., Oh, S., Yang, S., Fox, E.A. and Wildemuth, B. (2006), 'The Core: Digital Library Education in Library and Information Science Programs', *D-Lib Magazine* 12:11 (November). <http://www.dlib.org/>.

RUSA (2007), *Reference and User Services Association, Professional Development Online: 'The Reference Interview'*. <http://www.ala.org/ala/rusa/rusaevents/professionaldevelopmentonline/onlinereferenceinterviewcourse/refinterview.htm>.

APPENDIX 1

EDUCATION FOR DIGITAL LIBRARY PROGRAMS OFFERED IN THE US IN 2007

University of Illinois – Certificate of Advanced Study (CAS) 6th Year Degree – Digital Library Concentration.

<http://www.lis.uiuc.edu/programs/cas-dl.html#coursework>.

Required courses:

- Introduction to Digital Libraries
- Information Modeling
- Design of Digitally Mediated Information Services
- Metadata in Theory and Practice

Elective courses:

- Implementation of Information Storage and Retrieval Systems
- Architecture of Network Information Systems
- Agents and Multi-Agents for Dynamic Information Systems
- Current Topics in Collection Development
- Community Information Systems
- Computer Supported Co-operative Work
- Foundations of Data Curation
- Digital Humanities
- Document Modeling
- Document Processing
- Implementation of Distributed Information Systems
- E-Learning: Social and Technical Issues in E-Learning Research and Practice
- Electronic Publishing and Information Processing Standards
- Information Architecture
- Interfaces to Information Systems
- Information Policy

- Information Quality: Principles and Practices
- Knowledge Representation and Formal Ontology
- Rapid Prototyping and Evaluation
- Understanding Multimedia Information: Concepts and Practices
- Data Administration Concepts and Database Management (in co-operation with Syracuse University)
- Managing Information Systems Projects
- Creating, Managing, and Preserving Digital Assets

Indiana University – Masters Degree – DL Concentration

<http://www-slis.lib.indiana.edu/degrees/joint/dls.php>.

Indiana University offers the digital libraries concentration to those studying for the Masters in Library Science (MLS). In addition to the required Library Science Foundation course, they must take the following two courses for three hours of credit each:

- Representation and Organization
- Digital Libraries

They must also take three of the following four courses:

- Information Architecture for the Web
- User Interface Design for Information Systems
- Metadata
- Internship Related to Digital Libraries

Other courses may be selected in consultation with an academic advisor. Indiana also offers a Masters in Information Science which substitutes an additional Information Architecture course and a course in Database Design for the Representation and Organization and Digital Libraries courses required for the Masters in Library Science.

Rutgers University – Masters Degree – Digital Libraries Concentration Online

<http://www.scils.rutgers.edu/programs/lis/OnlineMLIS.jsp>.

Two required non-credit classes:

- Introduction to Library and Information Professions
- Colloquium of Library and Information Studies

Electives: at least 12 of the following courses:

- Human Information Behavior
- Interface Design
- Organizing Information
- Cataloging and Classification
- Metadata for Information Professionals
- Principles of Searching
- Reference Sources and Services
- Information Retrieval
- Information Technology for Libraries and Information Agencies
- Digital Libraries
- Information Visualization and Presentation
- Field Experience
- Digital Library Technology
- Multimedia Production
- Management of Libraries and Information Centers
- Information Technology for Libraries and Information Agencies

Syracuse University – Certificate of Advanced Study in Digital Libraries

<http://ischool.syr.edu/academics/graduate/mls/digitallibraries/curriculum.asp>.

Three required courses

- Digital Libraries
- Creating, Managing, and Preserving Digital Assets
- Planning and Designing Digital Libraries Services

Electives:

- Information Architecture for Internet Services
- Distributed Computing for Information Professionals
- Technologies in Web Content Management
- Data Mining
- Managing Information Systems Projects
- Licensing Digital Information
- Digital Information Retrieval Services
- Theory of Classification and Subject Representation
- Indexing and Abstracting Systems and Services
- Behavior of Information Users
- Human Interaction with Computers
- Introduction to Telecommunications and Network Management
- Database Management for Library Systems

- Database Administration Concepts and Database Management
- Metadata
- Basics of Information Retrieval Systems
- Information Technology for Libraries and Information Centers
- Knowledge Organization Structures
- Designing Web-Based Database Systems
- Advanced Database Management

INDEX